lonely planet

Virgin
Islands

Randall Peffer

LONELY PLANET PUBLICATIONS
Melbourne • Oakland • London • Paris

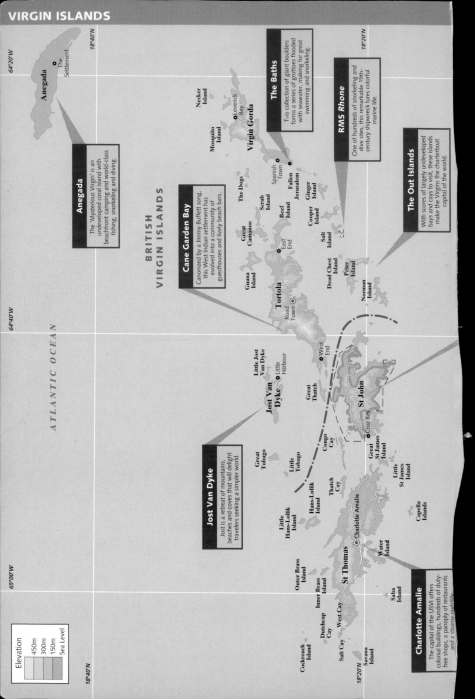

VIRGIN ISLANDS

ATLANTIC OCEAN

BRITISH
VIRGIN ISLANDS

Anegada

The 'Mysterious Virgin' is an undeveloped coral island with beachfront camping and world-class fishing, snorkeling and diving.

Anegada

The Settlement

Cane Garden Bay

Canonized by a Jimmy Buffett song, this West Indian settlement has evolved into a community of guesthouses and lively beach bars.

The Baths

This collection of giant boulders forms a series of grottoes flooded with seawater, making for great swimming and snorkeling.

RMS Rhone

One of hundreds of snorkeling and dive sites, this remarkable 19th-century shipwreck lures colorful marine life.

The Out Islands

With scores of largely undeveloped bays and cays to visit, these islands make the Virgins the charterboat capital of the world.

Jost Van Dyke

Jost is a retreat of mountains, beaches and coves that will delight travelers seeking a simpler world.

Charlotte Amalie

The capital of the USVI offers colonial buildings, hundreds of duty-free shops, a panoply of restaurants and a steamy nightlife.

Necker Island

Mosquito Island

Leverick Bay

Virgin Gorda

Spanish Town

The Dogs

Scrub Island

Beef Island

Great Camanoe

Guana Island

East End

Fallen Jerusalem

Ginger Island

Cooper Island

Salt Island

Dead Chest Island

Peter Island

Norman Island

Tortola

Road Town

West End

Little Harbour

Jost Van Dyke

Little Jost Van Dyke

Great Thatch

St John

Cruz Bay

Great Tobago

Little Tobago

Congo Cay

Thatch Cay

Great St James Island

Little St James Island

Capella Islands

Hans-Lollik Island

Little Hans-Lollik Island

St Thomas

Charlotte Amalie

Water Island

Outer Brass Island

Inner Brass Island

West Cay

Dutchcap Cay

Cockroach Island

Salt Cay

Savana Island

Saba Island

Elevation	
	450m
	300m
	150m
	Sea Level

18°40'N
18°20'N
18°20'N
18°40'N
65°00'W
64°40'W
64°20'W

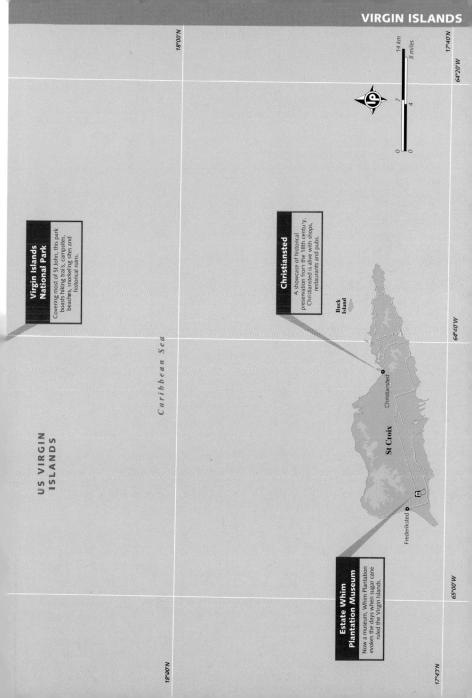

Virgin Islands National Park

Covering most of St John, this park boasts hiking trails, campsites, beaches, snorkeling sites and historical ruins.

Christiansted

A showcase of historical preservation from the 18th century, Christiansted is alive with shops, restaurants and pubs.

Estate Whim Plantation Museum

Now a museum, Whim Plantation evokes the days when sugar cane ruled the Virgin Islands.

US VIRGIN ISLANDS

Caribbean Sea

St Croix

Christiansted

Buck Island

Frederiksted

18°00'N

17°40'N

17°45'N

18°00'N

18°05'N

65°00'W

64°40'W

64°20'W

0   4   8 miles

0   7   14 km

Virgin Islands
1st edition – September 2001

Published by
Lonely Planet Publications Pty Ltd ABN 36 005 607 983
90 Maribyrnong St, Footscray, Victoria 3011, Australia

Lonely Planet Offices
Australia Locked Bag 1, Footscray, Victoria 3011
USA 150 Linden St, Oakland, CA 94607
UK 10a Spring Place, London NW5 3BH
France 1 rue du Dahomey, 75011 Paris

Photographs
Many of the images in this guide are available for licensing from
Lonely Planet Images.
email: lpi@lonelyplanet.com.au

Front cover photograph
Stars & Stripes, America's Cup challenge, St John (Steve Simonsen)

ISBN 0 86442 735 2

text & maps © Lonely Planet 2001
photos © photographers as indicated 2001

Printed by Colorcraft Ltd, Hong Kong

Contents

INTRODUCTION 11

FACTS ABOUT THE VIRGIN ISLANDS 13

History 13
Geography & Geology . . . 18
Climate 19
Ecology & Environment . . 20
Flora 21
Fauna 21
National Parks 22
Government & Politics . . . 23
Economy 24
Population & People 24
Education 25
Arts 25
Society & Conduct 28
Religion 29
Language 29

FACTS FOR THE VISITOR 31

Highlights 31
Suggested Itineraries 31
Planning 32
Responsible Tourism 33
Tourist Offices 33
Visas & Documents 34
Embassies & Consulates . . 35
Customs 35
Money 36
Post & Communications . . 37
Internet Resources 39
Books 39
Films 41
Newspapers & Magazines 41
Radio & TV 41
Video Systems 41
Photography & Video . . . 41
Time 42
Electricity 42
Weights & Measures 42
Laundry 42
Health 42
Women Travelers 46
Gay & Lesbian Travelers . . 47
Disabled Travelers 47
Senior Travelers 48
Travel with Children 48
Useful Organizations 48
Universities 48
Dangers & Annoyances . . 49
Emergencies 50
Legal Matters 50
Business Hours 51
Public Holidays 51
Cultural Events 51
Special Events 52
Activities 52
Work 54
Accommodations 55
Food 56
Drinks 58
Entertainment 59
Spectator Sports 60
Shopping 60

YACHT CHARTER BASICS 61

GETTING THERE & AWAY 65

Air 65
Sea 72
Organized Tours 73

GETTING AROUND 75

Air 75
Bus 75
Car & Motorcycle 76
Bicycle 77
Hitchhiking 77
Boat 77
Taxi 81
Organized Tours 81

ST THOMAS 82

Charlotte Amalie 92
Around Charlotte Amalie 107
Red Hook & East End . . . 112
North & West Island . . . 118

ST JOHN   120

Cruz Bay 127   North Island 135   Coral Bay & South Island 140

ST CROIX   144

Christiansted 153   West Island 167   East Island 173
Frederiksted 162

TORTOLA   178

Road Town 186   West Island 197   East Island 201
Cane Garden Bay Area . . 193

VIRGIN GORDA   205

Spanish Town & the Valley 209   North & East Island 214

JOST VAN DYKE   217

Great Harbour 221   Around Great Harbour . . 222

ANEGADA   225

The Settlement 228   Around the Settlement . . 228

OUT ISLANDS   232

Little Thatch Island 232   Necker Island 235   Peter Island 238
Guana Island 232   Fallen Jerusalem 236   Pelican Island 239
Marina Cay 234   Cooper Island 236   Norman Island 239
The Dogs 235   Salt Island 236
Mosquito Island 235   Dead Chest Island 237

GLOSSARY   241

INDEX   250

MAP LEGEND   256

MAP INDEX

OTHER MAPS
Virgin Islands at front of book
Locator page 11

Anegada page 226

ATLANTIC OCEAN

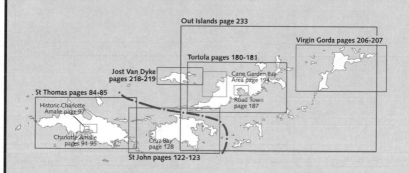

Out Islands page 233

Virgin Gorda pages 206-207

Tortola pages 180-181

Jost Van Dyke
pages 218-219

Cane Garden Bay
Area page 194

Road Town
page 187

St Thomas pages 84-85

Historic Charlotte
Amalie page 97

Charlotte Amalie
pages 91-95

Cruz Bay
page 128

St John pages 122-123

Caribbean Sea

St Croix pages 146-147

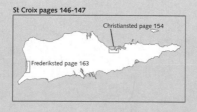

Christiansted page 154

Frederiksted page 163

| 0 | 7 | 14 km |
| 0 | 4 | 8 miles |

The Author

Randall Peffer

As a boy, Randy hopped a freight train out of his hometown of Pittsburgh, Pennsylvania, in search of the King of the Hoboes. He's been traveling ever since. Those travels have taken him into jobs as a commercial pilot, research schooner captain and teacher in a naval prison.

The Virgin Islands have enthralled him since he first cruised the archipelago aboard a family sailboat in the 1970s. Since then, he has returned many times to hike, camp, dive, sail and hide from the madding crowd.

A widely published feature writer, Randy has contributed to *National Geographic, Smithsonian, Islands, Travel Holiday, Sail, Reader's Digest* and most of the major US dailies. He is the author of Lonely Planet's *Puerto Rico* and coauthor of *Virginia & the Capital Region*. Randy is also the author of National Geographic's *New York, New Jersey and Pennsylvania* and two nautical memoirs, *Watermen* and *Logs of the Dead Pirates Society*. He now teaches literature and writing at Phillips Academy in Andover, Massachusetts.

FROM THE AUTHOR

First of all, thanks to senior editor David Zingarelli and project editor Suki Gear, who went beyond the call of duty to enrich the text. Senior cartographer Monica Lepe and her team have proven themselves wizards at their tasks.

Thanks also to research librarians Tim Spratller, Margaret Cohen, Bobbi McDonald and Rachael Penner at Phillips Academy's Oliver Wendell Holmes Library.

My field research in the USVI would not have been as trouble-free or as much fun without the support of Luana Wheatley of Marlin Public Relations. Tammy Peters of Foote, Cone & Belding was an invaluable resource in the BVI.

Dr Numi Mitchell of the Conservation Agency and Gloria Jarecki of Guana Island provided expert insights into the natural history and ecology of the islands.

Amy Ullrich, managing editor of *Sail* magazine, contributed the section on yacht chartering in this book and has shared her local knowledge and passion for the Virgins with me for a score of years.

I am also in debt to my student Ella Hoffman at Phillips Academy. A lifelong St Thomian, Ella and her parents not only consulted with me over the substance of this manuscript but also contributed a wealth of insights to my reportage.

Literally hundreds of other Virgin Islanders have welcomed me and my family to the islands over the years. One, Foxy Callwood, the infamous calypsonian of Jost Van Dyke, must be acknowledged specifically. The man's love for the islands infuses the Virgins.

Most importantly, thanks to my family – Jackie, Jacob and Noah – for being my shipmates as we plumbed every distant corner of the islands under sail. The adventure of seafaring and travel writing would be hollow indeed without having my family to share it.

This Book

This 1st edition of *Virgin Islands* was written by Randall Peffer. Amy Ullrich, managing editor for *Sail* magazine, contributed the Yacht Charter Basics chapter.

FROM THE PUBLISHER

Far from the Virgin Islands, this book was edited, mapped and designed by a crew of landlubbers in Lonely Planet's Oakland office. Suki Gear was the project editor, with editing help from Wendy Smith and Vivek Wagle. Wendy, Suki, Erin Corrigan and Gabrielle Knight proofread the text and maps. Senior editor David 'Z Man' Zingarelli stepped in with his much-appreciated guidance, and managing editor Kate Hoffman put in her two cents as well. Ken DellaPenta created the index.

The maps were carefully drawn by Herman 'Maple Leaf' So, with help from cartography champs Tessa Rottiers, Ed Turley and Dion Good. Senior cartographer Monica Lepe made sure the mapping rolled along smoothly.

On the design end, Henia Miedzinski laid out the book in record time and put together the lovely color pages as well as the book's cover. The illustrations were drawn by Justin 'Van Gogh' Marler, Henia Miedzinski, Jennifer Steffey, Mark Butler, Hugh D'Andrade, Hayden Foell and Rini Keagy and were coordinated by Beca Lafore. Susan Rimerman kept an eye on the whole design process.

Special thanks to the wonderful Randy Peffer for his jokes, compliments and easygoing demeanor. Thanks also to editor David Lauterborn for his insider scoop on the Virgins.

Foreword

ABOUT LONELY PLANET GUIDEBOOKS

The story begins with a classic travel adventure: Tony and Maureen Wheeler's 1972 journey across Europe and Asia to Australia. Useful information about the overland trail did not exist at that time, so Tony and Maureen published the first Lonely Planet guidebook to meet a growing need.

From a kitchen table, then from a tiny office in Melbourne (Australia), Lonely Planet has become the largest independent travel publisher in the world, an international company with offices in Melbourne, Oakland (USA), London (UK) and Paris (France).

Today Lonely Planet guidebooks cover the globe. There is an ever-growing list of books, and there's information in a variety of forms and media. Some things haven't changed. The main aim is still to help make it possible for adventurous travelers to get out there – to explore and better understand the world.

At Lonely Planet we believe travelers can make a positive contribution to the countries they visit – if they respect their host communities and spend their money wisely. Since 1986 a percentage of the income from each book has been donated to aid projects and human-rights campaigns.

Updates Lonely Planet thoroughly updates each guidebook as often as possible. This usually means there are around two years between editions, although for more unusual or more stable destinations the gap can be longer. Check the imprint page (following the color map at the beginning of the book) for publication dates.

Between editions, up-to-date information is available in two free newsletters – the paper *Planet Talk* and email *Comet* (to subscribe, contact any Lonely Planet office) – and on our Web site at www.lonelyplanet.com. The *Upgrades* section of the Web site covers a number of important and volatile destinations and is regularly updated by Lonely Planet authors. *Scoop* covers news and current affairs relevant to travelers. And, lastly, the *Thorn Tree* bulletin board and *Postcards* section of the site carry unverified, but fascinating, reports from travelers.

Correspondence The process of creating new editions begins with the letters, postcards and emails received from travelers. This correspondence often includes suggestions, criticisms and comments about the current editions. Interesting excerpts are immediately passed on via newsletters and the Web site, and everything goes to our authors to be verified when they're researching on the road. We're keen to get more feedback from organizations or individuals who represent communities visited by travelers.

Lonely Planet gathers information for everyone who's curious about the planet – and especially for those who explore it first-hand. Through guidebooks, phrasebooks, activity guides, maps, literature, newsletters, image library, TV series and Web site, we act as an information exchange for a worldwide community of travelers.

Research Authors aim to gather sufficient practical information to enable travelers to make informed choices and to make the mechanics of a journey run smoothly. They also research historical and cultural background to help enrich the travel experience and allow travelers to understand and respond appropriately to cultural and environmental issues.

Authors don't stay in every hotel because that would mean spending a couple of months in each medium-size city and, no, they don't eat at every restaurant because that would mean stretching belts beyond capacity. They do visit hotels and restaurants to check standards and prices, but feedback based on readers' direct experiences can be very helpful.

Many of our authors work undercover; others aren't so secretive. None of them accept freebies in exchange for positive write-ups. And none of our guidebooks contain any advertising.

Production Authors submit their raw manuscripts and maps to offices in Australia, the USA, the UK or France. Editors and cartographers – all experienced travelers themselves – then begin the process of assembling the pieces. When the book finally hits the shops, some things are already out of date, we start getting feedback from readers and the process begins again....

WARNING & REQUEST

Things change – prices go up, schedules change, good places go bad and bad places go bankrupt – nothing stays the same. So, if you find things better or worse, recently opened or long since closed, please tell us and help make the next edition even more accurate and useful. We genuinely value all the feedback we receive. Julie Young coordinates a well-traveled team that reads and acknowledges every letter, postcard and email and ensures that every morsel of information finds its way to the appropriate authors, editors and cartographers for verification.

Everyone who writes to us will find their name in the next edition of the appropriate guidebook. They will also receive the latest issue of *Planet Talk*, our quarterly printed newsletter, or *Comet*, our monthly email newsletter. Subscriptions to both newsletters are free. The very best contributions will be rewarded with a free guidebook.

Excerpts from your correspondence may appear in new editions of Lonely Planet guidebooks, the Lonely Planet Web site, *Planet Talk* or *Comet*, so please let us know if you *don't* want your letter published or your name acknowledged.

Send all correspondence to the Lonely Planet office closest to you:

Australia: Locked Bag 1, Footscray, Victoria 3011
USA: 150 Linden St, Oakland, CA 94607
UK: 10A Spring Place, London NW5 3BH
France: 1 rue du Dahomey, 75011 Paris

Or email us at: talk2us@lonelyplanet.com.au

For news, views and updates, see our Web site: www.lonelyplanet.com

HOW TO USE A LONELY PLANET GUIDEBOOK

The best way to use a Lonely Planet guidebook is any way you choose. At Lonely Planet, we believe the most memorable travel experiences are often those that are unexpected, and the finest discoveries are those you make yourself. Guidebooks are not intended to be used as if they provided a detailed set of infallible instructions!

Contents All Lonely Planet guidebooks follow the same format. The Facts about the Country chapters or sections give background information ranging from history to weather. Facts for the Visitor gives practical information on issues like visas and health. Getting There & Away gives a brief starting point for researching travel to and from the destination. Getting Around gives an overview of the transport options available when you arrive.

The peculiar demands of each destination determine how subsequent chapters are broken up, but some things remain constant. We always start with background, then proceed to sights, places to stay, places to eat, entertainment, getting there and away, and getting around information – in that order.

Heading Hierarchy Lonely Planet headings are used in a strict hierarchical structure that can be visualized as a set of Russian dolls. Each heading (and its following text) is encompassed by any preceding heading that is higher on the hierarchical ladder.

Entry Points We do not assume guidebooks will be read from beginning to end, but that people will dip into them. The traditional entry points are the list of contents and the Index. In addition, however, some books have a complete list of maps and an index map illustrating map coverage.

There may also be a color map that shows highlights. These highlights are dealt with in greater detail later in the book, along with planning questions. Each chapter covering a geographical region usually begins with a locator map and another list of highlights. Once you find something of interest in a list of highlights, turn to the index.

Maps Maps play a crucial role in Lonely Planet guidebooks and include a huge amount of information. A legend is printed on the back page. We seek to have complete consistency between maps and text, and to have every important place in the text captured on a map. Map key numbers usually start in the top left corner.

Although inclusion in a guidebook usually implies a recommendation, we cannot list every good place. Exclusion does not necessarily imply criticism. In fact, there are a number of reasons why we might exclude a place – sometimes it is simply inappropriate to encourage an influx of travelers.

Introduction

If you approach the Virgin Islands by sea, it isn't difficult to imagine what might have gone through Christopher Columbus' head in 1493 when he named this unspoiled collection of about 100 islands after the legendary Saint Ursula and her 11,000 virgins.

The 'Admiral of the Ocean Sea' had just completed a long Atlantic crossing from Spain, only to meet up with the poison arrows of hostile Carib Indians south of here. Perhaps Columbus was having second thoughts about the whole exploration and world-conquest business. But then, before his ship lay a compact archipelago of steep green slopes alive with bird songs and ripening fruit. There were shoals of fat fish on the islands' reefs as well as myriad protected bays where a mariner might anchor.

Here he found peace and plenty as far as the eye could see.

Visiting these islands 300 years later, Captain Thomas Southey offers a similar impression: He wrote that he had found 'a kind of Robinson Crusoe spot, where a man ought to be farmer, carpenter, doctor, fisherman, planter; everything himself.'

So you can excuse first-time visitors arriving on modern cruise ships when they hold their breath for a moment upon first glimpse of these emerald isles. After arriving among a clot of tourists in downtown Charlotte Amalie or nearly being run down in the traffic of Road Town, however, travelers may question if these islands still deserve their pristine name. The answer is still 'yes.'

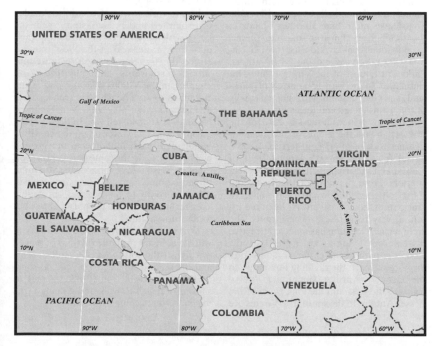

Over the last five centuries, the Virgins have been forced to dance, so to speak, with quite a few colonial powers. Those dances have left this tight little archipelago divided into two territories: the United States Virgin Islands (USVI) to the west and the British Virgin Islands (BVI) to the east. And during the last three decades of the 20th century, both territories have prospered as tourist destinations, attracting 2.5 million visitors per year. Today, with almost 60,000 people on an island just 12 miles long, St Thomas can hardly be considered rural – let alone pristine. And with more than 250,000 foreign companies registered to do business in the BVI (attracted by favorable tax incentives and privacy laws), these islands no longer qualify as an unknown paradise. Finally, there's nothing Edenic about the St Croix's Hess Oil facility, one of the largest refineries in the world.

Still, 95% of the Virgins' population, businesses and industry reside on the three islands of St Thomas, St Croix and Tortola. That leaves more than 90 other islands in the archipelago almost untouched. Thanks to individual conservationists, the US National Park Service and the BVI National Parks Trust, most of the Virgin Islands, including St John (with 9500 acres of parkland) and Guana Island, will remain partially or totally protected and forever wild.

Exploring this wilderness is easy for the traveler aboard the extensive and inexpensive network of interisland ferries, or on a vessel from the world's largest fleet of crewed and sail-it-yourself 'bareboat' yacht charters. From the days of the Taíno and Carib settlers right down to today's modern cruise ships, boats have always been the essential way to explore these islands. The archipelago's location has made it attractive to seafarers. Lying at 18° north latitude, along the path of the easterly trade winds, the Virgins mark the dividing line between the Greater Antilles (including Puerto Rico) to the west and the long chain of the Lesser Antilles to the south. The Virgins are geographically perfect for island-hopping by boat. The most numerous and most tightly packed island group in the Caribbean Sea, the Virgins fit into a triangle with sides of just 45 miles long. Anchorages are rarely more than a couple of miles apart, and the tropical climate and fresh breezes make boat travel exhilarating.

Each cove, snorkeling reef, beach and settlement has its own distinct character. Some places, such as Buck Island and Fallen Jerusalem, seem as pure as they were on the day volcanic action forced them above the sea. Other places, like the settlements on Jost Van Dyke, seem lost in 'de back times.' Marina Cay evokes out-island retreats of the 1950s, while Virgin Gorda, Caneel Bay, Peter Island and St Croix's Carambola Beach offer world-class resorts. You can step back into plantation society at Whim Plantation and Sprat Hall or live like the Swiss Family Robinson in campgrounds on St John or Anegada.

The historic towns of Charlotte Amalie, Christiansted and Frederiksted – with the largest collection of colonial structures (and duty-free businesses) in the West Indies – entice the traveler to explore museums, shops, restaurants and nightlife. And nightlife in the Virgins does not end at the city limits, as anyone who has seen a sunset at Cane Garden Bay, Jost Van Dyke or Norman Island will tell you. In these places, a young white wayfarer might dance with a middle-age black millionaire, and no one will bat an eye. In the same places, however, quite a few islanders will ask what you think of their home, and almost everyone will offer directions to the beaches, snorkeling sites, restaurants and nightspots that few but locals know about.

Wherever you go in these islands, you will never be far from the rhythms of reggae or calypso, the soft tones of Creole accents and the scent of thick, green *callaloo* soup. In these islands, a trail to hike, a reef to snorkel, a beach to walk and a mango tree to shade you become life itself.

Facts about the Virgin Islands

HISTORY
Early Peoples

Archaeologists date the Virgin Islands' habitation back to about 2000 BC. The first inhabitants were Pre-Ceramic Ciboneys, possible nomads from North America who drifted south to the Virgin Islands via a route through the Greater Antilles. The first wave of the Arawak Indians from South America, called Igneri, arrived here from South America in about AD 100. They traveled from the Orinoco Basin in Venezuela, island-hopping through the Lesser Antilles in swift, mammoth canoes that could carry 100 people. The Igneri settled on St Croix and brought with them well-developed skills in pottery making, fishing, canoe building and farming. There is evidence of an Igneri settlement on St Thomas as well, dating from about AD 900.

Around 1300, a second wave of Arawak, the Taíno, displaced the Igneri and set up a community at Salt River Bay on St Croix as well as settlements on the north shore of St John and St Thomas. These wayfarers were less skilled at pottery but better than their predecessors at grinding tools and procuring jewels from stones. The Taíno were also adept at agriculture. Archaeological evidence and reports from early European explorers indicate that the Taíno traveled through the West Indies, establishing scattered settlements as they went. Eventually, the Taíno centered their civilization in present-day Hispaniola and Puerto Rico, where they emulated the crafts and customs of the Igneri and evolved a sophisticated culture of their own.

Early Spanish chroniclers described the Taíno as short people with straight dark hair, high cheekbones and muscular, copper-colored bodies. Except in the case of the *caciques* (nobles) and married women – who wore apronlike garments called *naguas* – most of the Taíno wore no clothes. The copper coloring of their skin was actually a body paint made from plant and mineral dyes. In addition to these dyes, the Taíno favored red, white and blue hues for their faces. While the body paints were considered fashionable to some degree, they primarily functioned as protection against insects, the tropical sun and evil spirits.

But no body paint could protect the Taíno against the invasion of the Caribs. Master mariners and ruthless warriors, this tribe of Indians left the northern shoulder of South America during the 15th century and launched a reign of terror, wiping out the Taíno as the invaders moved north through the Lesser Antilles. By 1493, the Caribs had overrun and mingled with the major Taíno settlements in the Virgin Islands. The boundary between Carib and Taíno sovereignty lay between the Virgin Islands and Puerto Rico.

Christopher Columbus

Following his first voyage to the Caribbean in 1492, Christopher Columbus returned to the court of King Ferdinand and Queen Isabella of Spain. He had excellent news: By sailing 33 days west from the Azores, he had discovered the 'Indies,' a land where it was perpetually summer and the rivers flowed with gold. Upon hearing this report, the Spanish monarchs vested Columbus with the title 'Admiral of the Ocean Sea' and allowed him to assemble a fleet for a second voyage. So off he went with 17 ships and more than 1200 pilgrims, mariners and soldiers under the flagship nicknamed *Maríagalante*. The fleet departed the Spanish port of Cádiz on September 25, 1493, and sighted land on November 3 – an island in the Lesser Antilles that Columbus named 'Dominica' because it came into sight on Sunday morning. In the following weeks, the Spanish fleet worked its way north through the Leeward Islands, where it encountered the Caribs.

Taíno captives guided Columbus north and then west along the southern coast of the archipelago. He named these islands

Christopher Columbus

'Santa Ursula y Las Once Mil Vírgenes' (St Ursula and the 11,000 Virgins) in honor of a 4th-century princess (perhaps English) raped and murdered with an alleged 11,000 maidens in Cologne by marauding Huns. Historians believe that the great Admiral himself named the large islands in the group, but none can agree which he might have called 'Santa Ursula.' The earliest Spanish charts of the islands identify San Tomes (St Thomas), San Juan (St John), Tortola (Turtledove) and Virgen Gorda (Fat Virgin).

After sailing past the Virgins, Columbus traveled to the west to Vieques, Puerto Rico and Jamaica for the first time, and revisited Cuba and Hispaniola, which he had encountered on his first voyage.

The Age of Piracy

The Taíno and Caribs may have lived in peace on the Virgin Islands for another 15 years before the Spanish (who were establishing colonies to the west on Puerto Rico and Hispaniola) began raiding the Lesser Antilles for slaves. Rather than endure the wrath of Spain, the Indians who remained in the Virgin Islands fled south. But while the Virgins were abandoned by the Indians

before the middle of the 16th century, few Spaniards tried to colonize the islands. One exception was a mining operation for copper that developed on Virgin Gorda.

It's possible the Spanish adventurers were actually mining for that shinier precious metal that seemed to obsess them.

The islands of the Caribbean remained under Spanish control until the English defeated the Spanish Armada in 1588. In the aftermath of the destruction of the Spanish Navy, England, France and Holland were quick to issue letters of marque to mariners. These letters appointed the 'privateers' agents of the crown and gave them the rights to explore, claim territory and protect their claims in the name of the country that employed them. The letter of marque also gave the privateers rights to destroy or seize enemy shipping. One king's mercenary privateer was every other king's pirate.

By 1595, the famous English privateers Sir Francis Drake and Jack Hawkins were using the Virgin Islands as a staging ground for attacks on Puerto Rico and Spanish shipping. In the wake of Drake and Hawkins came French corsairs and Dutch freebooters as well. All knew that the Virgin Islands had some of the most secure and unattended harbors in the West Indies. Places like Sopers Hole at the West End of Tortola and The Bight at Norman Island are legendary pirates' dens.

Blackbeard (Edward Teach) was operating in the Virgin Islands before 1720, as were a collection of other rascals including Henry Morgan and Calico Jack Rackham with his female consorts and partners in plunder, Anne Bonny and Mary Read. Some historical observers claim that piracy was a way of life in these islands until the end of the Napoleonic Wars (1815); others claim the tradition of freebooting has never really disappeared.

The First Colonists

In 1621, the British established a colony on St Croix to raise tobacco, watermelons and sweet potatoes, but after four months

Spaniards from Puerto Rico ousted them. In 1625, the English were back on St Croix – and so were the Dutch, who set up a colony of their own. Squabbles between these settlements came to a head in 1645 with the murder of the Dutch governor, and the Dutch abandoned their colony. But England's sovereignty over the Virgins was far from a sure thing. Dutch buccaneers settled on Tortola in 1648, and in 1650 a force of 1200 Spaniards from Puerto Rico drove the English off St Croix. Within the same year, the French sailed from St Kitts and drove the Spanish off St Croix. During the next 83 years, the French governed St Croix and imported African slaves to work the tobacco and sugar plantations.

The Danes started their own initiative in 1665, when the Danish king granted a royal commission to establish a colony on St Thomas. The colony floundered from the start, and collapsed after English privateers plundered it. At about the same time, the English drove the Dutch off Tortola and brought that little settlement firmly under the rule of the British governor of the Leeward Islands. But the Danes returned to St Thomas in 1672. By 1680, St Thomas was under the rule of the Danish West India and Guinea Company and claimed 50 plantations with a population of more than 300, more than half of whom were slaves. In the same year, the British enticed planters from Anguilla to start tobacco and sugar farming on Virgin Gorda and Tortola. But on St Croix, planters grew discouraged, and in 1695, more

than 140 whites and 600 slaves abandoned the island to all but a dozen families.

Meanwhile, with English colonies in the Virgin Islands east of St John, and the Danes on St Thomas to the west, St John remained disputed territory. Finally, in 1717, the Danes sent a small but determined band of soldiers, planters and slaves to St John to drive the British out. The Narrows between St John and Tortola became the border that has divided the eastern Virgins from the western Virgins for more than 250 years.

Slavery & Plantocracy

When European nations signed the Treaty of Utrecht (1713), ending the War of the Spanish Succession and bringing peace between the major powers of Europe, the rivalries that had made the Caribbean a playing field for pirates ceased, and the West Indies began to grow rich producing sugar and cotton for Europe. In pursuit of profits, the Danish West India and Guinea Company declared St Thomas a free port in 1724 and purchased St Croix from the French in 1733. At this point, there were about 5000 African slaves in the Danish West Indies and fewer than 2000 in the British Virgin Islands. By the end of the century, the number of slaves exceeded 40,000, and estimates place the number of slaves brought to the islands at more than 220,000 persons. Something had to give. And it did.

In 1733, harsh living conditions and oppressive laws drove the slaves on St John to

First Blood at St Croix

On November 14, 1493, Columbus' ships anchored off Salt River Bay at the island Columbus named Santa Cruz (St Croix). When a landing party of 25 men headed for a Carib village on shore, the inhabitants scattered. But as the Spanish rowed back to their flagship, they surprised a Carib canoe coming around the point. The Caribs – four men and two women – let loose a flock of arrows on the Spaniards in their open boat.

Arrows wounded two sailors – one mortally – before the Spaniards rammed the canoe, forcing the Indians to swim. But the Caribs swam to a rock and fought on. At last, the Spaniards succeeded in taking the Caribs as prisoners, but they had gained respect for these fierce warriors. Columbus named the site of this conflict on St Croix *Cabo de Flechas* (Cape of Arrows).

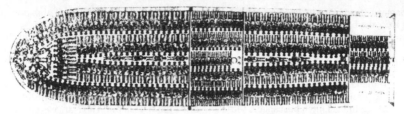

More than 220,000 slaves suffered through horrific conditions on the voyage to the VI.

revolt. After eight months, during which the slaves destroyed most of the plantations on the island and killed or drove off the white gentry, Danes and loyal slave militias as well as English and French forces brought the rebellion under control. Once again it was business as usual. The Danish Virgin Islands, in particular, turned a pretty profit supplying smuggled goods to support the American Revolution, which began in 1776. One of the emerging US leaders, Alexander Hamilton, spent much of his youth on St Croix.

Rebellion & Liberation

During the Napoleonic Wars, Denmark became an ally of France. In response, Britain's navy under the command of Lord Nelson occupied the Danish West Indies from 1801 to 1802. When the Napoleonic Wars flared again in 1807, the British Navy placed the Danish islands of St Thomas, St John and St Croix under military rule until the defeat of Napoleon in 1815. The English put an end to slave trading in their colonies (including the BVI) in 1803, and the empire decreed the abolition of the slave trade in 1808. This action closed the slave market in Charlotte Amalie and raised the hopes for emancipation among slaves throughout the islands.

At the same time, sugar beet production in Europe and American tariffs on foreign sugar cut into the islands' profits, and the deteriorating economy put islanders in a foul mood. On Tortola, slaves plotted a rebellion in 1831; white citizens barely quelled the revolt before it got started. Fearful and economically discouraged, half the whites abandoned the British Virgins for good. In

the Danish Virgins, the government began to create more options for slaves to gain their freedom but waffled over universal emancipation even as the English Parliament decreed the end of slavery in all British colonies (including the BVI) in 1834. Finally, during the summer of 1848, blacks on St Croix claimed by force their freedom and right to be treated as equal. (See the boxed text 'Caught in Freedom's Storm' in the St Croix chapter.)

The Victorian Era

Although 1848 brought the legal end to slavery in the Virgins, the black residents remained in economic bondage to an obsolete mercantile system. The old island plantocracy was barely competitive in what was quickly becoming a global economy.

Life in the islands was dismal. In one year, a cholera epidemic on St Thomas killed more than 1800 people. Average wages for field workers were less than 15¢ a day. Not surprisingly, a series of labor revolts broke out. The first came on Tortola in 1853, and a more violent one called the Fireburn erupted on St Croix in 1878. When it was over, half of Frederiksted had burned, two-thirds of all the plantations and mills were destroyed and more than 100 people were dead. In 1892, the coal carriers who worked the docks of St Thomas went on strike and threatened violence.

Meanwhile, the US was negotiating with Denmark to buy the Danish-controlled Virgins. President Abraham Lincoln's astute secretary of state, William Henry Seward, saw the islands' role as a waypoint and coaling station for steam ships and realized the strategic value of the Virgins relative to the Caribbean Basin. The deal was almost done in 1867, but the US Congress rejected the idea of paying $7.5 million (more than they paid for 'Seward's Folly,' Alaska) for the islands. The US made another bid in 1902, but this time the Danish parliament rejected the offer, hoping that the Germans might offer them a sweeter deal.

US Purchase & Democratization

A German presence in the Caribbean capable of controlling shipping to and from the Panama Canal scared the US. Concerns that German armies might easily invade Denmark and claim the Danish West Indies as a war prize made the Yanks particularly anxious as WWI began in Europe. So once again, US diplomats entered into negotiations with the Danes. But this time the Americans were pleading, and finally the Danes agreed to sell the Virgin Islands colony for $25 million in gold. This transaction makes the islands of St Thomas, St Croix, St John and their satellites the most expensive purchase of land by the US government – $290 per acre.

On March 31, 1917, the US Navy took control of the islands. Some local citizens had mixed feelings, but the majority of people were glad to see the Americans come: They had hopes that the US would improve health, education and social conditions on the islands. Meanwhile, the citizens of the neighboring British Virgins looked on with envy. Although they had felt pride when their own islands had been proclaimed a 'crown colony' in the 1870s, they had been largely ignored by England, and their Legislative Counsel had been stripped away in favor of rule by a governor working for the Leeward Islands Administration.

The people of the US colony soon had reason to be just as disappointed as their relatives and friends living on the British islands. The navy brought draconian rule, racism and gangs of misbehaving sailors to the islands. By the time the navy withdrew in 1931 in favor of a civil governor, most islanders had little good to say about living in a US colony. To make matters worse, the US

even tried to enforce Prohibition on these islands for a time before relenting – a bizarre twist for an economy linked to the production, sale and distribution of rum. In 1931, President Herbert Hoover traveled to the Virgins, stayed for less than six hours and made a speech in which he declared, 'It was unfortunate that we ever acquired these islands.'

In 1934, however, President Franklin Delano Roosevelt visited the islands and saw the potential that Hoover had missed. Soon, the US instituted programs in the Virgins to eradicate disease, drain swamps, build roads, improve education, create hotels for tourists, attract cruise ships and even sell rum under a label that Roosevelt himself designed. In 1936, the US Congress passed the Organic Act, which guaranteed US citizenship to all citizens in the US Virgin Islands. WWII, the associated sugar boom and the construction of naval and military bases in the islands brought full employment to the US islands for the first and only time since European colonization. During this era, social conditions in the BVI lagged behind the improvements in the USVI, and citizens from the sparsely populated British colony migrated to work in the USVI, particularly St Thomas – a trend that continued through most of the 20th century.

Following WWII, both British and US citizens in the islands clamored for more independence. In 1949, BVI citizens demonstrated for a representative government and got a so-called presidential legislature the next year. In 1954, the US Congress passed the second Organic Act, which established an elected legislature in the USVI. During the 1960s, Britain's administrative mechanisms for its Caribbean colonies kept changing shape, and by 1967, the BVI had become an independent colony with political parties, its own Legislative Council and an elected chief minister. The next year, the USVI won the right to elect its own governor, Cyril King.

The Bloom of Tourism

Morris de Castro, considered the USVI's first native appointed governor, took office in 1950 and saw that the government should be developing tourism in the islands. Within the first three years of his efforts, tourist visits in the USVI increased from 26,000 to 105,000. Seed money for advertising and loans to build hotels sustained this growth.

When Cuba's doors were closed to American tourists in 1959, the Virgin Islands were ready for the rush of sun seekers. And the advent of jet travel in the 1960s put the Virgins within a few hours of North America. Cruise ships began making St Thomas their featured stop, and yachties discovered the superb cruising in the islands east of St Thomas, particularly around St John and the BVI. And in the midst of this tourism boom, government incentives induced the Hess Oil company to establish a major refinery on St Croix, spurring further economic developments. In 1967, Britain's Queen Elizabeth II made the first of many royal visits to the BVI, casting a glow of celebrity on the islands that they enjoy to this day.

Presiding over the boom in the USVI was Ralph Paiewonsky, the governor appointed by President John F Kennedy. Paiewonsky came from an old rum-making family. He shepherded the islands through their greatest economic and political changes in centuries, not only oiling the tourism machine but also introducing social services that were part of the US 'War on Poverty.'

The past three decades in the islands brought unprecedented growth in the tourism industry, with dozens of luxury hotels and hundreds of guesthouses, condominiums and vacation villas popping up on the shores and hillsides of both the US and British Virgins. Concurrently, the islands' population mushroomed (see Population & People, later in this chapter).

The islands have endured more than their share of political corruption scandals – nepotism, cronyism and bribery have long been a way of life. Also, some unexpectedly violent crimes have rocked the Virgins, including the Fountain Valley Massacre on St Croix in 1972, drive-by shootings in Charlotte Amalie and the murder of a woman

vacationing on Tortola in 1999. But the biggest stories in recent years have been hurricanes. Four major storms have nailed the islands since 1989, when Hurricane Hugo laid waste to 80% of the buildings on St Croix. Yet each storm brings improvements in the building codes, and more conscientious preparedness (see the boxed text 'A High Wind Gonna Blow').

GEOGRAPHY & GEOLOGY

The Virgin Islands archipelago of more than 90 hilly islands lies 1100 miles southeast of Miami and 40 miles east of Puerto Rico. These are the northernmost islands in the Lesser Antilles chain, along the eastern edge of the Caribbean Sea. The Virgins archipelago is an irregular string of islands stretching west to east. The one exception to this string is the Virgins' largest island, St Croix (80 sq miles), which lies about 40 miles south of her sisters. The other major islands in the group are St Thomas (30 sq miles), Tortola (21 sq miles), St John (19 sq miles), Virgin Gorda (8 sq miles) and Jost Van Dyke (4 sq miles).

While the islands form a geographical unit, they are divided into two dependent territories. The islands in the southern and western part of the archipelago, the former Danish West Indies, are the United States Virgin Islands (USVI). The British Virgin Islands (BVI) compose the eastern end of the archipelago. The border between the two territories lies between the US island of St John and the British island of Tortola. Charlotte Amalie on St Thomas is the capital of the USVI. Road Town on Tortola is the capital of the BVI. All together, the islands have a total coastline of 166 miles and represent an area about twice the size of Washington, DC.

As with almost all of the islands ringing the Caribbean Basin, the Virgin Islands owe their existence to a series of volcanic events that took place along the dividing line between the North American and Caribbean Plates. These eruptions built up layers of lava and igneous rock, creating islands with three geographical zones: the coastal plain, coastal dry forests and the central mountains. For all of the Virgins except St Croix, the coastal plain is a narrow fringe, and for all of the islands except easternmost Anegada (a coral island), a ridge of moderately high mountains of 1000 feet or more run west to east across the islands and dominate their interiors.

Sage Mountain on Tortola is the highest point in the islands at 1780 feet. Except where houses have encroached, the mountain slopes are dense subtropical forests. All of the timber is second- or third-growth; the islands were stripped for sugar, cotton and tobacco plantations in the colonial era. Today, less than 7% of island land supports agriculture. The Virgins have no rivers and very few fresh-water streams.

Coral reefs of all varieties thrive in the shallow waters near the shores of all the islands. The shores host a few pockets of mangrove swamps, including Salt River Bay on St Croix.

CLIMATE

Virgin Islands' weather is reliably balmy with daily highs ranging between 77°F (25°C) in the winter and 82°F (28°C) in summer. Easterly trade winds of 15mph or more keep the humidity lower in the Virgins than on most other islands of the Caribbean. Rain usually comes in the form of brief tropical showers, and the islands average less than 50 inches of rain per year. The wettest months are July to October.

A High Wind Gonna Blow

The word 'hurricane,' denoting fierce cyclonic storms with winds in excess of 75mph, comes from the language of Taino Indians and their god of malevolence, Jurakán. Generally, the 'seeds' of these storms begin to grow off the west coast of Africa near the Cape Verde Islands. They migrate across the equatorial girdle of the Atlantic to the southern Caribbean as upperatmospheric disturbances driven by the easterly trade winds. Here, they linger and pick up moisture and energy until the Coriolis effect of

Earth's spinning propels the growing storms north through the Caribbean and/or the Gulf of Mexico. Eventually, many of these storms pose a threat to the southern and eastern US coasts.

The Virgin Islands suffered devastation from three storms – Hugo, Luis and Marilyn – in the 10 years preceding 1999. And just when islanders were beginning to think they could rest, Hurricane Lenny struck a direct blow in early November 1999. Sustained winds of more than 120mph raked through the islands, especially St Croix. But this time the Virgins were ready. No one was killed. Few structures sustained serious damage. Most telephone service was uninterrupted. Shipping and air traffic began flowing in and out of the islands within 24 hours, and all major roads were cleared of debris. Meanwhile, hotels kept their guests healthy, cool and happy with auxiliary generating systems and water supplies. Amazingly, government agencies restored water and electricity to most of the islands within two days (the less-powerful Hurricane Hugo disrupted basic services for more than two months in 1989).

Good, long-range storm predictions (broadcast widely on TV and radio and in newspapers), thorough preparation and the nearly universal practice of building new houses and public and commercial buildings with cement block or reinforced concrete have gone a long way toward reducing casualties and property damage.

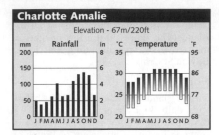

Charlotte Amalie
Elevation - 67m/220ft

Hurricane season in the Virgin Islands comes during the hottest and wettest months – July to October – with September being the most likely month for a storm. With the onset of global warming, hurricanes are more frequent than ever in the Caribbean. See the boxed text 'A High Wind Gonna Blow' for more information on the deadly phenomenon.

ECOLOGY & ENVIRONMENT

The Virgin Islands have long suffered from serious environmental problems, including population growth and rapid urbanization, deforestation, erosion of soil, mangrove destruction and a lack of fresh water. While islanders still have a long way to go toward undoing generations of environmental damage and preserving their natural resources, the past decade has seen a slight increase in the level of awareness, resources and action dedicated to conservation efforts.

Citizens on many of the Virgin Islands support government environmental agencies as well as environmental action groups. Contact one of these entities if you see a problem, or – better – want to collaborate with professionals and volunteers to save the Virgins.

Friends of the Virgin Islands National Park
(☎ 340-779-4940)

Bureau of Environmental Enforcement
(☎ 340-774-3320)

National Marine Fisheries Law Enforcement Division
(☎ 340-774-5226)

BVI National Parks Trust
(☎ 284-494-3904)

Population Growth & Urbanization

Without a doubt, population growth and rapid urbanization have long posed the greatest threats to the islands' environment. The Virgin Islands traditionally have had a very high birthrate and historically have been a sanctuary for immigrants.

As early as the 18th century, citizens complained that settlements such as Charlotte Amalie were bursting at the seams. Since 1970, the population has mushroomed from about 40,000 people to 140,000. On St Thomas and Tortola, almost all of the flat land has been developed, and houses hang on mountain slopes like Christmas ornaments. Such population growth and density have kept public utilities like sewage treatment plants in a constant scramble to keep the islands from soiling themselves.

Deforestation & Soil Erosion

During the 18th century, logging operations denuded many of the islands to make room for plantations. Subsequently, untold acres of topsoil have eroded. The demise of the agricultural economy in the late 19th century allowed the islands to reforest, and in recent years the island governments have set aside forest land as national parks (particularly on St John, Tortola and Virgin Gorda) and began work on a series of forest conservation projects to slow erosion.

Mangrove Destruction

As with the islands' other environmental problems, mangrove destruction was at its worst decades ago when the rush to develop business and housing lots saw the devastation of mangrove swamps around urban areas. Some bays now lined with marinas, hotels and businesses, such as the harbor at Road Town, were mangrove estuaries just 50 years ago. Environmentalists began fighting to preserve the Virgin Islands' remaining mangrove estuaries in the 1980s, and the late 1990s brought some victories in this arena, helping preserve the mangroves at Paraquita Bay on Tortola, Salt Pond Bay on St Croix and Mangrove Lagoon on St Thomas.

Poison Apples

In 1587, Sir Walter Raleigh paused at St Croix with a party of settlers on their way to North America. After the long sea voyage, the colonists were tempted by an abundance of fruit that looked like small light-green apples hanging from trees near shore. A number of Raleigh's men and women ate the poisonous fruit and 'were fearfully troubled with a sudden burning in their mouths and swelling of their tongues so big that some of them could not speak.'

The colonists' nemesis was the fruit of the manchineel or 'poison apple' tree. The sap of this tree is so toxic that the Caribs used it to poison their arrows. On French Caribbean islands, locals often mark the tree with a skull and crossbones. Although the manchineel has been eradicated from many public areas in the Virgins, it is still around, especially on St John and less developed islands.

Because touching any part of this tree can yield caustic burns (the sap takes paint off cars), humans must avoid the manchineel. Even rain dripping off the leaves and bark will burn if it touches your skin. Although manchineels can grow as tall as 40 feet and spread broad branches in a radius of 15 feet from the trunk, most trees are much smaller. You will always find these trees near beaches or salt ponds, and you will know a manchineel by its small, green apples and shiny green elliptical leaves.

Fresh-Water Shortage

If not for the miracle of desalination plants, which make fresh water out of seawater, the Virgin Islands could not support even a quarter of its population – let alone the hotel guests. When a hurricane strikes, islands lose power and desal facilities shut down. Islanders with enough foresight and money keep rainwater cisterns for such emergencies, but folks without these reserves suffer.

FLORA

Thousands of tropical plant varieties grow in the Virgin Islands, and a short drive can transport a nature lover between entirely different ecosystems. Mangrove swamps, coconut groves and sea grape trees dominate the coast, while mountain peaks support wet forest with mahogany, lignum vitae, palmetto and more than 30 varieties of wild orchid. Look for aloe, acacia, turpentine tree, gumbo limbo, century plant and dildo cactus in the coastal dry forests.

Exotic shade trees have long been valued in this sunny climate, and you will see yards and public parks with silk cotton trees, poincianas (with flaming red blossoms) and African tulip trees. Islanders often adorn their dwellings with a profusion of flowers such as orchids, bougainvillea and poinsettias, and tend lovingly to fruit trees that bear mango, papaya, carambola (star fruit), breadfruit, tamarind, plantain and gneps (a fruit the size of a large marble that yields a sweet, orange flesh).

Islanders also grow and collect hundreds of different roots and herbs, including japona, ginger root, anise and cattle tongue, as ingredients for 'bush medicine' cures. Psychoactive mushrooms grow wild (and are consumed) in the islands, particularly on Tortola (see 'Magic Mushrooms' in the Tortola chapter).

FAUNA

For a bibliography of sources of information on flora and fauna in the Virgin Islands, see Books in the Facts for the Visitor chapter.

Land Mammals

Very few of the land mammals that make their home in the Virgin Islands are natives; most mammal species have been accidentally or intentionally introduced to the island over the centuries. Virtually every island has a feral population of goats and burros, and some islands have wild pigs, white-tailed deer, cattle, horses, cats and dogs. Other prevalent land mammals a visitor will likely encounter include the mongoose and numerous species of bat. The mongoose was introduced to control the rat population in the days of the sugar cane plantations and has since overrun the islands.

Reptiles & Amphibians

The Virgins are home to just a few species of snake (none of which are poisonous), including the Virgin Island tree boa. Into this mix goes a host of small and not-so-small lizards – including the 6-foot-long rock iguanas of Anegada and the common green iguana found throughout the islands. Anoles and gecko lizards are ubiquitous. Numerous species of toad and frog populate the island, including the piping frog and the giant toad, which secretes a poisonous white venom from its eyes.

Birds & Insects

More than 200 species of bird – including the official bird, the bananaquit or 'yellow bird' – inhabit the Virgins. The coastal dry forest features more than 100 bird species, largely songbirds. Some of these are migratory fowl, such as the prairie warbler and the northern parula. Many are native species, like the Caribbean elaenia and the doctorbird. One of the joys of winter beach combing is watching the aerial acrobatics of brown pelicans as they hunt for fish. Wading birds such as egrets and herons are common at salt ponds.

The islands also have an ample supply of pesky and scary insects, including daytime-active mosquitoes that carry dengue fever, miniscule and sharp-biting no-see-ums, and a large ground spider often mistaken for a tarantula. Small scorpions are not uncommon.

Marine Life

Terrestrial species represent only a small portion of Virgin Island animal life. Much of what thrills nature lovers about the islands is found underwater. Mangrove estuaries and vast coral reefs are the nurseries and feeding grounds for hundreds of species of tropical fish. And not just sergeant majors, angelfish, groupers and lobsters – the islands are some of the best places in the world for divers to come face to face with large barracudas, manta rays, octopuses, moray eels and plentiful nurse sharks. Endangered giant sea turtles, including hawksbill, green and leatherback, nest on local beaches, particularly at St Croix. Game fish such as tuna and blue marlin patrol the deep. Schools of porpoises play in the bow waves of boats, and pilot whales frolic between the islands.

Endangered Species

In addition to the sea turtle, chief among the Virgin Islands' endangered species is the Anegada rock iguana *Cyclura pinguis* (see the boxed text 'Facing Extinction' in the Anegada chapter).

Once totally extirpated from the archipelago, American (also called Caribbean) flamingos have been reintroduced on Anegada and Guana Island and now have breeding colonies. A similar tale of rejuvenation surrounds the white-crowned pigeon and the red-legged tortoise (see the Anegada chapter and the Guana Island section of the Out Islands chapter).

NATIONAL PARKS

Both the USVI and the BVI have good reason to be proud of their national parks. Probably no country or territory in the Lesser Antilles has set aside so much land to remain forever wild. On the US islands, the National Park Service oversees the vast Virgin Islands National Park, which includes more than 9500 acres of wilderness on St John, 5600 acres of surrounding bays and sea gardens and Hassel Island in St Thomas Harbor.

The National Park Service also oversees Buck Island and the Christiansted National Historic Site, including Fort Christiansvaern, the Old Danish Scale House, the Old Customs House, the Danish West India and Guinea Company Warehouse and the Steeple Building.

Coral Ecology

A coral is a tiny animal with a great gaping mouth at one end, surrounded by tentacles for gathering food. The polyps, which resemble flowers or cushions upholstered with plush fabric, live protected by external skeletons, the production of which is dependent upon algae that live inside the polyps' tissue. The creatures live in vast colonies that reproduce both asexually by budding, and sexually through a synchronous release of spermatozoa that turns the surrounding sea milky. Together they build up huge frameworks – the reefs.

A reef is usually composed of scores of coral species, each occupying its own niche. However, all corals can flourish only close to the ocean surface, where they are nourished by sunlight in clear, unpolluted waters above 70°F (21°C). Each species has a characteristic shape – bulbous cups bunched like biscuits in a baking tray for the star coral and deep, wending valleys for the well-named brain coral. Deeper down, where light is scarcer, massive corals flatten out, becoming more muted in color. Deeper still, soft corals – those without an external skeleton – predominate. These lacy fans and waving cattails look like plants, but a close perusal shows them to be menacing animal predators that seize smaller creatures such as plankton.

Coral reefs are the most complex and sensitive of all ecosystems. Taking thousands of years to form, they are divided into life zones gauged by depth, temperature and light. When a coral polyp dies, its skeleton turns to limestone that another polyp may use to cement its own skeleton. The entire reef system is gnawed away by parrotfish and other predators.

Tourism in the form of careless divers, snorkelers and yachts have threatened Virgin Island reefs, but diver education and the placement of mooring buoys by park rangers have stemmed the tide in recent years (see 'Considerations for Responsible Diving' in the Facts for the Visitor chapter).

The BVI National Parks Trust has 15 parks and several more under consideration. Parks include 96 acres of so-called rain forest around the Virgin Islands' highest peak, Sage Mountain, and more than six islands including the Dogs and Fallen Jerusalem, which are excellent dive sites. The entire southwest coast of Virgin Gorda is a collection of national parks that include the giant boulder formations at the Baths and Spring Bay.

GOVERNMENT & POLITICS

The Virgin Islands of the United States is an unincorporated territory of the USA, and the islands participate in the US democracy by sending an elected, nonvoting representative to the US House of Representatives. All citizens of the USVI are citizens of the USA, but they cannot vote in US presidential elections unless they live in one of the 50 states of the union. Islanders elect a territorial governor every four years as well as 15 senators every two years. Currently, a movement is afoot to reduce the number of senators, whom many people view as 'fat cats.'

Four political parties represent the islands, with Democrats and Republicans holding almost equal power and representation. Although any USVI citizen can run for public office, history shows that only persons of African descent have a chance at winning an election. Laws in the USVI are based on US law. The Territorial Court interprets the law in the USVI, and judges are appointed by the governor. The US District Court judges federal issues.

As a Crown Colony of England, the British Virgin Islands have a governor appointed by the Queen. The governor in turn appoints a local administrator, known as the chief minister, from the elected members of the 13-seat Legislative Council. Each council member serves a five-year term. Four political parties hold sway in the BVI, with the Virgin Islands Party holding the most seats on the council as well as the seat of the chief minister. Britain's Eastern Caribbean Supreme Court oversees justice on the islands based on English law. One Supreme Court justice resides in the islands to preside over the local High Court.

ECONOMY

In the US Virgins, tourism dominates the economy. The islands host upwards of two million travelers a year, and the resulting income represents about 70% of the gross domestic product (GDP). The manufacturing sector produces jobs and revenue from petroleum, pharmaceuticals, textiles, rum, electronics and watches. The Hess Oil refinery on St Croix exports nearly $2 billion worth of petroleum products annually.

Meanwhile, agriculture contributes less than 7% to the economy. Service industries employ 62% of the workforce, and the largest employer in the islands is the territorial government. Per capita income is among the highest in the Caribbean at about $13,000 per year. For years, the USVI have depended on US aid to keep the government and its services going. Expenditures for massive capital projects during the final years of the 20th century resulted in $1 billion in debt for the territorial government. As the 21st century unfolds, US lawmakers continue to wrestle with how to bail out the islands. Territorial officials want the US to simply forgive the debt. Fat chance!

The BVI has seen its economy bloom in recent years. Tourism still leads the way to prosperity by contributing 45% of the GDP. About 70% of the nearly 400,000 tourists who visit the BVI each year come for yacht charters. But tourism may soon be overshadowed by the income generated by offshore businesses incorporating in the BVI. During the 1980s, the BVI passed laws that offered tax incentives to foreign businesses incorporating in the islands. By the end of the 20th century, more than 250,000 businesses had registered. A comprehensive insurance act that passed in 1994 provides registered corporations with blanket confidentiality, and some observers see the possibility of the BVI becoming an offshore financial haven for many businesses because all money earned through the BVI office of a corporation will be tax-free and confidential.

Agriculture – mostly cattle raising – constitutes about 7% of the GDP. Concrete-block-making and rum distilling are two of the islands' few industries. The annual per capita income exceeds $10,000.

POPULATION & PEOPLE

Since 1970, the BVI's population has more than doubled to more than 19,000 and the USVI's population has quadrupled to about 120,000. But the islands' population seems to have hit a plateau, with the current population growth rate at less than 2% per year. That rate would certainly be higher if not for the fact that large numbers of US Virgin Islanders move 'off island' to the US mainland each year.

In recent decades, many immigrants have been drawn to the Virgins (by the economic opportunities) from other parts of the West Indies. Other émigrés are 'continentals' (US mainlanders). Quite a few of these continentals are older, wealthy 'snowbirds' who have come here to retire in the sun. Other expats include young Brits, Canadians, French and Americans attracted by jobs in resorts, restaurants and water sports. While a few islands such as St Thomas, St Croix and Tortola are densely populated, many of the islands like Jost Van Dyke have less than 200 inhabitants.

As has been the case in these islands for hundreds of years, blacks outnumber whites by more than four to one. The difference today is that the descendants of the former slaves have control of their own destinies, with people of African heritage dominating the political and professional arenas in the islands. These islanders can trace their ancestry and traditions to the Yoruba, Hausa, Woloff, Ibo, Ashanti, Fula, Amin and Mandinka tribes.

Descendants of European Jews have long been leaders in import and export businesses, particularly in Charlotte Amalie. French immigrants from St Barts have

Women: First from Chains

The 1803 'Proceedings and Register of the Free Colored' shows how extensively many black women (and a few men) had successfully thrown off the shackles of slavery and were part of the mainstream of St Thomas society. The 1803 Proceedings list and describe the 'free coloreds' living in three-quarters of Charlotte Amalie.... Indeed, many of the women in the 1803 census are listed without an accompanying male name.

The census also suggests that women were more successful at working their way up the occupational ladder than men after gaining their freedom. For example, Anna Johanna (age 25) sold dry goods for a living; Lettys purchased her own freedom at age 30 and was a housemaid; Maria Rosina supported two children as a seamstress; Maria Foncado was a dancing girl; and Maria Theresa was a cigar maker.

—**Ella Hoffman**, from *Amazing Women of the Virgin Islands*

traditionally been fishers on St Thomas. And many of the shopkeepers on St Thomas and St Croix have a Middle East background. Some islands in the archipelago have significant white populations, including St John, St Croix and Virgin Gorda. One-third (more than 20,000) of St Croix's population claims Puerto Rican ancestry.

Unlike in the USA, or the Caribbean in the past, social status today on the islands has very little to do with a person's ancestry or the color of her skin. Social status is rooted in a person's level of education, profession and income. People who are island-born or children of island-born parents, often called 'belongers,' claim a special social status. In the USVI, belongers hold the bulk of government jobs. In the BVI, belongers get first priority when it comes to the purchasing of land or getting a job.

EDUCATION
Both the USVI and the BVI have compulsory education through age 16. In the USVI, schools follow the US system of education. The BVI follow the British system.

The University of the Virgin Islands on St Thomas enrolls approximately 2400 full-time and part-time students. The St Croix branch of the university teaches 1000 full-time students and 600 part-time students working toward a dozen different masters, bachelors and associate degrees. Many students come here to prepare for careers in service industries, technology, teaching, agriculture and marine/wetlands management.

In the BVI, the H Lavity Stoutt Community College on Tortola celebrated its 10th anniversary in 2000. The college serves about 900 students, including many people returning for higher education in the fields of marine science, culinary arts and tourism. Online classes with US partner schools like the New England Culinary Institute and the University of North Carolina complement courses taught on the campus.

ARTS
Music
The Virgin Islands have a rich musical heritage. Most of the music has roots in West African folk music and drumming with influences from the musical traditions of colonists from England, Ireland, Spain, France, Denmark and Holland.

Reggae and calypso are the two types of music heard most often today on the islands. Their catchy, singable tunes blast from vehicles and emanate from shops, restaurants and beach bars.

Quelbe and fungi (pronounced FOON-ghee, like the island food) are two types of Virgin Island folk music. The best time to experience a host of island bands and the variety of their accomplishments is during the 'jump up' parades and competitions associated with major festivals like carnival on St Thomas and St John, BVI Summer

Festival on Tortola and the Virgin Gorda Easter Festival.

Calypso This music originated in Trinidad in the 18th century as satirical songs sung in a French patois by slaves working the plantations. Many of the songs mirrored their discontent and mocked their colonial masters, while other songs were competitions in which two singers tried to top each other's insults. Lyrics were generally ad-libbed. Contemporary calypso is almost always sung in English and composed and rehearsed in advance. The most popular songs contain biting social commentary, political satire or sexual innuendos, laden with double entendres and local nuances. In most cases, the melodies and rhythms of the songs are well established. Mainly the lyrics change from song to song.

Calypso and carnival have been linked for well over 100 years in Trinidad, and that link is equally strong in the Virgin Islands, where festivals always feature a contest for the 'King of Calypso.' Among the classic calypsonians popular throughout the islands are the Mighty Sparrow, Shadow and David Rudder, who are all from Trinidad. Foxy Callwood of Jost Van Dyke is the BVI's legendary 'calypso mon.'

Reggae Born in Jamaica and derived from a mix of ska (a 1950s blend of R&B with calypso), blues, calypso and rock, reggae is the famous back-beat sound of social protest popularized by Bob Marley and Jimmy Cliff. Today, the reggae sound dominates the airways as well as the clubs of the Virgin Islands. VI bands not only cover all the Marley classics, but some of the great local bands like the Star Lights, O-2 and Xtreme have a lot of fresh and original works that add to the canon.

Soca Blend soul and calypso and you get soca, a dance music with bold rhythms, heavy on the bass sound. Soca started in Trinidad in the 1970s, and you are sure to hear its rhythms in Virgin Island clubs. Listen for songs by Arrow and Super Blue.

Quelbe This indigenous folk music of the Virgin Islands is a blend of jigs, quadrilles, military fife and drum music, with *bamboula* rhythms from the Ashanti in West Africa and *cariso* lyrics (often biting satire) from slave field songs. The music evolved when self-taught island musicians playing in the colonial fife and drum bands (basically colonial propaganda machines) blended their skills with the illegal cariso songs of the field.

As Quelbe bands evolved in the 19th and early 20th centuries, they turned into an ensemble of banjo, flute, guitars, steel triangle, squash (dried gourd) and 'ass pipe' (bass). Since the 1960s, Quelbe bands have added alto saxophone and electric guitar. The sound of the music remains percussive and distinctly rustic. Tapes and CDs of popular Quelbe groups, like Stanley and the Ten Sleepless Knights and Jamsie and the Happy Seven, are widely available in Virgin Island stores.

Fungi Fungi is the Virgin Island variation on scratch band music played throughout the West Indies. Bands use a host of home-made percussion instruments like washboards, ribbed gourds and conch shells to accompany a singer and melody played on a recorder or flute. Like calypso, fungi music favors satirical lyrics. You can hear (and make) fungi music at a number of restaurant/bars on Tortola, such as the North Shore Shell Museum and Mrs Scatliffe's Restaurant.

Steel Pan Another import from Trinidad, this music

began in the 1940s when musicians began hammering out the bottoms of steel oil drums, tuning different sections to different pitches. In the Virgin Islands, pan drum players usually perform as soloists, as background music in restaurants and bars. But like Trinidad, the USVI also have huge steel pan bands like the Rising Stars Young Steel Orchestra, which plays at festivals and tours internationally.

Dance

A predecessor of square dancing in the USA, quadrille dancing in the islands descends from the formal dances of the European planters in the 18th century. Denied the public practice of African dances like the bamboula, slaves imitated the formal dances of their masters during holiday celebrations. But, of course, the blacks put an African spin on the music using the banjo, ukulele and flute to create pulsating rhythms. Dancers in full skirts transformed the jumpy steps of the European dance into smooth, hip-swaying movements. Today, the world-touring Caribbean Dance Company of St Croix preserves quadrille dancing (and revives the bamboula) for public entertainment at festivals and the centers for performing arts on the islands.

Architecture

The towns of Charlotte Amalie and Christiansted are the largest showcases in the Caribbean of what is often thought of as traditional West Indian architecture. In fact, this architecture is a loose adaptation of English Georgian (neoclassical) style from the late 18th century. At their best, these West Indies classics are two or three stories tall with arched galleries for pedestrians on the 1st and 2nd floor verandas, 'welcoming arms' exterior staircases and hipped roofs. Construction materials are a mix of ship-ballast brick, 'rubble' (a blend of coral, molasses and straw) and wood.

Exteriors feature soothing pastel shades of yellow, turquoise, lime and sometimes pink. Window shutters keep out inclement weather and hot sunlight. Large rooms with high ceilings help buildings 'breathe' the trade winds. Frederiksted, rebuilt in the late Victorian era after it was destroyed by labor riots, is a repository of Victorian buildings.

Literature

While the Virgin Islands have been the setting for quite a few works of imaginative literature (see Books in the Facts for the Visitor chapter), no islanders have produced a blockbuster yet. But it might be just a matter of time. The University of the Virgin Islands sponsors the journal *The Caribbean Writer*. This journal offers a compendium of poems and short fiction by major Caribbean writers including Nobel laureate Derek Walcott from St Lucia, author of the epic poem *Omeros*.

The oral tradition of storytelling reaches all the way back to Africa and is still alive and well in the Virgins. Cultural festivals in the islands often feature modern storytellers who call children and the young at heart to the lawn under a shade tree for 'tim-tim time.' At these gatherings, you are likely to hear stories about the adventures of Anansi de Trickster. Anansi is the hero of the Bruh Nancy Tales, a series of West African folkloric stories that also gave rise to the US slave stories of Uncle Remus and Br'er Rabbit, recorded by Joel Chandler Harris.

Painting & Sculpture

The most celebrated painter to come from the Virgin Islands is Camille Pissarro. Born in St Thomas in 1830 as Jacob Pizarro, the son of Spanish Jews, the young Jacob grew up on Main St in Charlotte Amalie. Eventually, he became an accomplished painter, moved to Paris and changed his name to Camille Pissarro. The Virgin Islands, particularly St Thomas Harbor, inspired the painter. His tropical pastoral paintings feature a dreamy sense of line and sunwashed colors. Because of his subjects and his interpretations, Pissarro won recognition as one of the founders of the French Impressionist movement. Some pieces of the painter's work are on display at Government House in Charlotte Amalie.

In recent years, the Virgins have become home to first-rate sculptors such as Aragorn

Dick-Read at Trellis Bay, Tortola, and the woodworkers at the St Croix Leap project. Tillett Gardens on St Thomas houses the studios of superb printmakers, crafters and artists working in watercolors and oils.

SOCIETY & CONDUCT

Generalizing about national character is always dangerous, and West Indians (including Virgin Islanders) have suffered from unfortunate stereotypes perpetrated by Hollywood, advertising campaigns and pop music. The stereotype of West Indian men as happy-go-lucky beach bums addicted to rum, ganja (marijuana) and calypso/reggae, and West Indian women as matronly market vendors with head scarves, is so strong that many first-time visitors to the islands are more than a little surprised by the complex people and culture they find.

One of the best places to meet islanders is at one of the mom-and-pop restaurant/bars that West Indian entrepreneurs are fond of erecting in their homes along the country roads and in the settlements. Generally run by vivacious souls like Vie Mahabir of Vie's Snack Shack on St John, these gathering places attract a clutch of neighbors to drink bush tea (from leaves, roots and herbs), soft drinks or Carib beer and linger at tables and benches outside to discuss the news of the day – especially the latest twist in a political or commercial corruption scandal.

It is at these local restaurant/bars that you can get answers to all of your questions about island mysteries. You can also catch a few laughs, watch a basketball or cricket match on TV, hear the proprietor's newest calypso or reggae tapes and sense the love of life that infuses Virgin Islanders. You can pick up on a value system that places a high priority on family, friends and a love of the islands as well as the time to enjoy them. In the islands, you get a sense that work is often not an end in itself, nor a necessity. Work is a means of expanding one's social network; you do it with an eye toward entertainment, both for yourself and the folks around you. Laughter is worth more than gold.

In the BVI, you sense the strong influence of a British colonial heritage in the institutions of the government, education, religion and the law, whereas the US islands wear a veneer of mainstream American culture with its emphasis on conveniences like shopping malls and fast food.

Throughout the Virgins, you feel the strong presence of West Africa in music, dance, cooking and family life. And on these islands where everyone has arrived trailing a culture from somewhere else, there is – at last – a respect for differences. The islands' turbulent history of cultural and racial clashes is a constant reminder to everyone that only through respect for differences can blacks and whites, Jews and Palestinians, belongers and continentals survive and thrive in this tropical paradise they all love.

It is a sign of the times that many young Virgin Islanders embrace friends from black, white and Puerto Rican backgrounds. Biracial romances, long a tradition in these islands, are now rooted in mutual respect and not colonial concepts of master and slave.

Dos & Don'ts

Good manners are prized possessions in the islands. Taking the time to greet people with a 'good morning,' 'good day' or 'good evening' while making eye contact is the only courteous way to start a relationship with anyone in the islands, whether they are strangers or familiars.

And don't stop with the greeting; take time to acknowledge something special about the person you are meeting like her choice of blouse or his new shoes. Let a conversation develop, and do not be impatient to state your agenda. Eventually, the two of you will get around to putting that breakfast order together or exchanging money for some baked goods. When parting, always offer some remark of genuine, specific gratitude (not a generic 'thanks') and take time to wish the other person well.

Keep in mind that the tropical climate slows things down, and most islanders take life at a pace that keeps their bodies from overheating. So don't expect things to run like clockwork in the islands. Whether having a meal, catching a flight or doing some banking, always allow more time than you would back home.

Also see Clothing, below.

Clothing

One way islanders show their respect for each other is through dressing neatly. Both men and women wear rather conservative and formal attire when at work or out and about the islands during the day.

Skirts, dresses and neatly pressed slacks are common dress for island women. Men generally wear long pants (not jeans). Shorts are reserved for sport or leisure time at the beach.

To wear bathing suits, short shorts, skimpy outfits or dirty clothing when you are out in public (except at the beach or on hiking trails) is to blatantly reject the Virgin Islanders' sense of decorum. If you dress and act like you are at a beach party, you will eventually find yourself shunned in social interactions and dealt with last in shops, restaurants and pubs where islanders are in charge. Topless and nude sunbathing are generally frowned upon except at a few discreet beaches.

RELIGION

A number of different Protestant faiths dominate the Virgin Islands. The Baptist faith is the largest religious force in the USVI, with 42% of worshipers. Episcopalians constitute 17% of worshipers. And Roman Catholics (mostly Puerto Rican and Dominican immigrants) make up 34% of all worshipers.

In the BVI, the Methodist church claims 45% of all worshipers, whereas the Anglican church has 21%. Most other worshipers belong to Pentecostal faiths such as Seventh-Day Adventist. On St Thomas, the Jewish temple dates back more than 200 years.

The islands have a strong tradition of spiritual worship, and Sunday mornings bring legions of islanders dressed in their finery to church in family cars, taxis and church-owned buses. Services are packed, long and musical, and on Sunday mornings you cannot help but hear the singing of the congregations pouring through communities large and small. Church ministers hold substantial respect and power in island communities.

Quite a few islanders also practice obeah. This is not a religion per se but a set of beliefs that derive from West African ancestral worship, animism, spirit worship and sorcery. Like voodoo in Haiti, and Santería in the Spanish Caribbean, obeah uses fetishes, herbs, potions and rituals to invoke spirits of ancestors to work power magic in favor of the practitioner. For believers, these *jumbies* or *duppies* (spirits) are often considered the source of both good and bad fortune and capable of bringing everything from love and wealth to an outrageous electric bill or a bad hair day. After centuries of keeping obeah away from the prying eyes of imperial moralists and the Christian church, Virgin Islanders are still shy when it comes to talking about their beliefs in spiritualism. Nevertheless, plenty of islanders consult the 'obeah man' or 'obeah woman' when they are about to make an important decision like buying a house or getting married. If you are living in a West Indian neighborhood, you will no doubt hear adults tell unruly children that 'de jumbies gonna getcha.'

LANGUAGE

English is the main language spoken throughout the Virgin Islands, although you will hear quite a bit of Spanish if you visit St Croix. For the most part, islanders speak Standard English but with an accent that is lyrical and euphonious. The accent derives from the traditional dialect of the islands – so-called Creole, Calypso or West Indian – that is a blend of West African grammar and speech patterns with colonial English, Danish, French and Dutch. Creole varies significantly from island to island in both tones and in its use of local slang. But what is common across the islands is that islanders 'sing' their English, giving vowels a number of shades and dropping or changing consonants to syncopate the phrasing.

Island Proverbs & Witticisms

Buddy, me a walkin' behin'
  Discretion is the better part of valor

Yo' mout' is a one-room house
  Speak up, or, used ironically, You talk too much

If yo' put yo' ear a mango root, yo' will hear de crab cough
  Patience is a virtue

Bettah fo' sure dan for sorry
  Haste makes waste

Man got two wife; him sleep hungry
  You can get too much of a good thing

Yo' a run from de jumbie a' meet de coffin
  Out of the frying pan, into the fire

Not so cat walk dey does mouse
  Don't judge a book by the cover; literally, 'The idle cat may pounce on the mouse'

De longes' prayer got amen
  Nothing lasts forever

The difference between a Creole accent and a standard American accent is something like the difference between Brazilian Portuguese and Continental Portuguese. And the differences from island to island are remarkable as well. For example, the Standard English command 'Come here, man' becomes 'Coam yah, mahn' in the Creole of St Croix. The same request becomes 'Cahm heh, mon' on St Thomas.

One distinct feature of Creole is the use of the pronoun 'me' to replace 'I.' In addition, helping verbs often disappear from Creole sentences. Blended sounds like 'ing' get softened and simplified in Creole so that the standard English sentence 'I am running all day long' becomes 'Me runnin' all day long' in Creole.

The 'th' sound in the Standard English words 'this,' 'that' and 'the' soften to 'dis,' 'dat' and 'da' (or 'de') in Creole. 'With' becomes 'wit'; 'thing' is 'ting'; 'thanks' is 'tanks'; 'three' is 'tree'; and 'what' is 'wah.' 'Those' gets replaced by 'them' and pronounced 'dem.' 'Their' becomes 'they,' pronounced 'dey.' The 'er' sound at the end of a word like 'butter' softens to 'buttah.' A 'horse' on St Croix is a 'hahs' and a 'hoas' on Tortola.

Another change from Standard English to Creole is replacing the pronouns 'him' and 'her' with 'he' and 'she.' A major grammatical change between standard English and Creole is the forming of plural nouns using the word 'dem' instead of an 's' at the end of the word. In Creole, the standard plural noun 'boys' becomes 'boy dem.' Put all of these changes together (and many others) and a Standard English complaint like 'I am running all day long for those three boys, and I have no horse to help, father!' becomes in Creole, 'Me runnin' all de day long for tree boy dem and me have no hahs to he'p, faddah!'

Creole is easy to understand when spoken slowly, but sometimes islanders turn their language into code when they speak to each other quickly and sprinkle in a strong dose of slang (see the glossary at the end of this book). Doan worry. Dem jus' limin' and fowl bus'ness no cockroacy. (Don't worry. They are just relaxing, and it's best to mind your own business.)

Facts for the Visitor

HIGHLIGHTS
Historic Charlotte Amalie
With the largest concentration of colonial buildings in the Caribbean, the capital of the US Virgin Islands also has hundreds of duty-free shops, a panoply of restaurants and a steamy nightlife.

Water Island
The US government transferred this large island, a former military reservation in St Thomas Harbor, to the territory of the USVI in 1996. Though just a quarter-mile from the urban frenzy of Charlotte Amalie, Water Island remains a 490-acre oasis with only 125 residents, plenty of vacant beaches and roads ripe for biking.

Virgin Islands National Park
This park covers three-quarters of the island of St John (more than 9500 acres) and 5000 acres of adjacent reefs and cays. There are dozens of hiking trails, beaches and snorkeling sites as well as historical ruins, including the Annaberg Plantation. You can camp at Cinnamon Bay and Maho Bay on the north coast.

Historic Christiansted
This 18th-century town served as the capital of the Danish West Indies for more than 100 years. Today the National Park Service, merchants and citizens have made Christiansted a showcase of historic preservation, alive with shops, restaurants and pubs.

Buck Island
This small island (176 acres) lies 1½ miles off St Croix and sits at the center of an 880-acre marine sanctuary. The National Park Service controls its use and preserves the natural habitat of the island and its surrounding reefs. It is a prime example of a complete, wild Caribbean ecosystem. Several tour operators run trips to the island that include excellent snorkeling on the reef.

Estate Whim Plantation Museum
One of St Croix's most striking reminders of its colonial sugar cane history, Whim Plantation survives as a museum at mid-island. The grounds evoke the days when 'King Cane' ruled the island.

Jost Van Dyke
This island north of Tortola has developed a reputation that far exceeds its mere 4 sq miles of land. Jost's retreat of mountains, beaches and coves will delight visitors seeking a simpler world. A few guesthouses, a campground and a few infamous beach bars cater to travelers.

The Baths,
Spring Bay & Devil's Bay
This collection of giant boulders near the southwest corner of Virgin Gorda marks the BVI's most popular tourist attraction. The rocks form a series of grottoes that flood with seawater. The Baths will stir the imagination, but the place is generally overrun with tourists. Neighboring Spring Bay and Devil's Bay have the same landscape but without the crowds.

Snorkeling
The Virgins have hundreds of beaches, and almost all of them offer snorkeling opportunities. St John, Anegada and the smaller cays of the BVI have world-class reefs and fish.

Sailing to the Out Islands
The Virgin Islands are the charterboat capital of the world, with hundreds of bareboat (uncrewed) and crewed yachts to rent. Sailing aboard one of these boats for a day, week or longer is a good way to explore the largely undeveloped bays and cays like Peter, Cooper and Norman Islands.

SUGGESTED ITINERARIES
Someone looking at a one-week vacation may well opt to spend the whole time on just one island or select a destination, such as St

Thomas, St John or Tortola, that offers easy access to ferries for day trips to other islands. With a couple of weeks or more, travelers can begin to do some serious island-hopping.

Even if you crave sun and surf, plan on spending at least a day exploring the sites, museums, shops and nightlife of Charlotte Amalie, St Thomas. If you love restored colonial towns and shopping, take a sea-plane to Christiansted, St Croix, and spend two or more days exploring this large, historic island.

If you seek a Margaritaville atmosphere, spend a few days on the East End of St Thomas before taking the short ferry ride to St John. On St John, you can hit scores of wild beaches, snorkel, dive or hike the trails of the Virgin Islands National Park by day and fall into the Cruz Bay cafe/pub/restaurant/shopping groove by night. You haven't experienced St John unless you've spent a few nights in one of the campgrounds.

When you are ready to see the BVI, grab a ferry to Jost Van Dyke and kick back in the barefoot ambience of an island with fewer than 200 residents. The campground and several guesthouses here are good values, and for entertainment you have the famous Foxy's Tamarind Bar among other beach bars. Eventually, you can take a ferry to Red Hook on Tortola – home to more than half of the BVI's 19,000 people. This island has an amazing collection of beaches and guesthouses, particularly on the North Shore around Cane Garden Bay, which can be party central.

From Tortola, take a ferry, daysail (a one-day trip on a commercial excursion boat) or bareboat or crewed yacht to the many barely inhabited cays in the BVI, such as Peter, Cooper and Norman Islands. Here, life is reduced to the pleasures of snorkeling and diving, sleeping under a shade tree and finding a beach bar with a West Indian cook to make your tummy smile. If you like small-boat sailing and boulder-strewn landscapes, be sure to spend some time on Virgin Gorda. Finally, if you want to really get away from it all, take one of the scheduled flights to Anegada ($60 roundtrip). Here you'll find miles of empty beaches, funky campgrounds and probably the best snorkeling in the islands.

If you have a cruising boat, or if you charter one in the islands, you can follow this itinerary in your own craft.

PLANNING
When to Go

There are only good and better times to visit the Virgin Islands. They have one of the most congenial year-round climates in the world. Daily average temperatures range from the mid-70°s F (low to mid 20°s C) in January and February to the low 80°s F (mid to high 20°s C) from July to September. The hottest months are also the rainiest. Hurricane season runs from July to October (see Climate in the Facts about the Virgin Islands chapter).

For most travelers, the key to a great trip is successfully navigating the tourist season. 'The season' runs from Christmas week until the beginning of May. During these months, crowds of sun-loving tourists from Europe, the USA and Canada descend on the main islands. Many of these travelers arrive on cruise ships. Accommodations can be difficult to come by during the peak winter months, and they're 30% more expensive than at other times of the year. If you are planning to visit the islands during the winter, you should make reservations a minimum of three months in advance to get a decent selection and price.

Off-season travelers (those visiting May to November) will find good weather – barring a fall hurricane – and deep discounts on things such as hotel rooms and rental cars.

What Kind of Trip

If your main purpose in coming to the Virgin Islands is to vacation for a week or two with sun and surf, you will find it cheaper and easier to book a package tour that includes flights, transfers, accommodations and some meals.

If you have the time and inclination to explore, purchase a super-APEX fare in one of the 'shoulder season' months such as May or November. You might be able to negotiate a good rate for a multi-day stay in one of the guesthouses in Charlotte Amalie and use this site as your base. When you have had enough bright lights, big city, take off for the other islands on ferries or commuter flights.

Maps

The USVI Department of Tourism (☎ 340-774-8784, 800-372-8784) publishes free maps for visitors. The BVI Tourist Board (☎ 284-494-3864, 800-835-8530) distributes free color maps sponsored by AT&T; they are perfectly adequate for navigating Road Town and the main islands.

International Travel Maps (☎ 604-879-3621) of Vancouver, British Columbia, has a map to the US and British Virgin Islands published on heavy paper. This map is widely available through Rand McNally bookstores for $8. It offers excellent detail of topographical contours and hiking trails.

What to Bring

One of the joys of the islands is that travelers do not need to lug in a lot of clothes, gear, supplies, medicines, favorite foods, etc. Light cotton clothes and a couple of bathing suits will meet almost all of your daily garment needs. (Be sure to read the Clothing section in Facts About the Virgin Islands before you go.)

You might bring along a somewhat fancier dress, sport shirt, jacket or slacks if you plan on strutting your stuff at a posh resort or stepping out with the professional crowd in Charlotte Amalie or Christiansted on a Saturday night.

Comfortable walking shoes are essential for exploring. You may want a sweater for cool or windy nights. An inexpensive plastic rain jacket (or at least a travel umbrella) can come in handy during tropical showers, and a flashlight is essential for dark nights.

Pack some toiletries, a good book, a sketchpad and a beach towel. If you forget something, buy it on one of the islands.

RESPONSIBLE TOURISM

Travelers should remember that discarded fishing line, plastic bags and six-pack rings can entangle and kill birds and other sea creatures, some endangered. Avoid buying jewelry made from endangered species, such as black coral and sea turtles, as this threatens the existence of the remaining animals.

Divers' etiquette teaches that standing on, hanging from or carrying away live coral all cause damage to reef ecosystems that takes decades for nature to repair. To avoid hitting or killing endangered turtles, boaters must not travel at high speeds over seagrass beds.

Discharge of fuels, oils and cleaning bleaches kills all kinds of marine organisms, as well as the birds that feed on them. Remember too that taking plants or animals as souvenirs from a forest reserve is theft. When possible, recycle – failure to recycle paper, plastic containers, bottles and aluminum cans destroys global resources just as surely as a logging operation in a rain forest.

TOURIST OFFICES
Local Tourist Offices

The US Virgin Islands Department of Tourism (USVI DOT) and the BVI Tourist Board (BVI TB) are the territories' official agencies for tourism. Both are good sources for brochures on island accommodations, restaurants, sports, shopping and festivals. All of the most populated islands have tourist offices.

On St Thomas, the main visitors bureau (☎ 340-774-8784, 800-372-8784) is across the street from Vendors' Plaza and Emancipation Park on Tolbod Gade in Charlotte Amalie. A second office is on the cruise ship dock in Havensight.

On St John, the visitors bureau (☎ 340-776-6450) is a small building next to the post office on Dronningens Gade (across the street from the ferry dock) in Cruz Bay.

On St Croix, the visitors bureau (☎ 340-773-0495) is located at 52 Company St in Christiansted.

On Tortola, the main BVI Tourist Board office (☎ 284-494-3864, 800-835-8530) is in the Akara Building in Road Town, on Wickhams Cay 1. There is also a small office (☎ 284-494-7260) at the ferry terminal in Road Town.

On Virgin Gorda, the tourist board (☎ 284-495-5181) is in the Yacht Harbour mall at Spanish Town.

Tourist Offices Abroad

The following are USVI Department of Tourism and BVI Tourist Board offices abroad.

Canada
USVI DOT (☎ 416-233-1414) 3300 Bloor St West, Suite 3120, Center Tower, Toronto, Ontario MBX 2X3

Denmark
USVI DOT (☎ 45-86-181933) Park Alle 5, DK-80000, Arhus Center

England
USVI DOT (☎ 44-171-978-5262) Molasses House, Clove Hitch, Quay Plantation Wharf, London SW11 3TW
BVI TB (☎ 44-171-027-1183) 110 St Martin's Lane, London WC2N 4DY

Germany
USVI DOT (☎ 089 236 6210) Herzodspital-strasse 5, Munich D-80331
BVI TB (☎ 49 210 271 1183) Wallstrasse 56, Dusseldorf/Ratingin D-480878

Italy
USVI DOT (☎ 39-02-3310-5842) Via Gherardini 2, Milan 20145
BVI TB (☎ 39-02-6671-4374) AIGO Comunicazione, Piazza Caiazzo 3, Milan 20124

Puerto Rico
U*SVI DOT* (☎ 787-722-8023) 60 Washington St, San Juan 00907

USA
USVI DOT: (☎ 340-773-0495) 245 Peachtree Center Ave, Marquis One Tower, Suite MB-05, Atlanta, GA 30303
(☎ 312-670-8784) 500 North Michigan Ave, Suite 2030, Chicago, IL 60611
(☎ 213-739-0138) 3460 Wilshire Blvd, Suite 412, Los Angeles, CA 90010
(☎ 305-442-7200) 2655 LeJeuene Rd, Suite 907, Coral Gables, FL 33134
(☎ 212-332-2222) 1270 Ave of the Americas, Suite 2108, New York, NY 10020
(☎ 202-624-3590) The Hall of States, 444 North Capital St NW, Suite 298, Washington, DC 20001
BVI TB: (☎ 212-696-0400) 370 Lexington Ave, New York, NY 10017
(☎ 415-775-0344) 1804 Union St, San Francisco, CA 94123

VISAS & DOCUMENTS

Although student and senior cards rarely earn discounts in the islands, they can be useful identification and may bring occasional discounts at hotels.

Passport & Visas

Both the USVI and the BVI permit US and Canadian citizens to enter the islands with proper proof of citizenship (such as a driver's license with photo ID), a passport or a birth certificate. Visitors from other countries must have a valid passport, and many visitors are also required to have a US visa if heading for the USVI.

Check the US State Department Web site (http://travel.state.gov/visa_services.html) for detailed, current information about visa requirements, immigration and related topics. You do not need a visa if you are staying in the BVI for less than six months, but you must have a return or ongoing ticket.

Travel Insurance

No matter how you're traveling, make sure you take out travel insurance. This should cover you not only for medical expenses and luggage theft or loss, but also for cancellations or delays in your travel arrangements, and you should be covered for the worst possible case, such as an accident that requires hospital treatment and a flight home.

Coverage depends on your insurance and type of ticket, so ask both your insurer and your ticket-issuing agency to explain the finer points. STA Travel (☎ 800-777-0112) and Council Travel (☎ 800-226-8624) offer travel insurance options at reasonable prices. Ticket loss is also covered by travel insurance. Make sure you have a separate record of all your ticket details – or better still, a photocopy of the tickets. Also make a copy of your policy in case the original is lost.

Buy travel insurance as early as possible. If you buy it the week before you fly, you may find, for instance, that you're not covered for delays to your flight caused by strikes or other industrial action that may have been in force before you took out the insurance. Insurance may seem very expensive, but it's nowhere near the cost of a medical emergency in the islands. (Also see Health Insurance, later in this chapter.)

Driver's License

You will need your home driver's license to rent a car in the US and British Virgin Islands, and most visitors can legally drive here for up to a year with their home license. In the BVI, law requires that the rental agencies charge you $10 for a temporary (three months) BVI driver's license.

Photocopies

All important documents (your passport data page and visa page, credit cards, travel insurance policy, air/bus/train tickets, driver's license, etc) should be photocopied before you leave home. Leave one copy with someone at home and keep another with you, separate from the originals.

EMBASSIES & CONSULATES

With the exception of Danish (☎ 340-776-0656) and Swedish (☎ 340-774-6845) consulates on St Thomas, there are no foreign embassies or consulates in the Virgin Islands. The closest cache of foreign embassies and consulates is in nearby San Juan, Puerto Rico.

US diplomatic offices representing the USVI abroad and providing visa service include the following.

Australia
(☎ 2-9373-9200) Level 59 MLC Center, 19-29 Martin Place, Sydney NSW 2000
(☎ 3-9526-5900) 553 St Kilda Rd, Melbourne, Victoria

Canada
(☎ 613-238-5535) 100 Wellington St, Ottawa, Ontario K1P 5T1

France
(☎ 0142 96 12 02) 2 rue St Florentin, 75001 Paris

Germany
(☎ 228 33 91) Deichmanns Aue 29, 53179 Bonn

Ireland
(☎ 1-687-122) 42 Elgin Rd, Ballsbridge, Dublin

Netherlands
(☎ 70-310-9209) Lange Voorhout 102, 2514 EJ, The Hague

UK
(☎ 020-7499-9000) 5 Upper Grosvenor St, London W1

British diplomatic offices representing the BVI abroad include the following.

Australia
(☎ 02-9254-7521) Level 16, the Gateway, 1 Macquarie Place, Sydney NSW 2000

Canada
(☎ 416-593-1290) Suite 2800, 777 Bay St, College Park, Toronto, Ontario M5G 2G2

France
(☎ 01 44 51 31 00) 35 rue de Faubourg Saint Honeré, 75008 Paris

Germany
(☎ 022 891 670) Freidriech-Ebert Allee 77, 53111 Bonn
(☎ 030 201 840) Unter den Linden 17/34, 10117 Berlin

Ireland
(☎ 01-205-3822) 29 Merrion Rd, Ballsbridge, Dublin

Netherlands
(☎ 070-427-04-27) Lange Voorhout 10, 2514 ED, The Hague

USA
(☎ 212 745 0444) 27th floor, One Dag Hammarskjold Plaza, 885 2nd Ave, New York, NY 10017

As a tourist, it's important to realize what your own embassy – the embassy of the country of which you are a citizen – can and can't do. Your embassy won't be much help in emergencies if the trouble you are in is remotely your own fault. You are bound by the laws of the country you are in.

In genuine emergencies, you might get some assistance, but only if other channels have been exhausted. For example, if you need to get home urgently, a free ticket home is exceedingly unlikely – the embassy would expect you to have insurance. If you have all of your money and documents stolen, your embassy might assist in getting you a new passport, but a loan for onward travel is out of the question.

CUSTOMS

US citizens (including children) can bring home, duty-free, 5 liters of liquor and $1200 worth of goods from the USVI every 30 days. US citizens can bring back $400 worth of goods duty-free from the BVI.

Canadian citizens can bring back C$500 of goods duty-free, 200 cigarettes and 40oz of strong spirits.

UK citizens traveling from non-EC nations can bring back £145 in goods duty-free, 200 cigarettes and 1 liter of strong spirits.

Australian citizens over 18 can return with A$500 in goods, 250 cigarettes and slightly more than 1 liter of strong alcohol.

New Zealand citizens over 17 can return with NZ$700 in purchases, 200 cigarettes and 1.125 liters of strong spirits.

You must have receipts for all of your purchases to present to customs agents.

MONEY
Currency
Both the US and British Virgin Islands use US currency. The US dollar is divided into 100 cents (¢). Coins come in denominations of 1¢, called the penny; 5¢, called the nickel; 10¢, called the dime; 25¢, called the quarter; and the seldom-seen 50¢ (half dollar) coin. Quarters are the most commonly used coins in vending machines, so it's handy to have a stash of them.

Notes, commonly called bills, come in $1, $2, $5, $10, $20, $50 and $100 denominations – $2 bills are rare but perfectly legal. There are also two $1 coins that the government has tried to bring into mass circulation. One looks like a large quarter; the other is gold, with an image of Sacagawea on it.

Exchange Rates At press time, exchange rates were as follows:

country	unit		US dollar
Australia	A$1	=	$0.48
Canada	C$1	=	$0.63
East Caribbean	EC$	=	$0.37
European Union	€1	=	$0.88
France	FF1	=	$0.13
Germany	DM1	=	$0.45
Japan	¥100	=	$0.80
New Zealand	NZ$1	=	$0.40
UK	UK£1	=	$1.42
Venezuela	Bs 1000	=	$1.4

Exchanging Money Some banks on the islands will exchange cash or traveler's checks in major foreign currencies, but it may take them some time.

If you are flying into San Juan, Puerto Rico, on your way to the Virgins, it is less of a hassle to exchange foreign currency in the San Juan airport.

Cash & Traveler's Checks Though carrying cash is more risky, it's still a good idea to travel with some for the convenience. It's useful for tipping, and some smaller, more remote places may not accept credit cards or traveler's checks.

Traveler's checks offer greater protection from theft or loss and in many places can be used as cash. American Express and Thomas Cook are widely accepted in the Virgins and have efficient replacement policies.

ATMs In the Virgin Islands, you will find ATMs at most banks and in a few shopping malls. Some of these are available 24 hours a day. The ATM networks Plus and Cirrus are the predominant networks on the islands.

For a nominal service charge, you can withdraw cash from an ATM using a credit card or a charge card.

Credit & Debit Cards Major credit cards are accepted at hotels, restaurants, shops and car rental agencies throughout the Virgin Islands. In fact, you'll find it hard to perform certain transactions, such as renting a car, without one.

Carry copies of your credit card numbers separately from the cards. If you lose your credit cards or they get stolen, contact the company immediately (contact your bank if you lose your ATM card).

Following are toll-free numbers for the main credit card companies.

American Express	☎ 800-528-4800
Diners Club	☎ 800-234-6377
Discover	☎ 800-347-2683
MasterCard	☎ 800-826-2181
Visa	☎ 800-336-8472

Security

Carry your money (and only the money you'll need for that day) inside your clothing (in a money belt, a bra or your sock) rather than in a handbag or an outside pocket. Put the money in several places. Most hotels provide safekeeping, so you can leave your money and other valuables where you're staying. Hide (or don't wear) any valuable jewelry. A safety pin or key ring to hold the zipper tags of a day pack together can help deter theft.

Costs

The cost of accommodations in the Virgin Islands varies seasonally. Rates are highest between the December holidays and the end of the spring holidays (which include Easter, Passover, public school vacations and college spring break). With only a few exceptions, the cheapest rates are in the $50 to $60 range. Rustic camping is inexpensive, $20 or less per night, but you will have to pay a lot more at camping areas with amenities like tents and hot showers.

Food prices are about 20% higher than in the USA. The occasional splurge at a first-rate restaurant will cost from $20 to $50, but plenty of good meals in restaurants can be found for less than $10. If you purchase food and alcoholic beverages at markets and large supermarkets, you can get by more cheaply. Public transportation is relatively inexpensive; island buses generally cost $1 or less, depending on distance and the system.

On many islands, a car is the only easy way to get around; weeklong rentals can cost $275 and up. Gasoline costs about the same as it does in the USA. For more information on renting and operating a car, see the Getting Around chapter.

Tipping

Taxi drivers, hairdressers and baggage carriers expect tips. In restaurants, waitstaff rely upon tips for their livelihoods. Tip 15% unless the service is terrible (in which case a complaint to the manager is warranted) or up to 20% if the service is great. Never tip in fast-food, take-out or buffet-style restaurants where you serve yourself. Taxi drivers expect 10%, and hairdressers generally get 15% if their service is satisfactory. Baggage carriers (skycaps in airports and attendants in hotels) get $1 for the first bag and 50¢ for each additional bag. In budget hotels, tips are not expected.

Taxes

Many things you pay for in the Virgin Islands – except duty-free items like jewelry, liquor and china – are taxed. Frequently, the tax is included in the advertised price. Tax rates vary from item to item, and almost no one in the islands except the tax collectors can tell you the difference between the tax included in the cost of your airline ticket versus the tax on a round of Foxy's Lager at the bar. If you stay in a hotel, you will pay an 8% tax in the USVI, 7% in the BVI.

There is no departure tax in the USVI. In the BVI, you pay $10 departing by plane, $5 departing by boat. Unless otherwise stated, the prices given in this book don't reflect local taxes.

Special Deals

Although bargaining is not generally accepted in the Virgin Islands, there are ways to cut costs. At hotels in the off-season, casually and respectfully mentioning a competitor's rate may prompt a manager to lower the quoted rate. Artisans may consider a negotiated price for large purchases. Discount coupons are widely available – check circulars in tourist publications, supermarkets and tourist offices.

POST & COMMUNICATIONS
Post

In the US Virgin Islands, rates for 1st-class mail to the US and its territories are 34¢ for letters up to 1oz (21¢ for each additional ounce) and 20¢ for postcards. International airmail rates (except to Canada and Mexico) are 80¢ for a 1oz letter and 75¢ for each additional ounce. International postcard rates are 70¢. Letters to Canada and Mexico cost 60¢ for a 1oz letter, 85¢ for a 2oz letter and 50¢ for a postcard. Aerogrammes cost 70¢.

In the British Virgin Islands, you pay 30¢ for a postcard and 45¢ for a 1st-class letter (up to half an ounce). Usually, post offices in main towns are open 8 am to 5 pm weekdays and 8 am to 1 pm Saturday.

Hotels and other businesses on all but the most populated islands often have no street address or post office box. When no address is given in this book, you can address correspondence by simply writing the name of the business followed by the name of the town and the territory.

You can have mail sent to you, addressed as 'c/o General Delivery,' at any post office that has its own zip (postal) code. Mail is usually held for 10 days before it's returned to the sender; you might request that your correspondents write 'hold for arrival' on letters. Alternatively, have mail sent to the local representative of American Express or other private service (see the Information sections in the individual island chapters).

Telephone

All phone numbers in the USVI consist of a three-digit area code – ☎ 340 – followed by a seven-digit local number. In the BVI, the area code is ☎ 284. If you are calling locally, just dial the seven-digit number. If you are calling long distance, dial ☎ 1 + the seven-digit number. To call the islands from the USA (or between the USVI and the BVI), dial ☎ 1 + area code + the seven-digit number. Call the islands from other overseas destinations the same way, after dialing for an international line.

For directory assistance, dial ☎ 411. For US directory assistance outside the islands, dial ☎ 1 + the three-digit area code of the place you want to call + 555-1212. For example, to obtain directory assistance for a toll-free number, dial ☎ 1-800-555-1212 or 1-888-555-1212. The 800 and 888 area codes are designated for toll-free numbers within the USA and Virgin Islands.

Local calls cost 25¢ at pay phones, which are most easily found in hotels. Long-distance rates vary depending on the destination and which telephone company you use – call the operator (☎ 0) for rate information. Don't ask the operator to put your call through, however, because operator-assisted calls are much more expensive than direct-dial calls.

Generally, nights (11 pm to 8 am), all day Saturday and 8 am to 5 pm Sunday are the cheapest times to call (60% discount). Evenings (5 to 11 pm Sunday to Friday) are mid-priced (35% discount). Day calls (8 am to 5 pm weekdays) are full-price calls within the USA and the islands.

International Calls To make a direct international call from the islands, dial ☎ 011, then the country code, followed by the area code and the phone number. You may need to wait as long as 45 seconds for the ringing to start. International rates vary depending on the time of day and the destination. Call the operator (☎ 0) for rates. The first minute is always more expensive than extra minutes.

Phone Debit Cards There's a wide range of local and international phonecards available. Lonely Planet's eKno global communication service provides low-cost international calls – for local calls you're usually better off with a local phonecard. eKno also offers free messaging services, email, travel information and an online travel vault, where you can securely store all your important documents.

You can join eKno online at www.ekno .lonelyplanet.com, where you will find the local access numbers for the 24-hour customer service center. (In the Virgin Islands, call ☎ 877-503-0287.) Once you have joined, always check the eKno Web site for the latest access numbers for each country and updates on new features.

Fax & Telegraph

Fax machines are available at businesses like Nisky Mailboxes on St Thomas, Connections on St John and the Cable & Wireless office on Tortola. You can also find fax machines at computer service shops and hotel business-service centers, but be prepared to pay high prices (more than $2 a page). American Telegraph (☎ 800-343-7363) handles wire service in the islands.

Email & Internet Access

A lot of individuals and most businesses are online in the islands. However, because email and Internet addresses here seem to change constantly, they are not listed in this guide.

A few hotels have Internet connections as standard features in rooms, and cybercafes are popping up throughout the Virgin Islands. Check out www.netcafeguide.com for an up-to-date list of cybercafes worldwide. Local libraries are also online.

INTERNET RESOURCES

There's no better place to start your Web explorations than the Lonely Planet Web site (www.lonelyplanet.com). Here you'll find succinct summaries on traveling to most places on earth including the Virgin Islands, postcards from other travelers and the Thorn Tree bulletin board, where you can ask questions before you go or dispense advice when you get back.

You can also find travel news and updates to many of our most popular guidebooks, and the subWWWay section provides you with links to the most useful travel resources elsewhere on the Internet.

A quick search on the Web turns up literally thousands of sites trying to sell accommodations, tours and services in the Virgin Islands. To cut through the dross, try the following sites.

USVI Department of Tourism www.usvi.net
The department of tourism gives you an introduction to the islands, with links to island-specific tourism and business information, water sports and shopping.

BVI Welcome On-Line http://bviwelcome.com
This is the BVI Tourist Board's monthly magazine, with the scoop on items ranging from accommodations to 'Virgin Waters.'

OnePaper http://onepaper.com
Featuring three newspapers from the USVI – the *St Thomas Source*, the *St Croix Source* and the *St John Source*, – this site has extensive coverage from daily news and sports to editorials and entertainment.

Tradewinds http://stjohntradewindsnews.com
St John's newspaper is an excellent source of island news and villa rentals.

The BVI Home Page www.britishvirginislands.com
This Web site has complete coverage of island attractions plus a traveler's bulletin board and classified ads for jobs.

BOOKS

Most books are published in different editions by different publishers in different countries. As a result, a book might be a hardcover rarity in one country and readily available in paperback in another. Fortunately, bookstores and libraries can search by title or author, so your local bookstore or library is the best place to find out about the availability of the following recommendations. If you find that a title is out of print, a good used bookstore or your library may still have copies.

Lonely Planet

If you are combining your visit to the Virgin Islands with travels to other Caribbean islands, check out Lonely Planet's *Puerto Rico*, also by Randall Peffer; *Cuba*, by David Stanley; *Jamaica* and *Bahamas, Turks & Caicos*, both by Chris Baker; *Dominican Republic & Haiti*, by Scott Doggett and Leah Gordon; and *Eastern Caribbean*, by Glenda Bendure and Ned Friary.

Diving & Snorkeling British Virgin Islands, by Mauricio Handler, points you to all of the best dive sites and also provides the practical information you will need.

Caribbean Reef Ecology, by William S Alevizon, gives you the underwater picture.

World Food Caribbean, by Bruce Geddes, is a spicy, four-color introduction to Caribbean cuisine.

Travel

If you like the lilt of West Indian dialogue and slice-of-life stories about the contemporary Caribbean, check out Bob Shacochis' *Easy in the Islands,* a collection of short stories that won an American Book Award. Rob White's tropical memoir *Our Virgin Isle* describes his life as one of the first modern innkeepers in the Virgins, running the hotel on Marina Cay in the BVI.

Take a look at *Travelers' Health: How to Stay Healthy All Over the World,* by Dr Richard Dawood. The text is comprehensive, easy to read, authoritative and generally highly recommended. Unfortunately, it's rather large to lug around. You might read it before your trip and make copies of the sections you anticipate needing while you're away.

Activity Guides

Contemporary mariners will want *The Cruising Guide to the Virgin Islands,* by Nancy and Simon Scott, and *Street's Cruising Guide to the Eastern Caribbean.*

Aviators should carry a copy of Paul Fillingham's *Pilot's Guide to the Lesser Antilles.* Birders will want to check out *A Guide to the Birds of Puerto Rico & the Virgin Islands,* by Herbert Rafaela. The Lonely Planet diving guide listed above is essential for anyone contemplating an underwater adventure in these seas.

History, Politics & Sociology

To picture the Virgin Islands through the eyes of the conquistadors and read about the joys and tribulations of the first European encounters with the Caribbean, pick up Samuel Eliot Morison's *Admiral of the Ocean Sea* and *Caribbean the Way Columbus Saw It. From Columbus to Castro,* by Eric Williams, provides a historical view of the West Indies from colonial times to their struggle for independence in the 1980s.

The Virgin Islands: America's Caribbean Outpost, by James Bough and Roy Macridis, investigates the US role in the Virgin Islands' destiny.

Many US Virgin Islanders consider local author Harold Willocks' thick tome *The Umbilical Cord* the best portrait of their islands past and present. Florence Lewisohn has two short but well-researched volumes on the islands' history, *St Croix Under Seven Flags* and *Tales of Tortola and the British Virgin Islands.*

For a fascinating look at the evidence supporting early African exploration of the Caribbean, have a look at *They Came Before Columbus: The African Presence in Ancient America,* by Ivan Van Sertima.

Flora & Fauna

The Nature of the Islands and *Plants & Animals of the Eastern Caribbean,* by Virginia Barlow, are excellent guides to the flora and fauna of the Lesser Antilles, including lots of illustrations.

Eugene Kaplan's *Field Guide to the Coral Reefs of the Caribbean and Florida* (Petersen's Guides) and the boxed *Reef Set,* by Paul Humann, are comprehensive guides to the terrain and fish you will meet underwater in the Virgins. (Also see the Lonely Planet reef guide, listed earlier.)

Penelope Honeychurch has written an informative study of 'bush medicine' in *Caribbean Wild Plants and Their Uses. Common Trees of Puerto Rico and the Virgin Islands,* by EL Little and FH Wadsworth, has everything you ever wanted to know about the manchineel, the mango and more.

Reptiles and Amphibians of the Virgin Islands, by WP MacLean, is your guide to frogs, snakes and turtles in the islands. Bug lovers will want a peek at *Butterflies and Other Insects of the Eastern Caribbean,* by PD Stilling.

General

Herman Wouk wrote *Don't Stop the Carnival,* a comic yet tragic novel about a New York public relations man who 'drops out' at an inn on a small Caribbean island,

possibly Hassel Island (St Thomas) or Protestant Cay (St Croix). Derek Walcott's
Omeros is the Nobel Prize–winning Caribbean author's lauded epic poem about life
in the Lesser Antilles.

Caribbean Cooking, by Judy Bastry, and
Virgin Islands Native Recipes, by Mildred
Anduze, unfold the mysteries of Creole
cuisine. (Also see the Lonely Planet section,
earlier, for another guide to Caribbean
food.)

*Caribbean Carnival: Songs of the West
Indies,* by Irving Burgie, evokes the island
celebrations and traditional songs, including music and lyrics.

George Hunt, a Barbadian, gives an
insider's view of West Indian culture in *The
West Indies Islands. African Sources in New
World Black Music,* by Laz Ekwene, identi-
fies African influences in Caribbean and
North American music.

FILMS

The Virgin Islands regularly appear as settings for film and print advertisements and
commercials. In 1999, the BVI made a big
international splash as the setting for the
Sports Illustrated swimsuit issue.

Feature films have come to the BVI re-
cently as well with the shooting of *The Old
Man and the Sea,* starring Anthony Quinn,
at the west end of Tortola. Recent films shot
in the US islands include *Christopher
Columbus – The Discovery,* set at Hull Bay,
St Thomas, *The Four Seasons,* with Carol
Burnett and Alan Alda, and *The Big Blue,*
starring Rosanna Arquette, set at Hurricane
Hole on St John.

St Croix's Davis Bay was a setting for
The Island of Dr Moreau as well as *Trading
Places,* with Eddie Murphy and Dan
Aykroyd. In addition, the islands have been
settings for a plethora of TV shows and spe-
cials including *The Bold and the Beautiful,
Charlie's Angels* and *The Young and the
Restless.*

NEWSPAPERS & MAGAZINES

International editions of the *Miami Herald*
and *USA Today* are widely available on
the islands. *Caribbean Travel and Life* is a
four-color monthly magazine about travel
in the area.

The *VI Daily News* and *The Independent*
are the daily papers on St Thomas. The *St
Croix Avis* is this island's daily paper. *St
Thomas This Week* and *St Croix This Week*
are tourist tabloids with lots of relevant information about traveling in the islands.

In the BVI, the *Island Sun* has been
around Tortola for more than 40 years. It
comes out twice a week. Another major
news source is the *BVI Beacon.* The free
Limin' Times is a weekly entertainment
tabloid that gives you the best sense of
where to find the action throughout the
British Virgins.

RADIO & TV

WIVI (96.1 FM) is probably the most
popular rock & roll station. JAMZ (105.3
FM) is the station for continuous R&B. FM
stations like The Heat (94.3), ZGold (91.7)
and ZRod (103.7) serve up a mix of rock,
country, hip-hop, R&B and reggae. True
reggae lovers tune to Reggae 97.3 FM.
Puerto Rico's WOSO, at 1030 AM, has national and international news and commentary and excellent weather/storm coverage
in case of a hurricane.

As for TV, Channel 12 is St Thomas'
ABC affiliate. Channel 8 comes from St
Croix. For BVI news, check Channel 3,
which is the BVI local-access cable channel.

VIDEO SYSTEMS

Like the US, the Virgin Islands use the Na-
tional Television System Committee (NTSC)
color TV standard, which unless converted
is not compatible with other standards
(Phase Alternative Line, or PAL; Systeme
Electronique Couleur avec Memoire, or
SECAM) used in Africa, Europe, Asia and
Australia.

PHOTOGRAPHY & VIDEO
Film & Equipment

Print film is widely available at supermarkets and drugstores, but it is harder to find
slide film. Drugstores are a good place to
get your film cheaply processed; a few offer
same-day returns. In terms of photographic

equipment, it is wise to bring everything you need, although St Thomas has a few good camera shops.

The high air temperatures and humidity in the tropics accelerate the deterioration of film. If you are only in the islands for a week or two, don't worry about your film. But if you plan to stay longer, you should try to have your exposed film developed. To compensate for the bright light of the tropics, adjust your f-stop and/or use a polarizing filter. The best technique for managing light and contrast is to shoot before 9:30 am and after 3:30 pm.

Photographing People

It is common courtesy to ask people's permission before you photograph them. One good approach in markets is to buy something from the person whose picture you wish to take.

Airport Security

All airline passengers have to pass their luggage through X-ray machines. Today's technology doesn't jeopardize lower-speed film. If you are carrying high-speed (1600 ASA and above) film, you may want to carry film and cameras with you and ask the X-ray inspector to check your film visually.

TIME

The Virgin Islands are on Atlantic Standard Time. The time in this zone is an hour later than in the Eastern Standard Time zone, which encompasses US East Coast cities (New York, Miami, etc). During Daylight Saving Time in those cities – from 1 am on the first Sunday in April until 2 am on the last Sunday of October – the time is the same in the islands. There is no Daylight Saving Time in the Virgins. When it is noon on the islands, it's 4 pm in London, 8 am in Los Angeles and 2 am in Sydney.

ELECTRICITY

As in the USA, voltage in the Virgin Islands is 110V and plugs have two (flat) or three (two flat, one round) pins. Plugs with three pins don't fit into a two-hole socket, but adapters are easy to buy at hardware stores and drugstores.

WEIGHTS & MEASURES

The Virgin Islands use the imperial system. Distances are in feet, yards and miles; volume is usually measured in ounces for containers of beer and other beverages, and in gallons for gasoline. You will find the weight of grocery items such as meat measured in ounces and pounds. See the conversion chart at the back of the book for help converting to/from metric.

LAUNDRY

There are self-service laundry facilities in most towns and a few campgrounds in the islands. Washing a load usually costs about $1.50 and drying it costs another $2. Some laundries have attendants who will wash, dry and fold your clothes for you for an additional charge.

HEALTH

For most foreign visitors, no immunizations are required for entry to the Virgin Islands, though cholera and yellow fever vaccinations may be required of travelers from areas with a history of those diseases. There are no unexpected health dangers on the islands; good medical attention is readily available, and the only real health concern is that a collision with the medical system can cause severe injuries to your finances. St Thomas, St Croix and Tortola have modern hospitals. You will find walk-in clinics on virtually every inhabited island, as well as pharmacies – some open 24 hours a day.

In a serious emergency, call ☎ 911 or ☎ 999 (in the BVI) for an ambulance to take you to the nearest hospital's emergency room. ER charges are usually incredibly expensive unless you have valid medical insurance.

Predeparture Preparations

Make sure you're healthy before you start traveling. If you are embarking on a long trip, make sure your teeth are in good shape. If you wear glasses, take a spare pair and your prescription. You can get new spectacles made up quickly and competently for less than $100, depending on the prescription and frame you choose. If you require a particular medication, take an adequate supply and bring a prescription in case you lose your medication.

Health Insurance

A travel insurance policy to cover theft, lost tickets and medical problems is a good idea, especially in the USVI, where some hospitals will refuse care if you don't have evidence of insurance.

Policies vary widely; your travel agent should have recommendations. International student travel policies handled by STA Travel and other student travel organizations are usually a good value. Some policies offer lower and higher medical expense options, and the higher one is chiefly for countries that, like the US, have extremely high medical costs. Check the fine print.

Some policies specifically exclude 'dangerous activities' such as scuba diving, motorcycling and even trekking. If these activities are on your agenda, avoid this sort of policy. You may prefer a policy that pays doctors or hospitals directly rather than making you pay first and claim later. If you have to claim later, keep *all* documentation. Some policies ask you to call back (reverse charges) to a center in your home country for an immediate assessment of your problem. Check whether the policy covers ambulance fees or an emergency flight home. If you have to stretch out, you will need two seats, and somebody has to pay for it!

Food & Water

A crucial health rule is to be careful with what you eat and drink. Stomach upsets are the most common travel-related health problem (between 30% and 50% of travelers in a two-week stay experience one), but the majority of these upsets will be relatively minor. In the Virgin Islands, standards of cleanliness in places serving food and drink are generally high.

Bottled drinking water, both carbonated and noncarbonated, is widely available on the islands. Tap water is usually OK to drink, but ask locally.

Everyday Health

Normal body temperature is 98.6°F (37°C); more than 4°F (2°C) higher indicates a 'high' fever. The normal adult pulse rate is 60 to 80 per minute (children 80 to 100, babies 100 to 140). You should know how to take a temperature and a pulse rate.

Respiration (breathing) rate is also an indicator of illness. Count the number of breaths per minute: Between 12 and 20 is normal for adults and older children (up to 30 for younger children, 40 for babies). People with a high fever or serious respiratory illness (such as pneumonia) breathe more quickly than normal. More than 40 shallow breaths a minute usually means pneumonia.

Travel & Climate-Related Problems

Motion Sickness Eating lightly before and during a trip will reduce the chance of motion sickness. If you are prone to motion sickness, try to find a place that minimizes disturbance; for example, near the wing on aircraft or near the center on buses. Fresh air usually helps. Commercial anti-motion sickness preparations, which can cause drowsiness, have to be taken before the trip commences; once you feel sick, it's too late. Ginger, a natural preventative, is available in capsule form from health-food stores.

Jet Lag This condition is experienced when a person travels by air across more than three time zones (each time zone usually represents a time difference of one hour). Many of the functions of the human body are regulated by internal 24-hour cycles called circadian rhythms. When we travel long distances rapidly, our bodies take time to adjust to the 'new time,' and we may experience fatigue, disorientation, insomnia, anxiety, impaired concentration and/or a loss of appetite. These effects will usually be gone within three days of arrival, but there are ways of minimizing the impact of jet lag.

- Rest for a couple of days prior to departure; try to avoid late nights and last-minute dashes for traveler's checks or your passport.
- Try to select flight schedules that minimize sleep deprivation; arriving in the early evening means you can go to sleep soon after you arrive. For very long flights, try to organize a stopover.
- Avoid excessive eating (which bloats the stomach) and alcohol (which causes dehydration) during the flight. Instead, drink plenty of noncarbonated, nonalcoholic drinks such as fruit juice or water.
- Make yourself comfortable by wearing loose-fitting clothes and perhaps bringing an eye mask and ear plugs to help you sleep.

Sunburn Most doctors recommend the use of sunscreen with a high protection factor (SPF) for easily burned areas such as your shoulders and, if you'll be on nude beaches, areas not normally exposed to sun.

Heat Exhaustion Dehydration or salt deficiency can cause heat exhaustion. Take time to acclimatize to high temperatures, and make sure that you get enough liquids. Salt deficiency is characterized by fatigue, lethargy, headaches, giddiness and muscle cramps. Salt tablets may help. Vomiting or diarrhea can also deplete your liquid and salt levels. Anhydrotic heat exhaustion, caused by the inability to sweat, is quite rare, but unlike the other forms of heat exhaustion, it is likely to strike people who have been in a hot climate for some time rather than newcomers. Again, always carry – and use – a water bottle on long trips.

Heat Stroke Long, continuous periods of exposure to high temperatures can leave you vulnerable to this serious, sometimes fatal, condition, which occurs when the body's heat-regulating mechanism breaks down and body temperature rises to dangerous levels. Avoid excessive alcohol intake or strenuous activity when you first arrive in a hot climate to help prevent heat stroke.

Symptoms include feeling unwell, lack of perspiration and a high body temperature of 102° to 105°F (39° to 41°C). In extreme cases, hospitalization is essential, but meanwhile get victims out of the sun, remove their clothing, cover them with a wet sheet or towel and fan them continually.

Fungal Infections

These infections, which occur with greater frequency in hot weather, are most likely to occur on the scalp, between the toes or fingers (athlete's foot), in the groin (jock itch or crotch rot) and on the body (ringworm). You get ringworm (which is a fungal infection, not a worm) from infected animals or by walking on damp areas such as shower floors.

To prevent fungal infections, wear loose, comfortable clothes, avoid artificial fibers, wash frequently and dry carefully. If you do get an infection, wash the infected area daily with a disinfectant or medicated soap and water, and rinse and dry well. Apply an antifungal powder and try to expose the infected area to air or sunlight as much as possible. Change underwear and towels frequently, and wash them often in hot water.

Infectious Diseases

Diarrhea A change of water, food or climate can all cause the runs; diarrhea caused by contaminated food or water is more serious. Despite all your precautions, you may still have a mild bout of traveler's diarrhea from exotic food or drink.

Dehydration is the main danger with any diarrhea, particularly for children, in whom dehydration can occur quite quickly. Fluid replacement remains the mainstay of management. Weak black tea with a little sugar, soda water and soft drinks diluted 50% with water are all good. With severe diarrhea, a rehydrating solution is necessary to replace lost minerals and salts. Such solutions, like Pedialyte, are available at pharmacies.

Hepatitis This is a general term for inflammation of the liver. There are many causes of this condition: Poor sanitation, contact with infected blood products, drugs, alcohol and contact with an infected person are but a few. The symptoms are fever, chills, headache, fatigue, and feelings of weakness, aches and pains, followed by loss of appetite, nausea, vomiting, abdominal pain, dark urine, light-colored feces and jaundiced skin. The whites of the eyes may also turn yellow.

Hepatitis A is the most common strain. You should seek medical advice, but there is not much you can do apart from resting, drinking lots of fluids, eating lightly and avoiding fatty foods. People who have had hepatitis should avoid alcohol for some time after the illness, as the liver needs time to recover. Viral hepatitis is an infection of the liver, which can have several unpleasant symptoms or no symptoms at all, and the infected person may not even know that he or she has the disease.

HIV/AIDS The human immunodeficiency virus, HIV, develops into acquired immune deficiency syndrome, AIDS, which is a fatal condition. Any exposure to blood, blood products or body fluids may put an individual at risk. The disease is often transmitted through sexual contact or dirty needles – vaccinations, acupuncture, tattooing and body piercing can potentially be as dangerous as intravenous drug use.

Fear of infection by HIV should never preclude treatment for serious medical conditions. A good resource for help and information is the US Center for Disease Control AIDS hotline (☎ 800-342-2437, 800-344-7432 in Spanish).

Cuts, Bites & Stings

Skin punctures, such as those caused by coral, can easily become infected in hot climates and heal slowly. Treat any cut by first washing it with soap and fresh water, then cleaning it with an antiseptic such as Betadine. Finally, smear the wound with triple-antibiotic salve to prevent the further introduction of infection. When possible, avoid bandages and Band-Aids, which can keep wounds wet.

The stings of bees and wasps and nonpoisonous spider bites are usually painful rather than dangerous. Calamine lotion will give relief, and ice packs will reduce the pain and swelling.

Dastardly Dengue

This insect-borne disease may be the biggest threat to your health in the islands. At the onset of the 21st century, the Virgins and nearby Puerto Rico have been experiencing an epidemic of more than 24,000 cases of dengue per year.

A particular species of daytime mosquito spreads the disease. The best way to avoid dengue is to use mosquito repellents liberally, as there is no treatment for the disease once it is in your system. A sudden onset of fever and muscle and joint pains are the first signs of the disease before a rash starts on the trunk of the body and spreads to the limbs and face. Hospitals can treat your symptoms, so by all means seek medical attention if you suspect that you have contracted dengue.

The fever and other symptoms usually begin to subside after a few days. Serious complications are not common, but persisting weakness, returning fever and fits of depression can last a month or more.

If you get caught in jellyfish tentacles, peel off the tentacles using paper or a towel to protect your fingers. Wash the area with alcohol (rum works). To alleviate the itchy sting, cover the affected area with meat tenderizer, ammonia (bleach) or even urine.

Ticks are parasitic arachnids that may be in brush, forest and grasslands, where hikers often get them on their legs or in their boots. The adults suck blood from hosts by burying their head into skin, but they are often found unattached and can simply be brushed off. However, if one has attached itself to you, pulling it off and leaving the head in the skin increases the likelihood of infection or disease, such as typhus, Rocky Mountain spotted fever or Lyme disease.

Always check your body for ticks after walking through a high-grass or thickly forested area. To remove an attached tick, use a pair of tweezers, grab it by the head and gently pull it straight out – do not twist it. (If no tweezers are available, use your fingers, but protect them from contamination by using a piece of tissue or paper.) Do not touch the tick with a hot object such as a match or cigarette – this can cause it to regurgitate noxious gut substances into the wound. Don't rub oil, alcohol or petroleum jelly on it. If you get sick in the next couple of weeks, consult a doctor.

See the 'Poison Apples' boxed text in the Facts about the Virgin Islands chapter for information on the toxic manchineel tree.

WOMEN TRAVELERS
Bookstores are good places to find out about gatherings, readings and meetings. The university campuses are also good sites to network, and their social centers often have bulletin boards where you can find or place travel and short-term housing notices.

Annoyances
Dressing for the public in the Virgin Islands can be problematic for women travelers. If you wear comfortable shorts, a sleeveless top and walking shoes, you will be stereotyped as a cruise ship passenger and treated to persistent badgering from touts. Salespeople and restaurant staff may assume you have bundles of money you can't wait to give them.

On the other hand, if you try to wear the formal, conservative dresses and suits preferred by many local women, you may feel hot or constrained. A lot of island women who are spending a day of leisure at the shops and restaurants avoid extremes of dress and go with loose, comfortable cotton slacks, a matching top and sandals. Some younger women wear jeans, but you might find them hot until your body acclimates to the tropical temperature and humidity.

Women find themselves most vulnerable to harassment when they're working out. If you are jogging or power-walking along public thoroughfares, you must prepare yourself to get whistles, catcalls, clapping and the like from local men. The best way to avoid such displays of male chauvinism is to exercise in a setting where other people are exercising as well, like the grounds of a resort or a college campus.

Men may interpret a woman drinking alone in a bar as a bid for male company, whether you intend it that way or not. If you don't want the company, most men will respect a firm but polite 'no thank you.'

Safety Precautions
Women often face different situations when traveling than men do. If you are a woman traveler, especially a woman traveling alone, it is a good idea to travel with a little extra awareness of your surroundings. In general, you must exercise more vigilance in large cities than in rural areas. Try to avoid the 'bad' or less safe neighborhoods or districts; if you must go into or through these areas, it's best to go in a private vehicle (car or taxi). It's more dangerous at night, but crimes also occur in the daytime. Solo women travelers and small groups should avoid isolated beaches at any time of day or night. If you are unsure which areas are considered less safe, ask at your hotel or telephone the tourist office for advice.

Tourist maps can sometimes be deceiving, compressing areas that are not tourist attractions and making the distances look shorter than they are. In Charlotte Amalie on St Thomas, high-crime areas turn up with surprising frequency right next to tourist zones. For example, the dangerous Savan neighborhood lies right next to the town's major shopping district.

Try to avoid hiking or camping alone, especially in unfamiliar places. Hikers all over the world use the 'buddy system,' not only for protection from other humans, but also for aid in case of unexpected falls or other injuries or encounters with potentially dangerous wildlife.

Women face the extra threat of rape. Using common sense will help you avoid some problems. You're more vulnerable if you've been drinking or using drugs than if you're sober; you're more vulnerable alone than if you're with company; and you're more vulnerable in a high-crime urban area than in a 'better' district.

Don't hitchhike, and don't pick up hitchhikers if you're driving alone. If you get stuck on a road and need help, it's a good idea to have a pre-made sign to signal for help. At night, avoid getting out of your car to flag down help; turn on your hazard lights and wait for the police to arrive. Be extra careful at night on public transit, and remember to check the schedule of the last bus or ferry before you go out at night.

To deal with threats, many women protect themselves with a whistle, mace, cayenne-pepper spray or some self-defense training. If you do decide to purchase a spray, contact an island police station to find out about local laws, regulations and training classes. One law that doesn't vary is carrying sprays on airplanes. Because of their combustible nature, it is a federal felony to carry them on board.

If you are a victim of violence or rape in the islands, call the police (☎ 911 or ☎ 999 in the BVI). Telephone directories do not list rape crisis centers, but police can refer you to counselors.

GAY & LESBIAN TRAVELERS

The gay scene in the Virgin Islands is evolving. Along with Puerto Rico, the Virgin Islands are among the most gay-friendly islands in the Caribbean. St Croix has a well-developed gay scene in Frederiksted, where there are gay clubs and a hotel that advertises as a gay oasis. St Thomas has a large population of local gays as well.

But old religious prejudices against homosexuality die hard in these islands, and few gays are officially 'out.' In fact, the BVI had laws against the practice of homosexuality – albeit rarely enforced – until Great Britain struck down these laws in 2001. You will not see public displays of affection between gay people in the Virgin Islands except at known gay beaches, gay hotels and gay clubs. Many reputed 'gay bars' in Charlotte Amalie are dangerous dens of prostitution.

Resources & Organizations

The Damron Women's Traveller, with listings for lesbians, and *Damron Address Book,* for men, are both published by Damron Company (☎ 415-255-0404, 800-462-6654), PO Box 422458, San Francisco, CA 94142-2458. Ferrari's *Places for Women* and *Places for Men* are also useful. These can be found at any good bookstore.

Another good resource is the Gay Yellow Pages (☎ 212-674-0120), PO Box 533, Village Station, NY 10014-0533, which has a national edition and regional editions.

Try these resource numbers in the US: Lambda Legal Defense Fund (☎ 212-995-8585 in New York City, ☎ 213-937-2728 in Los Angeles), National AIDS/HIV Hotline (☎ 800-342-2437) or National Gay and Lesbian Task Force (☎ 202-332-6483).

DISABLED TRAVELERS

Travel in the Virgin Islands is not particularly easy for those with physical disabilities. There is little or no consciousness of the need for curb cuts, jet ways or other easy access onto planes, wheelchair lifts on buses, or rental vehicles for the disabled. Things are particularly primitive in this regard in the BVI.

Tropic Tours (☎ 340-774-1855) and DIAL-A-RIDE (☎ 340-776-1277) have island tours and transport for disabled travelers on St Thomas; Wheel Coach Services (☎ 340-719-9335) services is in St Croix. Aqua Action Dive Shop (☎ 340-775-6285) and Admiralty Dive Center (☎ 340-777-9802) both offer scuba programs for disabled people.

Some hotels have suites for disabled guests. All major airlines allow service animals to accompany passengers and frequently sell two-for-one packages for seriously disabled passengers who require attendants. Airlines also provide assistance for connecting, boarding and deplaning the flight – just ask for assistance when making your reservation. All airlines must accept wheelchairs as checked baggage and have an onboard chair available, though some advance notice may be required on smaller aircraft.

While land and air travel present significant obstacles, cruises can be a good handicapped-accessible option in the Caribbean (see Cruise Ship in the Getting There & Away chapter).

Resources & Organizations

A number of organizations and tour providers specialize in the needs of disabled travelers.

Mobility International USA (☎ 541-343-1284, fax 343-6812, infomiusa.org) PO Box 10767, Eugene, OR 97440. This organization advises disabled travelers on mobility issues but primarily runs an educational exchange program. www.miusa.org

Moss Rehabilitation Hospital's Travel Information Service (☎ 215-456-9600, TTY 456-9602) 1200 W Tabor Rd, Philadelphia, PA 19141-3099

Society for the Advancement of Travel for the Handicapped (SATH) (☎ 212-447-7284) 347 Fifth Ave, No 610, New York, NY 10016

Twin Peaks Press (☎ 360-694-2462, 800-637-2256) PO Box 129, Vancouver, WA 98666. This press offers a quarterly newsletter and publishes directories and access guides. www.pacifier.com /~twinpeak

SENIOR TRAVELERS

While the Virgin Islands make an attractive destination for seniors, the senior discounts that are prevalent in North America and Europe are rare in the islands except for some hotel package tours.

Some national advocacy groups that can help in planning your travels and finding discounts on travel to the islands include the following.

American Association of Retired Persons (AARP) (☎ 800-424-3410) 601 E St NW, Washington, DC 20049. This is an advocacy group for Americans 50 years and older and a good resource for travel bargains. US residents can get one-year/three-year memberships for $8/20. Citizens of other countries can get the same memberships for $10/24.

Elderhostel (☎ 617-426-8056) 75 Federal St, Boston, MA 02110-1941. Elderhostel is a nonprofit organization that offers seniors the opportunity to attend academic college courses throughout the USA, Canada and – occasionally – the Virgin Islands. Programs last one to three weeks, include meals and accommodations, and are open to people 55 years and older and their companions.

TRAVEL WITH CHILDREN

West Indians love, and have a high tolerance for, children. This cultural predisposition combines with the congenial climate, first-rate accommodations, beaches, casual dining opportunities and array of outdoor activities to make the Virgins a great place to travel with children. In fact, taking kids to the Virgin Islands is an excellent way to meet island families at beaches, playgrounds and low-key restaurants.

A number of resorts like the Sapphire Beach Resort on St Thomas offer camp-style programs for children three to 15 (see Places to Stay in the individual island chapters). For information on enjoying travel with young ones, read *Travel with Children,* by Lonely Planet cofounder Maureen Wheeler.

USEFUL ORGANIZATIONS

See also the organizations listed above for women, gays and lesbians, seniors and disabled travelers.

The National Park Service (NPS), part of the US Department of the Interior, oversees the Virgin Islands National Park as well as Buck Island and the historic sites in Christiansted. Current information about the national parks can be obtained from the Park Service Headquarters (see the St Thomas and St Croix chapters) and the visitors center (see the St John chapter). National park campground and reservation information can be obtained by calling ☎ 800-280-2267.

The BVI National Parks Trust (see the Facts About the Virgin Islands chapter) in Road Town is the agency that manages more than 14 national parks and associated mooring fields in the BVI. The agency publishes an excellent guide to the national parks.

UNIVERSITIES

The people of the USVI are justifiably proud of the University of the Virgin Islands

(☎ 340-776-9200), on Route 30 across from the airport at Brewers Bay. The university opened in 1962 and has added many programs and services, including the Reichhold Center for the Arts, the Eastern Caribbean Center and the William P MacLean Marine Science Center. The St Croix branch of the University of the Virgin Islands (☎ 340-778-1620) is a modern, 125-acre campus on Centerline Rd in midisland.

The H Lavity Stoutt Community College (☎ 284-494-4994), at Paraquita Bay on the south shore east of Road Town, is the institution of higher education in the BVI. Also see Education in Facts about the Virgin Islands.

DANGERS & ANNOYANCES
Drugs & Drug Trafficking
The Virgin Islands' poorest neighborhoods (and some secluded beaches) are to some extent havens for lawlessness and drug trafficking. While most of these drugs are bound for the US, more than enough are left behind to upset the lives of islanders. Recent statistics cite drugs as the cause of more than 60% of all crimes in the islands.

Personal Security & Theft
A growing number of the islanders carry weapons and may be prone to violence when it comes to resolving a dispute. House break-ins are commonplace on the three largest islands. Muggings occur in Charlotte Amalie after dark; personal articles left out on the beaches are never safe.

Even though street crime is a serious issue in urban areas, a few commonsense reminders should help keep you secure. Lock cars and put valuables out of sight, whether you're leaving the car for a few minutes or longer, and whether you are in a town or in the remote backcountry. Rent a car with a lockable trunk or glove box. Do not walk on dimly lit streets at night, particularly when alone. Walk purposefully.

Avoid unnecessary displays of money or jewelry. Divide money and credit cards to avoid losing everything. Aim to use ATM machines in well-trafficked areas. In hotels, don't leave valuables lying around your room. Use safety-deposit boxes or at least place valuables in a locked bag. Don't open your door to strangers – check the peephole or call the front desk if unexpected guests try to enter.

Recreational Hazards
In wilderness areas, the consequences of an accident can be very serious, so inform someone of your route and expected time of return.

Wildlife As more and more people spend time in the islands' wilderness, attacks on humans are becoming more common. Wild burros, for example, roam many of the Virgin Islands, and although they look gentle, they can kick, bite and trample. Even small animals are capable of inflicting serious injury or even fatal wounds on unsuspecting tourists. Keep your distance from all wild animals.

Many of the islands' recreational hazards lie in the sea. Water conditions around the Virgin Islands are perfect for the growth of coral, and the islands offers divers and snorkelers a plethora of fringe, ribbon, barrier and bank-type coral reefs. But remember that coral is an animal whose beautiful, calcified shell can cut easily and cause painful infections. Fire coral – the rust-colored branches with the white tips – actually packs a sting.

Other animals that swimmers and divers might see – and should keep at a distance – are the moray eel, a fierce biting denizen of the reef; stingrays, which like to bury themselves beneath the sand in shallow areas (such as popular beaches); and the spotted scorpionfish, which lurks around the bottoms of reefs and rocks. Spiny black sea urchins have the power to pierce a swim fin when stepped on.

Small sharks and large barracuda are plentiful in island waters, and swimmers should be cautious not to attract these predators with jerky movements or flashy metallic watches and jewelry. As threatening as the razor-toothed fish look, they account for far fewer injuries to humans than the innocent-looking jellyfish. The chief villain

Beware of the Portuguese man-of-war.

of this group is the Portuguese man-of-war, whose whiplike stinging tentacles can extend 40 feet or more from the animal's balloon-shaped float. And these tentacles can still sting hours after they have detached from the animal's body or washed up on the beach. Watch where you swim and where you plant your feet on the beach during jellyfish season (August to October).

Pests Mosquitoes are ubiquitous, and they do not restrict their activities to the hours around sunset. One type of daylight mosquito carries dengue fever (see 'Dastardly Dengue,' earlier). The only good thing that can be said about the islands' mosquitoes is that they do not carry malaria.

Anegada has a mosquito species called 'Gallon Nippers,' which can appear in swarms thick enough to kill wild goats. Be prepared with strong repellent. Stinging red ants can also be a problem, especially for trekkers and campers.

Another flying pest is a nearly microscopic sandfly, the no-see-um, which penetrates screens and sets off sharp little itches every time it lands on bare human skin. Traveling in the Virgin Islands without an arsenal of your favorite bug repellent is tantamount to offering up your body as a human sacrifice to the Lord of the Flies. (The 1963 version, incidentally, was filmed on neighboring Vieques.)

EMERGENCIES

Throughout the Virgin Islands, call ☎ 911 for emergency service of any sort. This is a free call from any phone. On a few islands in the BVI such as Virgin Gorda, the police number is ☎ 999.

Carry a photocopy of your passport separately from your passport. Copy the pages with your photo and personal details, passport number and US visa. If your passport is lost or stolen, this will make replacing it easier. In this event, you should call your nearest consulate or embassy (which is probably in Puerto Rico). To reach your embassy, call directory assistance for Washington, DC (☎ 202-555-1212).

Similarly, always carry copies of your traveler's check numbers and credit card numbers separately. If you lose your credit cards, contact the company immediately (see Credit & Debit Cards, earlier in this chapter, for company phone numbers). Contact your bank if you lose your ATM card.

LEGAL MATTERS

If you are stopped by the police for any reason, bear in mind that there is no system of paying fines on the spot. Attempting to pay the fine to the officer may compound your troubles by resulting in a charge of bribery. For traffic offenses, the police officer will explain your options to you. Should the officer decide that you should pay up front, he or she can take you directly to the magistrate instead of allowing you the usual 30-day period to pay the fine.

If you are arrested for more serious offenses, you are allowed to remain silent. There is no legal reason to speak to a police officer if you don't wish to, but never walk away from an officer until given permission. All persons who are arrested are legally allowed (and given) the right to make one phone call. If you don't have a lawyer or family member to help you, call your embassy. The police will give you the number upon request.

The drinking age is 18 in the islands – three years younger than in the USA! Legally, you need photo identification to prove your age. Servers and police on patrol have the right to ask to see your ID and may refuse service or arrest you if you are drinking without an ID. But in practice the drinking age is only loosely enforced in the Virgin Islands. Unlike the USA, the islands have few 'blue laws' prohibiting the times and places where alcohol can be consumed. This means that drinking (even underage drinking) is rampant during public holidays.

Driving under the influence of alcohol or drugs is a serious offense, subject to stiff fines and even imprisonment. For more information on driving and road rules, see the Getting Around chapter.

BUSINESS HOURS

Businesses are generally open 8 am to 5 pm, but there are certainly no hard-and-fast rules. Shops are usually open 9 or 10 am to 5 or 6 pm (often until 8 pm in shopping malls like Mongoose Junction on St John), except on Sunday, when hours are 11 am to 5 pm (sometimes later in malls).

Post offices are open 8 am to 4 or 5:30 pm weekdays; some are also open on Saturday and Sunday. Banks are usually open 8 am to 2:30 pm weekdays.

PUBLIC HOLIDAYS

US public holidays are celebrated along with local holidays in the USVI. Banks, schools and government offices (including post offices) are closed, and transportation, museums and other services are on shorter schedules. Holidays falling on weekends are usually observed the following Monday.

US Virgin Islands

January & February

New Year's Day January 1

Three Kings Day (feast of the Epiphany) January 6

Martin Luther King Jr's Birthday third Monday in January

Presidents' Day third Monday in February

March, April & May

Transfer Day March 31

Holy Thursday & Good Friday before Easter

Easter & Easter Monday late March or early April

Memorial Day last Monday in May

July, September & October

Emancipation Day July 3

  Island slaves were freed on this date in 1873.

Independence Day (aka Fourth of July) July 4

Supplication Day in July (date varies)

Labor Day first Monday in September

Columbus Day second Monday in October

November & December

Liberty Day November 1

Veterans' Day November 11

Thanksgiving Day fourth Thursday in November

Christmas Day & Boxing Day December 25 & 26

British Virgin Islands

New Year's Day January 1

Commonwealth Day in March (date varies)

Good Friday Friday before Easter (in March or April)

Whit Monday in May or June (date varies)

Sovereign's Birthday in June (date varies)

Territory Day in July (date varies)

Festival Monday, Tuesday, Wednesday early August (dates vary)

St Ursula's Day October 21

Birthday of Heir to the Throne November 14

Christmas Day & Boxing Day December 25 & 26

CULTURAL EVENTS

In addition to the holidays above, the Virgin Islands celebrate a number of other occasions, including the following widely observed ones. (Businesses stay open.)

Valentine's Day (February 14) No one knows why St Valentine is associated with romance, but this is the day to celebrate.

St Patrick's Day (March 17th) This holiday celebrates the patron saint of Ireland and has become the occasion for major-league pub crawling in Christiansted.

Mother's Day (second Sunday in May) Children send cards and flowers (or make a phone call) to Mom. Restaurants are likely to be busy.

Father's Day (third Sunday in June) Same idea, different parent.

SPECIAL EVENTS

Below is a list of island events that have cultural as well as entertainment value. The telephone numbers listed will connect travelers with event organizers or local tourist offices.

Virgin Gorda Easter Festival Held on the four days preceding the Christian Lent in mid-February, this festival (☎ 284-495-5181) is a true carnival event. Spanish Town fills with *mocko jumbies* (costumed stilt walkers representing spirits of the dead), scratch bands, calypsonians, a food fair, vendors' booths, parades and floats.

St Croix Agricultural Festival Held in mid-February, this three-day event features island crafters, food stalls, bands and more.

International Rolex Cup Regatta World-class racing boats and crews gather at St Thomas for this regatta (☎ 340-775-6320), a three-day event in early April.

Annual Spring Regatta The yachties sail again in mid-April. This time it's from Road Town in the Annual Spring Regatta (☎ 284-494-3286).

St Thomas Carnival This event (☎ 340-774-8774), in the last two weeks of April, stems from West African masquerading traditions. The St Thomas carnival is the second-largest carnival in the Caribbean after the one at Port-of-Spain, Trinidad, and throws St Thomas into nonstop party mode for weeks. The Carnival Village takes over Vendor's Plaza in Charlotte Amalie. Parades, calypso contests, food fairs and beauty pageants snake through the capital.

St Croix Half-Ironman Triathlon This triahlon (☎ 340-773-4470) takes place in early May (see Spectator Sports, later).

HIHO Races Windsurfers converge on the BVI for these Hook In, Hold On Races (☎ 284-494-7963). The competition lasts seven days, and a gaggle of cruisers follow the racers in a week-long portable party in late June.

St John Carnival This carnival (☎ 340-776-6450) begins around July 1 and climaxes on July 4 or 5. It's basically a smaller version of the St Thomas Carnival, with mocko jumbies, steel pan bands, parades and musical competitions.

BVI Summer Festival This festival (☎ 284-494-7963) occurs over three weeks at the end of July and the beginning of August. During this time,

Tortola rocks with everything from a beauty pageant and car show to 'rise & shine tramps' (noisy parades led by reggae bands in the back of a truck starting at 3 am).

Atlantic Blue Marlin Tournament This tournament (☎ 340-775-9500) draws sportfishers from all over the world in late August to participate in this tag-and-release event benefiting the islands' Boy Scouts.

Crucian Christmas Fiesta This festival (☎ 340-773-0495) puts a West Indies spin on the holiday shopping hype that seems to have spread the world over. Most of the decorations and events focus on Christiansted December 17 to January 7.

ACTIVITIES

The tropical climate and variety of land and seascapes make the islands a mecca for outdoor activities. See the Yacht Charter Basics chapter for information on sailing. See the Getting Around chapter for a listing of tour operators that provide activity-oriented trips on the islands. See the island chapters for more information on the activities described below.

Swimming

With more than 90 islands, the Virgin Islands offer travelers a host of swimming beaches. All beaches, except those on private islands, are open to the public. In general, if a beach and its clientele do not seem safe to you, they probably are not. Many travelers find it worth paying a few dollars to rent beach chairs and an umbrella for the relative security of a resort's beach and facilities.

See Recreational Hazards, earlier in this chapter, for things to watch out for in and around the ocean.

Diving & Snorkeling

Both diving and snorkeling here are superb, with nearshore reefs and more than 100 major dive sites. Water temperatures range between 76°F (24°C) in the winter and 84°F (29°C) in the summer, while visibility sometimes exceeds 100 feet. Fringing, bank, spur-and-groove and barrier reefs lie off the islands' shores. Almost all the major types of coral flourish on Virgin Islands reefs.

Considerations for Responsible Diving

The popularity of diving is placing immense pressure on many sites. Please consider the following tips when diving, and help to preserve the ecology and beauty of reefs.

- Do not use anchors on reefs, and take care not to ground boats on coral. Encourage dive operators and regulatory bodies to establish permanent moorings at popular dive sites.

- Avoid touching living marine organisms with your body or dragging equipment across the reef. Polyps can be damaged by even the gentlest contact. Never stand on corals, even if they look solid and robust. If you must hold onto a reef, touch only exposed rock or dead coral.

- Be conscious of your fins. Even without contact, the surge from heavy fin strokes near the reef can damage delicate organisms. When treading water in shallow reef areas, do not kick up clouds of sand. Settling sand can easily smother delicate reef organisms.

- Practice and maintain proper buoyancy control. Divers who descend too fast and collide with a reef can do major damage. Make sure you are correctly weighted and that your weight belt is positioned so you stay horizontal. If you have not dived for a while, take a practice dive in a pool before taking to the reef. Be aware that buoyancy can change over the period of an extended trip. Initially, you may breathe harder and need more weight; a few days later you may breathe more easily and need less weight.

- Take great care in underwater caves. Spend as little time as possible within them, as your air bubbles may be caught within the roof and thereby leave previously submerged organisms high and dry. Taking turns to inspect the interior of a small cave lessens the chances of damaging contact.

- Resist the temptation to collect or buy corals or shells. Aside from the ecological damage, taking home marine souvenirs depletes the beauty of a site and spoils others' enjoyment. The same goes for marine archaeological sites (mainly shipwrecks). Respect their integrity; some sites are even protected from looting by law.

- Take home all your trash and any litter you may find as well. Plastics in particular are a serious threat to marine life. Turtles can mistake plastic for jellyfish and eat it.

- Resist the temptation to feed fish. You may disturb their normal eating habits, encourage aggressive behavior or feed them food that is detrimental to their health. Minimize your disturbance of marine animals. In particular, do not ride on the backs of turtles, as this causes them great anxiety.

Most of the common Caribbean reef fish species are present. You may also see turtles, octopuses, rays, moray eels and nurse sharks. Snorkelers will find opportunities off almost every beach. Several dozen dive operators run day trips out of the major ports and resort hotels around the islands (see the individual island chapters for details).

Fishing

The Virgin Islands host several deep-sea fishing tournaments, including the popular Atlantic Blue Marlin Tournament and the Virgin Islands Game Fishing Club Annual Tournament.

Marlin is a spring/summer fish, sailfish and wahoo run in fall, and dorado show up in winter. You can fish for tuna all year long.

Anegada has excellent bonefishing. Many charters run out of American Yacht Harbor in Red Hook (see the island chapters, particularly St Thomas).

Surfing & Windsurfing
The three largest islands have healthy contingents of surfers. In general, winter is the best surfing season, when swells roll in out of the northeast and set up some point breaks of 6 feet and higher at places like Hull Bay on St Thomas and Josiahs Bay on Tortola. Bring your own board; it is hard to find rental equipment in the islands.

Windsurfing has its practitioners at favorite locations on every populated island (see the island chapters). The Bitter End Yacht Club (☎ 284-494-2745) on Virgin Gorda specializes in water-sports vacations and has excellent windsurfing conditions and equipment.

Golf & Tennis
With three championship golf courses, the Virgin Islands offer sufficient challenges for dedicated golfers. Two of the top courses are on St Croix (see that chapter); the other is the well-known Mahogany Run (☎ 340-777-6006) championship course designed by the Fazio brothers (see the St Thomas chapter).

The islands boast more than 50 tennis courts, mostly at resort hotels. Court fees for nonguests generally run $10 an hour or more.

Hiking
Among both tourists and islanders, the most popular hiking area is the 9500-acre Virgin Islands National Park on St John, with about 23 miles of hiking trails. St Croix, Jost Van Dyke and Virgin Gorda also have attractive hiking trails. In general, the Virgin Islands are each small enough that it is feasible to explore on foot if you are acclimated to the warm weather, or if you take to the cooler mountains. For more information, see the island chapters.

Horseback Riding
All of the major islands have horseback-riding operations. Rates are as low as $25 an hour at Shadow's Ranch (☎ 284-494-2262) on Tortola and as high as $45 an hour at Half Moon Stables (☎ 340-777-6088) on St Thomas (see the island chapters).

Bird-Watching
The best sites for bird-watching are the salt ponds on St Croix and Anegada, and the mountains of St John and Tortola.

Bicycling
The high volume of automobiles on islands like St Thomas, St Croix and Tortola makes bike touring difficult. Furthermore, rugged terrain and frequently slick turf (from tropical showers) on the prime mountain-biking trails make biking without a guide risky.

Because there is safety in numbers, most travelers do their touring or mountain biking through one of the adventure tour operators (see Organized Tours in the Getting Around chapter). If you like tooling around on a bike, head to the less-densely populated islands of St John, Water Island, Anegada or Jost Van Dyke, where there are few cars, plenty of open roads and rural scenery. You can rent bikes through guesthouses and vendors; see the island chapters for details.

WORK
Travelers with skills – such as diving instructors or those with a US commercial captain's license – can find seasonal work in tourist areas. Consider out-of-the-way resort areas like St John, where there are relatively few islanders who should rightly get the resort jobs first.

If you are good at carpentry, you might find work in the restoration of buildings in Charlotte Amalie or Christiansted. There is also a boom in new construction on St John and St Croix. Experienced cooks, bartenders, waitstaff and salespeople will find work in the tourist areas throughout the islands.

If you are not a US citizen and you want to work in the USVI, you need to apply for a work visa from the US embassy in your home country before you leave. The type of visa varies depending on how long you're staying and the kind of work you plan to do. Generally, you'll need either a J-1 visa, which you can obtain by joining a visitor-exchange program, or a H-2B visa, which you get when sponsored by a USVI employer. The latter can be difficult to obtain (the employer is required to prove that no US citizen or permanent resident is available to do the job); the former is issued mostly to students for work in summer camps.

To work in the BVI, people who are not citizens of the BVI must first find employment in the BVI. Once you have accomplished this, your employer will apply to the Labour Department for your work permit. The wait for processing your permit is usually four to six weeks. You cannot work legally until you have the permit in hand, unless your employer can obtain a waiver.

ACCOMMODATIONS

Lodging rates in the Virgin Islands can vary more than 30% from season to season and even from day to day, as hotels adjust rates according to the perceived demand.

In general, rates are highest from December 15 to the end of April. Rates are lowest from August 1 to December 14 (hurricane season). Rates that are listed in this book are for the high winter season unless otherwise noted, and they do not reflect room taxes, which are 8% in the USVI and 7% in the BVI.

If you are planning to visit the islands during the winter season, you should make your reservations a minimum of three months in advance to get a decent selection and price. Special events and conventions can fill up an island's hotels quickly, so call ahead to find out what will be going on. The local tourist office is always a good resource.

Travelers will not find any youth hostels in the Virgins, but a number of campgrounds and camping areas offer accommodations at prices equivalent to hostel prices and attract a youthful and adventurous backpacker crowd.

Web sites and email addresses have not been included in this guide because they change frequently and are not yet a reliable method for booking accommodations.

Camping

Camping is the cheapest, and in many ways the most enjoyable, approach to a vacation. Visitors with a tent (or who are willing to rent one from a campground) can take advantage of a scattering of campgrounds throughout the islands, many near beaches.

Prices run from about $20 for a basic site with no tent to more than $115 for a deluxe tent that looks like a treehouse at the Maho Bay Campground. A few of the larger camping areas also have rustic cabins for rent for about $100. In addition, camping is permitted on most beaches in the USVI that are not part of a national park. Backpackers take advantage of this opportunity, particularly on St Croix.

Costs given in this book are per site. A site normally accommodates two people. If you're in a group, you pay extra. Popular campgrounds like the one at Cinnamon Bay on St John have 14-night limits during the winter season and require reservations.

Guesthouses & Inns

Island guesthouses and inns offer alternatives to the high prices and insularity that come with rooms in resort hotels in the tourist zones. Virgin Islands guesthouses are not always the casual, inexpensive sort of accommodations found under the name of 'guesthouse' or 'B&B' in Europe. Some places may have as few as two rooms for travelers; others may boast as many as 20.

The cheapest establishments, with rooms for about $50, may have clean but unexciting rooms with a shared bathroom. Pricier places have rooms with private baths and balconies, sundecks and public dining rooms (at extra cost). Rooms at most guesthouses fall in the $60 to $100 range, but some cost more than $100. The best are distinguished by friendliness and attention to detail from the owners or hosts, who can provide you with local information and contacts and other amenities. All guesthouses and inns generally require advance reservations.

Hotels

There are just a few accommodations on the islands with rooms for less than $50, and almost all of these are found in unsavory neighborhoods of urban areas. Rooms are usually small, and beds may be saggy, but the sheets should be clean. Expect scuffed walls, atrocious decor, old furniture and strange noises from your shower. These places normally have a private shower and toilet in each room. None have air-conditioning.

Your best bets for moderately priced hotels are in Charlotte Amalie, Christiansted, Frederiksted, Road Town and Cane Garden Bay. These towns have a number of medium-size, well-tended hotels with pools and rates running $75 to $130. For the most part, island hotels categorize themselves as 'luxury' or 'deluxe' establishments, and rooms run more than $150 per night in high season unless you have a tour package. In addition, the Virgin Islands offer several truly exclusive retreats on private cays like Nicker Island and Guana Cay.

The prices advertised by hotels, called 'rack rates,' are not written in stone. If you ask about any specials that might apply, you can often save quite a bit of money. Booking through a travel agent can also save you money. Members of AARP or AAA can qualify for a 'corporate' rate at several hotel chains.

Because of changing marketing strategies and seasons, the prices in this guide can be only an approximate guideline at best. Also, in addition to taxes, you might need to add a 10% service charge to quoted rates. Children are often allowed to stay free with their parents.

Rental Accommodations

Condominiums, villas and apartments are the fastest-growing segment of the lodging business in the Virgin Islands, offering travelers some of the best values if they are willing to settle in one place for a week or more. Rental rates tend to be as low as $45 a night and as high as $300. But whatever you pay, you will be getting a lot for your money – perhaps even a housekeeper or cook.

During the last 20 years, the Virgin Islands have seen a boom in vacation condo/villa construction on all of the larger islands. Because the owners use these condos/villas for only a fraction of the year, renting them is a way to defray expenses. In the off season (generally May or June to mid-December), these rentals are readily available. The properties are in prime resort areas and include attractive, well-furnished homes with spectacular views. For a list of reliable local agents, see Places to Stay in each island chapter.

FOOD

Usually eaten between about 7 and 9 am, typical island breakfasts are light and simple except on weekends and holidays, when people have more time to cook egg dishes or French toast. One item common to a traditional West Indian breakfast is the johnnycake, the islands' most famous bread. Johnnycakes are made from fried or baked flour, and they make a tasty breakfast meal when lathered with homemade fruit preserves. Almost all restaurants serve US-style breakfasts.

Lunch is available between 11:30 am and 2 pm. Many islanders favor long leisurely lunches, and you will find that the 'business' lunch is alive and well, with crowds of local professionals and merchants filling the more popular restaurants of Charlotte Amalie, Christiansted and Road Town.

Dinner is served between about 6 and 10 pm. Prosperous islanders and snowbirds (in addition to flocks of tourists) have developed a tradition of going out to restaurants – especially on Thursday, Friday and Saturday – as a prelude to a long night on the town. At popular spots, call ahead for reservations or be prepared to wait for a table. (Many better restaurants require reservations days in advance.)

Snacks

If you are counting your calories or cholesterol level, watch out for island finger foods. Most of them are deep-fried in animal fat, contain coconut meat or oil and taste like your next addiction.

Pate (pronounced PAW-tay) is the islands' most popular finger food. It is a fried pastry of cassava (yucca) or plantain dough stuffed with spiced goat, pork, chicken, conch, lobster or fish.

Another popular dish is *roti* (pronounced ROOT-ee), a relative of the Mexican burrito. Roti are flatbread envelopes stuffed with curried meat, fish or poultry, often served with a tangy mango chutney.

Main Dishes

A crossroads today as well as 500 years ago, the Virgin Islands have restaurants featuring most of the major cuisines of the world. Until recently, travelers were more likely to find restaurants serving Japanese, French or Mediterranean dishes than local recipes. But a new generation of island cooks has begun seeking 'mo roots,' and you will find plenty of West Indian dishes on menus these days.

West Indian cooking, more properly called Creole cuisine, as practiced in the Virgin Islands is far from the peas-and-rice or goat-on-a-stick stereotypes often associated with Caribbean food. Creole cuisine is, perhaps, the most sophisticated fusion cuisine on the planet. West Indian dishes draw on breads and roots from the Carib and Taíno Indians, meats from the Europeans, spices and vegetables from Africa, India and China and cooking styles from the Slave Coast of western Africa and Asia.

Soup and stew are staples in West Indian cooking. Many soups use unique island vegetables, *ground provisions* (roots) and fruits to add texture, taste and vitamins. Some plants include okra (a favorite smuggled in from Africa by slaves), squash, plantain, eggplant, *christophene* (like a potato/cucumber cross), *paw paw* (green papaya), scallions, mamey apple, *batata* (tropical sweet potato), tannia and the West Indian pumpkin. *Dasheen* (taro root) is a tuber with the taste of a potato. The green leaves of this plant are a primary ingredient in the islands' famous *callaloo* soup, which also may contain okra, hot pepper, pork and fish (see the boxed text).

Generally, cast-iron pots are used for 'boilin' down' soups or stews such as *pepperpot*, combining oxtail, chicken, beef, pork and calf's foot with a hot pepper and *cassareep*

(from cassava). Tannia soup is another traditional offering, as is *calabeza* (pumpkin soup).

Starch is also a main ingredient of islanders' diets. You get starch in the form of ground provisions that are boiled, mashed or steamed. You also get this in *fungi* (pronounced FOON-ghee), which is made from cornmeal and has the look and texture of polenta. Island cooks usually serve fungi with fish and gravy, and many West Indian families eat 'fish-n-fungi' weekly. Another popular dish is *accra,* a fried mixture of okra, black-eyed peas, pepper and a little salt.

Meat dishes are primarily curried or barbecued with tangy spices. Islanders also serve the Jamaican-style 'jerked' barbecue, using meat marinated in lime, ginger, sugar and Scotch bonnet peppers and cooking over pimento wood. *Daube meat* is a pot roast seasoned with vinegar, native seasonings, onion, garlic, tomato, thyme, parsley

The Secret of Callaloo

The thick green soup known as callaloo, or kallaloo, has achieved legendary status among West Indians as a culinary art form. Each cook has his or her secret ingredients. Here is a recipe gathered during a conversation with several St Thomas matriarchs:

One small salted turkey
1½lbs of red snapper
Meat of two crabs or one conch
3lbs of spinach or dasheen leaves
12 okra
One large onion
One clove of garlic
One sprig each of thyme and parsley
Several pieces of hot pepper
One stalk of celery
2 tablespoons of vinegar

Boil the meat of the turkey in 3 quarts of water until the meat is tender. Boil the fish, remove bones and add fish to the stock. Add the crab meat. Add the vegetables and spices *after* they have been put through a grinder. Boil rapidly for 30 minutes. Serve with fungi.

and celery. *Souse* is another spicy one-pot dish made from boiled pig's feet and head with a sauce of limes and hot pepper.

All manner of fish and shellfish make it to the local table, including old wife (triggerfish), doctorfish, flying fish, grouper, grunt, red snapper, squid, West Indian topshell (welk), crab and lobster. The cooks bake, grill, stew and boil the daily catch. Queen conch that is tenderized, marinated and diced into salads is a local favorite, as is grilled mahimahi (dorado). Fish lovers should also try a bowl of conch stew made with onion, tomato, sweet pepper and sherry. Salt cod is an ingredient and a taste left over from the days of the islands' trade with sailing ships from New England.

Almost all of these dishes arrive at your table with the popular johnnycakes and flavored with 'native seasoning,' homemade mixtures of salt, ground hot pepper, cloves, garlic, mace, nutmeg, celery and parsley.

Vegetarian Options

You can live a veggie lifestyle on the island, but you may have to work at it. The popularity of meat dishes and meat flavoring among islanders and the use of animal fat to cook fried foods pose a problem for vegetarians. Even when cooks use high-quality vegetable oils for frying, they are likely to fry your food in the same oil they used for pork or beef.

Creative vegetarian cooks can find ways of using the islands' fruits and seasonings to spice up basic platters of rice and beans. If you are eating out, you will discover a few Asian restaurants and other establishments featuring vegetarian cooking, or at least one or two vegetarian alternatives.

Desserts

Some of the islands' most popular after-dinner treats are homemade ice creams, which are actually frozen custards flavored with fresh mango, soursop, papaya or coconut. For special occasions, bakers serve up sweet potato pie, sweet potato pone (a mix of mashed sweet potatoes, sugar, eggs, lemon, dry wine, cinnamon, chopped almonds and raisins) and a fried dough covered with powdered sugar called Maria Boombe.

Fruit

Thanks to the nearly perfect tropical climate and enterprising traders during colonial times, the Virgin Islands are a fruit lover's paradise today. The plantain is an important fruit of the island diet. Like most of the fruits in the islands, it was first introduced as an exotic import.

Mangos are probably the most popular fruit and fruit tree in the islands, and the practice of kicking back under the nearest mango tree to taste some of the windfall is alive and well throughout the islands.

Coconuts, limes, lemons, cocoplums, soursop, guava, gneps and carambola (star fruit) are big sellers in the local produce markets. Many of these fruits are combined with the juice of hot peppers, salt and sugar to produce a dozen different varieties of chutney and hot sauce that islanders consume with enthusiasm.

DRINKS
Nonalcoholic Drinks

The Virgin Islands have all the soft drinks and many of the juices found in mainland USA, which means travelers could miss trying the beverages that are unique to the islands.

Ginger beer is a nonalcoholic beverage that comes from a fermented mix of gingerroot, water and sugar. Maubi (like Puerto Rico's *mauvi*) is the foamy juice made from the fermented bark of the carob tree, with spices and brown sugar. The islands' traditional practice of 'bush medicine,' descended from Africa, has created bush teas, made from more than 400 of the islands' leaves, roots and herbs. Many of these teas come with names like 'sorrel,' 'tamarind,' 'worry vine,' 'worm grass' and 'Spanish needle.' Each tea cures specific illnesses like gas, menstrual pain, colds or insomnia. Bottled water is also widely available.

Alcoholic Drinks

Because the USVI and BVI governments have not levied outlandish taxes on alcohol,

Rum by Gum

As is the case throughout the former sugar-cane islands of the Caribbean, rum is the national drink. Neighboring Puerto Rico is the largest producer of rum in the world, and the Virgin Islands still have a few distilleries such as the historic Callwood distillery on Tortola and the modern Cruzan Rum factory on St Croix.

With at least 20 brands of rum marketed in the islands, a drinker might be overwhelmed by the options. Beyond brand-name preferences, the choice of which rum to drink boils down to three options: white (like the local Cruzan offering), gold or añejo (aged, often from Puerto Rico). Dark rums are largely the products of Jamaica and other former British colonies such as Barbados.

White rums are the lightest. They are distilled and aged for as little as a year and are often mixed with orange or tomato juice. Gold rums must be distilled and aged for three years, and this beverage is often an ingredient in the popular piña colada or the 'Painkiller.' The longest aged, most flavorful and expensive rums are añejo. These amber beverages are often sipped straight or on the rocks and can be 'called' by a patron in a bar who wants to show a touch of class.

Adventuresome drinkers may want to take a risk and imbibe a bit of 'pinch.' These are homemade, illegal rums that can be either blinding firewater or the smooth, treasured drinks of connoisseurs.

Here's the traditional islands' recipe/poem for rum punch:

One of sour (lime juice)
Two of sweet (granadine)
Three of strong (rum)
Four of weak (7up or other soda)

the Virgin Islands are among the cheaper places to drink in the Caribbean. And alcohol plays a major role in island social life.

Although the laws are only loosely enforced (particularly in smaller settlements), people younger than 18 (minors) are prohibited from consuming alcohol in the islands. Carry a driver's license or passport as proof of age to enter a bar, order alcohol at a restaurant, buy alcohol or drink on the beaches as well as streets.

You can get many US, Mexican, Canadian and European beers with ease in the islands. Foxy's Lager and Blackbeard's Ale are two microbrews from St Croix. Carib, the Eastern Caribbean's most popular beer, is brewed in Trinidad, Granada and St Kitts. Expect to pay about $3 for a beer in most pubs or restaurants.

Rum is the island specialty – see the boxed text.

ENTERTAINMENT

The wit, good humor and pleas for freedom that pulsate through calypso and reggae music say it all: Here is a culture that loves unfettered leisure time.

Pubs & Bars

The West Indian culture of the Virgin Islands is very social, and many travelers come to the islands looking for a good time. That combination breeds a lively bar scene, which often features superb reggae and calypso music.

Many of the legendary haunts like Foxy's Tamarind Bar on Jost Van Dyke, Bomba's Surfside Shack on Tortola, the Green House on St Thomas, Boz's Cane Bay Beach Bar and the schooner *Willie T* at Norman Island are waterfront operations. But some great gin mills show up in unlikely settings, such as a mall parking lot where you will find

Duffy's Love Shack in Red Hook. There is absolutely no place in the Virgin Islands where the races, classes, genders, 'belongers' and 'nonbelongers' mix more freely.

Nightclubs

The Virgin Islands are not rich clubbing territory for travelers. A few major resort hotels like Marriott's Frenchman's Reef Beach Resort on St Thomas have resort discos that also feature live bands and cater to tourists. But spacious, high-tech clubs are hard to find in the islands, with the exception of the Old Mill in St Thomas. Many of the dance clubs found in the islands appeal to a young West Indian crowd.

Live Music, Theater & Dance

The Reichhold Center for the Arts (☎ 340-693-1500), at the University of the Virgin Islands on St Thomas, is the primary concert venue in the islands, hosting local performing arts and international stars like Itzak Perlman. The Island Center for the Performing Arts (☎ 340-778-5272) is St Croix's venue for theater, cabaret and performances by local and internationally recognized stars like the Boston Pops and the Temptations.

Cinemas

Movies are not an exceedingly popular form of entertainment in the islands, and theaters are rare even on the largest islands. The few cinemas are in malls or shopping districts of St Thomas, St Croix and Tortola.

Casinos

Casino gambling came to the Virgin Islands in 2000 with the opening of the Divi Carina Bay Casino on the east end of St Croix. If the experiment is successful, more casinos may follow. But so far, no one is betting on a bonanza: In its first year of operation, the Divi Casino attracted a lot more locals than tourists. You must be at least 21 to enter the casino.

SPECTATOR SPORTS

Although the USVI and BVI host a plethora of yachting regattas like the presti-gious International Rolex Cup (☎ 340-773-9531) in early February and fishing contests like the Atlantic Blue Marlin Tournament (☎ 340-774-2752) in August, true spectator sports are rare.

The St Croix Half-Ironman Triathlon (☎ 340-773-4470) takes place in early May and features qualifying spots for the Ironman World Championship in Kona, Hawaii. This is the first event in the World Professional Triathlon tour. Each event includes running, swimming and biking.

The Doc James Race Track (☎ 340-778-1395), on St Croix, is an old, small-scale thoroughbred racing operation.

SHOPPING

The US Virgin Islands are a duty-free destination, and you can save up to 40% on gems, watches, cameras, crystal, china, fabrics, liquor and other items. In particular, the historic areas of Christiansted and Charlotte Amalie have hundreds of shops to tempt you. Travelers looking for souvenirs are drawn to the islands' folk arts (see the Facts about the Virgin Islands chapter). In the BVI, shoppers often purchase island-made cooking spices and batik fabric. As the Caribbean is the leading producer of rum in the world, you would be right to expect that many travelers find this beverage the one thing they must buy in the islands. Most bottles cost between $4 and $10, depending on size and quality.

Sea turtle shells make beautiful jewelry – too beautiful, in fact, for the welfare of the turtles, which are endangered worldwide. Buying any turtle products increases the demand for hunting the turtles. Turtle shell jewelry, as well as sea turtle taxidermy and food products, is prohibited entry into the USA, Canada, Australia and most other countries.

Also note that the importation of black coral is banned in more than 100 countries. The purchase of other corals, which are often taken live from their fragile reef ecosystems and sold in chunks or made into jewelry, should also give pause to the environmentally conscious.

YACHT CHARTER BASICS

A felicitous combination of geography and geology has positioned the Virgin Islands as sailing's Magic Kingdom. Here you have a year-round balmy climate, steady trade winds, little to worry about in the way of tides or currents, a protected thoroughfare in the 35-mile-long Sir Francis Drake Channel, and hundreds of anchorages, each within sight of another. These factors make the Virgins one of the easiest places to sail – easy, that is, for capable sailors with piloting skills – and quite a bit lower on the seasickness scale than other Caribbean cruising grounds.

Thirty years ago, Ginny and Charlie Cary had the vision to start up the Moorings as the type of company they themselves would like to charter from. Since then, sailboat chartering has grown from a refuge for eccentric dropouts (though there are still plenty of them around) to a real industry (which still occasionally runs on 'island time'). The boats are well equipped and reliable, charts of the area are accurate, and the cruising guides are excellent. Today, 20 or so companies in St Thomas and Tortola offer around 800 monohulls and catamarans in sizes ranging from the low 30s to 50 feet. More than a third of visitors to the Virgins come to sail. In addition to the sandy beaches, waving palm trees and multihued waters, they find all the beach bars, ecologically sensitive moorings and purveyors of luxury groceries they could want in a week or two.

You have three basic options: a sailing school or other instructional situation; a bareboat charter (bare of crew but fully equipped to sail, lodge and cook for two to eight people), with or without a skipper; or a more luxurious crewed charter, complete with captain, cook and sometimes other crew. While a sailing school will offer a formal program of instruction leading to certification by a recognized sailing association, many of the bareboat charter companies and a good number of the crewed boats also offer certification programs or as much instruction as the client chooses to absorb, given the other distractions available.

Most charterers head for the British Virgin Islands; a typical weeklong itinerary involves a sampling of the islands as part of a circumnavigation

STEVE SIMONSEN

of Tortola, with a lunch stop at one anchorage and an overnight at another. The attraction of a sailing vacation is you can sail or stay put as long as you want, look for quiet anchorages or head for the party spots, and add on diving or hiking or shopping at will. There are about 100 islands, islets, rocks and cays in the 45 miles between St Thomas and Anegada; note that you can't hit them all in a week.

If you're in the mood for a longer passage, many companies will let you sail to St Croix, about 40 miles from St Thomas or St John, and back. Another option is to arrange a one-way charter to the Spanish Virgins (Puerto Rico's Vieques and Culebra Islands and their surrounding cays). Going west from St Thomas to drop off in Fajardo (on the Puerto Rican mainland) avoids a nasty upwind slog going the other way. Anegada's reef-strewn approaches have claimed many boats, but if you can demonstrate appropriate experience or are willing to take a skipper, it's more than worth the effort.

Qualifications

For your protection and theirs, all bareboat charter companies require you to fill out a sailing résumé to demonstrate your ability to handle the boat and the sailing conditions. A physical demonstration of your skills will be required upon arrival. In practical terms, you should have a reasonable amount of recent coastal-cruising experience in an auxiliary sailboat more than 30 feet long (this need not be a boat you own, however). You should be able not only to sail the boat, but to dock and anchor it, to run its systems and to deal with minor problems and routines (for example, checking battery and oil levels). In addition, you must be competent in basic piloting and able to deal with passing squalls and winds.

Many charter companies consider the résumés of the group as a whole when deciding if you're qualified to take one of its boats. Be honest; feeling underprepared when you're under way can spoil your vacation. One option – one that the charter company may require – is to bring along an instructional skipper for a few days.

When to Charter

The time of year affects two major considerations – weather and cost. Winter winds average 15 to 22 knots from the northeast; the 'Christmas winds,' which have been known to extend into January and even February, are the strongest of the year. When the wind is northeast, northside anchorages, including Tortola's Cane Garden Bay, are uncomfortable to impossible. In spring and summer, the wind swings around through the east to the southeast and declines to an average of 10 to 18 knots; many sailors prefer the milder and somewhat warmer conditions of spring. In September and October, when the trade winds are at their weakest, the weather tends to be more unsettled. September is the most likely month for hurricanes, so it's probably the best month to avoid. (Also see Planning in the Facts for the Visitor chapter.)

Another seasonal consideration is cost. Many charter companies offer a variety of prices, which may change from week to week depending on seasonal demand. Most companies offer summer (low-season) deals involving extra 'free' days.

Costs

The cost of chartering a boat is a function of the vessel's size and age and the time of year. A new 50-foot sloop with room for eight averages $6000 a week at peak season and roughly half that in low season; an older boat of the same size would be around $3000 a week (low season) to $4000 a week (high season). For a fully crewed boat, expect to pay $5000 a week and up.

All charter companies in the Virgin Islands offer provisioning packages; the most popular type includes all breakfasts, all lunches and three or four dinners, and averages $22 per person. Doing your own provisioning (there are large markets in St Thomas, St John and Tortola) is always an option; it costs time but can save money. You'll also have to pay insurance ($20 to $30 a day). You can hire a skipper ($100 to $125 a day; add $25 a day for an instructional skipper) or a cook ($100 to $125 a day). If you do, you'll have to provide sleeping space and food. Though not compulsory, trip insurance is recommended. You may be responsible for the whole charter fee if you cancel less than 45 days before your booking.

Optional add-ons include rental equipment (a kayak or cruising spinnaker), a cell phone (often comes with larger boats) and a delivery fee for a one-way charter. Diving is usually arranged by rendezvous with a local dive company; they pick you up and return you to your boat.

Choosing a Company

Charter companies depend on their reputations. Ask for references from recent clients and spend some time talking with the company's representatives. They should be able to answer your questions about the charter area, the sailing conditions, their fleet, a suggested itinerary (you'll get more information at the chart briefing) and whatever else you want to know. Web sites can provide a good deal of useful information, but there's no substitute for personal communication. If you're not satisfied, call another company.

The following is a list of respected charter services based in the Virgin Islands. For an up-to-date list of services, prices and equipment check the *Sail* magazine Web site, www.sailmag.com.

St Thomas & St Croix

Annapolis Sailing School (☎ 800-638-9192), on King Cross St in Christiansted, books three-day and five-day learn-to-sail vacations.

Caribbean Sailing Charters (☎ 800-824-1331), at American Yacht Harbor in Red Hook, has 18 boats.

CYOA Yacht Charters (☎ 340-777-9690, 800-944-2962), at the French town Marina, has 15 boats.

Island Yacht Charters (☎ 340-775-6666, 800-524-2019), at American Yacht Harbor, has 15 boats.

Virgin Island Power Yacht Charters (☎ 340-776-1510), at Benner Bay, has a fleet of cruising motor yachts for weekly rentals as bareboats. It also has 20 sailboats.

Tortola

The Catamaran Company (☎ 954-566-9806, 800-262-0308), at Nanny Cay Marina, has 40 boats.

Conch Charters (☎ 284-494-4868, 800-521-8939), at Fort Burt Marina, maintains 30 boats.

Footloose Sailing Charters (☎ 800-814-7245), in Road Town, rents 30 boats.

Horizon Yacht Charters (☎ 284-494-8787), at Nanny Cay Marina, has 16 boats.

The Moorings (☎ 727-530-5424, 800-535-7289), on Wickhams Cay 2 in Road Town, started the bareboat business in these islands. It has more than 200 sailing yachts, most less than two years old.

Offshore Sailing School (☎ 800-221-4326), at the Prospect Reef Resort, has learn-to-cruise courses and 46-foot boats.

Stardust Yacht Charters (☎ 207-253-5400, 800-772-3500), at Maya Cove, operates about 100 vessels.

Sunsail Sailing Vacations (☎ 410-280-2553, 800-327-2276) maintains a large base in Sopers Hole, with 140 boats.

Trade Wind Yacht Charters (☎ 284-494-6892, 800-825-7245), at Fat Hogs Bay, has 30 boats.

Tortola Marine Management (☎ 284-494-2751, 800-633-0155) has 41 boats at Road Reef Marina on Fat Hogs Bay.

Crewed Boats

If you're looking for luxury accommodations that move from island to island, look no farther than the fleet of privately owned boats with skipper, cook and any other crew needed for proper ship handling and your personal pampering. Meticulously maintained and often exquisitely decorated, these boats offer all the water toys (and electronic connections to your office) you might imagine, plus cuisine that tops most luxe resorts. In fact, the food served on board is the primary means by which the companies compete with one another.

Crewed boats are booked by brokers who get to know the boats and their crews at boat shows. They will get to know you, too, before making a recommendation based on your budget, the size of your party and your preferences for all those little things that make your vacation special. All this splendor comes, of course, at a price.

People looking for a crewed-yacht vacation in the US or British Virgin Islands can contact the Virgin Islands Charterboat League (☎ 340-774-3944, 800-524-2061), 5100 Long Bay Rd, St Thomas. Following is a list of reputable brokers who know the boats and crews.

Caribbean Sailing Charters (☎ 800-824-1331)
Ed Hamilton & Co (☎ 800-621-7855)
Lynn Jachney Charters (☎ 800-223-2050)
Sailing Vacations (☎ 800-922-4880)
Virgin Island Sailing Ltd (☎ 800-382-9666)

—Amy Ullrich, Managing Editor, *Sail* magazine

Getting There & Away

AIR

Airfares to the Virgin Islands vary tremendously depending on the season you travel, the day of the week you fly, the length of your stay and the flexibility the ticket allows for flight changes and refunds. Nothing determines fares more than demand, and when things are slow, regardless of the season, airlines will lower their fares to fill empty seats.

Airports

The Cyril E King International Airport on St Thomas, with its state-of-the-art terminal, is the busiest airport in the islands. More than half of all flights to and from the Virgin Islands pass through this facility. Some are direct flights from the US; most are commuter flights from San Juan, Puerto Rico, the hub for air travel in the Caribbean.

Two other airports in the islands see significant commercial traffic. St Croix's Henry

Warning

The information in this chapter is particularly vulnerable to change: Prices for international travel are volatile, routes are introduced and cancelled, schedules change, special deals come and go, and rules and visa requirements are amended. Airlines and governments seem to take a perverse pleasure in making price structures and regulations as complicated as possible. You should check directly with the airline or with a travel agent to make sure you understand how a fare (and ticket you may buy) works. In addition, the travel industry is highly competitive, and there are many lurks and perks.

The upshot of this is that you should get opinions, quotes and advice from as many airlines and travel agents as possible before you part with your hard-earned cash. The details given in this chapter should be regarded as pointers and are not a substitute for your own careful, up-to-date research.

E Rohlsen Airport can handle jumbo jets and has a new, expanded terminal as well. Direct service to St Croix from the US has been an intermittent proposition. Most travelers fly here via connecting flights through San Juan or St Thomas.

Off Tortola, Beef Island International Airport is the BVI major point of entry, but the airport cannot accommodate large jets. Travelers coming from overseas arrive at San Juan, Puerto Rico or St Thomas and take smaller aircraft to Tortola.

Virgin Gorda has an airstrip that receives a few commuter flights a day. The harbors at Christiansted and Charlotte Amalie serve as seaplane bases for Seabourne Aviation's Twin Otter floatplanes, a commuter service between the two islands.

Airlines

The following list includes some of the more popular airlines serving the Virgin Islands from the Americas and Europe, often via connections through nearby Puerto Rico. (The 800 and 888 telephone numbers are toll-free calls from the US, Canada, Mexico and the Caribbean.)

Air Canada	☎ 800-776-3000
Air France	☎ 800-237-2747
Air St Thomas	☎ 800-522-3084
American Airlines	☎ 800-433-7300
British Airways	☎ 800-247-9297
Canadian Airlines	☎ 800-426-7000
Condor (Lufthansa)	☎ 800-524-6975
Continental Airlines	☎ 800-525-0280
Delta Air Lines	☎ 800-221-1212
Iberia	☎ 800-722-4642
KLM	☎ 800-374-7747
LIAT	☎ 787-791-3838
Martinair Holland	☎ 800-627-8462
Northwest Airlines	☎ 800-225-2525
TWA	☎ 800-221-2000
United Airlines	☎ 800-241-6522
US Airways	☎ 800-842-5374

Buying Tickets

It pays to do a bit of research and shop around before purchasing your airline ticket. If you are buying tickets in the US, the *New York Times, Los Angeles Times, Chicago Tribune, San Francisco Chronicle, Boston Globe* and other major newspapers all produce weekly travel sections with numerous travel agents' ads.

Council Travel (☎ 800-226-8624) and STA Travel (☎ 800-777-0112) have offices in many major cities; visit their Web sites at www.counciltravel.com and www.sta-travel .com. The magazine *Travel Unlimited* (PO Box 1058, Allston, MA 02134) publishes details on the cheapest airfares and courier possibilities. Those coming from outside the US might start their search for cheap fares by perusing the travel sections of magazines such as *Time Out* and *TNT* in the UK, or the Saturday editions of newspapers such as the *Sydney Morning Herald* and *The Age* in Australia.

Your plane ticket will probably be the single most expensive item in your budget, and buying it can be intimidating. It is always worth putting aside a few hours to research the current state of the market. Start shopping for a ticket early – some of the cheapest tickets must be bought months in advance, and some popular flights sell out early. You can also use the Internet to hunt for low fares. Phoning a travel agent is still one of the best ways to dig up bargains. Roundtrip (return) tickets are usually cheaper than two one-way fares – sometimes *much* cheaper. Note that high season in the Virgin Islands is mid-December to late April (winter). The lowest rates for travel to and from the islands are found from May 1 to about December 20.

Cheap tickets are available in two distinct categories: official and unofficial. Official tickets have a variety of names, including advance-purchase, APEX, budget and promotional fares. Unofficial tickets are simply discounted tickets that the airlines release through selected travel agencies (not through airline offices). The cheapest tickets are often nonrefundable, and they require an extra fee for changing your flight (usually US$50 or more). Many insurance policies will cover this loss if you have to change your flight for emergency reasons.

In some places, especially the UK, the cheapest flights are advertised by obscure bucket shops whose names haven't yet reached the telephone directory. Many such firms are honest and solvent, but some will take your money and disappear. If you feel suspicious about a firm, don't give them all the money at once – leave a deposit of 20% or so and pay the balance on receiving the ticket. If they insist on cash in advance, go elsewhere. Once you have the ticket, call the airline to confirm that you are booked on the flight.

You may decide to pay more than the rock-bottom fare by opting for the safety of a better-known travel agent. Established firms such as STA Travel and Council Travel (see above), both of which have offices internationally, and Canada's Travel CUTS/ Voyages Campus (☎ 800-667-2887), with a Web site at www.travelcuts.com, offer good prices to most destinations.

Use the fares quoted in this book as a guide only. They are approximate and are based on the rates advertised by travel agencies and airlines at press time. Quoted airfares do not necessarily constitute a recommendation for the carrier.

Once you have your ticket, make a copy of it and keep the copy separate from the original ticket. This will help you get a replacement if your ticket gets lost or stolen. Remember to buy travel insurance as early as possible to protect against any penalties for an unavoidable cancellation. (See Travel Insurance under Visas & Documents in the Facts for the Visitor chapter.)

Round-the-World Tickets RTW tickets can be a great deal if you want to visit other regions as well as the US and Puerto Rico. Although the Virgin Islands do not presently qualify as a stopover point on any carrier's round-the-world itinerary, RTW tickets are often real bargains and can get you to Miami (the nearest US entry point).

Getting Bumped On oversold flights, the gate agent will first ask for volunteers to be

Air Travel Glossary

Alliances Many of the world's leading airlines are now intimately involved with each other, sharing everything from reservations systems and check-in to aircraft and frequent-flyer schemes. Opponents say that alliances restrict competition. Whatever the arguments, there is no doubt that big alliances are the way of the future.

Courier Fares Businesses often need to send urgent documents or freight securely and quickly. Courier companies hire people to accompany the package through customs and, in return, offer a discount ticket that is sometimes a bargain. However, you may have to surrender all your baggage allowance and take only carry-on luggage.

Fares Airlines traditionally offer 1st-class (coded F), business-class (coded J) and economy-class (coded Y) tickets. These days, there are so many promotional and discounted fares available that few passengers pay full fare.

Lost Tickets If you lose your airline ticket, an airline will usually treat it as a travelers check and, after inquiries, issue you with another one. Legally, however, an airline is entitled to treat it as cash, so if you lose it, then it could be gone forever. Take very good care of your tickets.

Onward Tickets An entry requirement for many countries is that you have a ticket out of the country. If you're unsure of your next move, the easiest solution is to buy the cheapest onward ticket to a neighboring country or a ticket (from a reliable airline) that can later be refunded if you do not use it.

Open-Jaw Tickets These are return tickets used to fly out to one place but return from another. If available, this can save you from having to backtrack to your arrival point.

Overbooking Since every flight has some passengers who fail to show up, airlines often book more passengers than they have seats. Usually excess passengers make up for the no-shows, but occasionally somebody gets 'bumped' onto the next available flight. Who is it most likely to be? The passengers who check in late. If you do get 'bumped,' you are normally offered some form of compensation.

Reconfirmation Some airlines require you to reconfirm your flight at least 72 hours prior to departure. Check your travel documents to see if this is the case.

Restrictions Discounted tickets often have various restrictions on them – such as mandatory advance payment and penalties for alterations or cancellations. Others have restrictions on the minimum and maximum period you must be away.

Round-the-World Tickets RTW tickets give you a limited period (usually a year) in which to circumnavigate the globe. You can go anywhere the carrying airlines go, as long as you don't backtrack. The number of stopovers or the total number of separate flights is decided before you set off, and these tickets usually cost a bit more than a basic return flight.

Ticketless Travel Airlines are gradually waking up to the realization that paper tickets are unnecessary encumbrances. On simple one-way or return trips, reservations details can be held on computer, and the passengers merely show identification to claim their seats.

Transferred Tickets Airline tickets cannot be transferred from one person to another. Travelers sometimes try to sell the return half of their tickets, but officials can ask you to prove that you are the person named on the ticket. On an international flight, the name on the ticket is compared with the name on the passport.

bumped in return for a later flight plus compensation of the airline's choosing. (If there aren't enough volunteers, some passengers will be forced onto a later flight. Each airline has its own method of choosing which customers will be bumped.)

When you check in at the airline counter, ask if the flight is full and if there may be a need for volunteers. Get your name on the list if you don't mind volunteering. Depending on how oversold the flight is, compensation can range from a discount voucher toward your next flight to a fully paid roundtrip ticket or even cash. Be sure to try to confirm a later flight so you don't get stuck in the airport on standby. If you have to spend the night, airlines frequently foot the hotel bill for their 'bumpees.' You don't have to accept the airline's first offer; you can haggle for a better deal.

However, be aware that, due to this same system, being just a little late for boarding could get you bumped with none of these benefits.

Baggage

On most domestic and overseas flights to the Virgin Islands, you are limited to two checked bags, or three if you don't have a carry-on. There could be a charge if a bag exceeds the airline's size limits. It's best to check with the individual airline if you are concerned about this. On some international flights, the luggage allowance is based on weight, not size; again, check with the airline.

If your luggage is delayed upon arrival (which is rare), some airlines will give you a cash advance so you can purchase necessities. If sporting equipment is misplaced, the airline may pay for rentals. Should your luggage get lost, it is important to submit a claim. The airline doesn't have to pay the full amount of the claim; rather, they can estimate the value of your lost items. It may take them anywhere from six weeks to three months to process the claim and pay you.

Smoking

Smoking is prohibited on all domestic flights within the US, and this includes the US Virgin Islands. Many international flights are following suit, so be sure to call and find out. Many airports in the US and the islands also restrict smoking.

Illegal Items

Items that are illegal to take on a plane, either checked or as carry-on, include aerosols of polishes, waxes, tear gas and pepper spray, camp stoves with fuel, divers' tanks that are full and mercury thermometers.

Travelers with Special Needs

If you have special needs of any sort – a broken leg, dietary restrictions, dependence on a wheelchair, responsibility for a baby, major fear of flying – you should let the airline know as soon as possible so it can make arrangements accordingly. You should remind the airline when you reconfirm your booking (at least 72 hours before departure) and again when you check in at the airport. It may also be worth calling several airlines before you make your booking to find out how they can handle your needs.

Airports and airlines can be surprisingly helpful, but they do need advance warning. Most international airports can provide escorts from the check-in desk to the plane, and there should be ramps, lifts, accessible toilets and reachable phones. Aircraft toilets, on the other hand, are likely to present a problem; travelers should discuss this with the airline at an early stage and, if necessary, with their doctor.

Guide dogs for the blind often have to travel in a specially pressurized baggage compartment with other animals, away from their owners, though smaller guide dogs may be admitted to the cabin. Guide dogs are not subject to quarantine as long as they have proof of being vaccinated against rabies.

Deaf travelers can ask that airport and in-flight announcements be written down for them.

Children younger than two travel for 10% of the standard fare (or for free on some airlines) if they don't occupy a seat. They don't get a baggage allowance with this deal. 'Skycots' should be provided by the airline if requested in advance; these will hold a child weighing up to about 22lb. Children between two and 12 years old can usually occupy a seat for one-half to two-thirds of the full fare and do get a baggage allowance. Strollers can sometimes be taken on as hand luggage. Occasionally, there is a child's rate on a discounted fare. It can be cheaper for a child to fly on an adult discounted fare than on a child's fare at two-thirds of the full adult rate. For pricing purposes, the child's age is reckoned at the time of departure on the first leg of the flight.

Departure Tax
All passengers passing through Puerto Rico en route to the Virgins must pay a US$12 airport departure tax. Passengers entering Puerto Rico or the US are charged an additional US$12 North American Free Trade Agreement (NAFTA) tax. These taxes are normally included in the cost of tickets bought in the US (thus they're 'hidden' taxes added to a ticket's purchase price). Tickets purchased abroad may or may not include these taxes. There is a US$10 departure tax due when leaving the BVI, but no tax when leaving the USVI.

The Caribbean & Latin America
American Eagle (☎ 880-474-4884) is a major carrier for those traveling from San Juan, Puerto Rico, to the US Virgin Islands. You can also take the smaller planes of Cape Air (☎ 800-352-0714), Air Sunshine (☎ 340-778-8900), Gulfstream International (☎ 800-457-4838), Vieques Airlink (☎ 340-778-9858) or Continental Connection (☎ 284-495-1044, 800-231-0856).

LIAT (☎ 340-778-9930) offers service to the other Lesser Antilles islands, as does Coastal Air Transport (☎ 340-773-6862).

Many flights to the Virgin Islands from Central and South America are routed through San Juan, Miami, Houston or New York. Some countries' international flag carriers, such as Aerolíneas Argentinas (☎ 800-333-0276), LACSA (☎ 800-225-2272) and Mexicana (☎ 800-531-7921), fly directly to San Juan from Latin American cities.

The USA
The most popular routings to the Virgin Islands from the USA are via New York, Boston and Miami, but flights from about a dozen other cities in the continental US also serve the islands. Most major US carriers – including American, Continental, Delta, Northwest, United and US Airways – fly to Puerto Rico, where travelers board commuter flights to the islands. St Thomas has a number of direct flights to and from major hubs in the US daily. American Airlines has the most frequent service to and from the islands, with more than 50 scheduled flights a day to St Thomas, St Croix and Tortola.

For toll-free telephone numbers of airlines serving the Virgin Islands from the US, see Airlines, earlier.

Discount Tickets Many discount ticket agencies sell reduced-rate tickets to the Caribbean. One of the leading brokers specializing in the area is Pan Express Travel (☎ 212-719-9292), 25 W 39th St, New York, NY 10018. Other leading discount agencies include Express Holidays (☎ 619-283-6324, 800-266-8669), 5945 Mission Gorge Rd, No 2, San Diego, CA 92120, and the Vacation Store (☎ 212-465-0707, 800-825-3633, fax 212-594-6711), 101 W 31st St, New York, NY 10001.

Charter Flights These generally offer the lowest fares for confirmed reservations (sometimes one-third or more off airline prices) and can be booked through most travel agencies. You can sometimes book one-way tickets with charter airlines for less than half the roundtrip fare. Often the charter price includes accommodations.

Charter flights are usually direct, without the hub stop common on standard airlines. Few charters are listed in airline reservation systems, as they're operated by wholesale tour operators with whom you or your travel agent will have to deal directly.

Although you can buy the ticket without an advance-purchase requirement, you do have to fix your departure and return dates well in advance, and a substantial fee may apply for any changes or cancellations. Consider cancellation insurance to protect yourself in the event of illness (see Travel Insurance under Visas & Documents in the Facts for the Visitor chapter). Also, seating on charter flights may be more cramped, as planes tend to be full, and flights are often at inconvenient hours.

While US charter operators are bonded with the US government, if the tour operator or airline defaults, you may have difficulties getting your money back. Finally, charter airlines are often less organized than standard carriers, and processing at airport counters tends to be more confused and time-consuming, even when the charter operator uses the service desk and aircraft of a major airline.

Before buying, compare charter prices with the airlines' current 'sale' fares and with the cost of a discount ticket from a consolidator. Check the Sunday travel sections of major city newspapers or ask a travel agent. A good resource is the *Worldwide Guide to Cheap Airfares,* by Michael McColl, which provides a comprehensive listing of charter tour operators.

Some wholesale tour companies operating charters to the Virgin Islands include Apple Vacations (☎ 800-727-3400), 7 Campus Blvd, Newtown Square, PA 19073; Globetrotters (☎ 800-999-9696), 139 Main St, Cambridge, MA 02124; and GWV International (☎ 800-225-5498), 300 First Ave, Needham, MA 02494.

Courier Flights If you're willing to fly at short notice and travel light, courier flights are one of the cheapest ways to go – normally about half the standard fare, but often much less.

As a courier, you are responsible for delivering an item such as a parcel or document on behalf of a company. Usually, the handling of the item is taken care of by the courier company; you merely act as its agent by occupying a seat. The traveler is usually allowed only one piece of carry-on baggage, and the checked-baggage allowance is taken by the item to be delivered.

Unfortunately, there are very few courier options to the Caribbean. For information,

try NOW Voyager (☎ 212-431-1616), 74 Varick St, No 307, New York, NY 10013, the leading booking agency for courier companies. You must pay a one-time US$50 registration fee.

Two good resources are the *Courier Air Travel Handbook,* by Mark Field, and the *Worldwide Guide to Cheap Airfares,* by Michael McColl.

Last-Minute Flights If you can fly at very short notice (usually within seven days of travel), consider buying a ticket from a 'last-minute' ticket broker. These companies buy surplus seats from charter airlines (and sometimes standard carriers) at hugely discounted prices. The airline would rather fill the seats than fly empty, so you reap the reward. Discounts can be as great as 40% for a confirmed seat.

One of the leading distress-sale brokers is Last Minute Travel Club (☎ 617-267-9800, 800-527-8646), 1249 Boylston St, Boston, MA 02215, which specializes in air/hotel packages to the Caribbean. Other last-minute ticket agencies require you to become a member of their clubs; annual fees are about $40, for which you receive regular updates.

Companies to consider for last-minute tickets include Moment's Notice (☎ 212-486-0500), 425 Madison Ave, New York, NY 10017, and Worldwide Discount Travel Club (☎ 305-895-2082), 1674 Meridian Ave, Miami Beach, FL 33139.

Canada

No Canadian carriers fly direct to the Virgin Islands, but Air Canada (☎ 800-776-3000) offers connections (via Continental and American flights) from Montreal, Ottawa and Toronto.

Travel CUTS/Voyages Campus (☎ 416-614-2887, 800-667-2887 in Canada) has offices in all major cities.

City newspapers such as the Toronto *Globe and Mail* and *Vancouver Sun* carry travel agents' ads. The magazine *Great Expeditions,* PO Box 8000-411, Abbotsford, BC V2S 6H1, is also useful.

Australia & New Zealand

STA Travel has offices in major cities throughout Australia and New Zealand. STA sells tickets to everyone but offers special deals to students and travelers under 30. Head offices are at 224 Faraday St, PO Box 75, Melbourne, VIC 3053, Australia (☎ 1-300-360-960, 3-9347-6911) and 10 High St, Auckland, New Zealand (☎ 9-309-0458).

Flight Centres International (☎ 2-9584-9133, fax 2-9235-2871) is a major dealer in cheap airfares. Check the travel agents' ads in the yellow pages and phone around.

The cheapest tickets to US destinations have a 21-day advance-purchase requirement, a minimum stay of seven days and a maximum stay of 60 days. Flying with Air New Zealand is slightly cheaper, and Qantas and Air New Zealand offer tickets with longer stays or stopovers, but you pay more.

Flying from Australia or New Zealand to the Virgin Islands is difficult. As no airline offers direct service, travelers and their travel agents will have to do a bit of work to get a good deal. One common option is to fly from Melbourne to Mexico City with Japan Air Lines (JAL) and then fly from Mexico City to San Juan, Puerto Rico, on Mexicana. From there, you can take a commuter flight to the islands. The fare in low season is around A$2350; in high season, it's A$2650 or more.

The UK & Ireland

British Airways offers direct service to San Juan from Gatwick on Saturday and Sunday, with daily connecting flights through Miami. BA and British West Indies Airlines (BWIA) feed the islands of Antigua, St Lucia, Barbados, Grenada and Trinidad from the UK. A commuter flight will carry you on to the Virgin of your choice.

Trailfinders (☎ 020-7937-5400), 194 Kensington High St, London W8 7RG, produces a lavishly illustrated brochure that includes airfare details. Other good, reliable agents for cheap tickets in the UK are Council Travel (☎ 020-7437-7767), 28a Poland St, London W1; and STA Travel (☎ 020-7581-4132), 86 Old Brompton Rd, London SW7 3LQ. One of the leading air-only travel specialists is Caribbean Gold (☎ 020-8741-8491).

Look in the magazines *Time Out* and *City Limits,* the Sunday papers, and *Exchange & Mart* for ads. Also look out for the free magazines that are widely available in London – start by looking outside the main railway stations.

Most British travel agents are registered with the ABTA (Association of British Travel Agents). If you have paid for your flight through an ABTA-registered agent that goes out of business, ABTA guarantees a refund or an alternative. Unregistered bucket shops are riskier but sometimes cheaper. The Globetrotters Club, BCM Roving, London WC1N 3XX, publishes a newsletter called *Globe* that covers obscure destinations and can help in finding travel companions.

Continental Europe

In Denmark, Cruise & Travel (☎ 45-33-119-500, fax 45-33-119-501), Bredgade 35C, Copenhagen, 1260 K, specializes in travel to the Caribbean.

In Amsterdam, NBBS is a popular travel agent. Martinair Holland flies from Amsterdam to San Juan on Monday and Saturday.

A good source in Paris is Council Travel (☎ 01 44 41 89 80), at 1 place de l'Odeon, 75006. For great student fares, contact USIT Voyages (☎ 01 42 34 56 90), at 6 rue de Vaugirard, 75006 Paris.

In Germany, try STA Travel (☎ 069 43 01 91), Berger Strasse 118, 60316 Frankfurt, or contact either of the Council Travel offices at Graf Adolph Strasse 18, 40212 Düsseldorf (☎ 0211 36 30 30) or Adalbert Strasse 32, 80799 Munich (☎ 089 39 50 22). Lufthansa's subsidiary line Condor flies from Frankfurt to San Juan and back on Saturday.

If you plan to travel from Spain, Iberia offers one or two direct flights per week from Madrid to San Juan. From here, you can catch a half-hour flight to the Virgin Islands.

Asia

Bangkok and Singapore are the discount ticket capitals of the region, but their bucket shops can be unreliable. STA Travel, which is dependable, has branches in Hong Kong, Tokyo, Singapore, Bangkok and Kuala Lumpur. Reaching the Virgin Islands from Asia is much the same as traveling to the islands from Australia, with connecting flights through the US or Mexico City.

SEA
Cruise Ship

St Thomas is the most popular cruise ship destination in the Caribbean, with more than 900 arrivals each year. For the most part, these ships dock at the West India Company dock in Havensight on the eastern edge of St Thomas Harbor. A lot of them move on to the Frederiksted pier at St Croix and the cruise ship dock in Tortola. A few even anchor in Pillsbury Sound off St John.

Prices vary according to the standard of the ship, but you will be lucky to pay less than $1500 for a seven-day cruise to the Virgin Islands. However, this price will probably include your airfare and transfers to the cruise ship, as well as all your meals and entertainment.

The Cruise Line International Association (CLIA; ☎ 212-921-0549, fax 212-921-0549), 500 Fifth Ave, No 1407, New York, NY 10110, provides information on cruising and individual lines. Or you can contact the cruise lines directly at the following toll-free numbers.

Carnival Cruise Lines	☎ 800-327-9501
Celebrity Cruise Lines	☎ 800-437-3111
Commodore Cruise Lines	☎ 800-237-5361
Costa Cruise Lines	☎ 800-462-6782
Crystal Cruise Lines	☎ 800-446-6620
Cunard Lines	☎ 800-528-6273
Disney Cruise Lines	☎ 800-511-1333
Holland American Line	☎ 800-426-0327
Norwegian Cruise Line	☎ 800-327-7030
Royal Caribbean Cruise Line	☎ 800-327-6700
Seabourn Cruise Line	☎ 800-929-9595
Star Clippers	☎ 800-442-0551

Yacht

Crewing aboard a yacht destined for the West Indies from North America or Europe is a popular way of getting to the Virgins. You will need impressive offshore sailing experience to make (or be hired for) an Atlantic passage. Most sailors heading to West Indian destinations do so from Florida or the shores of other eastern states. Winds and currents favor the passage south through the Bahamas. If you plan to travel in summer, keep fully abreast of weather reports, as July to October is hurricane season (see Climate in the Facts about the Virgin Islands chapter).

Marinas are located at some major resorts and at principal ports throughout the islands. Upon reaching the USVI, you *must* clear immigration and customs unless you are coming directly from a US port or Puerto Rico. You can clear US customs at Charlotte Amalie (St Thomas), Cruz Bay (St John) or Christiansted or Frederiksted (St Croix). To clear customs and immigration in the BVI, you must stop at Great Harbour (Jost Van Dyke), Spanish Town (Virgin Gorda) or one of two ports on Tortola, Sopers Hole or Road Town. The Virgin Islands' drug-smuggling problem is such

that you should anticipate the possibility of being boarded and searched by the US Coast Guard.

There are now numerous online clearinghouses for those seeking yacht crew positions (both experienced and inexperienced mariners). These services usually charge a registration fee of US$25 to US$40. One operation known for its professionalism is the Yacht Crew Registry (☎ 604-990-9901), with a Web site at www.yachtregister.com. In the UK, contact Alan Toone of Compass Yacht Services (☎ 020-8467-2450) at Holly Cottage, Heathley End, Chislehurst, Kent BR7 6AB. Alan arranges yacht charters and may be able to help assist you in obtaining a crewing position.

During both the winter and summer seasons, there is a lot of boat traffic between the east end of Puerto Rico and Charlotte Amalie on St Thomas as well as the island of St Croix. Inquire at the yacht marinas in these ports if you want to take a slow boat to the Virgins or do some island-hopping. In early November, after hurricane season, you will find a lot of vessels bound for the USVI from US yachting centers, including Newport, Rhode Island; Annapolis, Maryland; Beaufort, North Carolina; Charleston, South Carolina; and Fort Lauderdale and Miami, Florida. See the Yacht Charter Basics chapter for a list of companies offering crewed or bareboat yacht charters.

You'll need accurate maps and charts for any voyage through the Caribbean's reef-infested waters. British Admiralty charts, US Defense Mapping Agency charts and Imray yachting charts are all accurate. You can order them in advance from Bluewater Books & Charts (☎ 305-763-6533, 800-942-2583), 1481 SE 17th St Causeway, Fort Lauderdale, FL 33316. Consult the Books section in the Facts for the Visitor chapter and the Sailing special section for additional information and resources.

ORGANIZED TOURS

For overseas visitors, the most reliable sources of information on the constantly changing tour offerings are major international travel agents such as Thomas Cook and American Express.

Elderhostel occasionally offers special tours for seniors. (See Senior Travelers in the Facts for the Visitor chapter.)

Dozens of companies offer package tours to the Virgin Islands, using charter airlines and common carriers. The largest companies may operate on a regular basis, often every week.

Many companies offer a range of hotels to choose from, with package prices varying accordingly. Most per-person rates are quoted based on double occupancy. An additional charge (called a 'single supplement') is usually applied to anyone wishing to room alone.

The USA

The following US tour operators are among those most active in the Virgin Islands market.

Adventure Tours USA (☎ 214-360-5000, 800-999-9046) 5949 Sherry Lane, Dallas, TX

American Airlines FlyAAway Vacations (☎ 800-433-7300, fax 817-967-4328) Mail Drop 1000, Box 619619, DFW Airport, TX 75261

Apple Vacations (☎ 610-359-6700, 800-727-3400, fax 610-359-6624) 7 Campus Blvd, Newtown Square, PA 19073

Delta Dream Vacations (☎ 800-872-7786) 110 E Broward Blvd, Fort Lauderdale, FL

TWA Getaway Vacations (☎ 800-438-2929, fax 609-985-4125) 10 E Stow Rd, Marlton, NJ 08053

US Airways Vacations (☎ 407-857-8533, 800-455-0123) 7200 Lake Ellenor Dr, No 241, Orlando, FL 32809

Canada

Canadian package tour operators include the following.

Air Canada Vacation Tours (☎ 514-876-4141, 800-263-0882) 1440 Ste Catherine St W, Montreal, QC H3G 1R8

Canadian Holidays (☎ 416-620-8687, 800-661-8881, fax 416-620-9267) 191 The West Mall, 6th floor, Etobicoke, ON M9C 5K8

Sunquest Vacations (☎ 416-485-1700, fax 416-485-9479) 130 Merton St, Toronto, ON M4S 1A4

Other Countries

Contours Travel (☎ 3-9670-6900, fax 3-9670-7558), 466 Victoria St, North Melbourne, VIC 3051, is currently Australia's largest tour operator and wholesaler to Caribbean destinations.

In New Zealand, contact Innovative Travel & Promotions (☎ 3-365-3910, fax 3-365-5755), PO Box 21, 247 Edgeware, Christchurch, which is about the only tour operator with a Caribbean specialty.

In the UK, contact the Caribbean Centre (☎ 020-8940-3399, fax 020-8940-7424), 3 The Green, Richmond, Surrey TW9 1PL; or consider Uncle Sam Travel Agency (☎ 0121-523-3141, fax 0121-554-7315), at 295 Sotto Rd, Birmingham B21 95A.

In Japan, Island International (☎ 03-3401-4096, fax 03-3401-1629), 4-11-14-204 Jingumae, Shibuya-ku, Tokyo 150, specializes in package tours and special-interest travel to the Caribbean.

Getting Around

The Virgin Islands are each small enough that it is feasible to explore on foot if you are acclimated to the warm weather or if you take to the cool mountains.

AIR

Air travel in the Virgin Islands is easy, with frequent (and sometimes inexpensive) flights. For example, flights between St Thomas and St Croix or Tortola run more than six times a day and cost as little as $60.

Within the islands, air travelers look to American Eagle (☎ 800-474-4884), which operates out of its hub at San Juan, Puerto Rico. Recent fares between San Juan and the Virgins have dropped as low as $85 one way, $140 roundtrip. Cape Air (☎ 800-352-0714) runs 13 flights a day between St Thomas and San Juan, and six flights a day between St Croix and St Thomas. Gulfstream International (☎ 800-457-4838) also flies the San Juan–St Thomas run. LIAT (☎ 340-774-2313) offers service to the other Lesser Antilles. Air Sunshine (☎ 340-778-8900) serves St Thomas, Tortola and San Juan.

Air St Thomas (☎ 340-776-2722) flies between St Thomas and Virgin Gorda. The seaplanes of Seabourne Aviation (☎ 340-773-6442) fly between Charlotte Amalie and Christiansted. Fly BVI (☎ 284-435-9284) and Clair Aero (☎ 284-495-2271) make the run from Tortola to Anegada.

Bohlke International Airways (☎ 340-778-9177) has charter service between St Croix and St Thomas and San Juan. For charter flights in the BVI, try Fly BVI (☎ 284-435-9284) and Clair Aero (☎ 284-495-2271).

BUS

The USVI Division of Transportation (VITRAN; ☎ 340-774-5678) operates air-conditioned buses over the length of St Thomas, St John and St Croix. Buses travel the islands seven days a week from about 5:30 am to 8:30 pm. The fare for anyone under 55 is $1 for all or part of the ride. You must have exact change!

In Charlotte Amalie, city buses run from the hospital (east of town) through town to the airport (west of town) about twice an hour.

On Tortola, Scato's Bus Service (☎ 284-494-2365) roams the island. These vehicles are heavy-duty pickup trucks with bench seats in the truck bed and an awning overhead. There is no set schedule. Passengers

Don't worry – VITRAN buses have come a long way since Fleming's (in St Croix, 1941).

wishing for a ride just stand by the side of the road and hail the driver as he or she approaches. Expect to pay between $1 to $4, depending on the length of the ride. See the island chapters for more details.

CAR & MOTORCYCLE

Driving is undoubtedly the most convenient way to get around individual islands. Unlike some other Caribbean islands, the Virgin Islands have no tradition of moped or motorcycle rentals to travelers.

See Visas & Documents in the Facts for the Visitor chapter for information on driver's licenses.

Driving Conditions

Motoring in the Virgin Islands is rarely a leisurely 'Sunday drive.' The major problem is that residents on the larger islands have adopted the belief that it is every person's divine right to own and operate an automobile. To complicate matters, island roads are narrow, steep and twisting. The potholes on St Thomas, St John and St Croix can be a real hazard for people on motorcycles or mopeds Furthermore, stray cows, goats, donkeys and chickens constantly wander onto the roads on all of the islands.

A further challenge for many visitors to the islands is that traffic proceeds along the *left-hand side of the road*. The good news is that because of these challenging conditions, most traffic proceeds slowly, and drivers are generally attentive and courteous.

There is no AAA or other emergency road service, but most car rental agencies will provide service to a customer with a breakdown.

Road Rules

You must be at least 16 years old to drive in the Virgin Islands. Traffic keeps to the left-hand side of the road, and proceeds clockwise at traffic roundabouts. The speed limit on most island roads is 30mph or less. However, roads are not heavily patrolled. Road signs and speed-limit signs are rare, but do watch for speed bumps, which are common.

Note that drivers don't always heed the rules of the road here, often stopping dead with no warning in the middle of the road to talk to friends or reversing their cars in the opposite lane of traffic if they've missed their turn. A common gesture you should know is the flap: When drivers are about to do something (stop, turn, etc), they may extend their arm horizontally out the window and waggle their hand up and down like a flapping bird.

Gasoline

Esso, Texaco and a few other oil companies maintain gasoline (petrol) stations throughout the islands. Stations generally stay open until 7 pm or so and sell fuel by the gallon; at press time, the price was about $1.60 per gallon for economy gas. You can use credit cards for fuel purchases on some islands but not others (such as St John).

Rental

Many of the major international car rental companies operate in the Virgin Islands, along with plenty of local firms. Most rental companies require that you have a major credit card, that you be at least 21 years old and that you have a valid driver's license (your home license will do). Car rental agencies are listed in the local yellow pages and most of the tourist literature provided by the islands. You will find some rental companies at the airports on St Thomas and St Croix but not on Tortola. Many other agencies will meet you with a car at the airport if you make arrangements in advance. See the individual island chapters for local rental agencies.

High-season rates begin at about $40 per day and can run as high as $100. You can get a much better price for a weekly rental, with major rental companies offering subcompact cars for about $250 a week with unlimited mileage. The prices may get even better the longer you keep the car. Many firms require a deposit of at least $500 but will accept a credit card imprint. Keep copies of all your paperwork.

You can reserve a car upon arrival, but a better plan is to make your reservation several months in advance if you need a car during peak weeks such as the December and February school breaks and the Easter holiday. Before arrival, it's wise to reconfirm the date and time your car will be delivered to the airport (or your hotel). Before signing the rental agreement, go over the vehicle carefully to identify any dents and scratches. Make sure they are all clearly noted on your contract. Otherwise, you're likely to be charged for the slightest trace of damage. You can return cars to the rental office, or they can be left at an airport parking lot.

Types of Vehicle Most car rental companies on St Thomas and St Croix utilize modern Japanese sedans. A small sedan is perfectly adequate for most conditions; a big car is a liability on the islands' crowded streets and winding roads. Companies also rent 4WD vehicles (particularly on St John and in the BVI), which you will want for backcountry exploration. Your options are standard (stick shift) or automatic transmission, and vehicles with or without air-con. Standard transmission is preferable because of the constant and sudden gear changes required on the hilly, winding roads.

Insurance There are several types of insurance to consider. Liability insurance is required in the Virgin Islands, but it is not always included in rental contracts because many drivers are covered for rental cars under their home car liability insurance. Check this carefully.

Insurance against damage to the car, called Collision Damage Waiver (CDW) or Loss Damage Waiver (LDW), is usually optional ($8 to $12 per day) but will often require you to pay for the first $100 or $500 of any repairs. This cost, called the deductible, may be avoided if you pay additional premiums. A number of credit card companies, including Gold MasterCard or American Express, will cover your CDW if you rent for 15 days or less and charge the full value of the rental to your card. Check with your credit card company before you leave home to determine if this service is offered and find out the extent of coverage.

BICYCLE
The lack of shoulder on most roads, the steep hills, the blind curves and the high number of cars on the largest islands conspire to make bike touring somewhat risky. Conditions for cycling are better on less-populated islands, such as Jost Van Dyke, Anegada and Water Island. Consider arranging a bike tour through one of the adventure tour operators described under Organized Tours, later in this chapter. See Bicycling in the Facts for the Visitor chapter for more information.

HITCHHIKING
Hitchhiking is never entirely safe in any country in the world, and we don't recommend it. Travelers who decide to hitchhike should understand that they are taking a risk – creeps and criminals might see a hitchhiker as easy prey. People who do choose to hitchhike will be safer if they travel in pairs and let someone know where they are planning to go.

Hitchhiking on St Thomas and St Croix is impractical and can be very dangerous. It's safer and more convenient on St John, as it's a small island and there are only two main roads connecting Cruz Bay and Coral Bay.

BOAT
The Virgin Islands have frequent and inexpensive ferry service connecting the main islands and many smaller islands (see 'Inter-island Ferries'). Note: You must have a passport to travel between USVI ports and the BVI. (US and Canadian citizens can carry a voter's registration card or birth certificate in conjuction with a photo ID.)

Major islands have marinas where you can charter sailing yachts or powerboats, either bareboat or with a crew. Crewed boats come with a skipper and crew, so you don't need any prior sailing experience. Also see the Yacht Charter Basics chapter and Yacht in the Getting There & Away chapter.

Interisland Ferries

These schedules are subject to change. Call the ferry companies in advance for current departure times. Except where noted, the ferries carry passengers only. For fares between islands, see the Getting There & Away section in each island chapter.

Car Ferry from Red Hook (St Thomas) to Cruz Bay (St John)
Boyson, Inc (☎ 340-776-6294)
   Departs Red Hook every hour on the half-hour 6:30 am to 6:30 pm daily
   Departs St John 6 am (except Sunday), 7 am (except Sunday), 8:30 am, then every hour on the half-hour to 5:30 pm daily

Republic Barge (☎ 340-997-4000)
   Departs Red Hook every two hours from 7 am to 7 pm daily
   Departs St John 6:15 am, 8 am, then every two hours to 4 pm, 6:15 pm, (8 pm Saturday) daily

From Red Hook (St Thomas) to Cruz Bay (St John)
Transportation Services (☎ 340-776-6282)
   Departs Red Hook 6:30 am, 7:30 am, then hourly from 8 am to midnight daily
   Departs St John hourly from 6 am to 11 pm daily

From Charlotte Amalie (St Thomas) to Cruz Bay (St John)
Transportation Services (☎ 340-776-6282)
   Departs Charlotte Amalie 9 am, 11 am, 3 pm, 4 pm, 5:30 pm daily
   Departs St John 7:15 am, 9:15 am, 11:15 am, 1:15 pm, 2:15 pm, 3:45 pm daily

From St Thomas to Tortola & St John
Smith's Ferry and Native Son alternate service and departure times between St Thomas and Tortola.

Smith's Ferry Services (☎ 284-495-4495, 284-494-2355)
Charlotte Amalie to Road Town (Tortola), stopping at West End (Tortola)
Weekdays
   Departs Charlotte Amalie 8:25 am, 11:15 pm, 2 pm, 4:30 pm
   Departs Road Town 6:15 am, WE 7 am, 10 am, (2:15 pm Wednesday), 3 pm
Saturday
   Departs Charlotte Amalie 8:25 am, noon, 2 pm, 3 pm, 4:30 pm
   Departs Road Town 6:15 am, 9 am, 2 pm, 5:30 pm, WE 7 am, 10 am, 2:30 pm, 6 pm
Sunday
   Departs Charlotte Amalie 8 am, 10:45 am, 2:15 pm, 5:15 pm
   Departs West End 9:15 am, 12:20 pm, 3:35 pm, 4:05 pm

Red Hook to West End, stopping at St John
   Departs Red Hook 8 am, 11:15 am, 2:55 pm, 5:30 pm daily
   Departs West End 6:30 am, 8:50 am, 12:20 pm, 3:45 pm daily

Native Son, Inc (☎ 284-495-4617)
*Charlotte Amalie to West End and Road Town (*check for availability)*
Weekdays
   Departs Charlotte Amalie 8:25 am, 1:30 pm, 2:30 pm, 4 pm
   Departs Road Town 6:15 am, WE 7 am, 10 am, (2:15 pm Wednesday), 3 pm
Saturday
   Departs Charlotte Amalie 8:25 am, noon, 2:30 pm, 4 pm, 5 pm
   Departs Road Town 6:15 am, *8:45 am, 2 pm, WE 7 am, 10 am, 2:30 pm, 5:45 pm

Sunday
  Departs Charlotte Amalie 8 am, 10:45 am, *2:45 pm, *4 pm, 5:45 pm
  Departs West End 9:30 am, 3:50 pm, RT 3:15 pm
Red Hook to West End, stopping at St John
  Departs Red Hook 7:45 am, 11:15 am, 3:20 pm, 5 pm daily
  Departs West End 6:45 am, 8:30 am, 12:30 pm (continues to Charlotte Amalie),
     4 pm daily

Nubian Princess (☎ 284-495-4999)
Red Hook to West End, stopping at St John
  Departs Red Hook 10:45 am, 2:30 pm, 4:30 pm Sunday to Friday
  Departs West End 8:00 am, 11:30 am, 3:30 pm Sunday to Friday

Inter-Island Boat Services (☎ 284-495-4166)
St John to West End
Monday to Saturday
  Departs St John 8:30 am, 11:30 pm, 3:30 pm, (5 pm Friday)
  Departs West End 9:15 am, 12:15 pm, 4:15 pm, (5:30 pm Friday)
Sunday
  Departs St John 8:30 am, 11:30 am, 4:30 pm
  Departs West End 9:15 am, 12:15 pm, 5:15 pm

From Tortola to Virgin Gorda
Speedy's (☎ 284-495-5240)
Road Town to Virgin Gorda
Monday to Saturday
  Departs Road Town 9 am, noon, 1:30 pm, 4:30 pm
  Departs Virgin Gorda 8 am, 10 am, 11:30 am, 3:30 pm
Tuesday & Thursday
  Departs Virgin Gorda 6:30 am, 2:45 pm
  Departs Road Town 10 am, 6:15 pm
Sunday
  Departs Road Town 9 am, 5:15 pm
  Departs Virgin Gorda 8 am, 4:30 pm

Smith's Ferry Services (☎ 284-495-4495, 284-494-2355)
Also goes to St John and St Thomas, stopping at West End
Monday to Saturday
  Departs Road Town 7 am, 8:50 am, 12:30 pm, (3:15 pm weekdays), (4:15 pm Saturday)
  Departs Virgin Gorda *7:50 am, *10:15 am, *2:15 pm, (4 pm weekdays), (*3 pm and 5 pm
     Saturday)
Sunday
  Departs Road Town 8:50 am, 12:30 pm, 4:15 pm
  Departs Virgin Gorda 10:15 am, 3 pm, 5 pm

North Sound Express (☎ 284-495-2138)
Beef Island (Tortola) to Spanish Town and Bitter End (Virgin Gorda); reservations required
  Departs Beef Island 8:15 am, 11:15 am, 1 pm, 3:45 pm, 5:30 pm, 7:30 pm daily
  Departs Spanish Town 8:30 am, 11:30 am, 4:00 pm, 5:45 pm daily
  Departs Bitter End 6:45 am, 9 am, noon, 2:45 pm, 4:30 pm, 6:15 pm daily

[Continued on page 80]

Interisland Ferries

[Continued from page 79]

From Charlote Amalie (St Thomas) to Tortola & Virgin Gorda
Speedy's (☎ 284-495-5240)
Charlotte Amalie to Virgin Gorda, stopping at Road Town (Tortola)
Tuesday & Thursday
  Departs Charlotte Amalie 8:45 am, 5 pm
  Departs Road Town 7:15 am, 3:25 pm
  Departs Virgin Gorda 6:30 am, 2:45 pm
Saturday
  Departs Charlotte Amalie 3:30 pm
  Departs Virgin Gorda 8:30 am, RT 9:15 am

From Beef Island (Tortola) to Marina Cay (☎ 284-494-2174)
  Departs Beef Island 10:30 am, 11:30 am, 12:30 pm, 3 pm, 4 pm, 5 pm, 6 pm, 7 pm daily
  Departs Marina Cay 10:15 am, 11:15 am, 12:15 pm, every hour from 2:45 pm to 6:45 pm
    (later for restaurant guests) daily

From West End (Tortola) to Jost Van Dyke
Jost Van Dyke Ferry Service (☎ 284-494-2997); available for charter
Monday to Saturday
  Departs West End 7:30 am, 9:45 am, 1:30 pm, 4 pm
  Departs Jost Van Dyke 8:30 am, 11 am, 3 pm, 5 pm
Sunday
  Departs West End 9:30 am, 1:30 pm, 4 pm
  Departs Jost Van Dyke 1 am, 3 pm, 5 pm

From Red Hook (St Thomas) to St John & Jost Van Dyke
Inter-Island Ferry Services (☎ 340-776-6597, 284-495-4166)
Red Hook to Jost Van Dyke, stopping at Cruz Bay
Friday, Saturday & Sunday
  Departs Red Hook 8 am, St J 8:30 am, RH 2 pm, St J 2:20 pm
  Departs Jost Van Dyke 9 am, 3 pm

From Road Town (Tortola) to Peter Island
Peter Island Ferry (☎ 284-495-2000)
  Departs Road Town 7 am, 8:30 am, 10 am, noon, 2 pm, 3:30 pm, 5:30 pm, 7 pm, 8 pm,
    10:30 pm daily
  Departs Peter Island 8 am, 9 am, 11:30 am, 1:30 pm, 2:30 pm, 4:30 pm, 6 pm, 7:30 pm,
    10 pm, 11:30 pm daily

TAXI

Almost all of the populated islands have taxi services. St Thomas alone has about six, and none of them is cheap. All cabs on the major islands have rates set by the territorial governments. This means you must consult a rate sheet for your trip and establish an agreed price before you get in a cab. See the island chapters for vendors and local rates.

The best reason to take a cab is to connect with islanders. Local politics, police crackdowns on drug smugglers and the islands' relationship to the US are topics that always seem to be on drivers' minds. West Indians are friendly people and they usually have a fierce pride in their islands, which they like to share. During your $12 ride from the airport to your hotel, a gregarious driver may impart a lot of local knowledge about restaurants, beaches, clubs, dangerous neighborhoods and upcoming festivals.

St Thomas has an association of gypsy cabs, which are open-air pickup trucks with bench seats and an awning. Drivers cruise the major roads, traveling between the capital and the ends of the island. To hail one, stand by the side of the road and wave when a cab approaches. The fare is $1.

ORGANIZED TOURS

The Virgin Islands have a plethora of tour operators. Tours are geared to travelers who have limited time but want to see a lot. Operators usually pick up clients at their hotels or at the cruise-ship docks in Charlotte Amalie, Frederiksted or Road Town. From there, clients are whisked off in open-air trucks with bench seats to popular tourist sites around the islands.

Many tour operators offer hiking, birding, kayaking, snorkeling, horseback riding and diving adventures. While nothing can compete with the adventure of planning and executing a wilderness trip on your own, these tour operators can take a lot of the worry out of the adventure and give you a chance to interact with fellow adventure travelers. See the island chapters for specific tour information.

St Thomas

Beloved darling of the cruise ship industry, as well as the capital and economic center of the US Virgin Islands, St Thomas is the place most people picture when they think of the West Indies. And why not? You have to go to Rio de Janeiro to find an anchorage to rival the drama of St Thomas Harbor and its port, Charlotte Amalie (pronounced a-MALL-ya). No town in the Caribbean can top Charlotte Amalie's number and density

Highlights

- Exploring & shopping in historic Charlotte Amalie
- Wining & dining in Frenchtown
- Bicycling on Water Island
- Walking on the floor of the Caribbean Sea at the Coral World Marine Park
- Picnicking & sunbathing at Hull Bay
- Dancing in the streets during the St Thomas Carnival in April

of shops selling pretty things. Furthermore, the fringe of the island offers uncrowded, world-class beaches, turquoise waters and trade winds to soothe body and soul.

These assets draw three or four cruise ships and a dozen jumbo jets to St Thomas every day during the high season, between Christmas and Easter. And the money those travelers spend each day on shopping, dining, sightseeing and entertainment has brought four decades of prosperity and development. Resort hotels and vacation condos now dominate most of the eastern half of the island. New homes speckle the island's hillsides. During the weekday evening rush hour, you can spend an hour in traffic just trying to get through Charlotte Amalie. Nearly 60,000 citizens (80% West Indian, 15% continental, 5% other) pack this 30-sq-mile island. Though St Thomas has its quiet corners, the island is as thickly settled as Bermuda or Capri.

In recent years, the island's reputation for being densely populated and mobbed with tourists in the throes of a shopping frenzy has turned some travelers away. Add to this reputation the undeniable fact that Charlotte Amalie has a crime problem, and you can see that St Thomas has a small public relations dilemma. Some people call it an identity crisis; they say that inept political leaders and greedy entrepreneurs have sold out their island's land and West Indian character to multinational cruise ship and hotel conglomerates, the US's car culture, fast-food chains and consumerism.

There is a silver lining to this story: The citizens of St Thomas seem to have looked up from counting their money to take stock. Island newspapers, radio and TV run daily news and editorial coverage of citizens speaking up against government corruption, crime and the selling out of the island's remaining open spaces and historic architectural heritage. Preservation groups are waging fights to stop development on the remaining beaches without resort hotels.

Until the positive changes reverse the island's tarnished image, independent travelers can benefit from lower hotel prices as hotels and guesthouses compete for a nearly static number of overnight guests. Sure, there are crowds of cruise ship passengers roaming the island by day, but most of the ships sail in the evening. And when the cruise ships have gone, the islanders – both West Indians and continentals – step out to reclaim their island. If you follow these locals in their chosen rounds, you will discover restaurants, pubs and clubs where the good times roll on like a redemption song under an indigo sky.

As they say on the island, 'Night bring day, mon' – out of the gloom comes brightness.

History

St Thomians owe their history to their island's position as a crossroads. St Thomas stands as the gatekeeper to the Virgin Passage, probably the safest sailing route for vessels moving between the Atlantic Ocean and the Caribbean Sea. In addition, St Thomas stands directly on the path followed by ships sailing the trade route between North America and South America.

Early Peoples While historians know that the Ciboney or 'Pre-Ceramic' Indians were in the Virgin Islands on St Croix perhaps as early as 2000 BC, the first evidence of human habitation on St Thomas dates to about AD 900. The evidence comes from excavations at Hull Bay and Magens Bay on the north shore. (See 'The Hull Bay Find,' later in this chapter.) For years, islanders had been finding shards of pottery scattered around the area. But archeologists first hit pay dirt at Magens Bay early in the 20th century when a hurricane uprooted a turpentine tree and exposed the kitchen midden from an Indian settlement of Caribs and Taíno.

We know that after Christopher Columbus had his encounter with the Indians on St Croix, he sailed north, skirting the south coast of the Virgin Islands archipelago and naming the island group in November 1493. He did not stop at St Thomas, but the Spanish adventurers and colonists who followed shortly thereafter did, and by 1555 they had totally depopulated the island by kidnapping, murdering and driving off the indigenous Taíno and Caribs (see History in the Facts about the Virgin Islands chapter).

Danish Colonization Except for Spanish raiders and marauding buccaneers, few Europeans gave much thought to St Thomas during the 16th and early 17th centuries. But after 1625, the nations of Europe became hell-bent on acquiring colonies in the New World. And while the English, Dutch and French fought over plums like St Croix, the Danes tried to stake a claim on a piece of forgotten fruit, St Thomas.

In 1665, a Danish mariner named Erik Schmidt (also spelled Smit) received a commission from Danish King Christian V to become governor of St Thomas and establish a colony. Schmidt's voyage to his island proved disastrous as storms and a fire wracked his ship, the *Eindragt*. But he arrived at what seemed to be a propitious moment in late 1665 or early 1666. War between England and the Netherlands had spread to the Caribbean, and Dutch settlers were eager to migrate from islands under English siege to Schmidt's little colony on St Thomas, which seemed beyond the scope of the English attacks. Unfortunately, the Dane's good fortune in establishing a colony was short-lived as English privateers plundered the island. Schmidt himself died of disease six months after his arrival. After the deaths of many colonists from the same disease, in addition to a hurricane and more raids by the English, the settlers abandoned St Thomas.

In 1671, Danish nobles formed the Danish West India and Guinea Company and hired George Iverson to establish a colony on St Thomas. Initially, the English protested such a plan, contending that they had rights to the island, but eventually English King Charles II retracted his country's claims. Iverson assembled 91 settlers, mostly indentured servants and prisoners (promised freedom and land) and sailed from Copenhagen aboard the *Frego*.

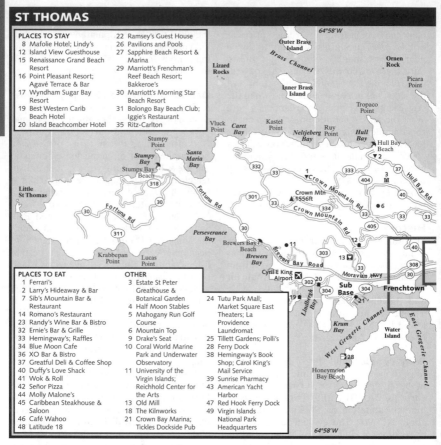

ST THOMAS

PLACES TO STAY
8 Mafolie Hotel; Lindy's
12 Island View Guesthouse
15 Renaissance Grand Beach Resort
16 Point Pleasant Resort; Agavé Terrace & Bar
17 Wyndham Sugar Bay Resort
19 Best Western Carib Beach Hotel
20 Island Beachcomber Hotel

22 Ramsey's Guest House
26 Pavilions and Pools
27 Sapphire Beach Resort & Marina
29 Marriott's Frenchman's Reef Beach Resort; Bakkeroe's
30 Marriott's Morning Star Beach Resort
31 Bolongo Bay Beach Club; Iggie's Restaurant
35 Ritz-Carlton

PLACES TO EAT
1 Ferrari's
7 Larry's Hideaway & Bar
7 Sib's Mountain Bar & Restaurant
14 Romano's Restaurant
23 Randy's Wine Bar & Bistro
32 Ernie's Bar & Grille
33 Hemingway's; Raffles
36 Blue Moon Cafe
36 XO Bar & Bistro
37 Greatful Deli & Coffee Shop
40 Duffy's Love Shack
42 Wok & Roll
42 Señor Pizza
44 Molly Malone's
45 Caribbean Steakhouse & Saloon
46 Café Wahoo
48 Latitude 18

OTHER
3 Estate St Peter Greathouse & Botanical Garden
4 Half Moon Stables
5 Mahogany Run Golf Course
6 Mountain Top
9 Drake's Seat
10 Coral World Marine Park and Underwater Observatory
11 University of the Virgin Islands; Reichhold Center for the Arts
13 Old Mill
18 The Kilnworks
21 Crown Bay Marina; Tickles Dockside Pub

24 Tutu Park Mall; Market Square East Theaters; La Providencia Laundromat
25 Tillett Gardens; Polli's
28 Ferry Dock
38 Hemingway's Book Shop; Carol King's Mail Service
39 Sunrise Pharmacy
43 American Yacht Harbor
47 Red Hook Ferry Dock
49 Virgin Islands National Park Headquarters

A leak compelled the ship to stop for repairs in the Norwegian port of Bergen, where the former prisoners jumped ship, forcing Iverson to recruit some new prisoners from the Bergen jails. As if these troubles were not enough, disease set in aboard ship, and by the time the *Frego* reached St Thomas, most of the potential colonists had died.

Some historians claim that there were Dutch settlers on the island when Iverson arrived; others maintain that these settlers joined the colony shortly after the Danes. Whatever the case, the colonists got down to business, sending a party to Tortola to get sugar cane shoots for planting and starting the construction of Fort Christian (named in honor of the reigning Danish monarch) on the harbor shores. In 1774, Iverson imported the island's first African slave, a master stonemason, to help finish the fort. The essential infrastructure for colonial exploitation was now in place.

During the next 10 years, the island settlement prospered, largely by trading with St Croix. The Cruzan planters supplied sugar, and the St Thomians sold finished goods to the Cruzans without the formality of customs declarations and duties.

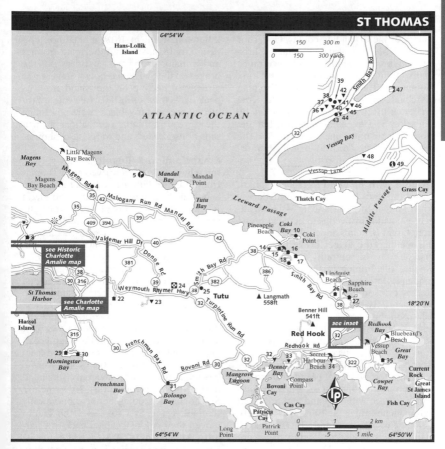

St Thomas established its identity as a way station and sanctuary for the wild at heart. The epoch of the pirates of the Caribbean had begun. Perhaps nothing signaled this era more clearly than the appointment of Adolph Esmit – a noted brigand and harborer of runaway servants, debtors, mariners and criminals – as governor. At this point, there were 331 people on the island, 175 of them slaves.

The Trading Post The early years of the 18th century were a time of revolving governors, political corruption and financial troubles. But by 1716, the little colony had begun to prosper as Denmark asserted its neutrality in the European wars and advertised St Thomas as an open and safe haven for ships of all nations of Europe. King Frederick of Denmark put his stamp on this role by reducing import duties on the island. In less than 40 years, St Thomas had become a community of merchants and traders who now included a diversity of nationalities and religions, including English, Dutch, Danes, Germans and Jews, including the governor Gabriel Milan.

The 1730s were a thrilling time for Danish rule in the Virgin Islands as neighboring

St John suffered a major slave rebellion and France sold St Croix to the Danes. The architect of the expanding colony, Governor Frederick Moth, moved the capital to Christiansted, his newly built model town on St Croix. While the economy of St Croix bloomed, St Thomas stagnated. St Thomian merchants and traders appealed to King Frederick to save their island economy by declaring St Thomas a free port, but the monarchy did not cooperate until 1764. The rest of the century proved to be an extraordinary period of prosperity.

Trouble with England In 1800, Denmark joined the so-called Northern Confederacy with Russia, Sweden and Prussia, an alliance aimed at protecting national interests from Great Britain's imperial ambitions. In this manner, the Danes broke from more than 35 years of neutrality and began supporting the French in their war against England. On March 6, 1801, the Brits retaliated by blockading St Thomas Harbor with six frigates. By the end of the month, English troop ships arrived, and the Danes surrendered the island (along with St John and St Croix) in the face of an occupational army of 4000 soldiers. For 10 months, the British Navy ruled the Danish West Indies, building a fort on Hassel Island to guard the mouth of the harbor, but in 1802 the Danes signed a truce with England and promised to remain neutral in the European conflicts.

The English returned St Thomas to Danish rule, but the island's glory days were over. In Europe, the Danes found themselves pressured by Napoleon to side with the French in their war with England. Once again – on December 22, 1807 – the British sailed into St Thomas Harbor to take control of the Danish West Indies. This time the English stayed until the end of the Napoleonic Wars in 1815. During the English occupation, ships from the US and many European nations steered clear of their British enemy at St Thomas.

After getting the West Indies colony back as part of the peace treaty with England, the Danes tried to jump-start the island economy by once again proclaiming St Thomas a free port. The measure brought a new wave of prosperity to the island, but a killer hurricane in 1819, a smallpox epidemic in 1820, sundry other catastrophes and a major drop in sugar prices put the brakes on the St Thomas boom. Slavery was already in decline on the island from its peak of 5900 slaves in 1803; free colored (of mixed race) and free blacks were now filling the slave's traditional occupations as artisans, housekeepers and warehouse laborers.

Emancipation & Revolt On July 4, 1848, the schooner *Vigilant* arrived at St Thomas from St Croix with the news that Peter von Scholten, the Danish governor of the Virgin Islands, had been forced to proclaim the emancipation of all slaves on Danish territory. The news was read with accompaniment of drumrolls to a crowd of people in the Charlotte Amalie common ground on the waterfront – thereafter known as Emancipation Garden. The rum bottles came out, and dancing in the streets ensued. (See 'Caught in Freedom's Storm' in St Croix.)

Except for a brief period during the American Civil War (1861–65) when St Thomas thrived as a supply depot and coaling station for smuggling goods to and from the US South through the North's naval blockade, the island's economy stagnated during the late 19th century. Nevertheless, St Thomas was doing better economically than its sister, St Croix, and the Danes moved their colonial capital back to Charlotte Amalie in 1871. Meanwhile, the island's economy evolved to meet modern shipping needs, establishing itself as a major coaling station for steamships. By the last decade of the century, the largest employer on the island was the West India Company, which sold coal to steamers. The coal was transported in baskets by legions of black women who earned about $1 a day. Finally, pushed to the brink by fatigue, humiliation and poverty, the coal carriers rocked St Thomas with a strike led by a dancer called Queen Coziah. Fearing a labor riot and 'fireburn' like one on St Croix in 1878, the steamship agents quickly agreed to the workers' demands.

US Purchase & Hurricanes Maritime commerce was still bringing enough sailors to St Thomas Harbor to keep the brothels and bars of 'Back Street' hopping when the US bought the islands in 1917. The number of sailors only increased during the subsequent US Navy rule of the island. With the departure of the US Navy by the 1950s, the US Congress and the territorial government saw St Thomas' status as a free port and commercial center as potential for developing the island as a major tourist attraction. The naval port facilities and former air base became the crucial infrastructure for facilitating the flow of tourists to and from the island. Land values soared, foreign investors (mostly wealthy continentals) showed up in droves, hotel construction ensued and St Thomians began their quest for the Yankee dollar.

During the next five decades, a few foreign investors cleaned up, and quite a lot of islanders did 'very well, thank you.' St Thomas got a cable car ride, an underwater theme park, a four-fold growth in population, a whole lot of cars and a healthy dose of street crime.

In 1989, Hurricane Hugo wreaked havoc on the island. Then, in 1995, Hurricanes Luis and Marilyn dealt a back-to-back blow. The storms caused extensive structural damage, sank dozens of boats, and the islands were declared a federal disaster area.

Orientation

If you picture a fish swimming east, 40 miles away from Puerto Rico, you have a pretty good idea of the shape and location of St Thomas. Home to the capital of the USVI, this is the second-largest island in the Virgin Islands archipelago (after St Croix). St Thomas stretches about 12 miles from west to east and averages about 3 miles north to south. A steep spine of mountains runs down the center of the island, with peaks like Crown Mountain reaching more than 1500 feet.

Charlotte Amalie, the largest city in the Virgin Islands, and the seat of the territorial government for the USVI, rims the well-protected harbor on the island's south shore. The bulk of St Thomas' resorts and attractions lie along the beaches of the East End, many within a mile or two of the business district and ferry terminal, Red Hook. The northwest coast has a string of spectacular bays including world-renown Magens Bay. The airport is 2 miles west of Charlotte Amalie.

The island is a maze of roads. Route 30 follows the south shore along the length of the island and is the easiest route for getting around St Thomas, despite having various names (including Veterans Dr and Frenchman Bay Rd). Route 38 is a shortcut between the East End and Charlotte Amalie. This broad road (sometimes four lanes) scales the mountains and is the major commercial artery, lined with businesses and malls as it passes through the island's interior. To reach the less-developed north shore beaches, you follow a series of roads, including Routes 40 and 33, along the island's spine. St Thomians refer to this chain of mountaintop roads as Skyline Dr.

The St Thomas/St John Chamber of Commerce (☎ 340-776-0100) and the Virgin Islands Department of Tourism's Visitors Bureau (see below) publish free maps for visitors. You can pick up these maps at displays at most inns and many restaurants as well as at the visitors bureau. There are also useful maps of Charlotte Amalie in two widely available tourist publications, *St Thomas This Week* and *Virgin Islands Playground*. The best of these maps is a four-color affair published by the government.

Information

Tourist Offices For years, the Department of Tourism's Visitors Bureau (☎ 340-774-8784) stood in the Grand Hotel on the north side of Charlotte Amalie's Emancipation Garden, and it may return there. But while the Grand Hotel building is being restored, the visitors bureau has moved to a spot on Tolbod Gade across the street from Vendors' Plaza and Emancipation Garden, in the heart of Charlotte Amalie. The staff here is friendly and well informed.

There is also a welcome center and visitors bureau satellite office on the West India

Company Dock, where the cruise ships land in Havensight. Both offices are open 8 am to 5 pm weekdays, 9 am to 1 pm Saturday.

The National Park Service runs the Virgin Islands National Park headquarters (☎ 340-775-6238) at the end of a dirt road skirting the south shore of Vessup Bay, though these offices have little to offer travelers. There is a wharf where some tour operators land their boats to shuttle tourists to St John. The headquarters are open 8 am to 4:30 pm daily.

Money St Thomas is an easy place to take care of your finances. Chase Manhattan, Citibank, First Bank, Scotiabank and Banco Popular de Puerto Rico are all on the island, and most have a number of branch offices. If you are coming off a cruise ship, the best place to get cash is the Chase Manhattan ATM right on the West India Company wharf. You will also find Chase and Banco Popular ATMs in Red Hook on the East End. All the banks have central locations in the vicinity of Main St in Charlotte Amalie. Although hours may vary slightly, most banks are open 9 am to 2:30 pm Monday to Thursday, 9 am to 2 pm and 3:30 to 5 pm Friday.

Post & Communications The main post office in Charlotte Amalie is on the west side of Emancipation Garden (☎ 340-774-3750). There are satellite post offices in the Havensight Mall, Frenchtown, Sugar Estate and Tutu Park Mall. Most post offices are open 7:30 am to 5:30 pm weekdays and 7:30 am to 2:30 pm Saturday.

In Red Hook, a lot of travelers and cruising sailors use Carol King's Mail Service (☎ 340-779-1890) for sending mail and receiving forwarded mail. The office is on the 2nd floor of the Red Hook Plaza and is open 8 am to 6 pm weekdays and 9 am to 4 pm Saturday.

The AT&T Calling Center (☎ 340-777-9201), in Havensight next to the tram station, has more than 15 phone booths plus fax and copying services for travelers to use.

Beans, Bytes & Websites (see Places to Eat under Charlotte Amalie) is the least-expensive place to reconnect with your electronic mailbox on the island. Fifteen minutes of online time costs $2.50. The Greatful Deli & Coffee Shop (see Places to Eat under Red Hook & East End) also offers Internet access (four keyboards, $2 for 15 minutes online).

Travel Agencies St Thomas has well over a dozen travel agencies. Two that are particularly convenient are Discount Travel (☎ 340-777-8273), in the Holiday Inn Windward Passage, and Caribbean Travel Agency (☎ 340-774-1855), in the Guardian Building in Havensight.

Bookstores & Libraries For a complete collection of fiction and nonfiction titles, including books about the Virgin Islands and the West Indies, stop at the Dockside Bookshop (☎ 340-774-4937) in the Havensight Mall. In Red Hook, Marty Klenberg runs Hemingway's Book Shop (☎ 340-775-2272) on the 2nd floor of the Red Hook Plaza. You'll find used paperbacks for $3. It's open 9 am to 5 pm weekdays, to 4 pm Saturday.

The Enid M Baa Public Library (☎ 340-774-0630), Dronningens Gade at Guttets Gade, is housed in a classic West Indian version of a Georgian public building.

Newspapers The *VI Daily News* and *The Independent* are the island's daily papers, with local, national and international news. The *Daily News* is a Pulitzer Prize–winning mouthpiece, advocating for social reform and exposing business and government corruption. Travelers interested in island scandals should consult *The Independent* for a second opinion. *St Thomas This Week* is a free monthly tabloid that covers the island's tourist attractions from art to water sports.

Laundry Many of St Thomas' laundries are located in dodgy areas. If you want to feel safe while doing your laundry, head to La Providence (☎ 340-777-3747) at the Tutu Park Mall, on Route 38 in the center of the island, open 6 am to 11 pm daily.

Medical Services & Emergencies The Roy Schneider Community Hospital

(☎ 340-776-8311), 48 Sugar Estate Rd at Route 313, stands on the east side of Charlotte Amalie. There are 160 beds in this facility, an emergency room, recompression chamber and doctors in all major disciplines.

All the shopping areas of the island have pharmacies. Travelers generally favor the Havensight Pharmacy (☎ 340-776-1235) at the Havensight Mall. If you are at the east end of the island, try the Sunrise Pharmacy (☎ 340-775-0600) in the Red Hook Shopping Center.

For police, ambulance or fire call ☎ 911. You can reach the US Coast Guard by calling ☎ 340-776-3497.

Dangers & Annoyances St Thomas has a reputation for crime. That said, savvy travelers who take reasonable precautions should have no fear for their safety or their belongings on St Thomas. Millions of travelers pass through this island each year without incident.

To be safe, travelers should avoid a number of areas in Charlotte Amalie, especially at night. The island's underworld takes its deepest hold on the Savan section of town, a well-known red-light district. Savan is the area surrounding Main St (Dronningens Gade) west of Market Square and north of the Holiday Inn Windward Passage hotel. There is no reason for travelers to wander into this area except to use Savan as a shortcut from a guesthouse on the west side of town to the business/entertainment district. Don't risk it. If you are a night owl, sooner or later someone will offer you a walk on the wild side (drug dealers or prostitutes of either gender) in one of Savan's bars. Pursuing such an adventure could be suicide.

Travelers are more likely to put themselves at risk by wandering into Back St after dark. This street actually has several different Danish names – Wimmelskafts Gade, Torvet Strade and Prindsesse Gade – but travelers will recognize it as the street that parallels Main St a block north. In recent years, a number of shops and popular restaurants and pubs have moved to the east end of Back St, and there are several budget guesthouses in the neighborhood.

A few travelers get mugged here each year, and shootings occasionally take place.

Several local bars and clubs near the intersection of Domini Gade and Commandant Gade have a reputation for attracting unsavory characters. New Town is a neighborhood just east of town that spreads out around the base of Bluebeard Hill. There is a large federal housing project here that has a bad reputation for violence and crime. Bustling with shoppers and businesspeople by day, Charlotte Amalie's Main St grows desolate after about 5 pm, when the shops begin to close, and travelers have been mugged here. Most of Charlotte Amalie's bars and restaurants are on the safe strip along Waterfront Dr and in the virtually crime-free Frenchtown.

You and your belongings are relatively safe out on the island. Most hotels and guesthouses have excellent security. Nevertheless, if you leave valuables unguarded in your room or in your vehicle, you are risking robbery. The same caveat extends to beaches. By law, all beaches are open to the public in the USVI. Even the most exclusive resorts must open their gates to anyone wishing to use the beach, and enterprising thieves use a day at the beach as an excuse to fleece a few tourists. During daylight, personal safety on St Thomas beaches has not been an issue for travelers or islanders *except* at Lindquist Beach and at Little Magens Bay (later in this chapter).

The first thing to know about driving on St Thomas is that traffic proceeds on the left side of the road, as it does throughout the Virgin Islands. The speed limit is 20mph on most of the island's thoroughfares. Roads are narrow, steep and etched with sharp curves. An additional challenge to drivers is that there is significant traffic on most of the main roads, most of the time. Unless sitting in traffic for an hour is your idea of really experiencing the soul of a place, avoid traveling through Charlotte Amalie between 4 and 6 pm, even on weekends.

Organized Tours

St Thomas has more than a dozen tour operators offering island tours and day trips to

St John and the British Virgin Islands. Almost all of these tours are geared to cruise ship passengers on a tight schedule. Expect to pay $25 and up for a two-hour circuit of St Thomas sites. You will spend $60 or more for a day trip and tour of St John. Of course, you can visit St John on your own by ferry from Red Hook ($3) or Charlotte Amalie ($5). (See 'Interisland Ferries' in the Getting Around chapter.)

The *Atlantis* submarine (☎ 340-776-5650), at Havensight Mall, carries passengers on a tour of St Thomas Harbor before making a dive to explore coral reefs. Trips last two hours and cost $72.

Tropic Tours (☎ 340-774-1855), in the Guardian Building, gets high marks from disabled customers for its island tour.

Destination Virgin Islands Tours (☎ 340-776-2424), at 19 Norre Gade in Charlotte Amalie, is another popular operator with a variety of St Thomas and St John tours.

Limnos Charters (☎ 340-775-3230), at American Yacht Harbor, runs day trips to BVI attractions, including the Baths on Virgin Gorda and the Treasure Caves on Norman Island.

High Performance Charters (☎ 340-777-7545), in Nazareth, offers similar trips aboard a 38-foot luxury speedboat.

Special Events

Although the US Virgin Islands claim more than 20 public holidays, the celebration of these occurs largely at the family level and consists of little more than feasting at home or on a beach.

In early April, world-class racing boats and crews gather at St Thomas for the International Rolex Cup Regatta (☎ 340-775-6320), a three-day event.

Carnival (☎ 340-774-8774), the last two weeks of April, is the one holiday that consumes the island, with costume designers and musicians gearing up almost a year in advance. Officially, carnival lasts two weeks, but in recent years, the various contests and celebratory events have taken up the better part of a month. The festival is rooted in West African masquerading traditions. Slaves appended their African rituals to celebrations of Christian Lenten traditions as early as 1783 in Trinidad, and the custom has spread throughout the West Indies. Today, St Thomas' carnival is the second-largest celebration in the Caribbean after the one at Port-of-Spain, Trinidad. Carnival Village takes over Vendors' Plaza in Charlotte Amalie. Parades, calypso contests, food fairs and beauty pageants snake through the capital to the Carnival Village and adjacent Emancipation Garden. You'll see *mocko jumbies* (costumed stilt walkers representing African spirits), 50-piece steel bands and literally thousands of lavishly costumed parade marchers who dance their way through the streets to the rhythms of reggae, Quelbe and scratch bands mounted on floats and in the back of pickup trucks.

Late August brings the Atlantic Blue Marlin Tournament (☎ 340-775-9500), which draws sportfishers from all over the world to participate in this tag-and-release event benefiting the island Boy Scouts.

Getting There & Away

Air St Thomas' Cyril E King Airport is a modern facility less than 2 miles west of the USVI capital, Charlotte Amalie. Large, air-conditioned and easily accessible, this airport handles direct flights from the major hubs of the US as well as other Caribbean destinations. See the Getting There & Away and Getting Around chapters for specifics.

A thrilling way to get between Charlotte Amalie and Christiansted is to take a Seabourne Aviation floatplane (☎ 340-773-6442) for the half-hour commute from town to town (about $60 each way). The seaplane wharf is near the west end of the inner harbor in Charlotte Amalie.

Ferry St Thomas has two very active ferry terminals that run frequent services to and from St John, Tortola, Jost Van Dyke and Virgin Gorda. Charlotte Amalie's ferry terminal is on Waterfront Dr across from the Windward Passage hotel. This terminal serves passengers only (no cars) and has no convenient parking lot.

The other ferry landing is on the waterfront at the east end of the business district in Red Hook. This is the place to catch a car ferry to St John, as well as a number of passenger ferries to the other islands. There is a parking lot here where you can leave your car for $5 a day. Expect to pay $3 to St John from Red Hook, $5 from Charlotte Amalie. Ferries to the BVI run around $40 round-trip. For schedules, see 'Interisland Ferries' in the Getting Around chapter.

Getting Around

Hitchhiking is not safe on St Thomas. Your best bet is to rent a car, hop on a bus or hail a taxi.

To/From the Airport If you are in a hurry, a taxi is your best bet. The fare for one passenger going between Charlotte Amalie and the airport is $4.50, $10 to/from Red Hook. Cabs are readily available at the airport.

You can also get bus service from the airport to Charlotte Amalie and vice versa. Buses run about every 30 minutes and cost 75¢. The first bus from town (from the stop on Waterfront Dr near Emancipation Garden) leaves at about 6:45 am. The last bus to leave the airport at night departs at 9:30 pm.

Bus The territorial Division of Transportation (VITRAN; ☎ 340-774-5678) operates air-conditioned buses for the length of the island. Look for the VITRAN bus stop signs on Routes 30 and 38. Country buses travel the island seven days a week between 5:30 am and 8:30 pm, departing their stops at 50- or 60-minute intervals. The fare for people under 55 is $1 for all or part of the ride. You must have exact change!

City buses run from the hospital (east of town) through Charlotte Amalie to the airport (west of town) about twice an hour between 6:15 am and 10:15 pm. The fare is 75¢ per ride.

Car St Thomas has a handful of car rental agencies, some of which have outlets at the airport and resort hotels. You can sometimes rent cars for about $30 a day with unlimited mileage, but don't be surprised to hear vendors quote rates of $45 and up. A lot of rental agencies pitch Jeeps to tourists (which may be handy if you want to go off on back roads or take the vehicle over to St John on the ferry), but be aware that a Jeep lacks a trunk in which to secure your valuables. Some agencies prohibit you from taking their cars to St John, and they claim they know you've been there if they see St John's distinct yellow dust on the car.

Dependable Car Rentals (☎ 800-522-3076) offers clean, new vehicles and discount rates. It also offers free pick-up and drop-off at the airport.

Other vendors on the island include Avis (☎ 800-331-1084), Discount Car Rentals (☎ 340-776-4878), Budget (☎ 800-626-4516), Hertz (☎ 800-654-3131) and National (☎ 340-776-3616).

Taxi Territorial law requires that taxi drivers carry a government-set rate sheet. Because taxis are not metered, you must set your fare before embarking. Ask your driver for the rate sheet or get yourself a copy of the readily available free tourist guide *St Thomas This Week*, which lists the rates between principal places on the island.

Note that a $1 to $1.50 surcharge applies to cabs called between midnight and 6 am. The minimum fare within town limits is $2. Additional bags (after the first one) cost 50¢. The taxi stands in Charlotte Amalie are at Emancipation Garden, the Windward Passage hotel and the Havensight Mall. There are also always taxis at the airport. Usually there are taxis waiting at the ferry landing in Red Hook.

Many taxis are vans that carry eight to 10 passengers. These service multiple destinations and may stop to pick up passengers along the way, so their rates are usually charged on a per-person basis. Following are current per-person rates for some of the island's most popular destinations from Charlotte Amalie.

destination	cost
Frenchtown	$2
Havensight	$4
Magens Bay	$6.50
Red Hook	$9

The following taxi services get good marks from islanders: Independent Taxi (☎ 340-775-1006), VI Taxi Radio Dispatch (☎ 340-774-7475), VI Taxi Association (☎ 340-774-4550) and Wheatley Taxi Service & Tours (☎ 340-775-1959).

Because taxis are generally too expensive and VITRAN buses too few to meet islanders' needs for getting around St Thomas, an association of gypsy cabs has developed to fill the void. These vehicles are heavy-duty pickup trucks with bench seats in the truck bed and an awning overhead. Drivers roam the major roads, traveling to both ends of the island.

To hail one of these cabs, simply stand by the side of the road and wave when one approaches. The fare is $1.

Ferry Larry's Ferry to Water Island leaves Crown Bay Marina in Sub Base at 7:15, 8:15 and 11:15 am, 12:15, 2:15, 4:15, 5:15 and 6 pm. Ferries usually return from the island 45 minutes after departing Crown Bay. Tickets cost $7 roundtrip, $4 one way.

Travelers can ride the Ferry Around Mangrove Lagoon at the East End on Friday and Saturday nights during the high season. Ticket costs $5. You can ride all night, and they give you a coupon good for two free rum drinks at any one of the six restaurant/pubs where the boat stops.

CHARLOTTE AMALIE

With more than 900 cruise ship visits a year, Charlotte Amalie is the most popular cruise ship destination in the Caribbean. To many travelers, the mere mention of the town spawns images of a festive shopping bazaar. The image is accurate to a point. Yet this town of about 12,000 people is much more than an exotic mall. The setting of Charlotte Amalie could hardly be more dramatic. Protected by the green peaks of Water and Hassel Islands, St Thomas Harbor makes a deep indentation on the south shore of the most famous Virgin. And from the harbor's edge, the buildings of the town, whitewashed with red-hipped roofs, spread over the narrow coastal plain, blossom over a

cluster of pointed hills in the foreground and dot the slopes of the island's mountains rising in the background.

Charlotte Amalie not only has the largest number of boutiques, perfume venders and jewelry shops in the Caribbean, it also has the largest collection of colonial buildings in the West Indies. Most of these buildings are classic Caribbean adaptations of the English Georgian architecture (the Danes loved it), dating from the 1830s. No other town in the Lesser Antilles can boast such an extensive collection of restaurants and chic bistros and nightspots, especially in the Frenchtown quarter. Charlotte Amalie's pubs and clubs offer a sophisticated collection of entertainment, from serene piano bars and jazz caves to bars packed with a cast of hundreds getting their boogie on to reggae, rock and hip-hop.

Furthermore, Charlotte Amalie has become a jumping-off place for the other US and British Virgin islands. Every year, there are more high-speed ferries leaving Charlotte Amalie for St John, Tortola and points east. The capital's waterfront even sports a seaplane base with scheduled flights to St Croix.

But all is not sweetness and light in Charlotte Amalie. A pirates' den almost from its inception (see History, below), this town today has some big-city problems including drugs, poverty, prostitution and street crime (see Dangers & Annoyances, earlier). It's not enough to spoil your adventure, but enough to remind you that this definitely is not Kansas, Toto.

History

In 1672, more than five years after Denmark laid claim to St Thomas, the Danes began the construction of Fort Christian on St Thomas Harbor. Three years later, the colonists constructed four pubs near the water's edge on the western side of the fort, and in 1778, the Danes strengthened their military position here by building Blackbeard's and Bluebeard's Castles as lookout towers on the crests of two hills. People of the time called the colony Taphus, Danish for 'brew pub,' and the settlement outside the fort on St Thomas Harbor was, by all accounts, a rustic, free-spirited pirates' den.

A series of governors and investors tried to bring the port under control, turn a profit for the Danish West India and Guinea Company and get islanders to pay taxes. Their efforts met with only marginal success, as there were more freebooters on the island than people interested in developing cane or tobacco plantations. One enterprise did take hold: slave trading. In 1685, the Brandenberg Company contracted with the Danes to create a factory on the west side of the settlement for the manufacture and trade of furniture, silver and 'merchandise.' While the factory did indeed produce these goods, it did so with slave laborers imported from a Danish slave-trading outpost in West Africa.

In subsequent years, the secret of the company's success lay in the profits it made from importing slaves to St Thomas for sale throughout the Caribbean and North America. Not to be outdone, the Danish West India and Guinea Company began to compete with the Brandenbergers for profits in the slave trade. Despite an earthquake, hurricanes and brutal raids by the French, the town on St Thomas prospered as a slave market and a neutral port. During these years, the settlement gained the name of Charlotte Amalie in honor of Denmark's queen.

In 1755, the Danes moved their capital from Charlotte Amalie to Christiansted, St Croix. But even this slight could not hamper Charlotte Amalie's growth, as its aggressive and independent-minded merchants profiteered in slave, rum and arms trades to belligerent nations. Supplying the needs of North America and the subsequent American Revolution meant good news for Charlotte Amalie's businessfolk, and the town continued to fill with immigrants from Europe, Africa and the other islands of the Lesser Antilles. In 1764, Denmark's King Frederick V declared Charlotte Amalie a free port, and the town became one of the busiest harbors in the world.

In 1804, a fire in the town destroyed 1200 homes and warehouses. Two more fires struck in 1805 and 1806, and the densely settled island town lost another 800 buildings. Eventually, the town recovered and was rebuilt, and even as most of the West Indies suffered from the recession in the sugar industry and the end of slavery, Charlotte Amalie rose from its ashes and prospered. Many of the buildings in the town's historic district date from this era. The town's high point came when it flourished as a coaling station and smuggling center for ships running the Federal blockade of Confederate ports during the American Civil War (1861–65). As acknowledgment of the port's success, the Danes moved their colonial capital back to Charlotte Amalie in 1871.

The ills of overpopulation plagued the town during the latter half of the 19th century, as cholera epidemics infested Charlotte Amalie. In 1854, one epidemic alone killed more than 1500 people. Charlotte Amalie fell into a queasy dormancy until the US bought the Danish West Indies in 1917. The US Navy took control of the islands and made Charlotte Amalie its headquarters. Navy presence in the town truly overwhelmed Charlotte Amalie during WWII, when the harbor became a naval base to protect allied shipping to and from the Panama Canal. During this era, Charlotte Amalie lived up to its old name of Taphus, as drunken sailors spread their money (and racism) around the island.

Over the last 50 years, St Thomas has experienced extraordinary economic growth, largely as a consequence of cruise ship visits, which initially meant hasty conversion of historic homes and commercial buildings into shops and restaurants. Fake West Indian buildings and modern structures sprouted on the perimeter of the historic district. And for more than 30 years, historic preservation and restoration of the town beyond the business district stirred up little enthusiasm. However, during the 1990s, a social and historical consciousness emerged. Each year, historic buildings are restored to how they looked 180 years ago.

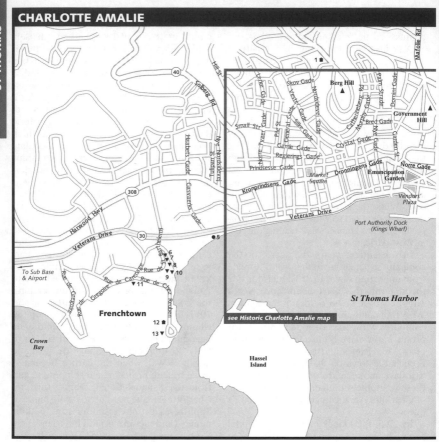

CHARLOTTE AMALIE

The restoration of the Grand Hotel, the Haagensen House and L'Hotel Boynes are good examples of what will happen if the current impulse toward historic preservation continues.

Orientation

Located mid-island on the south shore, Charlotte Amalie stretches about 1½ miles around St Thomas Harbor from the Havensight district (where the cruise ships land) in the east, to Frenchtown and the Sub Base neighborhoods on the west. The red walls of the Danish Fort Christian and the open

space of Emancipation Garden and the Vendors' Market are the center of the old town. Many of the city's historic homes and businesses stand on the slopes of Government Hill just to the north of Emancipation Garden. This area is traditionally known as Kongens (Kings) Quarter.

To the west, spanning the area between Waterfront Dr and Main St, stand a score of alleys, each lined with colonial warehouse buildings that have been turned into upscale shops and urban malls. Havensight is another popular shopping area, with several malls adjacent to the cruise ship docks.

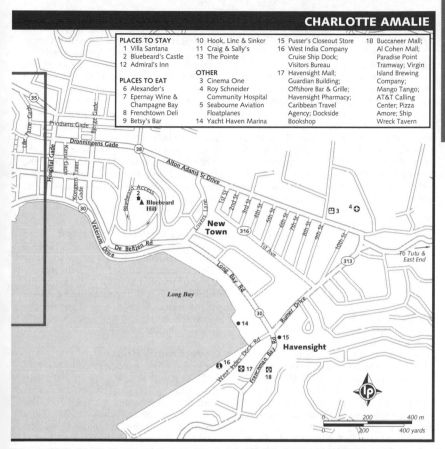

CHARLOTTE AMALIE

PLACES TO STAY
1 Villa Santana
2 Bluebeard's Castle
12 Admiral's Inn

PLACES TO EAT
6 Alexander's
7 Epernay Wine &
   Champagne Bay
8 Frenchtown Deli
9 Betsy's Bar

10 Hook, Line & Sinker
11 Craig & Sally's
13 The Pointe

OTHER
3 Cinema One
4 Roy Schneider
   Community Hospital
5 Seabourne Aviation
   Floatplanes
14 Yacht Haven Marina

15 Pusser's Closeout Store
16 West India Company
   Cruise Ship Dock;
   Visitors Bureau
17 Havensight Mall;
   Guardian Building;
   Offshore Bar & Grille;
   Havensight Pharmacy;
   Caribbean Travel
   Agency; Dockside
   Bookshop

18 Buccaneer Mall;
   Al Cohen Mall;
   Paradise Point
   Tramway; Virgin
   Island Brewing
   Company;
   Mango Tango;
   AT&T Calling
   Center; Pizza
   Amore; Ship
   Wreck Tavern

Frenchtown, across the harbor, has become the city's restaurant district, where strollers can window-shop for the eatery or pub that fits their mood and purse. Of course, the historic district has its share of restaurants and pubs as well.

Visitors should be prepared to see all of the street signs in the historic district labeled with their original Danish names. North St, for example, is Norre Gade (pronounced GAA-da, which is 'street' in Danish). Main St and Back St have signs in English as well as Danish and are generally called by their English names.

Emancipation Garden

This park, with its trees, benches and gazebo is the center of Charlotte Amalie. Here, on July 3, 1848, town officials read the emancipation proclamation to the people of St Thomas after receiving word that Governor Peter von Scholten had freed the slaves on St Croix. There is a replica of the Philadelphia Liberty Bell in the corner.

Carnival celebrations and band concerts take place here, but most of the time it is a place for folks to kick back with a cold drink from the Vendors' Plaza. Travelers will find this park a convenient rallying point and the easiest place to catch a cab. VITRAN buses and gypsy cabs stop close by on Waterfront Dr.

Fort Christian

Built with blood-red brick, Fort Christian (☎ 340-776-4566), east of Emancipation Garden, is the oldest colonial building in the Virgin Islands. The core of this fort dates from 1666. Most of the ramparts were added in the 18th century. The clock tower came during an 1870s renovation of the fort to celebrate the colonial government returning to St Thomas. Over the years, the fort has functioned as a bastion, jail, governor's residence and a Lutheran church.

The museum inside is one of the best places to gain a visual sense of Virgin Islands history. Exhibits include artifacts from the Taíno and Carib occupation to the present. Many photos illustrate life on the island over the last 150 years. The fort is open 8:30 am to 4:30 pm weekdays. Admission is free, but a $1 donation is encouraged.

Kings Wharf & Legislature Building

This government compound (☎ 340-774-0880), on Veterans Dr across from Fort Christian, is the original ship landing for the Danish colony. Today, the US Coast Guard shares the ground with the territorial legislature. The USVI governing body meets in the pale-green neoclassical building that dates from 1874.

Once a barracks for Danish and, subsequently, US troops, this building is where the Danes officially turned over the islands to the US. Island politicians have assembled here since the 1950s. Although the building is not open for tours, you can come and sit in a gallery when the legislature is in session.

Grand Hotel Complex

Dating to 1839, this collection of four buildings in a neoclassic/Tuscan design occupies the entire block north of Emancipation Garden. Artisans began a major restoration of the complex in 1999. The buildings now house popular shops and restaurants.

Frederik Lutheran Church

This church (☎ 340-776-1315), at 7 Norre Gade across the street from the Grand Hotel, is one of Charlotte Amalie's architectural gems. Most of the present structure was built between 1789 and 1793. The original structure was Georgian, but after two major reconstructions in the 19th century, the church now has Gothic Revival elements, including a gable roof and tower. The entrance has a West Indian 'welcoming arms' stairway (a reference to the way the stairway flares at the base). During the 19th century, the church had two segregated congregations – one West Indian, the other Danish. The church is open 8 am to 5 pm Saturday. You can attend services on Sunday.

Frederik Church Parsonage

This large building at 23 Kongens Gade is the large structure on your left as you scale Government Hill. Built in 1725, the parsonage with its double balcony is one of the oldest private residences in continuous use on the island. Constructed of rubble masonry, this house still has vestiges of slave quarters and a cookhouse.

Government House

The grand white mansion (☎ 340-774-0001), at 21-22 Kongens Gade opposite the parsonage, has two floors of cast-iron verandas. With three stories and a hipped roof, this edifice is one of St Thomas' most famous buildings, built between 1865 and 1867. Restored in 1994, the building currently houses the offices of the territorial governor. The 1st-floor reception area and the 2nd floor are open to the public. During your visit, you will see paintings by noted local artists, including island-born Camille Pissarro. Visiting hours are 9 am to noon and 1 to 5 pm weekdays. Admission is free.

Seven Arches Museum

This 18th-century artisan's home (☎ 340-774-9295) sits in a tiny alley off Kongens Gade just to the east of Government House. The museum takes its name from the seven arches that support the welcoming arms staircase. You can admire the antiques in

STEVE SIMONSEN

Atop Charlotte Amalie, St Thomas

LEE FOSTER

Duty-free shopping, St Thomas

LEE FOSTER

Magens Bay, St Thomas, has a mile-long beach and calm water, perfect for water sports.

DANI VALENT

Bluebeard's Castle, St Thomas

DANI VALENT

LEE FOSTER

Biking on Water Island, off St Thomas

DANI VALENT

99 Steps in historic Charlotte Amalie, St Thomas

DANI VALENT

Synagogue in Charlotte Amalie, the second-oldest Jewish temple in the Western Hemisphere

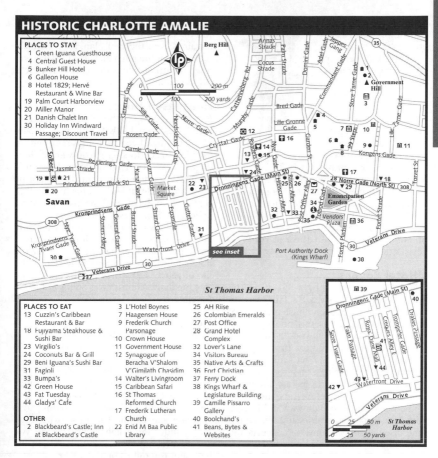

HISTORIC CHARLOTTE AMALIE

PLACES TO STAY
1 Green Iguana Guesthouse
4 Central Guest House
5 Bunker Hill Hotel
6 Galleon House
8 Hotel 1829; Hervé Restaurant & Wine Bar
19 Palm Court Harborview
20 Miller Manor
21 Danish Chalet Inn
30 Holiday Inn Windward Passage; Discount Travel

PLACES TO EAT
13 Cuzzin's Caribbean Restaurant & Bar
18 Fujiyama Steakhouse & Sushi Bar
23 Virgilio's
24 Coconuts Bar & Grill
29 Beni Iguana's Sushi Bar
31 Fagioli
33 Bumpa's
42 Green House
43 Fat Tuesday
44 Gladys' Cafe

OTHER
2 Blackbeard's Castle; Inn at Blackbeard's Castle

3 L'Hotel Boynes
7 Haagensen House
9 Frederik Church Parsonage
10 Crown House
11 Government House
12 Synagogue of Beracha V'Shalom V'Gimilath Chasidim
14 Walter's Livingroom
15 Caribbean Safari
16 St Thomas Reformed Church
17 Frederik Lutheran Church
22 Enid M Baa Public Library

25 AH Riise
26 Colombian Emeralds
27 Post Office
28 Grand Hotel Complex
32 Lover's Lane
34 Visitors Bureau
35 Native Arts & Crafts
36 Fort Christian
37 Ferry Dock
38 Kings Wharf & Legislature Building
39 Camille Pissarro Gallery
40 Boolchand's
41 Beans, Bytes & Websites

St Thomas Harbor

---

the great room and take in a view of the harbor before heading out back to the separate Danish kitchen and cistern and sipping a free tropical drink in the walled garden. The house is open 10 am to 3 pm Tuesday to Sunday. Admission is $5.

Crown House

If you climb the steep stairs up Government Hill past Government House, you reach Dronningens Gade. Crown House, 26-27 Dronningens Gade, is the house to your left with the broad gambrel roof and narrow dormer windows. Built in 1740, the house

was once home to two island governors. One was Peter von Scholten, who is credited with freeing the slaves some years after he left St Thomas and moved to St Croix. A museum for a while, Crown House is once again a private residence and does not allow visitors inside.

Blackbeard's Castle

At the top of Government Hill stands the five-story masonry watchtower known as Blackbeard's Castle. This turret stands on the grounds of a boutique hotel (see Places to Stay, later) of the same name. Originally built as a watchtower in 1678, it was called Skytborg by the Danish.

In the 18th century, the tower was allegedly the lookout post of the pirate Edward Teach, alias Blackbeard, who found St Thomas a haven from which to ambush unsuspecting merchant ships. As the romance of the pirate legend seems to be what sticks in the popular consciousness, the brigand is memorialized by the tower's popular name. It's worth the climb up Government Hill (come in the cool of the morning) for the vista of St Thomas Harbor and the red roofs of Charlotte Amalie.

Blackbeard

L'Hotel Boynes

L'Hotel Boynes (☎ 340-774-5511), on the upper slope of Blackbeard's Hill, was an elegant B&B that is becoming a museum of architectural history as this book goes to press. In 2000, the Historic Trust of the Virgin Islands purchased the property and plans to restore it. The 1785 townhouse features period furnishings, airy rooms, a secluded pool and an upper gallery and was a favorite retreat of celebrities including Muhammad Ali, Cab Calloway and Eartha Kitt. Jazz ensembles and local poets sometimes use the public rooms for concerts and gatherings.

99 Steps

Halfway down Government Hill from Blackbeard's Castle, a steep set of stairs leads through a canopy of trees back to the commercial district. These are the so-called 99 Steps. There are actually 103 steps, but no matter. People count them when bounding uphill on hot days because every step is a victory.

The steps are a classic example of the step streets built throughout Charlotte Amalie of ship-ballast brick during the mid-18th century. It seems that Danish city planners back in Copenhagen drew up an orderly grid of streets for Charlotte Amalie without ever witnessing the steepness of the terrain. Given the grid plan, local builders realized that the pitch on some hills was too steep for streets; steps were the only practical solution.

Haagensen House

Poised at the top of the 99 Steps, this completely restored 1830s townhouse (☎ 340-774-9605) has become a museum and an excellent place to stop if you want a thorough evocation of Danish colonial life on St Thomas. The house's docents could not be more knowledgeable about the house, 19th-century colonial life and the historic district in general. Simply put, a stop here will give you all you want to know about Charlotte Amalie's history. Once the home of Danish banker Hans Haagensen and his family, the house and the tour thoroughly depict the life of gentry 150 years ago. It's open 9 am to 4 pm daily. Admission is $6 for adults, $3 for children.

Hotel 1829 & Yellow Brick Building

This hotel (see Places to Stay, later), at 30 Kongens Gade near the base of the 99 Steps, dates from 1829 and was once the mansion of French sea captain and merchant Alexander Lavalette. The building is distinctive for its 'U' shape, welcoming arms staircase and elliptical archway. The hotel bar includes the original kitchen, and you see the original owner's initials, AL, in the wrought-iron railing on the upper gallery.

The so-called Yellow Brick Building (1854) next door is a great example of ballast-brick construction with a marble-tiled porch. In recent years, it has housed shops and the Hervé restaurant (see Places to Eat, later).

St Thomas Reformed Church

This church (☎ 340-776-8255), at Crystal Gade at Nye Gade, dates from 1844 and is an uncommon example of Greek Revival architecture in the West Indies. The church is not open for casual viewing, but you can attend services on Sunday morning.

Synagogue of Beracha V'Shalom V'Gimilath Chasidim

The Synagogue of Blessing and Peace and Acts of Piety (☎ 340-774-4312), Crystal Gade at Raadets Gade, is the second-oldest Jewish temple in the Western Hemisphere (the oldest is on the island of Curaçao).

The current building dates from 1833, but Sephardic Jews from Denmark have worshipped on this site since 1796. In 2000, a major restoration of the temple was completed and the synagogue of the 600-person Hebrew congregation of St Thomas was formally designated as a National Historic Landmark. The floor of the temple is made of sand to symbolize the flight of the Israelites out of Egypt and across the desert. You will not see the Old Testament scrolls because they are secured in the temple ark, but you may see the 11th-century Spanish menorah that holds the Chanukah candles.

The Weibel Museum next to the synagogue has exhibits depicting 300 years of Jewish history in the West Indies. The temple and museum are open 9 am to 4 pm weekdays. Donations are encouraged.

Camille Pissarro Gallery

This building at 14 Dronningens Gade houses the Camille Pissarro Gallery (☎ 340-774-4621). Here in 1830, Jacob Pizarro was born as the son of Spanish Jews. As a young adult, Jacob became a very accomplished painter, moved to Paris, changed his name to Camille Pissarro and emerged as one of the founders of the French Impressionist movement in art. The gallery sells reproductions and posters of Pissarro's famous island scenes and shows the work of other island artists. Also see Arts in the Facts about the Virgin Islands chapter.

Market Square

The square and wrought-iron market shed on Dronningens Gade at Savan Gade is the site of Charlotte Amalie's legendary slave market. Possibly as many as 200,000 captive Africans arrived at this market to be sold as slaves during the 17th and 18th centuries. The actual auction block is difficult to find today because the square is a farmers'

market for flower and produce vendors. This is an excellent place to pick up a mango or gneps to slake your thirst.

Frenchtown

Occupying a peninsula on the western side of St Thomas Harbor, this former fishing village is now the hottest restaurant quarter on the island (see Places to Eat, later). Traditionally, the community of many brightly painted frame homes has been populated by the island's 'Frenchies,' Huguenots who immigrated to St Thomas in the mid-19th century from the French island of St Barts. Frenchtown was once a community of about 1500 people who spoke a mix of 18th-century Breton French and West Indian Creole. But in recent years, many of the neighborhood's French citizens have assimilated or moved away.

West India Company Cruise Ship Dock

A hundred years ago, this dock and the surrounding area known as Havensight on the east side of St Thomas Harbor was a wharf for steamships and a coaling station. Today, as many as six cruise ships tie up here at a time. When passengers disembark, they find Havensight Mall, a compound of buildings that house shops and restaurants. This mall, as well as the shops and restaurants across the street in the Al Cohen Mall and the Buccaneer Mall, constitute the largest shopping area on St Thomas outside the historic district of Charlotte Amalie.

Paradise Point Tramway

Built in 1994, this aerial tramway (☎ 340-774-9809) scales 700-foot Flag Hill to the scenic outlook on Paradise Point. From a base station across the street from the Havensight Mall, you ride in modern gondolas. The trip takes seven minutes each way. At the top, there is a restaurant, bar, gallery of shops, tropical bird show and a short nature trail. The tramway is open 9 am to 4:30 pm daily. Tickets cost $10 for adults, $5 for children under 12.

Every Wednesday, visitors can view the sunset over Charlotte Amalie on a free tramway ride (from 5 pm until dark). At the top of the mountain, guests receive a free beer or rum drink at the tramway's bar.

Places to Stay

Rack rates on St Thomas hotels look steep, but do not dismay. St Thomas gets the bulk of its tourists off the cruise ships during the busy winter/spring high season. The popularity of cruise ship travel has cut into the island's hotel business, particularly at budget and moderately priced accommodations. As a result, there is a lot of competition among island innkeepers to fill their rooms.

If you are willing to move around the island every two or three days, and go through the hassle of calling guesthouse and hotel managers, you can usually (except on prime holidays) pick up significant last-minute discounts on rooms. The biggest savings will most likely be found at resort hotels, where managers' careers rise and fall according to the house count. In addition, most of St Thomas' larger hotels offer constantly changing promotional deals that can save you up to 30% on the rack rate, but you won't get these deals unless you ask.

Another option, if you want to lock yourself into a single place to stay, and you have a rental car to get around, is to consider a villa rental. Like hotel managers, a lot of villa property managers start dropping their prices when places look like they may go unrented: $3000-a-week waterfront palaces with five bedrooms can go for $1200 when managers get nervous.

Although you can camp legally at any beach on St Thomas (except Magens Bay), no one does. The island is too densely populated to offer the off-the-beaten-track experience most campers desire, and the beaches can be unsafe. If your heart is set on sleeping under the stars on St Thomas, some locals favor the beach at Hull Bay or Stumpy Bay. Nearby St John, with thousands of acres of national park land and several campgrounds, is the place where most campers head.

Prices listed below are based on high-season occupancy unless otherwise noted.

Guesthouses On Commandant Gade about a hundred yards north of the intersection with Domini Gade in the heart of town, the *Central Guest House* (☎ 340-777-9746) has the cheapest rooms on the island. Margot Rodriguez has nine basic rooms with worn furniture in this multistory building. All rooms have air-con and cable TV. Some share baths. The advantage of this location is that it's in the center of Charlotte Amalie's historic and commercial district. The disadvantage is that it's in a dodgy part of town (near Back St). After dark, the area is frequented by drug users and local barflies. Rooms run $40 to $50. The clientele is largely transient West Indians with a few backpackers mixed in.

Miller Manor (☎ 340-774-1535, 26 Prindsesse Gade), on Frenchman's Hill, is a good value. Aida and Leo Miller have run this 26-room hillside establishment for decades, and it has the homey feel of your Aunt Josie's summer place. There is a 150-year-old Danish townhouse at the center of this complex with a bar and restaurant overlooking the town and harbor. Each room has a microwave and fridge as well as air-con. Many of the visitors are older couples, but children are welcome. Guests can use the pool at the neighboring Palm Court Harborview Hotel. Rooms start at about $50. While Miller Manor is in a safe neighborhood, the dicey Savan district lies between here and the heart of town. Do not walk this territory at night; take a cab.

The *Green Iguana Guesthouse* (☎ 340-776-7654), virtually attached to the Inn at Blackbeard's Castle, offers quaint accommodations overlooking St Thomas Harbor. All rooms were refurbished in 2000. The guesthouse has four rooms for short-term rentals and four condos for longer stays. Guesthouse rooms have twin-size beds, a coffeepot, a microwave, a small refrigerator and a toaster. All guests have access to the pool and restaurant at Blackbeard's Castle. Rates range from $89 to $99.

Galleon House (☎ 340-774-6972, 800-524-2052) may be the traveler's best value of all. This 14-room property spreads along the west side of Government Hill, behind the popular Hervé restaurant in the absolute heart of the town's historic district. With good vistas of town and the harbor, this place offers a sense of being in the middle of things, yet above it all. The staff is perky, and the property looks freshly painted and clean. All rooms have air-con, TV and private bath. You also get a full complimentary breakfast, and an attractive veranda, pool and deck look out on the red roofs of the historic district. Doubles run about $80 to $120.

The **Admiral's Inn** (☎ 340-774-1376, 800-544-0943, 3700 Villa Olga), next to the Pointe restaurant in Frenchtown, has the most romantic location of all the guesthouses and small hotels on St Thomas. The charm of this place rests in its location overlooking Hassel Island. The inn is also close to many of the island's most popular restaurants and bars. Each of the 12 rooms has a bath, air-con, kitchen and TV. There is a freshwater pool and sundeck here for guests. Doubles start at about $130.

Hotels The **Danish Chalet Inn** (☎ 340-774-5764, 9E-9 Solberg Rd) has three buildings with 13 rooms overlooking the town and harbor. About half of these rooms share baths, but all are neat, clean and alive with vibrant fabrics. Most rooms have a fridge and air-con. There is no pool, but there is an outdoor spa rife with the scent of bougainvillea. Expect to pay $85 and up.

The **Bunker Hill Hotel** (☎ 340-774-8056, 7 Commandant Gade) has been refurbished as a modern, spotless, three-story inn built around a sunny pool deck and courtyard. Each room has air-con, TV and bath. The furnishings were new and attractive in 2000. Full breakfasts are complimentary. Rooms start at about $85. You might ask for one of the rooms in the back to lessen the street noise.

Hotel 1829 (☎ 340-776-1829, 800-524-2002), located next to Galleon House, is a historic site and inn that blends the atmosphere of a Victorian gentlemen's club and a colonial villa. Exposed rubble walls, beamed ceilings, period West Indian furnishings and a profusion of flowers characterize the property. All rooms have air-con, TV, bath and phone. There is a free continental breakfast and a small pool for guests as well. Rooms start at $100 for a single and rise to more than $200 for a suite. No children under 12 are allowed.

The **Palm Court Harborview** (☎ 340-774-5292), across the street from Miller Manor on Solberg Rd, is a multistory concrete hotel with more than 30 rooms and a convention center. Rooms have all the amenities, including daily maid service. There is a large pool and deck overlooking the town and harbor. Rooms start at about $100, suites $130.

The **Inn at Blackbeard's Castle** (☎ 340-776-1234, 800-344-5771) stands on the grounds surrounding the pirate's watchtower on the hilltop above Charlotte Amalie. All rooms feature 1st-class amenities like period West Indian furnishings and private balconies. The huge pool right at the base of the historic tower seems designed for a hotel with five times the number of guests, and the restaurant/piano bar here is one of the most popular venues on the island for a romantic night out (see Places to Eat). Rooms run $110 to $225.

Villa Santana (☎ 340-776-1311), on Denmark Hill overlooking Charlotte Amalie, was the 19th-century estate of Mexico's famous General Antonio López de Santa Anna. Guests can stay in one of seven suites located around the property, in the villa's former wine cellar, kitchen, pump house and library. All rooms come with full amenities and Mexican decor. This is where you hear the Gypsy Kings on the stereo, rather than Bob Marley, while you are lounging poolside among well-traveled couples. Rates start at about $130 and go over $200.

For decades, the four-story, block-long **Holiday Inn Windward Passage** (☎ 340-774-5200, 800-524-5389), on Waterfront Dr, has been the centerpiece of Charlotte Amalie's harbor. Lit up at night by floodlights, the modern building is grand in its own 'International Style' way. With 151 renovated rooms, this place now has the feel of a 1st-class business hotel, and even at its busiest, the pool in the central courtyard seems tranquil. Guests can also take advantage of a free shuttle to the beach at Magens Bay. From the hotel, you have an easy walk along the waterfront to the restaurants and shopping in the historic district or Frenchtown. Avoid the crime-ridden district of Savan directly behind the hotel. Rates can run $130 to $300.

Bluebeard's Castle (☎ *340-774-1600*), with its sprawling white-stucco facade on Bluebeard's Hill, looks a lot like the fortress it once was. On the eastern edge of Charlotte Amalie, this is another visual landmark of the city. Fifty years ago it was the island's premier resort, and while it can no longer compete with the Ritz-Carlton and Marriott resorts for chic, Bluebeard's still offers 1st-class rooms, pools, restaurants and service. There is also a shuttle from here to Bluebeard's condo resort on the south coast at Frenchman Bay. Expect to pay at least $250.

Rental Accommodations St Thomas has hundreds of time-shared or individually owned vacation condos and villas that owners rent through property managers on the island. You will see advertisements for these rental agencies splattered throughout tourist brochures, newspapers, yellow pages and the Internet.

The following are some of the most respected property managers with rentals in desirable locations: Calypso Realty (☎ 340-774-1620) manages a wide range of condos and villas all over the island. Rates start at about $125. Paradise Properties (☎ 340-779-1530, 800-524-2038) is the agent for 60 homes, villas and condos that rent for $116 to $165 a night. McLaughlin Anderson Villas (☎ 340-776-0635, 800-537-6246), 100 Blackbeard's Hill, manages more than 35 island properties with rates starting at about $100 per night.

Places to Eat
Travelers could spend months eating their way around St Thomas. You'll find a lot of dining options in downtown Charlotte Amalie along with neighboring French-

town and Sub Base. Red Hook, at the east end of the island, has developed into an extensive restaurant zone as well. In addition, motorists will find an eclectic group of restaurants scattered along the twists and turns of the island's roads.

Historic Charlotte Amalie Also called the Buzz Club, ***Beans, Bytes & Websites*** (☎ 340-777-7089), in the Royal Dane Mall on the waterfront, has great prices for java junkies and email addicts. This chic little cyberbistro will sell you coffee for $1, espresso for $2 and 15 minutes of online time for $2.50. It also serves pastries and croissants. This is the least-expensive place on the island to reconnect with your electronic mailbox. It's also a good place to meet the cruise ship crews who come in to surf the Web.

Bumpa's (☎ *340-776-5674, 38-A Waterfront)* is a popular place for upscale St Thomians and travelers (particularly the cruise ship crowd) to linger over breakfast. This cheery second-story cafe looks out on the harbor and serves up scones for $2 and herbal tea for $1.50. Breakfast sandwiches with two eggs, sausage and cheese on a bagel cost about $6. Deli luncheon sandwiches cost about the same.

Gladys' Cafe (☎ *340-774-6604),* in the Royal Dane Mall just north of the waterfront, is also a good place to get a hearty breakfast. There is no view here, but the bistro setting in this restored warehouse building and the jazz on the stereo create their own mood. Expect to pay about $5 for a full breakfast with eggs, home fries, toast and a hot beverage. Gladys also cooks up some mean West Indian dishes for dinner. Try the Old Wife (triggerfish) with fungi for $14.

Fat Tuesday (☎ *340-777-8676),* Waterfront Dr at Palm Passage, is a lively hole-in-the-wall cafe on the waterfront, in the heart of the shopping district. The attraction here is cheap eats, 30 different flavors of frozen rum drinks and great people-watching. A lot of singles off the cruise ships stop here (see Entertainment, later). A taco costs $3; hot dogs run $2; nachos supreme cost about $6.

Cuzzin's Caribbean Restaurant & Bar *(☎ 340-777-4711, 7 Wimmelskafts Gade)* is almost everybody's favorite stop for West Indian cuisine on St Thomas. The scent of onions, peppers and curry will draw you to this place from half a block away. Drew Hilson and her husband, Brant Steele, have gathered together family recipes and some of the island's best cooks in this restored livery stable in the center of town. You can go light with the spicy calypso chicken wings for $3.50 or get into something more serious like the fresh curried conch for $13.

Coconuts Bar & Grill *(☎ 340-774-0099, 10 Main St)* is another happening lunch spot nearby. Owner Tammy LaVelle's corner pub spills over into a clutch of outdoor cafe tables and attracts a lively group of locals, such as Mr Claude Malone (who has a plaque marking his seat at the bar) and a lot of travelers. Tammy claims to run the best baby-sitting service on the island – for spouses deserted by their partners on a shopping binge in the downtown shops. You can get an 8-inch pizza here for under $6 and popcorn shrimp for $7.

The ***Green House*** *(☎ 340-774-7998)*, on Waterfront Dr in the heart of town, has been an oasis for both locals and travelers for years. Raised a half-story above the surrounding sidewalks, this cavernous, open-air restaurant overlooks the seaplane-landing zone, Hassel Island and the wharf where interisland trading boats tie up. The cuisine is predictable American pub fare, but the menu is extensive, with eight different kinds of burgers (about $7), individual pizzas ($7) and moderately priced seafood entrees like coconut shrimp ($15). After 10 pm, the Green House becomes a rocking dance scene (see Entertainment, later).

At ***Fujiyama Steakhouse & Sushi Bar*** *(☎ 340-714-2247)*, on Norre Gade two blocks east of the post office, you can seat your party at a *teppanyaki* table with its own grill and chopping board. The chef slices, dices and grills with considerable flourishing of knives as you watch from just inches away. Considering the show you get, the prices for things like chicken teppanyaki ($8) are quite reasonable.

Beni Iguana's Sushi Bar *(☎ 340-777-8744)*, in the Grand Hotel courtyard, is the most popular sushi place on the island for locals. You can find a lot of the island's rich and powerful here eating California rolls for $8. Other sushi platters can run $14.

Fagioli *(☎ 340-777-8116)*, Waterfront Dr at Guttets Gade, looks the part of a Roman cafe/restaurant set on Charlotte Amalie's waterfront. If your memories of a romantic Roman eatery include the sound and smell of autos, the gated courtyard here adjacent to the traffic jams on Veterans Dr can deliver. The ambience is quieter and cooler inside, where exposed brick walls, wine racks and jazz (live on weekends) set the scene. St Thomians swear that the talapia (fish) sautéed in lemons and capers ($21) is one of the delights on the menu.

Virgilio's *(☎ 340-776-4920, 18 Dronningens Gade)* is a popular upscale northern Italian restaurant in the Back St area of Charlotte Amalie. The vaulted ceilings, 18th-century furnishings and scent of garlic and Chianti might remind you of a place you would discover on an alley in Firenze. Most of Virgilio del Mare's dinner entrees run $20 to $35, but you can get a filling chicken Caesar salad here for $14.

Hervé Restaurant & Wine Bar *(☎ 340-777-9703)*, on Government Hill, specializes in Swiss-French cuisine and has been an island attraction for more than a quarter of a century. The setting is a rather formal terrace in a historic townhouse with views of the downtown rooftops and the harbor. Perhaps the best dinner value here is the fixed-price menu, which includes Norwegian salmon or veal roulade with all the side dishes for about $26. For lunch, catch the cold duck salad (about $10). You'll need reservations on weekends.

The ***Inn at Blackbeard's Castle*** (see Places to Stay, earlier, and Entertainment, later) cannot be beat for an elegant dinner. Cheese tortellini with roasted artichokes and sun-dried tomatoes runs $18, but you will pay more than $25 for most other entrees. Gourmands come for the $55 fixed-price menu, which includes soup, salad, entree and dessert. Penny pinchers come for a late lunch. Don't miss the roasted red snapper sandwich ($12). Reservations are a must on weekends.

Frenchtown & Sub Base In the tiny Frenchtown Mall, *Frenchtown Deli* (☎ 340-776-7211) is a popular takeout stop for breakfast and lunch with a view of Hassel Island and the harbor. You can get a bagel and cream cheese with a cup of coffee here for under $3.50. A thick turkey sandwich for lunch will run you about $7.

Alexander's (☎ 340-774-4349), on Rue de St Bathelemy, is actually two restaurants: a bar and grill where you can get pub fare, and a cafe that specializes in German and Austrian cuisine. The cafe entrees are particularly exciting; they run more than $24 at night, but you can get a filling platter of *jaegerschnitzel* (veal in a mushroom cream sauce) for about $14 during lunch hours. You will want reservations for dinner.

Betsy's Bar (☎ 340-774-9347), tucked behind Alexander's restaurant, is another great stop for cheap eats in Frenchtown. This place is a small indoor bar with a collection of tables on a large patio where a Jerry Garcia look-alike often plays guitar and covers Dead classics. The food is pub fare, served in generous portions at modest cost. Most platters, like the spicy chicken wings, run less than $7. After 9:30 pm, Betsy's has a lively bar scene (see Entertainment, later).

Hook, Line & Sinker (☎ 340-776-9708, 2 Honduras) serves a Sunday brunch ($12) that locals love. Owners Ted and Becky Luscz run this little place on the water as a mom-and-pop operation and welcome all people like old friends. Most entrees, such as the cornmeal-dusted catfish and jerked swordfish, are in the $19 range. Pastas run about $14. Expect to pay $8 for a sandwich.

Epernay Wine & Champagne Bay (☎ 340-774-5348), next to the Frenchtown Deli, is a favorite roost for the St Thomas in-crowd. The hip, the powerful and the beautiful come to hang at the bistro's bar, gnash appetizers like tuna tartare (about $11) and quesadillas ($9) before they settle at a shadowy table for oriental shrimp with bok choy ($15). On weekends, an after-dinner dance scene often develops upstairs (see Entertainment). You'll need dinner reservations most nights.

Craig & Sally's (☎ 340-777-9949, 22 Honduras) is another place where you will need reservations days in advance. Sally Darash lives up to the claims that she is a 'kitchen witch.' Her fusion cooking draws a crowd every night to the limited seating in the open-air alcoves of this 'Frenchie' cottage. The menu changes according to Sally's whim, but expect entrees like pan-seared jumbo scallops with avocado slices, garlic and a lemony avocado sauce served with mozzarella mashed potatoes for about $25.

The Pointe (☎ 340-774-4262), on Villa Olga overlooking Hassel Island, has replaced the Chart House restaurant. The setting on a large veranda of a 19th-century villa (once the Russian consulate) could not be more romantic, with the clatter of palm trees in the trade winds and hush of harbor waves. You can choose the mammoth salad bar as an entree for $17. Most hot entrees like the paella run $25 and up. There are plenty of tables here, but make reservations if you want a table with a view.

Tickles Dockside Pub (☎ 340-776-1595), at the Crown Bay Marina in the Sub Base district, appeals to wannabe Jimmy Buffett types. This open-air restaurant overlooks the harbor's maritime activities and serves up a selection of reasonably priced finger foods and sandwiches. The 'gator eggs' (deep-fried jalapeño peppers stuffed with cheese) beg for a two-beer chaser. You can get a cup of beef vegetable soup and half a turkey sandwich for about $7.

Elsewhere in Charlotte Amalie In Havensight at the Port O' Sail Mall, the *Offshore Bar & Grille* (☎ 340-779-6400) has become hugely popular since it opened in 2000. The attraction is the proximity to the cruise ship docks, lots of live music (particularly jazz), 1st-class pub fare, fast service and a lively crowd. Cruise ship crews like this place because they can catch a beer and a bite while collecting and sending their email at the cybercafe upstairs. Try the Vietnamese salad roll for $9.

Pizza Amore *(☎ 340-774-2822, 18 Estate Thomas),* across the street from the Havensight Mall, is probably Charlotte Amalie's favorite independent pizza joint, and they do a lot of takeout business. The large cheese pie will cost you about $14.

Entertainment

Much of the nightlife on the island gets going in local pubs and restaurants, but there are a few noteworthy clubs as well. The Virgin Islands' abundance of musical talent means you can find a variety of live entertainment playing at places around St Thomas almost every night, including jazz, calypso, reggae, funk, hip-hop, R&B, top 40, folk, acoustic and bluegrass. If you can sing along or dance to it, some musician will probably play it for you on the island.

The Reichhold Center for the Arts on Brewers Bay is the main concert arena (see Around Charlotte Amalie). If it's first-run Hollywood films you are seeking, head for ***Cinema One*** *(☎ 340-774-2855),* in Sugar Estate on Route 38 near the hospital.

Bars & Clubs When the cruise ships are in town, ***Fat Tuesday*** (see Places to Eat) is a lively party and pick-up scene on winter afternoons and evenings. A lot of transient singles discover that this is the cheapest place to catch a buzz in town and often have hit-and-run flirtations with no holds barred (see the snapshots on the bulletin board for the incriminating evidence). During happy hour, domestic beers run under $1.50. Women drink free on Tuesday night from 8 to 10 pm. Wednesday is Mexican Night, when tequila shooters cost $1.50, burritos $5.

The ***Green House*** (see Places to Eat) attracts a big dance crowd. The revelers are mostly under 30, West Indian and dressed in some fine threads. The DJ spins out hip-hop, R&B and Caribbean rhythms on Tuesday and Saturday. You get live reggae on Wednesday and Friday. Do not miss the Star Lights, a world-class reggae and R&B band

that usually plays on Wednesday night. The cover is $3.

Gladys' Cafe (see Places to Eat) turns into a classic jazz cave on weekend nights. The smoke is thick, the liquor sweet and the music way cool. The crowd is a mix of West Indians and continentals with some cruise ship folk dropping in.

The ***Inn at Blackbeard's Castle*** (see Places to Stay) may well be the top jazz venue in the islands. The live jazz starts at about 8 pm every night in high season. Acts come in regularly from the US as well as from around the islands. Friday night is the liveliest night here, when the tables and bar are packed to overflowing.

Epernay Wine & Champagne Bay (see Places to Eat) is a popular hangout for St Thomian professionals, politicians and snowbirds. Friday evening happy hour is the biggest scene. At about 11 pm, people begin to wander upstairs to get their dance on while the stereo cranks top 40 and some calypso. Cocktail dresses, slacks and collared shirts set the fashion.

Betsy's Bar (see Places to Eat) calls itself the 'Best Little Bar and Grill in Frenchtown,' and if you like cheap beer, friendly sailors, charterboat crews and carefree West Indians, you will probably agree with the advertising. There is no better place to network in the Virgin Islands if you are looking for a job as cook or crew on a yacht. Betsy brings in live music on Wednesday and weekend nights, usually a laid-back minstrel singing Buffett ballads and classic rock & roll.

The ***Offshore Bar & Grille*** (see Places to Eat), in Havensight, has become another hotspot since opening in 2000. After 9 pm, this restaurant turns clubby with live music every night. Sometimes you get cool or funky jazz; often you'll hear driving rock & roll. The crowd is a mix of cruise ship crews, continentals and some West Indians, all around 18 to 35. Dress is casual. Currently, this is one of the liveliest places to dance on the island.

Walter's Livingroom *(☎ 340-774-5025, 3 Trompeter Gade),* near the historic synagogue, draws a sophisticated middle-aged West Indian crowd. The owner, Walter

Springette, has a hot collection of West Indian CDs, and this place really hops on weekend nights after 11 pm, when the rum flows liberally. The cover is $3.

The *Ship Wreck Tavern* (☎ 340-777-1293), in Havensight at the Al Cohen Mall, has become one of the newest 'in' spots on the island. This place is your basic gin mill with pool tables, air hockey and a cast of the young and restless. Lots of cruise ship crew members favor this venue. It also appeals to local continentals. As the night goes on, the crowd gets younger, and the Ship Wreck has become a favorite late-night stop for the dance crowd on their way home from discos. (It's a good place to find a date.)

Gay & Lesbian Venues Gay people have been some of the island's most prominent entrepreneurs and politicians for decades, and St Thomas has a lot of gay and lesbian citizens. But few are out and about. A climate of 'don't ask, don't tell' has surrounded gay and lesbian life on this island more than on St Croix, which has openly gay hotels and entertainment venues. Nevertheless, there are a few places on the island where gay and lesbian travelers will feel comfortable.

The live jazz scene on Friday nights at the *Inn at Blackbeard's Castle* (see Bars & Clubs) has long made a popular evening out for gay and lesbian St Thomians and travelers, but the scene is far from totally gay.

Plenty of gay black men find a congenial mix with their straight West Indian counterparts at *Walter's Livingroom* (see Bars & Clubs).

Touts may offer to lead single men to 'gay bars' in Charlotte Amalie. Most of these bars exist side by side with the strip clubs and brothels in the Savan district and tender sex for money. Escaping one of these hellholes without becoming a victim to disease, robbery or violence is unlikely.

Shopping

As a duty-free port with a long tradition of importing pretty things from all over the world, St Thomas is a shopper's paradise. Because there are no taxes levied against a wide variety of luxury goods sold on St Thomas, you can save 50% or more on jewelry, fashions, fabrics, crystal, china, liquor, perfume, cosmetics, electronics, cameras and other items. Each US citizen can leave with up to $1200 worth of purchases without paying the customs agent.

Business hours in most of the island stores are 9 am to 5 pm Monday to Saturday. Charlotte Amalie and Havensight stores open on Sunday if cruise ships are in town.

Historic Charlotte Amalie is the island's main shopping district. Vendors' Plaza, in front of Fort Christian, is a bazaar for crafts, costume jewelry, African imports and T-shirts. The area around Main St, Back St and the colonial warehouses that stretch down to the waterfront has been converted into what amounts to a large outdoor mall. Here, you will find more than 100 elegant shops and boutiques cloistered in historic 18th- and 19th-century buildings and tucked along narrow alleys scented with spices and echoing with jazz and West Indian rhythms. The best place to park is in the large lot on the east side of Fort Christian.

Havensight Mall is a modern compound of buildings that houses shops adjacent to the cruise ship wharf on the east side of St Thomas Harbor. There are more than 50 businesses here and more right across Route 30 at the Buccaneer Mall, the Guardian Building and the Al Cohen Mall. All of these malls have plenty of parking.

Among the stores not to be missed is AH Riise (☎ 340-776-2303), 37 Main St, where you can buy everything from watches and jewels to tobacco and liquor.

Boolchand's (☎ 340-776-8550), 31 Main St, has been one of the largest retailers of cameras in the Caribbean for more than 50 years.

Colombian Emeralds (☎ 340-774-3400), on Main St, Havensight Mall and elsewhere, has a reputation throughout the Caribbean for offering good value on gems of extraordinary quality.

Caribbean Safari (☎ 340-777-8795), at 6 Wimmelskafts Gade (Back St), sells traditional Caribbean straw hats, tote bags, dolls, baskets and masks.

Native Arts & Crafts (☎ 340-777-1153), next to the visitors bureau on Tolbod Gade, is the place to buy dolls, lace and other traditional gifts made by St Thomian crafters.

Lover's Lane (☎ 340-777-9616), facing the waterfront from the 2nd floor at 33 Raadets Gade, carries a full line of erotica. Down Island Traders (☎ 340-776-4641), on the waterfront in the AH Riise Mall, has seasonings, jellies, teas, coffees, hot sauces and locally made jewelry.

Mango Tango Art Gallery (☎ 340-777-3060), at the Al Cohen Mall in Havensight, shows the prints, cards and original depictions of island life by the best of Virgin Island artists. The Camille Pissarro Gallery (see earlier in the chapter) shows the work of island artists and sells reproductions and posters of Pissarro's famous island scenes.

Virgin Island Brewing Company (☎ 340-777-8888), across from the Havensight Mall, has free samples and good prices on the Virgin Islands' only brews, Blackbeard Ale and Foxy's Lager.

Pusser's Closeout Store (☎ 340-774-9680), at 13 Estate Thomas near Kentucky Fried Chicken on Route 30, offers discounts of more than 50% on discontinued items from the company's line of outdoor and nautical apparel.

AROUND CHARLOTTE AMALIE

You can reach a multitude of attractions, beaches, accommodations and restaurants on the island from Charlotte Amalie in less than half an hour by car, taxi or inexpensive gypsy cab.

Tillett Gardens

This collection of artisan studios and shops (☎ 340-779-1929), off Route 38 in Tutu, east of Charlotte Amalie, is several cuts above most of the island's tourist attractions. English silkscreen artist Jim Tillett started this artists' compound on a Danish farm in 1959 as a 'peaceful sanctuary of creativity and wonderment.' Fifty years later, the compound is just that. You can stroll the grounds, eat in a cafe, meet working artists and buy handcrafted fabrics, jewelry and other objets d'art. The gardens sponsor an ongoing concert series that features performances by superb jazz, blues and classical musicians, so try to time your visit to coincide with a concert.

Drake's Seat

Legend has it that Sir Francis Drake came to this overlook, on a mountaintop just off Route 40 south of Magens Bay, to plot the passage of his fleet through the British Virgin Islands east of here. Unless you like tour buses and street vendors, you can skip this stop.

Mountain Top

This restaurant and shopping complex (☎ 304-774-2400), off Route 33 on St Peter Mountain, offers you vistas from 1500 feet above sea level. On a clear day, you can see almost all of the British Virgin Islands to the east and the Spanish Virgin Islands of Puerto Rico to the west. You might also share the view with a busload of folks stopping here as part of an island tour. The vistas you get by simply driving east from here on Crown Mountain Road (Route 33) may not be quite as spectacular, but you will have them all to yourself.

Estate St Peter Greathouse & Botanical Garden

This contemporary great house (☎ 340-774-4999), at the corner of Barrett Hill Rd and Route 40, is another of St Thomas' popular tourist attractions. The 11-acre property overlooking Magens Bay has been the retreat of a French consul, an island governor and the Johnson & Johnson Corporation. Largely destroyed by Hurricane Hugo, the great house and botanical gardens have been restored. The house has photos of hurricane damage, a local art collection and views of the north shore bays from an expansive deck. There are also a few shops, a bar and a cafe on the premises. The estate is open 9 am to 4 pm daily. Admission is $8 for adults, $4 for children.

Hassel Island

The 120-acre island in the middle of St Thomas Harbor was actually part of the main island until 1865. That year, the Danish dredged Haulover Cut to separate Frenchtown and Hassel Island in an attempt to help water flow more freely out of the harbor, thereby reducing the sewage build-up that promoted cholera epidemics.

Today, the entire mile-long island is on the National Register of Historic Places and under the jurisdiction of the National Park Service. During the late 19th century, Hassel Island was a coaling station and repair facility for Royal Mail Steam Packet Company and several other shipping lines. Ruins from that era and even earlier lie disintegrating under island vegetation. Some observers claim that the island's defunct Royal Mail Inn was the prototype for the Gull Reef Club in Herman Wouk's novel *Don't Stop the Carnival*. While the NPS has plans to preserve the ruins and develop Hassel Island as a recreational facility, nothing has been done yet. You need a private boat to get here.

Water Island

The so-called fourth US Virgin Island lies a quarter of a mile off Crown Bay Marina at the extreme western end of St Thomas Harbor. This 490-acre island takes its name from its freshwater pools, which are used to resupply visiting windjammers. From WWI to WWII, Water Island was a US military reservation. Following WWII, the US government used the island for a few years as a chemical warfare test facility before finally leasing the land to the St Thomas Development Authority. After about 1951, US expats began to trickle onto the island to build homes.

The only resort on the island, the Sugar Bird Hotel, blew away in Hurricane Hugo (1989). Since then, the expats have been living a quiet existence on the island. In 1996, the Feds finally ceded Water Island to the territory. The island has a low-key atmosphere in which most people travel by bike or golf cart and community messages are posted on a bulletin board at the ferry dock.

The island is ripe for bike exploration (see Activities, later) and relaxation on the pristine beaches like Honeymoon Bay.

There are no restaurants on the island, but islanders usually throw a Saturday night dinner and Sunday afternoon beach party (see Places to Eat, later). Two real estate agents on the island rent cottages and villas (see Places to Stay). A portion of Water Island's 125 residents commute back and forth by dinghy; others ride Larry's Ferries (☎ 340-774-8706) from Crown Bay Marina (see Getting Around, earlier in this chapter).

Beaches

St Thomas has more than 40 beaches, ranging from remote and barren strands to quite a few hotel beaches with a full array of vacationers and water sports. VITRAN buses run in the vicinity of only a few of these beaches. Many others lie near main arteries like Routes 30, 32 and 38, which have a steady flow of gypsy cabs.

The following are the beaches in the Charlotte Amalie vicinity.

Morningstar Bay A thin, beige strand just east of the Frenchman's Reef resort, this site is a manicured hotel beach with all the trimmings. Morningstar can be busy. And while most of the people you meet here are hotel guests, some West Indians and expats sunbathe here. Many are gay.

Bolongo Bay A long, broad golden crescent in front of the hotel of the same name, this beach adjacent to Route 30 has to be one of the most picturesque hotel beaches on the island. You have the hotel's beach bar and restaurant, Iggie's (see Places to Eat), and a water-sports operation to entertain you. The people who frequent the beach are largely young couples and families on package vacations.

Lindbergh Bay You reach this sheltered horseshoe beach by turning south off the airport access road. There are three moderately priced small resort hotels like the Island Beachcomber Hotel (see Places to Stay) on the strand and a couple of restaurants. The beach is steep and a bit narrow. Lots of families with children frequent the resorts, but the depth of the water drops off pretty quickly and can be dangerous for kids. There is some good snorkeling among the rocks and coral heads along the arms of the bay.

Honeymoon Bay This beach is a short walk from the ferry landing on Water Island (see earlier).

Located at the head of a cove, Honeymoon Bay beach appeals for several reasons: It is safe, never crowded and undeveloped, yet it's within St Thomas Harbor. Catch the weekend beach parties thrown by the local expats. Snorkelers will find plenty of fish along the southern shore of the bay.

Brewers Bay Located adjacent to the University of the Virgin Islands on Route 30, this long strand has almost no shade but features very sheltered water and plenty of shallow areas for kids. Brewers Bay is the one beach that can be reached easily by VITRAN buses that stop at the college campus. On weekends, lots of West Indian families come here to cool off. At such times, there are always mobile food-and-drink vendors set up along the highway at Brewers Bay. Quietude can be in short supply here because the airport's busy runway lies just across the bay.

Activities

Those interested in **diving** should stop by St Thomas Dive Club (☎ 340-776-2381) at Bolongo Bay, Underwater Safaris (☎ 340-774-1350) at the Yacht Haven Marina in Havensight, or Hi Tech Watersports (☎ 340-774-5650) at Crown Bay Marina.

Although the traffic on St Thomas makes **bicycling** on the island's roads dangerous (except early on Sunday morning), you can still get a good two-wheel workout here. Water Island Adventures (☎ 340-714-2186) offers a 3½-hour trail ride on Water Island that includes visits to island ruins such as old forts, a hotel and an abandoned plantation.

Lone Eagle in Paradise

Lindbergh Bay takes its name from Colonel Charles Lindbergh, who landed at a field here with his famous *Spirit of Saint Louis* in 1929. The 'Lone Eagle,' or 'Lucky Lindy,' was on a goodwill tour of the Caribbean and Latin America following his 1927 nonstop solo crossing of the Atlantic by airplane. Lindy definitely had luck with him when he plopped the *Spirit* down in a small open space between the sea and the mountains on the edge of the bay that now bears his name.

A year later, Lindbergh returned to the bay in a Sikorsky seaplane. Lindy became convinced that St Thomas was the perfect refueling stop for a commercial flight between the US and South America. And because of Lindbergh's visits, Pan American Airways' Flying Clippers began making regular stops at St Thomas in the 1930s. The Cyril E King Airport now has extended its runway to more safely accommodate modern jets. Of course, plenty of contemporary passengers may wish they were still landing aboard one of the Lone Eagle's graceful clippers after a brake-screeching, gut-in-the-mouth landing aboard a Boeing 757.

The end of the ride lands you at Honeymoon Bay for a swim and free drinks. Most bikes are Cannondales, and child-size bikes are available. Expect to pay around $50.

For **tennis** lovers, the Bolongo Bay Beach Club (see below) on the south coast has lighted courts that are free to guests. There are also two free courts with lights in Sub Base near Crown Bay Marina.

Places to Stay

Ramsey's Guest House (☎ 340-774-6521), on a residential street off Route 38 on Raphune Hill, is a safe, clean alternative for budget travelers. Leonard Ramsey has 22 rooms in his hillside compound with great views of Charlotte Amalie and the harbor. All rooms have a kitchen as well as air-con, TV and private bath. You can walk to a nearby shopping center from here, although you will pass through a dicey area. Expect to pay $55 to $75 and up for a double.

Mafolie Hotel (☎ 340-774-2790, 800-225-7035), on Mafolie Hill, offers a dramatic vista, the feel of a Danish colonial villa and Lindy's, a popular alfresco restaurant. Each of the 23 rooms has a private bath, air-con and TV. Room furnishings are reminiscent of one of the budget motel chains in the US. Some guests have complained about the cavalier management. Rates start at about $100 for a double.

The ***Island View Guesthouse*** (☎ 340-774-4270, 800-524-2023, 11-C Constant) is about a 10-minute drive west of Charlotte Amalie halfway up the mountainside, just off the Crown Mountain Rd. You will find 16 clean but simple units here, most with private baths. All have balconies overlooking the town and harbor, and catch the trade winds for ventilation (not all rooms have air-con). There is a small pool on the property. Expect to pay about $100 for a double. If you stay here, you will need a car or cab to get you everywhere except the Old Mill, the island's most popular disco (there's also a restaurant here), which is a two-minute walk down the road.

The ***Island Beachcomber Hotel*** (☎ 340-772-5250, 800-982-9898), at Lindbergh Bay, has long been touted (for good reason) as one of the best values for a beachfront stay in the Caribbean. While there is nothing very remarkable about the motel-like structure, and shade trees are few, the rooms are large, brightly furnished and equipped with air-con, TV, fridge, phone and private patio. The beach, restaurant and bar are just steps away from the rooms. With rates that run from $95 to $145, who cares if the departure end of the airport runway is only 300 yards away?

Best Western Carib Beach Hotel (☎ 340-774-2525, 70-C Lindbergh Bay) is another on-the-beach value near the airport. There are 60 oceanfront rooms with all the amenities you associate with this chain. You will also find a pool and a popular pool bar. A lot of travelers say this is a good stop for families with younger kids. Rates run from about $100 to $150.

Marriott's Frenchman's Reef Beach Resort (☎ 340-776-8500, 800-524-2000), 3 miles east of Charlotte Amalie's center on Flamboyant Pt, has more than 400 rooms. This place qualifies as a mega-resort, with three pools, five restaurants and eight bars (including the most popular resort disco on the island). You'll find Jacuzzis, four lit tennis courts, diving instruction and sailing trips offered here. A $58 million renovation recently spruced up this place. Rack rates run from $350 to $500, but the resort almost always has some promotional package to save you money.

Virtually next door, ***Marriott's Morning Star Beach Resort*** (☎ 340-776-8500, 800-524-2000, 5 Estate Bakkeroe) spreads out along the beach. There are 96 rooms in several cross-shaped villas tucked among shady palms. The serenity of this resort is an antidote to the crowds you may experience at the seven-story Frenchman's Reef, as long as you don't mind spending $350 to $450 a night.

The ***Bolongo Bay Beach Club*** (☎ 340-775-1800, 800-524-4746, 7150 Bolongo Bay) has been an attraction for travelers seeking value, resort ambience and a convivial, welcoming atmosphere since 1974. Its key to success is its setting on 1000 feet of crescent beach and the management by the Domeng family. All 75 rooms and 20 villas have ocean views, private patios and 1st-class amenities. On the waterfront is a complete array of water sports, and there are tennis courts, a fitness center and a 53-foot catamaran for daysails and diving trips. You can go cheap here by taking a room in the Bolongo Bayside Inn across the street from the resort for $110, or splurge for an all-inclusive package that runs about $450 a day per couple.

For **rental accommodations**, Mary Coe (☎ 340-774-2024) and Chuck Gidley (☎ 340-774-6043) have cottages and villas on Water Island.

Places to Eat

The **Lunch Box** (☎ 340-774-1739), at Honeymoon Bay beach on Water Island, is Helena Sudak's catering cart, bringing 1st-class alfresco dining to the 'fourth Virgin Island.' Helena is the cook at Betsy's Bar in Frenchtown, but this catering business is her own. She serves dinner on Saturday nights (about $22 for grilled fish and the trimmings) and lunch on Sunday afternoon ($7 and up).

Iggie's Restaurant (☎ 340-775-1800), at the Bolongo Bay Beach Club, is a cut above standard resort eateries. It's in a large open-air pavilion overlooking a broad beach. Most sandwiches, such as the grilled fish in mango chutney, run around $7. Lots of folks come for the open-face meatloaf sandwich, jerked chicken salad or pizza ($12 for a 12-inch pie).

Polli's (☎ 340-775-4550, 4125 Anna's Retreat), on Route 38 inside the Tillett Gardens complex, is one of the island's few Mexican offerings. The food here may remind you of a sunny cafe in Cozumel. Burritos start under $7.

Randy's Wine Bar & Bistro (☎ 340-775-5001, 4002 Raphune Hill), in Al Cohen's Plaza, is probably the most unlikely restaurant on all of St Thomas. You will never find it unless you make the effort. Located mid-island off Route 38, Randy's is a secret hideaway tucked in a building behind a paint store in a small plaza. The attraction is the scent of fresh basil, grilled mushrooms

and the best wine list on the island. Tables in the bistro are spread among crates of wine. You can drink by the glass from the house wine list or bring your own bottle and pay a $5 corkage fee. Sandwiches like the chicken and Brie run about $9. The pan-seared tuna with lentils and rice ($17) is not to be missed.

Sib's Mountain Bar & Restaurant (☎ 340-774-8967), on Mafolie Hill, is a small restaurant at a crossroads with a huge local following. Some folks come to drink and shoot pool (see Entertainment). Others claim you can't get better red snapper anywhere on the island. Expect to pay more than $20 for dinner, but you can get a burger for under $7.

Lindy's (☎ 340-774-8643), in the Mafolie Hotel (see Places to Stay) has alfresco dining. This restaurant has become popular with longtime expatriates, upscale West Indians and travelers for its cool breezes, intimate feel and striking vista of Charlotte Amalie from high on Mafolie Hill. Mary Russ and her chefs specialize in crab and lobster entrees (expect to pay $24 and up) as well as key lime pie.

Entertainment

The **Old Mill** (☎ 340-774-7782), on Crown Mountain Rd, is the island's hottest disco. There are already four separate bars with dance scenes in this place, and it's still expanding. This is definitely a youth scene where hip-hop and the driving West Indian rhythms prevail. Most of the clientele is upscale West Indians or island-born continentals. Everyone arrives dressed to kill and stays until about 4 am. The cover is usually $5.

Bakkeroe's (☎ 340-776-8500), at Marriott's Frenchman's Reef Resort, has live bands covering rock and reggae classics Wednesday to Friday. The clientele is upscale vacationers and lots of honeymooners. The DJ plays top 40 dance rhythms and some techno.

The **Reichhold Center for the Arts** (☎ 340-693-1500), at the University of the Virgin Islands on Brewers Bay, is the island's active concert arena. The outdoor amphitheater has seating for 1200 people. Any list of current artistic events on St

Thomas will include a number of events at the Reichhold Center, including concerts by international celebrity artists like Itzhak Perlman, dance troupes like the Oakland Ballet, and repertory theater groups. In addition, the center hosts a weekly film series. Events generally start at 8 pm.

Market Square East Theaters (☎ 340-776-3656), on Route 38 in Tutu, shows first-run films.

Shopping
The Tutu Park Mall, on Route 38 east of Charlotte Amalie, is the place where most St Thomians do their everyday shopping. The mall includes supermarkets, discount stores, a theater and a Kmart.

RED HOOK & EAST END
The East End has the bulk of the island's major resorts, an extensive collection of restaurants and entertainment options (particularly at Red Hook), the most popular tourist attraction (Coral World), well over a dozen beaches and easy access to neighboring St John. Here, the island has the feel of a vacation destination, rather than a multifaceted West Indian island.

Coral World Marine Park & Underwater Observatory
This 4½-acre marine park (☎ 340-774-1555), at Coki Point near East End, is the most popular tourist attraction on St Thomas. Probably the biggest draw here is the Underwater Observatory, which takes you down to a very active reef 15 feet below the water. Topside, you can visit a shark tank, turtle pool, touch pool, marine gardens and a mangrove lagoon. Kids love feeding the iguanas that run wild. A new attraction at Coral World is a walk on the floor of the Caribbean Sea, called Sea Trekkin'. On this underwater adventure, you wear a helmet as a guide leads you along a trail equipped with a handrail 12 to 30 feet below the crystal-clear water. The unique helmet provides air and allows you to communicate with the guide while keeping your head dry.

Coral World is open 9 am to 5:30 pm daily, but come early because the place can get swamped with cruise ship passengers by 10:30 am. Admission costs $18 for adults and $9 for children three to 12. You can find discount coupons in some of the free tourist guides as well as at hotel and cruise ship concierge desks.

Beaches
Coki Bay This beach is on a protected cove right at the entrance to Coral World Marine Park, near the northeast tip of the island. The snorkeling here is excellent, but the beach has been so highly promoted for so many years that it is usually mobbed with cruise-ship passengers here for a day of sun and fun. Mobile vendors set up in the parking area, adding to the general congestion.

Pineapple Beach A short, broad beach at the head of Water Bay about a half-mile off Route 38, this beach now sports the Renaissance Grand Beach Resort. The adjacent Point Pleasant Resort shares the beach as well. Trade winds often make the water choppy and cloudy, but the beach itself is spacious and manicured, with lots of room for children to play. In fact, the resort has a state-of-the-art children's playground at the south end of the beach. When the wind is calm, the snorkeling along the south shore of the bay is good.

Secret Harbour This west-facing beach in front of the eponymous resort could hardly be more tranquil. It is protected from breezes as well as waves, and the water remains shallow a long way offshore. The resort has a water-sports operation, and this is one of the best places to learn to windsurf. You will find good snorkeling off the rocks here, and the lagoon to the west makes for excellent exploration by kayak.

Bluebeard's Beach You will find this undeveloped beach by following Route 322 from Red Hook past the Ritz-Carlton resort to the bottom of the hill. For years, developers have been trying to put a hotel here, but they haven't succeeded yet. A lot of islanders come here on weekends for family picnics. If you come by car, do not leave anything in your vehicle, as your parking spot will be amid undeveloped jungle.

Vessup Beach To reach this long, broad strand overlooking St John and the BVI, follow a dirt road around the south side of the harbor at Red Hook until you reach Vessup Bay Marina. Park here and walk east. The beach is just 100 yards away. Serious windsurfers love this spot, as do a lot of continentals and travelers who have come to roost around Red Hook. The Latitude 18 bar and restaurant (see Places to Eat) is here at the marina, and one of the best sailboarding operations on the island works off the beach.

Sapphire Beach The Sapphire Beach Resort just off Route 38 is perhaps the most welcoming of all the island's resorts to transient beach visitors. On weekends, you will find a mix of resort guests (lots of families with young children), continentals and West Indians from the island. The beach volleyball games here can get spirited, as can the party scene on Sunday afternoon, when the resort brings in live bands. The beach affords a great view of St John, Jost Van Dyke and Tortola. An offshore reef slows the wave action but presents snorkeling opportunities.

Lindquist Beach This narrow strand along Smith Bay north of Sapphire Beach is probably the largest piece of undeveloped beach property on the island. Dirt roads lead to the beach off Route 38, and on weekends, plenty of West Indian families and groups of teens come here to bathe and party. At other times, the beach can be very lonely. The place has a reputation for attracting bad characters, and people have been raped here. Locals don't usually come to Lindquist without a large group.

Activities

The East End is a prime spot for outdoor activities.

Sailing During the last 25 years, the bulk of the Virgin Islands' bareboat yacht charters

have migrated to the BVI, but St Thomas still has a few charter operations (see the Yacht Charter Basics chapter). Expect to pay $55 a person for a four-hour trip and about $100 for a full-day adventure. The trips generally include a catered lunch, free drinks and snorkel gear.

True Love (☎ 340-779-1640), at Sapphire Beach Marina, is a classic 65-foot schooner. This is the boat on which Bing Crosby and Grace Kelly sang the song 'True Love' in the movie *High Society.* Daysails include seven hours on the water with stops for snorkeling and a picnic. The schooner also offers sunset and moonlight cruises.

Nightwind (☎ 340-775-4110), also at Sapphire Beach Marina, is a powerful 50-foot ketch offering daily trips to St John and the offshore cays.

Fantasy (☎ 340-775-5652), at American Yacht Harbor, is a Pearson 36 that carried President Clinton and his family out for a sail. You could have the same experience.

Windsurfing Most St Thomas resort hotels have windsurfing equipment for beginning and intermediate enthusiasts. The average rental price is $20 an hour. West Indies Windsurfing (☎ 340-775-6530) on Vessup Beach has advanced equipment and instruction.

Diving & Snorkeling St Thomas and neighboring St John feature more than a dozen premier dive sites, and most island resort hotels have a dive service on the property. Aqua Action Dive Center (☎ 340-775-6285) at Secret Harbour Beach Resort and Chris Sawyer Diving Center (☎ 340-775-7320) at American Yacht Harbor are established diving services that charge about $55 for a one-tank dive, $85 for two-tanks.

Captain Nautica (☎ 340-715-3379), at American Yacht Harbor, runs two-hour snorkeling expeditions aboard a 31-foot power raft for about $60. You can also take a 4½-hour trip to snorkel and hike on St John for $70.

Nauti Nymph Power Boat Rentals (☎ 340-775-5066), at American Yacht Harbor, rents 25-foot speedboats with snorkel gear for $175 a day and up.

Sea & Ski Power Boat Rentals (☎ 340-775-6265), at American Yacht Harbor, has similar boats and rates.

Virgin Islands Ecotours (☎ 240-779-2155), Route 32 at Holmberg's Marina on the East End, offers a 2½-hour guided kayak tour and snorkeling expedition. The trip takes you through a mangrove lagoon to a coral rubble beach for snorkeling. Rates run about $50.

Fishing The *Marlin Prince* (☎ 340-779-5939), at American Yacht Harbor, is Captain John Prince's 45-foot sportfisherman. The boat and crew consistently place among the top spots in local tournaments for marlin, tuna, wahoo and mahi mahi. In 1999, this boat began offering saltwater fly-fishing for marlin.

Prowler (☎ 340-779-2515), at American Yacht Harbor, is another tournament-winning boat. Captain Bill McCauley has been named Captain of the Year numerous times by the Billfishing Foundation.

Captain Al Petrosky's *Fish Hawk* (☎ 340-775-9058), at the East End Lagoon, is another tournament winner.

You can expect to pay about $400 for a half-day on any of these boats, around $700 for a full day.

Tennis Most of the island's large resort hotels have tennis facilities, and nonguests generally pay $10 an hour for the court fee. The Wyndham Sugar Bay Resort (☎ 340-777-7100) has a stadium court and lit Laykold courts.

Places to Stay

Prices listed are based on high-season occupancy unless otherwise noted.

Pavilions and Pools (☎ 340-775-6110, 6400 Estate Smith Bay), on Route 38, has a fresh concept. Set on a hill, this small hotel has a collection of 25 suites, each with its own pool, deck and vista of St John and the BVI. Suites have full kitchens, sliding doors that open from your bedroom right to your own pool. You can spend days here and never put on a stitch of clothing. When you come out, expect the staff to treat you like an old friend. Rates start at $180 and go to about $275.

Point Pleasant Resort (☎ 340-775-7200, 800-777-1700), on a steep hill overlooking Water Bay, started as a family-run property in the 1970s and was the first truly eco-sensitive resort on St Thomas. Thirty years later, this property still has a lot of charm. It spaces 95 suites in multiunit cottages throughout the hillside forest, which looks out toward St John and the BVI. Each unit has a full kitchen, separate bedroom, large porch and all the 1st-class amenities. The resort also has walking trails, several pools set at different levels and a beach. An added attraction is one of the island's most chic restaurants, the Agavé Terrace (see Places to Eat, later). Rates run from about $275 to $450.

The *Renaissance Grand Beach Resort* (☎ 340-775-1510, 800-421-8188), on Smith Bay Rd/Route 38, is Marriott's newest resort on the island. It has the squeaky-clean, manicured appearance that travelers have come to associate with this chain. There are 290 rooms here, many in high-rise units overlooking Water Bay and Pineapple Beach, but there are some rooms in villa settings around pools and close to the beach. In addition to offering a full selection of activities and water sports, this resort has a superb playground for children virtually at beach side. Expect to pay around $280 for a room.

Sapphire Beach Resort & Marina (☎ *340-775-6100, 800-524-2090*), on Smith Bay Rd/Route 38 close to Red Hook, is another attractive option for families with children. This is a place where you and your children can make friends with other parents and kids. Sapphire Beach itself is more than half a mile long. There is also a two-tier pool with waterfalls and a poolside restaurant that will prepare meals to go. Rooms are studio-style suites with all the amenities; there are about 170 separate guest quarters in a collection of large multi-story buildings facing the beach and the resort's marina. Rates start at about $300.

The *Wyndham Sugar Bay Resort* (☎ *340-777-7100, 800-996-3426*), at Smith Bay, is the island's newest and only truly all-inclusive resort. This high-rise hotel perches dramatically on a point of rock above a small sheltered beach, with 300 rooms, three interconnecting pools, a fitness center, tennis courts, water sports and a Kids Club program. All rooms have 1st-class amenities. Expect to pay about $350 a day per couple for the whole enchilada, including killer drinks.

The *Ritz-Carlton* (☎ *340-775-3333, 800-241-3333*), at Great Bay, is without a doubt the most chic resort on St Thomas. The 15-acre property with 152 guest quarters exudes European ambience with frescoed walls, imported pink marble and the continental accents of its concierge and front-desk staff. Accommodations are in multiunit villas peppered around the property and surrounded by extensive tropical gardens. The pools and sundecks are expansive, and the beach is broad and uncrowded. Rates start at about $450.

For *rental accommodations*, Red Hook Mountain Apartments (☎ *340-775-6669, 800-619-0005*) can sometimes come up with East End studios for around $100 a night. Caribbean Style Ocean Front Condos (☎ *340-715-1117, 800-593-1390*) has seaside, one-bedroom condos for $115 and up.

Places to Eat

The commercial center of Red Hook is all of about two blocks long. But during the 1990s, this area developed the highest concentration of restaurants on St Thomas. Almost all are geared to continentals – those roosting in East End resorts, condos or villas, and those who have come to work on the island. Few West Indians frequent these establishments.

The *Greatful Deli & Coffee Shop* (☎ *340-775-5160, 6500 Red Hook Plaza*), across from the ferry dock, can't be beat for breakfast or a sandwich. The male waitstaff are bearded, tattooed pirate-looking guys who are full of cheer and like to call customers 'amigo.' The place is redolent with the scent of 10 varieties of fresh-roasted coffee and grilled veggies, and the click of fingers on computers (four keyboards, $2 for 15 minutes online) as well as the sound of classic rockers like Neil Young. You can do breakfast for under $4. Sandwiches run about $7 and are huge: Try Fire on the Mountain with smoked turkey, pepper jack and avocado.

Wok & Roll (☎ *340-775-6246, 6200 Smith Bay*) is stuffed between Red Hook Plaza and the Marina Market and offers dine-in and takeout Cantonese and Szechuan food. These guys will deliver as well. The prices are very reasonable, with chicken and pork entrees running about $7. You can get chicken wings for under $4.

Señor Pizza (☎ *340-775-3030*), across from the ferry dock, can get very busy with takeout orders in the evening, when a lot of vacationers in East End condos decide they don't feel like cooking. Expect to pay $9 for a medium pie.

Duffy's Love Shack (☎ *340-779-2080, 650 Red Hook Plaza*), is without a doubt a legendary stopping place for travelers visiting the East End. This pub really is just a frame shack over a small bar in the middle of a paved mini-mall parking lot. But Duffy's creates its own atmosphere with high-volume rock & roll and crowds of attractive hard bodies in shorts and tank tops. The food is classic pub fare. Consider the Bahamian conch fritters or Pacific Rim skewers (satay) for under $6. The big attraction here is people-watching and the killer drinks, such as the 64oz 'shark tank.' After dark, particularly on Friday, Duffy's turns into the biggest frat party on the island (see Entertainment).

Molly Malone's (☎ *340-775-1270)*, on the lower level of the American Yacht Harbor commercial complex, makes a good waterfront stop for the family. Like all of the other venues in the complex, Molly's is a re-creation of a bygone era, in this case an Irish pub. The music is traditional Celtic riffs mixed with classic acoustical numbers. You can get a full American breakfast here for $4, a Caesar salad with grilled scallops for $12 and Danish babyback ribs for $17.

The ***Caribbean Steakhouse & Saloon*** (☎ *340-775-7060)*, in the American Yacht Harbor complex, is another major player in Red Hook's pub-and-grub scene. This second-story venue is a contemporary rendering of a classic beer garden. The prices match the upscale re-creation with a mere basket of fries running $4. A bowl of chili ($5.50) is perhaps the best value on the menu. Dinner entrees like the New York strip run about $20. Like its rival saloons up and down the street, this place can rock with a young crowd on winter nights.

XO Bar & Bistro (☎ *340-779-2069)*, in the Red Hook Plaza, is a great 'date' restaurant. This narrow little hideaway has only six tables and the most exclusive, romantic feel of any Red Hook eatery. Patrons come dressed in cocktail dresses and long slacks to sample the hot artichoke dip for $7 or entrees like the capellini pomodoro (angel hair pasta with garlic, basil, mushroom and tomatoes) for $11. The staff serves until midnight or later, when the bistro bar starts to hum (see Entertainment).

Latitude 18 (☎ *340-779-2495)*, down a dirt road around the south side of Vessup Bay, is Red Hook's funkiest bar and restaurant. The place is a patio protected by a roof of old sails and blue tarps that blow away in every hurricane. The decoration is a mix of marine flotsam, a huge plastic shark, Christmas lights and a pirate flag. Most of the clientele are world-cruiser types who come in off their boats and local continentals who are – or dream of being – seafaring ramblers. Locals rave about the inexpensive delicacies such as marinated lamb, quail and poached talapia in plum wine with crispy ginger (all under $15) coming from Alex Bar-Sela's little kitchen. Several nights a week, Alex brings in live entertainment and the local buckos get a little fired up (see the Entertainment section).

You get a gourmet dinner experience at ***Café Wahoo*** (☎ *340-775-6350, 6300 Estate Smith Bay)*, next to the ferry dock. This restaurant with its sushi and Euro-Caribe fusion cooking attracts a huge following, and you should definitely make reservations during the busy winter season. The setting is a large deck looking out on the yacht harbor. Imaginative appetizers like the tuna carpaccio run between $7 and $11. The Caribbean bouillabaisse with shrimp, scallops, local fish and green-tipped mussels in lobster bisque is not to be missed.

Amid Christmas lights and guitar music at La Vida Marine on Route 32 in Nazareth, ***Ernie's Bar & Grille*** (☎ *340-775-7716)* is nothing but a roofed patio on the edge of the marina's boatslips, but it has developed a loyal following since it opened in 1999. Cheap eats, cheap beer and welcoming conversation are the attractions here for boat folk and young continentals working on the island. The place can attract quite a pub crowd (see Entertainment). Try the French dip for $6.

Julie Peterson's ***Blue Moon Cafe*** (☎ *340-779-2262)*, at the Secret Harbour Beach Resort at the southeast end of the island, gets rave reviews from locals and travelers. This is not your average hotel restaurant. The attraction is the casual elegance of the waterfront setting overlooking the harbor and the care that goes into preparing dishes like veggie Napoleon (grilled vegetables on angel hair pasta with basil vinaigrette) for under $14. Fish, duck and pork entrees start at about $20. There is an extensive wine list with some decent grapes for under $25.

Hemingway's (☎ *340-777-1609)*, at the Compass Point Marina off Route 32, opened in 1999 to offer yachties and East End condo renters first-rate dinners at a moderate price. Entrees like the blackened mahimahi served with mango salsa run about $15.

Raffles (☎ 340-775-6004), next door to Hemingway's, has been around for years. This establishment advertises itself as a 'restaurant for pampered people' and charges prices to match. An entree like lemon sole stuffed with salmon, capers and onions runs $25. The hostess, who claimed to be Australian, never heard of Lonely Planet. Different strokes for different folks.

Off Route 38, **Romano's Restaurant** (☎ 340-775-0045, 97 Smith Bay Rd) gets many St Thomians' votes for the best Italian cuisine on the island. The setting is dark, without a view and rich with candlelight and violin music. Pasta dishes like the linguini con pesto start at about $17. Veal and seafood dishes cost about $26.

Greg Miller's **Agavé Terrace & Bar** (☎ 340-775-4142, 6600 Estate Smith Bay), at the Point Pleasant Resort, is one of the island's most respected restaurants. The deck here hangs out in thin air over a steep slope, giving diners a breathtaking view of St John and the BVI. This is a place to be dressed up. Expect candlelight, linen, crystal and professional waitstaff. Entrees like the stuffed lobster can cost $35 or more, but the black bean soup for $6 is a meal for light eaters. Make reservations early for weekend dining.

Entertainment

All of the following are also listed under Places to Eat, above.

Ernie's Bar & Grille is a little open-air pavilion with the feel of a local bar where everybody knows everybody. Happy hour starts at 3 pm and folks get fired up on $1 Coors. This is a good place to network for a job and meet some of the party animals you missed at Betsy's. There is live acoustical music from the likes of island legend Mighty Whitey on Saturday and Sunday evenings. He plays calypso, reggae and country.

Duffy's Love Shack rules! Almost every night of the week is a party scene here, but the crowd overflows into the parking lot on Ladies Night (Wednesday) and Friday. Saturday features themes like Bathrobe Night. On Tuesday and Thursday, Kevin, Patrick, Rabbit and Nitro work the bar and apply free tattoos (thighs and chests only) to willing damsels. Driving rock & roll (Sheryl Crow's the queen) fuels this crowd of under-30 continentals and travelers who pursue the rites of spring with bottomless gusto.

Latitude 18 is a down-and-dirty sailors' bar. Owner Alex Bar-Sela took over this gin mill in 2000, and life here under the blue tarp he calls a roof is 'chill.' You will usually find live music on Tuesday, Thursday, Friday and Saturday, when island legends like Mighty Whitey, Dick Solberg (also called the Fiddler) and the Sun Mountain Band show up to play acoustic, rock, bluegrass, country and folk. Open-mike nights with Mighty Whitey are a hoot. And so is the crowd. Just picture every character you have ever heard about in a Jimmy Buffett ballad.

XO Bar & Bistro gets going on weekends, when middle-aged continentals out for a night on the town stop in for cigars and martinis against a background of progressive jazz CDs. The crowd gets younger after about midnight, when you find owners, managers and employees from other local businesses drifting in to stir up the party.

Shopping

Since the development of the American Yacht Harbor complex, Red Hook has become the favorite shopping area for East Enders. This compound of multistory buildings is home to upscale shops and restaurants, and there are more shops across the street in the Red Hook Shopping Center. You can park for a fee in a protected lot at American Yacht Harbor or for free at the shopping center.

The Kilnworks (☎ 340-775-3979), on Route 38 at Smith Bay, is where you can pick up the imaginative pottery of Peggy Seiwart, which often features distinctive images of island lizards.

ST THOMAS

NORTH & WEST ISLAND

The north and west sides of St Thomas are the quieter sections of the island. In these areas, steep-sloped mountains rise almost from the water's edge. Large coves such as Magens Bay have exquisite, secluded beaches at their heads. Largely residential, the north shore and West End feature a mix of undeveloped forests and fields with middle- and upper-class villas perched on the mountainsides. Except for villa rentals, accommodations for travelers are nonexistent here. Restaurants and entertainment venues are rare and attract a lot more islanders than travelers.

Beaches

Magens Bay The mile of sand that fringes deeply cupped Magens Bay 3 miles north of Charlotte Amalie makes almost every travel publication's list of beautiful beaches. The seas here are calm, the bay is broad and the vista of the surrounding green hills is dramatic.

The beach and much of the surrounding land is protected as a territorial park. In a sense, Magens Bay is *the* public beach for St Thomas. It has picnic tables and changing facilities, as well as food vendors and a water-sports operation. On weekends, when the locals come to party, and on days when the cruise ships bus in loads of folks, you'll find a whole lot of people here. But the beach is so long that you may not feel claustrophobic. If you do, head for the west end, which is always sparsely populated.

The beach is open 6 am to 6 pm. Admission is $1 per car and $1 per person. No regularly scheduled public transportation stops here, and surprisingly, gypsy cabs are rare except on weekends.

Little Magens Bay This is the only nude beach on the island, and it is beautiful. But beware: The beach is on private property, and it has developed a reputation for rampant theft. To get here, take the dirt road that leads off Magens Rd to the right about a quarter-mile before the entrance to the beach at Magens Bay. Follow the dirt road for a couple hundred yards until you see rocks and a cliff to your left and a trail that leads down a steep embankment to the beach. Every year, the police get reports of robbed and vandalized rental cars here. Some thieves have actually descended to the beach to steal nude bathers' clothes and valuables while they are in the water.

Hull Bay Lying to the west around Tropaco Point from Magens Bay, Hull Bay is the island's most popular surfing beach and usually a gem of solitude when Magens Bay is overrun with cruise ship passengers and local families on picnics. This strand lies at the base of a steep valley and features excellent shade along its entire length.

There is a boat ramp here, which the 'Frenchie' fisherfolk use, as well as Larry's Hideaway & Bar (see Places to Eat). The surf is at its best during the winter, when the swells roll in out of the northeast and you get a 4-foot point break. On days when the surf is up, Hull Bay can be a major surf scene with youth from all over the island

---

The Hull Bay Find

Excavations at Hull Bay have turned up a significant Indian settlement on the shores there, this one a Taíno community predating the arrival of the Caribs. Archaeologists might have expected such a find, given what we already know about the Indian patterns for settlement in the Antilles, but the scientists were not prepared for the two skeletons they unearthed in 1974 at Hull Bay.

Testing by the Smithsonian Institution proved that these were African skeletons. One of the skeletons had chipped teeth, as was the custom in many parts of West Africa. The other skeleton was found among what appeared to be Indian pottery. These skeletons, known as the 'Hull Bay Find,' have touched off waves of disagreement between experts as to whether these skeletons (along with petroglyphs on St John) are evidence that African explorers visited the Virgins before Christopher Columbus.

abandoning jobs and schools to catch a wave. Locals complain about a lot of drug use and trafficking here after dark.

Hans-Lollik You can see 500-acre Hans-Lollik Island 2 miles north of Magens Bay and Hull Bay. For years developers have been trying to get approval for a luxury resort and condos on the island, but so far no one has given out building permits. Water taxis run here from Hull Bay and (sometimes) Magens Bay. The beach on the western side of the island is pristine and rife with shade trees. Expect to pay $6 or more per person roundtrip; give your money to the water-taxi captain.

Stumpy Bay If solitude is what you are seeking, head for Stumpy Bay near the northwest end of St Thomas. Look for the dirt road that leads off Route 30 and down a steep hill. The road ends after a half-mile, and beachgoers must park their cars here and then walk another half-mile down a trail to the beach. The beach features shade trees, brown sand and calm water within the arms of this northwest-facing bay. Some people risk nudism here, but they are a definite minority. As at Little Magens Bay, the car park at Stumpy Bay is wide open to vandals and thieves.

Activities
Mahogany Run Golf Course (☎ 340-777-6006), east of Magens Bay, is your only option for **golf**. But what an option it is. This 18-hole championship course owes its design to George and Tom Fazio and features the famous 'Devil's Triangle' seaside holes. Greens fees are $85, $70 after 2 pm. Carts run $15 per person. Club rentals cost about $20.

For **horseback riding**, Half Moon Stables (☎ 340-777-6088) offers a trail ride with vistas of Magens Bay and the BVI and a descent to a quiet beach. You can ride English or western saddles, but you cannot mount a horse if you weigh more than 180lbs. Expect to pay at least $45 an hour.

Places to Eat
Ferrari's (☎ *340-774-6800, 33 Crown Mountain Rd*) now has one of the island's legendary chefs, Pat La Court, presiding over the grill, so it's worth the trek over winding West End roads to taste her veal marsala. Most entrees run more than $20.

Larry's Hideaway & Bar (☎ *340-777-1898*), next to the entrance to the beach at Hull Bay, looks like a cross between a campground and a Mexican cantina. The chicken legs here cost $3, and you can carry your grub to the beach.

St John

St John has gained a reputation over the centuries as the 'wild virgin,' and today the island lives up to its reputation in more ways than one. This mountainous island lies less than 3 miles east of St Thomas, but the contrast between the two isles could not be more distinct. Whereas St Thomas is dotted with homes and businesses, St John is largely wilderness: Almost three-quarters of the island's 20 sq miles of land fall within the borders of the Virgin Islands National Park. While commuters cause traffic jams on St Thomas, feral burros stop Jeep traffic on the byways of St John. While about 60,000 citizens call St Thomas home, fewer than 4000 people live on St John. And while almost every beach on St Thomas has a luxury resort, many beaches on St John don't even have a parking lot.

The large tracts of wilderness, the interface of water with mountains and the sense of escape are the big attractions here. The fringe of St John has more than 35 harbors and coves, each with its own beach and coral garden. The interior of the island features steep slopes that rise from the sea to St John's backbone and 1277-foot Bordeaux Mountain. More than 20 miles of trails snake over the terrain, leading hikers from mountain vistas to the ruins of sugar plantations and vacant beaches. Besides snorkeling and hiking, St John offers scuba trips, sea kayak adventures and trail rides by bike, horse and burro. You will find an abundance of camping opportunities on St John, from sleeping under the stars at Cinnamon Bay to living like the Swiss Family Robinson in the luxury tents at Maho Bay or Estate Concordia.

Upscale travelers find privacy in mountainside villas and condos as well as three resort hotels, including Caneel Bay – the place that has made St John a chic destination for almost 50 years. Gentrification has changed other things as well. As recently as the 1970s, the population of St John was largely West Indian. Now St John is the 'whitest' of all the major Virgin Islands. Easily half of St John's residents are continentals. Many young statesiders have moved here to work in construction, retail, restaurants, accommodations, entertainment and water sports. In addition, both the east and west ends of the island have communities of older snowbirds who nest in their island villas each winter.

The other big change on the island is Cruz Bay, St John's only town. Thirty years

Highlights

- Swimming & snorkeling with ghosts at the secluded Jumbie Bay beach
- Hiking the Reef Bay trail past ancient petroglyphs
- Camping at Cinnamon Bay, Maho Bay or Estate Concordia
- Exploring the Annaberg Sugar Mill Ruins
- Grazing the restaurants & bars of Cruz Bay

ago, it was a dusty customs port where almost nothing moved in the midday sun. Now it is a hip collection of boutiques, restaurants and pubs. The new Virgin Islands National Park Visitors Center is here. Streets fill with day-trippers from St Thomas (and the cruise ships), arriving on six or so different ferries. If you have ever been to New England's Martha's Vineyard in the height of tourist season, you can picture Cruz Bay. At some point during the town's evolution, folks began calling it 'Love City.' The nickname came as an attempt to sum up the New Age aura of freedom, independence and upscale chic that now surrounds St John. But the nickname might allude to the nightlife in Cruz Bay as well. During the winter high season, the pubs and clubs of Cruz Bay pulse with the frenzy of Spain's Ibiza.

History

Scholars differ as to the date of earliest settlements on St John. Indians may have been on St John as early as 770 BC. But the evidence coming from the National Park Service's Ken Wild and his nearly two decades of excavation only offer conclusive proof of Taíno occupation of the island dating back about 500 years. (See Cinnamon Bay Archaeological Dig, later.)

Columbus did not stop at St John in 1493 on his sail along the south coast of the island. However, most scholars credit him with naming St John (San Juan) and putting the island on the map for Spanish adventurers, whose slave raids drove the Indians off the island by the 1650s. Few but itinerant pirates visited St John until 1684. In that year, merchants from Barbados attempted to set up a colony on St John, but the English drove them away. In 1687, the Danish West India and Guinea Company laid claim to St John, and in 1688, the Danish governor of St Thomas received instructions from his company to send four to six men to St John to begin cane plantations.

No Danes actually arrived on the island because British colonists from Tortola had a logging operation on St John and repelled any Danes who approached the island. In 1717, the Danish governor of St Thomas, Erick Bridel, sailed to St John from St Thomas on an armed vessel with 20 planters, 16 black slaves and five soldiers. They landed at Coral Bay, planted a flag, feasted, divided up the land into plantations and selected the site for the building of Fort Berg on the crest of a hilly peninsula. Fearing retaliation by the English from Tortola, the planters left, but the soldiers and slaves dutifully remained and began construction of the fort.

The British governor of the Leeward Islands dispatched a man-of-war to St Thomas to intimidate the Danes and force them to give up their claims on St John, but the Danish governor deflected the English by casting blame on his superiors. And while the British were ruminating over their options, the Danish governor secured 100 armed reinforcements from Denmark to stand guard on St John.

With this move, the Danes kept the English away from St John for the next 180 years, and the Danish West India and Guinea Company quickly set about selling plantations on St John. By 1720, 39 planters had deeds to St John. Northern Europeans and settlers from a score of countries applied for grants, and by 1733, St John had 109 plantations. There were 208 whites (planters and their families) and 1087 black slaves on the island at that time.

When planters arrived, they found that the soil was richer here than on St Thomas, and for a few years the colony prospered. But in 1733, the plantations suffered a drought, a severe hurricane and a plague of mosquitoes. These natural disasters plunged the inhabitants of St John into virtual survival conditions. The slaves suffered greatly, and the new Danish governor, Philip Gardelin, compounded their misery by issuing a manifesto of draconian punishments to be leveled on runaway slaves. Slaves fleeing or plotting to flee a plantation on Danish soil could be punished with hanging, 150 lashes or the chopping off of an ear or leg. With little food and water, hideous living conditions and huge deterrents against escape, some of the slaves felt

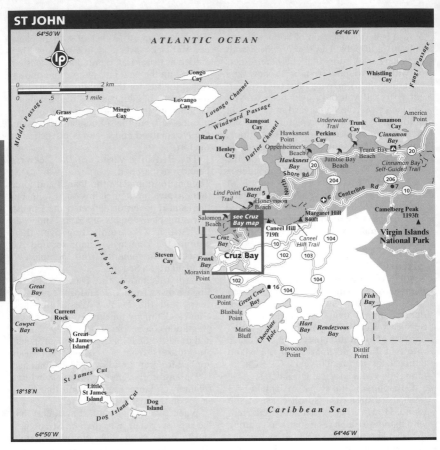

ST JOHN

that survival for them and their families meant revolution. The uprising that began in November 1733 brought murder and destruction to the families of St John's white planters for six months.

In spite of the devastation caused by the slave revolt and natural disasters, all 109 plantations were up and running again by 1739, and St John's population regenerated to more than 200 whites and 1400 slaves. The island's cane and cotton plantations began to mature, and St John gained a patina of civilization. The Moravian Mission built its first church at Coral Bay in the late 1750s. In 1760, the settlement at Cruz Bay became an official town, and a ferry began service between St Thomas and Cruz Bay.

When Britain claimed the Danish West Indies from 1801 to 1802 and again from 1807 to 1815 as spoils from the Napoleonic Wars, little changed on St John except the color of the uniforms of soldiers posted at Fort Berg. Economic conditions on the plantations worsened after the emancipation of slaves in 1848. When the US took possession of St John in 1917, the island's plantations had been abandoned, the island depopulated, and the landscape turned wild

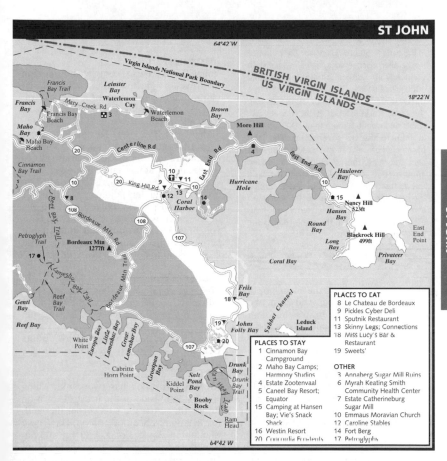

ST JOHN

PLACES TO EAT
8 Le Chateau de Bordeaux
9 Pickles Cyber Deli
11 Sputnik Restaurant
13 Skinny Legs; Connections
18 Miss Lucy's Bar & Restaurant
19 Sweets'

PLACES TO STAY
1 Cinnamon Bay Campground
2 Maho Bay Camps; Harmony Studios
4 Estate Zootenvaal
5 Caneel Bay Resort; Equator
15 Camping at Hansen Bay; Vie's Snack Shack
16 Westin Resort
20 Concordia Ecotents

OTHER
3 Annaberg Sugar Mill Ruins
6 Myrah Keating Smith Community Health Center
7 Estate Catherineburg Sugar Mill
10 Emmaus Moravian Church
12 Caroline Stables
14 Fort Berg
17 Petroglyphs

again. The last operating sugar mill, at Reef Bay, closed in 1918.

The last 40 years on St John have been the story of the island's development as an ecotourism attraction, a sanctuary for free thinkers and a vacation retreat for the upper-middle class. Historic St John with its poverty and racism are gone. Few people are grieving the loss.

Orientation

At 9 miles long and 5 miles wide, St John rises above the surrounding sea like a peaked green cap. All but the extreme east and west ends of the island lies within the borders of the national park and will remain forever wild. Cruz Bay at the West End is St John's port of entry, with constant ferry traffic and most of the island's shops, restaurants and pubs.

The settlement of Coral Bay at the East End is the sleepy domain of folks who want to feel like they're living on a frontier. Centerline Rd (Route 10) scales the island's heights and proceeds east-west along the mountain ridges to connect St John's two communities. The North Shore Rd (Route 20) snakes along the north coast

Becoming an Island Park

In the early 1950s, the US millionaire Laurence Rockefeller discovered and fell in love with the nearly abandoned St John (fewer than a 1000 citizens) and began purchasing large tracts of island land. Shortly after acquiring the land, Rockefeller built the Caneel Bay resort and donated more than 5000 acres of St John to the US government. The land became an official national park in 1956, and over the years the government has added another 4000 acres of island land to the park. In addition, the Park Service has extended the park borders to include 5650 underwater acres surrounding St John. Twenty-four-hour electrical service came the same year as the park, and paved roads followed.

and connects many of the most popular beaches, bays and campgrounds. A network of 22 hiking trails penetrates the island's wilderness. The wildest and least accessible areas of St John lie along the south shore and the extreme east end of the island.

The St Thomas/St John Chamber of Commerce (☎ 340-776-0100) and the Virgin Islands Department of Tourism's Visitors Bureau (☎ 340-774-8784), as well as some St John merchants, publish free maps for visitors. You can pick up maps at displays in most inns and many restaurants on the island as well as at the visitors center. The best of the maps for Cruz Bay is a cartoon-like map published by St John Guidebook.

A four-color map published by the National Park Service gives you excellent detail of the island and the national park and marks coral reefs for snorkeling. Pick up one at the park's visitors center (see below). The Park Service also publishes a trail guide.

International Travel Maps (☎ 604-879-3621) of Vancouver, British Columbia, has a map to the US and British Virgin Islands published on heavy paper. This map, which is widely available for $8 through Rand McNally bookstores, offers excellent detail of topographical contours and hiking trails.

Information

You will find the most complete information for travelers – including notebooks of restaurant menus and outdoor activity operators – in the concierge hut at the entrance to the Gallows Point Resort (see Places to Stay under Cruz Bay, later). To find out about current events on the island, go to the bulletin board in front of Connections (Prince St at King St), at the center of town.

US Customs & Immigration (☎ 340-776-6741) is in a building adjoining the wharf for ferries serving the BVI. If you arrive on one of these ferries or on a yacht from the BVI, you must clear customs and immigration here before proceeding into town. The office is open 8 am to noon and 1 to 5 pm daily.

Tourist Offices The visitors center (☎ 340-776-6450) is a small building next to the post office, across the street from the BVI ferry dock, in Cruz Bay. It's open 9 am to 5 pm daily.

The Virgin Islands National Park Visitors Center (☎ 340-776-6201) is on the north side of the harbor in Cruz Bay.

Money Cruz Bay has two banks, which stand side by side in the heart of town on Prince St, across the street from the landmark Woody's Seafood Saloon. The Chase Manhattan Bank is open 8:30 am to 3 pm weekdays for check cashing. The Bank of Nova Scotia keeps the same hours and has an outdoor ATM.

Post & Communications The post office on St John (☎ 340-779-4227) is directly across the street from the passenger ferry dock in Cruz Bay. It is open 7 am to 6 pm weekdays, 7 am to 5 pm Saturday and 11 am to 3 pm Sunday.

For phone calls, email and surface-mail forwarding, many travelers use Connections (☎ 340-776-6922 in Cruz Bay, ☎ 340-779-4994 in Coral Bay, connectvi@att.net). The Cruz Bay office is on the corner of Prince and King Sts. The Coral Bay office is in the small complex of shops surrounding Skinny Legs restaurant (see Coral Bay & South Island, later).

The Quiet Mon Pub in Cruz Bay and Pickles Cyber Deli in Coral Bay also have Internet access.

Bookstores & Libraries It is hard to believe that St John cannot support a bookstore, but this is an ugly fact. However, all the resorts, guesthouses and camping areas have shelves of used paperbacks. Bibliophiles take the ferry to Red Hook and shop at Hemingway's Book Shop (see the St Thomas chapter).

The Elaine Ione Sprauve Library (☎ 340-776-6359) is across from Marina Market on Route 104 just south of Cruz Bay center.

Newspapers Tom Oat puts together the weekly *Tradewinds* (☎ 340-776-6496). Make sure to pick up a copy to catch the latest news about island restaurants and entertainment as well as to get the inside scoop on current island controversies like development plans for the East End. The paper is also available online at http://stjohntradewindsnews.com, where you can arrange villa rentals.

Laundry Santos Laundromat (☎ 340-693-7733) is conveniently located on Route 104 next-door to the Marina Market in Cruz Bay and is open 7 am to 9 pm weekdays, 6 am to 10 pm Saturday. Wash loads cost under $2.

Medical Services & Emergencies The Myrah Keating Smith Community Health Center (☎ 340-693-8900), about 2 miles east of Cruz Bay on Centerline Rd, is the place to come for routine medical attention.

St John Drug Center (☎ 340-693-9093), across from the Texaco station in Cruz Bay, is open seven days a week.

There is an EMT station equipped to handle medical emergencies across from the ferry dock in Cruz Bay: Walk in or call ☎ 911. The same telephone number works for the fire department as well as the police station.

Dangers & Annoyances St John is largely crime-free. With just 4000 permanent residents on this island, and very few people living in desperate circumstances, street crime is not a big problem. This does not mean travelers should leave valuables exposed in cars or tents, keep hotel rooms unlocked or walk the streets of Cruz Bay drunk or alone in the wee hours. Thefts and muggings occasionally occur.

The feral burros and goats that wander onto the island's roads are a particular hazard to motorists (see the boxed text 'Wild Kingdom'). Drive with extreme caution.

Organized Tours
Now that St John attracts a lot of day-trippers from St Thomas and the cruise ships, the street and parking lot in front of the ferry dock at Cruz Bay swarm with cabs offering island tours. These cabs look like the gypsy cabs you see on St Thomas; they are large pickup trucks with bench seats in the bed and a sun awning. A two-hour circuit of the island, which takes you east on the North Shore Rd and brings you back west across the mountaintops on Centerline Rd, costs about $30 for one or two passengers. You pay $12 per person when three or more take the tour.

Limnos Charters (see Organized Tours in the St Thomas chapter) offers snorkeling trips around St John and to the BVI from the Westin Resort aboard its 53-foot power catamarans. Rates run $55 and up.

Special Events
The one big event on the island is St John's Carnival, which begins around July 1 and climaxes on July 4 or 5. The event aims to celebrate Emancipation Day (July 3) and the US Independence Day (July 4). Except for the costumes and floats that may depict elements and characters from these two historical events, the celebration has more to do with African-Caribbean celebrations of the spring equinox (never mind that it was

in March) and Easter. Basically, you get a smaller version of the St Thomas Carnival with mocko jumbies, steel pan bands, parades and musical competitions.

Wild Kingdom

Whether you are camping, hiking or driving on St John, it will not be long before you have a close encounter with one or more of the island's troublesome population of feral animals. According to rough estimates from the National Park Service, 300 burros, 500 goats, 200 pigs and hundreds of cats are the descendants of animals abandoned in the island jungle. North American white-tailed deer (about 300) and mongoose are two other exotic species that were imported to the island and now have successful breeding colonies.

Park rangers are most concerned with the goats and pigs, whose foraging wipes out underbrush and leaves hillsides prone to erosion. Their droppings also upset the balance of flora on the island by introducing seeds of exotic plants to pristine wilderness areas. Many of the colonies of burros and cats have grown adept at raiding garbage cans and food supplies in the camping areas, and the donkeys that often congregate and meander on island roads pose a serious hazard to drivers. Each year sees more dead burros and wrecked vehicles on island roads.

The population of feral animals on St John has grown so large that Park Service rangers are now exploring a number of management techniques, including relocation, limited hunting and sterilization. Do not tempt these animals by offering them food or leaving food or garbage where they can get at it. And do not approach them for petting or taking a snapshot. They may look harmless, but the current population is the result of decades, or in some cases centuries, of free-range breeding. The animals are all capable of aggression.

Getting There & Away
Passenger ferries between Charlotte Amalie and Cruz Bay run about every two hours and cost about $7 one way. Ferries run almost every hour between Red Hook and Cruz Bay, costing about $3 one way. Car ferries from Red Hook to Cruz Bay run hourly and cost $25 one way (see 'Interisland Ferries' in the Getting Around chapter).

Getting Around
Bus VITRAN (☎ 340-774-5678) operates air-conditioned buses over the length of the island via Centerline Rd. Buses leave Cruz Bay in front of the ferry terminal at 6 am and 7 am, then every hour at 25 minutes after the hour until 9:25 pm. The buses run to the clinic, Coral Bay and Salt Pond Bay, where they turn around and head back to town. The first westbound bus leaves Salt Pond Bay at 5 am, Coral Bay at 5:15 am. The fare for people under 55 is $1 for all or part of the ride. You must have exact change!

Car St John has a handful of car rental agencies. All have outlets in Cruz Bay. Rates generally run $45 and up per day. Vendors uniformly rent Jeeps, wannabe Jeeps and SUVs to handle the island's rugged terrain. Also see the boxed text 'Wild Kingdom.'

Try the following agencies: C & C Jeep Rentals & Taxi Service (☎ 340-693-8169), Hertz (☎ 800-654-3131), Hospitality Car & Jeep Rental (☎ 340-693-9160), O'Connor Car Rental (☎ 340-776-6343) or St John Car Rental (☎ 340-776-6103).

Taxi Territorial law sets the taxi rates on St John just as it does on St Thomas. Some taxis are passenger vans that carry 8 to 10 passengers. Many are open-air affairs like the St Thomas gypsy cabs. Taxi rates are reckoned on a per-person basis. Grab a cab at the waterfront in Cruz Bay or call the St John Taxi Association (☎ 340-693-7530) for a pick-up.

Following are current per-person rates to some of the island's most popular destinations from Cruz Bay.

destination	cost
Annaberg Sugar Mill Ruins	$10
Caneel Bay	$2.50
Cinnamon Bay	$5.50
Coral Bay	$10
Reef Bay trail	$6
Trunk Bay	$5
Westin Resort	$2.50

Hitchhiking Although Lonely Planet does not recommend hitchhiking under any circumstances, quite a few people use this method for traveling around St John. If you hitchhike, don't travel alone and always exercise caution.

CRUZ BAY

About half of St John's population lives in or around Cruz Bay. The heart of the settlement is a rectangle of roads at the harbor's edge, lined with shops and restaurants. Guesthouses, rental villas, hotels and the homes of St Johnians dot the hills and shores on the outskirts of the village.

The Battery

On the small peninsula to the left of the ferry dock stands a large Georgian building, rising on the foundation of an 18th-century fort that the Danes built to protect the island. Today, the battery houses government offices and is also the residence the governor uses when he visits St John.

Virgin Islands National Park

A large two-story building (☎ 340-776-6201) on the dock across from the Mongoose Junction shopping arcade is the visitors center for the Virgin Island National Park. Well over a million visitors a year stop at the park, making it the most popular single attraction in all of the Virgin Islands. In 2000, the Park Service enlarged and upgraded the visitors center to better serve guests. In addition to collecting brochures, maps, trail guides and books here, you can also see a video on the park and learn about craft demonstrations, evening campground programs, guided hikes to Reef Bay, the active archaeological dig and camping opportunities. The visitors center is open 8 am to 4:30 pm daily.

The center makes an essential first stop for all travelers interested in exploring the more than 9500 acres of national park land on St John and the 5600 acres of protected bays and sea gardens. This park ranks with Puerto Rico's El Yunque forest as one of the great wilderness preserves in the Caribbean. Virgin Islands National Park includes miles and miles of shoreline and pristine reefs as well as hiking trails (see 'Hiking on St John'). Among the attractions are the Cinnamon Bay Campground (see Places to Stay) and the underwater snorkeling trail at Trunk Bay. Beaches, including Francis Bay, Hawksnest Bay and Salt Pond Bay, are places most travelers will not want to miss. The Annaberg Sugar Mill Ruins and Reef Bay petroglyphs are also points of interest.

More than 30 species of tropical birds, including the bananaquit (or 'yellow bird,' the official bird of the Virgin Islands), hummingbirds and smooth-billed ani, nest in the park. Lizards such as the green iguana and gecko, hawksbill turtles and an assortment of feral animals and introduced species inhabit the park. Reef fish bring the island alive below the water. Largely regenerated after 18th-century logging and clearing, the island flora is a mix of introduced species

Bananaquit

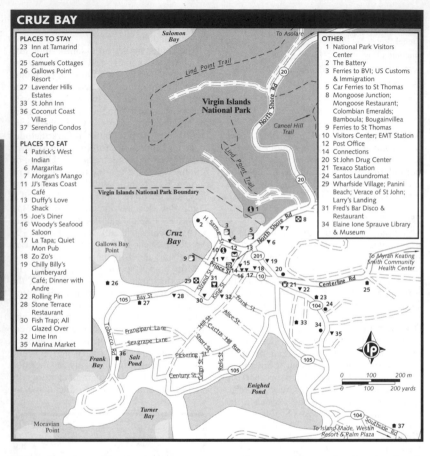

CRUZ BAY

PLACES TO STAY
23 Inn at Tamarind Court
25 Samuels Cottages
26 Gallows Point Resort
27 Lavender Hills Estates
33 St John Inn
36 Coconut Coast Villas
37 Serendip Condos

PLACES TO EAT
4 Patrick's West Indian
6 Margaritas
7 Morgan's Mango
11 JJ's Texas Coast Café
13 Duffy's Love Shack
15 Joe's Diner
16 Woody's Seafood Saloon
17 La Tapa; Quiet Mon Pub
18 Zo Zo's
19 Chilly Billy's Lumberyard Café; Dinner with Andre
22 Rolling Pin
28 Stone Terrace Restaurant
30 Fish Trap; All Glazed Over
32 Lime Inn
35 Marina Market

OTHER
1 National Park Visitors Center
2 The Battery
3 Ferries to BVI; US Customs & Immigration
5 Car Ferries to St Thomas
8 Mongoose Junction; Mongoose Restaurant; Colombian Emeralds; Bamboula; Bougainvillea
9 Ferries to St Thomas
10 Visitors Center; EMT Station
12 Post Office
14 Connections
20 St John Drug Center
21 Texaco Station
24 Santos Laundromat
29 Wharfside Village; Panini Beach; Verace of St John; Larry's Landing
31 Fred's Bar Disco & Restaurant
34 Elaine Ione Sprauve Library & Museum

and native plants like the bay rum tree, whose aromatic leaves were a principal ingredient in the Virgin Islands' cologne industry. Another curious native plant is the night-blooming cereus. Its vanilla scent attracts bats and moths to pollinate it by starlight. The south shore and East End are magnificent tropical dry forest; the uplands and West End get more rain.

Elaine Ione Sprauve Library & Museum

Cruz Bay's library (☎ 340-776-6359), across Route 104 from Marina Market, is also a

small museum. Photos, drawings, local crafts and a few Indian and colonial artifacts are presented in this restored manor house, dating from the 1750s. The library and museum are open 9 am to 5 pm weekdays; admission is free.

Beaches

With about 40 beaches, St John offers sunbathers, swimmers and snorkelers a lot of options.

An easy walk from town, **Frank Bay (Cruz Bay Beach)** offers snorkeling off the point near the desalination plant. But be careful,

Stars & Stripes, sailing near St John

STEVE SIMONSEN

Taking a snorkel break, St John

STEVE SIMONSEN

View from Lizard Hill (north shore), St John

STEVE SIMONSEN

Cruz Bay is St John's main hub, with a hopping nightlife and great beaches nearby.

The five-star Westin Resort, St John

Secluded Salomon Bay Beach, St John

You can hike the Lind Point trail down to quiet Honeymoon Beach, St John.

swimmers have been hit by speedboats in this area. To get here, head south of town past the Gallows Point Resort and down the hill. Along the road, you will see a thin beach with a few coconut palms. Beach houses line the other side of the street, and the island's desal plant chugs along at the far end of the beach.

Salomon Bay is the closest wild beach to Cruz Bay and one of the few you can walk to from town. To get here, follow the Lind Point trail (see 'Hiking on St John'), which heads northeast from the National Park Visitors Center. After about 1 mile, the trail descends to this secluded beach.

The beach is on national park land, where nude sunbathing is prohibited. Nevertheless, the beach is popular with nudists and gays, who slip into something when the 'Ranger' call echoes up the beach, announcing the arrival of a Park Service patrol. You will find good snorkeling at each end of the beach.

The broad but short **Great Cruz Bay** spans the head of the bay in front of the Westin Resort, about 1½ miles south of Cruz Bay. Some travelers staying on the West End come here to use the pool, swim up to the pool bar for an expensive buzz, soak in the hot tub and feel like a pampered guest.

Activities

For information on fishing, see the St Thomas chapter. The boats listed there will also arrange to meet you on St John. For hiking, see the 'Hiking on St John' boxed text on the next page.

Sailing The bulk of the US Virgin Islands' bareboat and crewed yacht charters run out of St Thomas. Nevertheless, each year during the winter season, a few crewed yachts arrive at Cruz Bay to carry passengers on daysails. See the Yacht Charter Basics chapter for more details on chartering.

Alcyone (☎ 340-776-6922) is a coast-guard-licensed fiberglass sloop that has been sailing these waters for 25 years. A daysail includes lunch, beverages and snorkel gear. Expect to pay about $75.

Diving, Snorkeling & Boating Low Key Watersports (☎ 340-693-8999), at Wharfside Village, is a great dive-training facility and has some of the most experienced instructors in the islands. A two-tank dive will cost $75 including all the rental gear. It offers wreck dives to the *General Rogers* and the RMS *Rhone* as well as night dives and dive packages.

Cruise Bay Watersports (☎ 340-776-6234), Palm Plaza, is a competing operation with a fleet of four impressive dive boats. Half-day snorkel trips to two different offshore cays cost about $40. You can make a full day of it on their trip to Jost Van Dyke in the BVI. The cost is $80 (including lunch, drinks and a stop at the legendary Foxy's Tamarind Bar). You can also rent snorkels (about $7) from these folks.

St John Adventures Unlimited (☎ 340-693-7730), at the Gallows Point Resort, can arrange an array of boat rentals, snorkel tours, daysails and more.

Low Key Watersports (see above) rents snorkels for the same rate. It also offers kayak tours ($40 for a half-day, $80 for a full day).

For the same price, Arawak Expeditions (☎ 340-693-8312) offers guided sea kayak tours that leave from Cruz Bay and paddle over to Henley Cay and Lovango Cay for snorkeling.

Noah's Little Arks (☎ 340-693-9030), at Wharfside Village, rents 10-foot inflatable dinghies with 15hp engines ($65 for a half day, $95 for a full day).

Ocean Runner Powerboat Rentals (☎ 340-693-8809), at Wharfside Village, rents larger speedboats for about $175 a day and up.

Bicycling & Tennis Arawak Expeditions (☎ 340-693-8312), at Wharfside Village, has guided mountain bike tours of the most remote areas of the national park. Half-day trips cost about $45; full-day trips run $80 and include lunch.

The Westin Resort has six lighted tennis courts. Nonguests pay $15 an hour. Lessons run $50 an hour. You will also find two public courts near the fire station in Cruz Bay.

Hiking on St John

With more than 9500 acres of national park and 22 maintained trails, St John is paradise for tropical hikers. The National Park Visitors Center has excellent maps, and a reasonably fit, cautious person with appropriate gear and familiarity with tropical trekking (see Hiking in the Facts for the Visitor chapter) can safely hit St John's trails for adventure without the company of a local guide. Nevertheless, joining a hiking tour led by a professional guide can be well worth the cost of participation because of the natural and human history you can learn from your leader.

The National Park Service sponsors a number of hikes, including birding expeditions and shore hikes, but its best-known offering is the Reef Bay Hike (☎ 340-776-6201 ext 238 for reservations). This begins at the Reef Bay trailhead, 4¾ miles from Cruz Bay on Centerline Rd. The hike is a 3-mile downhill trek through tropical forests, leading past petroglyphs and plantation ruins to a swimming beach at Reef Bay, where a boat picks you up and runs you back to Cruz Bay. The hike during the winter season usually runs 10 am to 3:30 pm every Monday, Thursday and Friday. You pay a $15 transportation fee on the boat.

Thunderhawk Trail Guides (☎ 340-776-6412) offers two-hour guided hikes on the island's trails to places like Lind Point, Honeymoon Beach and the Caneel Hill spur. Guides share information about history, culture, bush medicine and Taíno Indians. Expect to pay about $25.

Natural Adventures St John (☎ 340-776-6922) offers three educational trips. The two-hour tour includes an hour-long snorkeling session with lessons on coral-reef ecology, botany, island geology and birding. The early-bird special, a 1½-hour bird-watching tour, focuses solely on seabirds. Guests can also listen to the sounds of fish, dolphins and whales (when they are in season) through a hydrophone carried on the tour boat. Rates run from about $25.

Park trails include a number of old plantation roads that lead through wet forests and dry forests to ruins, archeological sites, mountain peaks and secluded shores. All trails have identifying signs at the trailheads. The following are some favorites.

Lind Point trail (1.1 miles, moderate) This trail starts at the visitors center and follows the coastline of the north shore east to Caneel Bay. There is a .4-mile climb through cactus dry forest to Lind Battery, once a British gun emplacement, 160 feet above the sea. The trail also takes you to secluded Salomon and Honeymoon Beaches.

Caneel Hill trail (2.4 miles, rugged) The trail links Cruz Bay with the North Shore Rd entrance to the Caneel Bay resort. The hike starts with a .8-mile climb to the top of Caneel Hill (719 feet), then climbs farther to the top of Margaret Hill (840 feet) before making a steep descent through the forest to the coast.

Cinnamon Bay self-guided trail (.5 miles, easy) You pick up the trailhead a few yards east of the entrance road to the Cinnamon Bay Campground and follow a shady trail among native tropical

Places to Stay

St John's accommodations appeal to two groups: One large group is upper-middle-class vacationers willing to pay hundreds of dollars a night for a villa/condo rental or a suite at one of the three exclusive resort hotels. The other group is adventure travelers keen on camping and ecotourism. The island has little to offer middle-class travelers looking for conveniences like hotel restaurants, swimming pools and waterfront activities at moderate prices. Low-cost, no-frills guesthouses, once staple accommodations on the island, are disappearing fast in the face of gentrification.

For camping options, see Places to Stay under the North Island and Coral Bay & South Island sections. Unless otherwise

Hiking on St John

trees to the ruins of a sugar factory. Placards along the way identify relevant vegetation and explain some local history. Takes about one hour.

Cinnamon Bay trail (1.1 miles, rugged) No question about it, this hike through tropical wet forest on an old plantation road is a challenging hill climb (unless you walk it one way downhill from Centerline Rd). You join the trail 100 yards east of the entrance to the campground and start your climb to the top of the island's spine, where the trail hits Centerline Rd. Serious trekkers continue east along the road for about a mile, where they join the Reef Bay trail.

Francis Bay trail (.5 miles, easy) You pick up the trail at the west end of the Mary Creek paved road. The trail follows the rim of a salt pond that usually harbors a good collection of wading birds. It also continues on a boardwalk through a mangrove forest before reaching the broad crescent beach at Francis Bay.

Reef Bay trail (2.2 miles, rugged) Probably the most famous of all the island trails, this one starts on Centerline Rd about 4.75 miles east of Cruz Bay and makes a steep descent from Bordeaux Mountain (1277 feet), the highest point on St John. Along your descent through tropical wet forest, you pass the ruins of four sugar plantations before reaching the south shore at Reef Bay.

Petroglyph trail (.2 miles, moderate) This is a spur that veers west 1½ miles down the Reef Bay trail. It leads to waterfalls and the mysterious petroglyphs that some attribute to Arawak Indians and others attribute to West Africans.

Lameshur Bay trail (.8 miles, moderate) If you want a sandy beach at the end or beginning of your assault on Bordeaux Mountain, follow this spur that breaks off the Reef Bay trail at the petroglyph trail intersection and heads east. Near the base of the trail, another spur breaks off to the coral rubble beach on Europa Bay.

Bordeaux Mountain trail (1.2 miles, rugged) This trail leaves from Little Lameshur Bay and climbs to an elevation of 1000 feet, where it joins the dirt Bordeaux Mt Rd that continues north 1.7 miles to Centerline Rd. The vistas and the challenge of this trail make it worthwhile.

Drunk Bay trail (.3 miles, easy) The trail leaves the beach at Salt Pond Bay and follows the rim of the salt pond to the extremely wild and rocky beach that faces east to Sir Francis Drake Channel and the BVI. Swimming is dangerous here, as the trade-wind-driven seas pile up on this shore. The waves carry all manner of flotsam and jetsam, including wrecked yachts. Beachcombing here can be fascinating.

Ram Head trail (1 mile, moderate) The trailhead is at the south end of the beach at Salt Pond Bay. You follow an exposed trail over switchbacks to the Ram Head, a promontory 200 feet above the seas at the southernmost tip of St John, a lonesome, windswept place.

stated, prices listed below are winter high-season rates.

Inns & Hotels In a friendly West Indian neighborhood less than a quarter-mile up Centerline Rd from Cruz Bay, *Samuels Cottages* (☎ 340-776-6643) has been Elaine Samuels' family-run operation for decades. There are three hillside cottages here that

look out over the town, Cruz Bay and Pillsbury Sound. Each cottage has one bedroom, a kitchen, living room and bath as well as fans, air-con and a deck. The accommodations are not fancy, but they are clean and private. Expect to pay about $100 a night.

The *Inn at Tamarind Court* (☎ 340-776-6368, 800-221-1637), along the busy Route 104, is within walking distance of Cruz Bay.

The central location (with laundry next-door) and economical rates make this inn popular with budget travelers. There are no water views or private decks here, but the shady courtyard with its casual bar and restaurant make for a good place to kick back with other guests, hoist a jar and exchange local knowledge. Most of the 20 rooms are small and simply furnished with two twin beds, a table and chairs. You get fans and air-con for cooling, but no TV or telephone. The smallest rooms with a single bed and shared bath rent for about $50. Standard rooms run about $110.

St John Inn (☎ 340-693-8688, 800-666-7688), a few blocks from the town center, looks down from the hillside on Enighed Pond. This small inn with 13 rooms got a makeover in 1998 and now sports pastel paints in brown and blue that give the inn a Southwest ranch aura. Handcrafted pine furniture and iron beds add ambience to the small rooms, which run from about $115 to $185. Travelers get phone, TV, air-con, fan and kitchen as well as private baths here. There is a sun deck and small pool.

Serendip Condos (☎ 340-776-6646, 888-800-6445), on the hill above Cruz Bay, offers a lot for a moderate price. But you must have transportation, or not mind the three-quarter-mile hike along Route 104 to town. There are 10 studios and one-bedroom units in three-story concrete buildings. Each unit has a private balcony with sea view, a full kitchen, TV, telephone, air-con and fans. Furnishings have a Pier 1 Imports contemporary flare, and most of the units were redecorated for the millennium. Studios start at about $115, but prices may be negotiable if you call at the last minute and there is space available.

Coconut Coast Villas (☎ 340-693-9100, 800-858-7989) stands right on the waterfront road on small Frank Bay. Cruz Bay is about a half-mile walk over the hill. There are nine units in this compound, including studios and townhouses. All the units come with local art, a kitchen, private deck, air-con, TV, telephone and private bath. There's a swimming pool. Rates start at $235 and rise to almost $500.

Lavender Hills Estates (☎ 340-779-6969, 800-348-8444), a short walk to the south of the business district, has 12 suites in a multi-story concrete building with a view of the harbor. These are privately owned condos, and many have been recently refurbished. The units are rather spacious, with tile floors, rattan furnishings and plastic deck furniture on the private porches. Guests enjoy the convenience of the pool and laundry on the premises. Rates start at about $275 for a one-bedroom unit. Extra people pay $35 per night.

Gallows Point Resort (☎ 340-776-6434, 800-323-7229), on the promontory at the south side of Cruz Bay, overlooks the harbor, Pillsbury Sound and St Thomas. The resort is just a three-minute walk from the shops, restaurants and nightlife in town. Each of the 14 villas stands amid lushly landscaped grounds that play host to a wandering flock of peacocks and include a swimming pool, sunning terrace, small beach and swimming raft. Each suite has private terraces and decks, a living room, full kitchen, one or two bedrooms and large bath. Many of the condo units have vaulted ceilings; all have a collection of French doors that open onto water views. Furnishings are wicker creations with vibrant floral patterns. The swank Ellington's restaurant is on the property. Rates run between $300 and $400.

The **Westin Resort** (☎ 340-693-8000, 800-808-5020), 2 hilly miles south of Cruz Bay on Route 104, has all the hallmarks of a contemporary five-star resort. The resort offers a quarter-acre pool, a palm-shaded beach on Great Cruz Bay, fitness center, spa, lit tennis courts and four restaurants. You will also find quite a few guests milling about as this resort has 285 rooms in the cedar-roof villas at seaside and 90 condo units on the hill across the road. Rooms feature all the 1st-class amenities, private decks and contemporary furnishings, but no cooking facilities. Rates start at $400 a night.

Rental Accommodations If you would like to search for or book a St John rental online, check out the *Tradewinds* Web site at www.stjohntradewindsnews.com.

Star Villas (☎ 340-776-6704) has a good selection of small and moderately priced villas in the Cruz Bay area. Caribbean Villas & Resorts (☎ 340-776-6152, 800-338-0987) is one of the island's most popular real estate agencies.

Other island real estate agents with a large rental stock include Cruz Bay Realty (☎ 340-963-8808), Pastory Estates (☎ 340-776-6152), Vacation Homes (☎ 340-776-6094) and Vacation Vistas (☎ 340-776-6462).

Places to Eat

Cruz Bay offers the traveler an unexpected range of distinctive eateries. They are all within an easy walk of each other, which makes window-shopping for a place to eat one of the joys of dining out on St John. Because of the easy and frequent ferry service between St Thomas and St John, a lot of people from St Thomas come to Cruz Bay for a night of restaurant- and bar-hopping.

Joe's Diner, just north of the intersection of Prince and King Sts at the center of the village, is a Cruz Bay institution. This is a hole-in-the-wall with about six streetside tables. It's a favorite place for locals and travelers to catch a fast bite, especially at breakfast. You will see a steady queue of folks lined up at the window after 7 am ordering juices, coffees, beers, bagels or egg sandwiches to start their day. Joe's percolates with a wealth of island gossip, and there are local and Miami papers for news junkies.

Chilly Billy's Lumberyard Café (☎ 340-693-8708, 13-38 Enighed Gade), as you start up the hill from the car-ferry dock, will fill your belly no matter what time you roll out of bed. Islanders swear by the strawberry pancakes ($7), but if you get here before 10:30 am, you can get two eggs, home fries, toast and coffee for less than $4. *Dinner with Andre* is the nightly incarnation of Chilly Billy's, switching its cuisine to French by starlight. There are only 24 seats in Andre Rosin's little bistro, so make reservations to dine on entrees like the salmon Trianon ($22), topped with thin slices of zucchini and a tarragon cream sauce.

The *Mongoose Restaurant* (☎ 340-693-8677), a sun-dappled terrace secreted in the heart of the Mongoose Junction shopping arcade, drips with laid-back ambience. Omelets start at about $8; cappuccino costs $3. For lunch, try the shrimp and mango quesadillas ($7).

JJ's Texas Coast Café (☎ 340-776-6908), facing the park on Cruz Bay's waterfront, has a breakfast burrito for about $5. The town's party animals often rejoin the world here to munch on steak and eggs ($9) after a night of reggae and calypso.

Woody's Seafood Saloon (☎ 340-779-4625), a block and a half up Prince St from the ferry dock, has inspired local legends (see Entertainment). While lots of folks show up at this cramped bar for cheap beer and a chance to rub shoulders with a first-rate collection of tan bodies, a traveler can actually get some reasonable pub food at Woody's. Spicy conch fritters ($6) are a staple here, but you can get a variety of grilled fish as well (over $10).

The *Rolling Pin* (☎ 340-779-4775), just past the landmark Texaco station at the start of Route 104, is the island's most popular pizza vendor. A large cheese pie costs $16; specialty pizzas run to $20. Calzones and subs cost about $6, and the Rolling Pin will deliver between 5 and 9 pm.

Patrick's West Indian, the ancient blue-panel truck that seems permanently parked at the passenger ferry dock, is a local institution. The tide of gentrification and local fashion police have been trying to push out squatters like Patrick for years, but so far he has maintained his status as a 'mobile' vendor. Lots of the West Indians and continentals who ride the ferries catch their daily meals at Patrick's. Get here by 5 pm before the rib platters ($6) run out. Kingfish stew (enough for two) costs $10.

The *Fish Trap* (☎ 340-693-9994), on King St, has been a popular travelers' stop for years. The restaurant stands on a sheltered deck. Consider the fish chowder ($5) or the vegetarian primavera pasta with a garlic Parmesan sauce over fettuccine for $13.

Margaritas (☎ 340-693-8400), on the North Shore Rd across from the car-ferry

ST JOHN

ramp, is an open-air cantina offering enchiladas with rice and beans for around $12. The gazpacho with jalapeño creme ($5) is a good bet if you want something cool and inexpensive.

Duffy's Love Shack (☎ 340-776-6065), across from Joe's Diner, came to a two-story building in the heart of Cruz Bay shortly after the millennium. The arrival stirred up a lot of negative emotions among St Johnians who resented the appearance of this off-island celebrity bar and restaurant. Nevertheless, Duffy's seems here to stay. You eat upstairs with a view over the roofs of the village. The jerked Caesar wrap is worth a try (under $8).

Morgan's Mango (☎ 340-693-8141), across from the car-ferry landing, is a mid-priced restaurant with imaginative Caribbean recipes. The terrace of this hillside restaurant offers a good view of the harbor while you dine on items such as voodoo snapper ($20), a Haitian specialty, or citrus chicken ($13) from Cuba.

The ***Lime Inn*** (☎ 340-776-6425), on King St, is a travelers' favorite for quality cuisine, ambience and service at moderate prices. Owner Rich Mayer has splashed his terrace restaurant with a mix of plants, wicker and tropical fabrics and hired some of the friendliest waitstaff in town. The New England clam chowder is a value at $4 a bowl. Both the shrimp Provençal and the shrimp dijon ($16) get rave reviews. Make reservations, or come right at 6 pm when the restaurant opens.

Panini Beach (☎ 340-693-9119), in Wharfside Village, offers northern Italian cuisine with indoor and outdoor harborside dining. Some of the attractions at this trattoria include pizza al pesto ($12) and linguini con vongole (pasta with clams and garlic), which is $21 for a large platter.

Zo Zo's (☎ 340-693-9200), next to the police station on Prince St, is largely an open pavilion. This streetside restaurant can offer a surprisingly romantic setting for first-rate Italian cuisine like osso bucco (veal shank simmered in red wine, tomato and veal stock). Most entrees cost more than $20.

La Tapa (☎ 340-693-7755), across the street from Scotia Bank and next-door to Woody's, has the look and smell of a sangría well you may have visited in Ibiza or Mallorca. Ceviche runs about $10. Paella for two will set you back $36.

The ***Stone Terrace Restaurant*** (☎ 340-693-9370), on the southern edge of the village, is all candlelight, linen and cocktail dresses. The menu here includes black peppercorn-encrusted tuna with fried artichoke hearts, cured olives and creamy lemon risotto for $24. Rack of lamb runs about $30.

Asolare (☎ 340-779-4747), perched on a hill overlooking Cruz Bay, offers the most exotic view and cuisine on St John. The chef here is constantly rotating menu items, frequently drawn from the Pacific Rim. Entrees can easily exceed $30, but you can get some fabulous appetizers, including Kampuchea shrimp ravioli and Indochine bouillabaisse for under $13.

Entertainment

Woody's Seafood Saloon (see Places to Eat) officially begins St John's daily party at 3 pm, when the price on domestic US beers drops to $1. By 4 pm, the crowd in this tiny place has spilled over to plastic cafe tables on both sides of the street. Female bartenders in shorts and tank tops pass beers out a streetside window. Meanwhile, the crowd basks in the glow of the tropical sun and listens to the Rolling Stones or Merle Haggard blasting from the sound system. Over the course of the night, the gang ebbs and flows, but by 11 pm, Woody's has a crowd inside and out. Part frat party, part college reunion, Woody's lets the good times roll. You probably will not meet the love of your life here, but you may well meet somebody to love.

Morgan's Mango (see Places to Eat) has a popular bar scene on Thursday night, when they bring in some impressive acoustic acts and sell two-for-one margaritas. This event can be a romantic stop for a date or a good place to meet someone for a beach rendezvous the following day.

Duffy's Love Shack (see Places to Eat) draws flocks of enthusiasts here just as it does at its original venue on St Thomas, but the two scenes are notably different. On St Thomas, Duffy's is the traditional hangout for local night owls; no such luck in Cruz Bay even though the bar here has an actual dance floor. Few locals or continentals working on the island visit Duffy's. The crowd is largely younger collegians or prep school kids out for a spree.

The *Quiet Mon Pub* (☎ 340-779-4799), above La Tapa restaurant, is the Irish pub next to Woody's. This is a great spot for women who want to go out for the night without getting hit on by the sharks. The tables on the 2nd-floor deck make for the best people-watching in town because you can see the crowds flowing in and out of Woody's and the neighboring gin joints. You can surf the Web ($3 for 15 minutes), and quite a few travelers have made friendships while checking their email. On Friday night, there is top-40 dance music and a crowd of under-30 continentals.

Larry's Landing (☎ 340-693-8802), in the Wharfside Village arcade, draws a young crowd – mostly male – to its pool tables and bar where you can pour your own drink ($3.50).

Fred's Bar Disco & Restaurant (☎ 340-776-6363), across the street from the Lime Inn on Kongens Gade, is a 'must visit' stop. This is the place to be if you crave reggae and calypso, if you want to party with a mix of euphoric West Indians and continentals, and if you're searching for the best dance scene on the island. The bands playing under the pavilion here really jam (especially Wednesday and Friday nights), and the energy and music are worth the $3 cover. Here you have authentic and welcoming West Indian culture the way you dreamed of it the first time you heard Bob Marley sing 'Stir It Up.'

Shopping

St John's shopping district is to a large extent Cruz Bay. Here you will find a collection of boutiques, galleries, studio shops and salons mostly located in two attractive shopping arcades. Wharfside Village is on the waterfront just to the south of the ferry dock. The larger Mongoose Junction is a place that looks like a collection of Italian palaces on the North Shore Rd near the National Park Visitors Center. Most shops have long hours, usually 9 am to 8 pm Monday to Saturday.

You will find fine island clothing at Bougainvillea (☎ 340-693-7160) in the Mongoose Mall. Bamboula (☎ 340-693-8699), also in Mongoose Mall, is a vibrant shop selling all manner of Caribbean art, fabrics, crafts and furniture. Colombian Emeralds (☎ 340-776-6007) has an outlet in the same arcade. Verace of St John (340-693-7599), in Wharfside Village, is possibly the most chic jewelry store in town.

For locally made pottery, check out All Glazed Over (☎ 340-693-9451), in the Raintree Court next to the Fish Trap restaurant.

Island Made (☎ 340-693-7575), in the Palm Plaza about a mile south of Cruz Bay, has an exceptional collection of island crafts such as carnival masks, stained-glass fish and beaded jewelry.

NORTH ISLAND

Travelers access this area using the North Shore Rd and Centerline Rd. Most of the national park's major attractions, trailheads and campgrounds lie along this route.

Annaberg Sugar Mill Ruins

These ruins at Leinster Bay are the most intact ruins of a sugar plantation in the Virgin Islands. The national park has done an excellent job preserving the structures and landscaping the grounds. A 30-minute, self-directed walking tour leads you through the slave quarters, village, windmill, horse mill, dripping cistern, oven, rum still and dungeon.

The drawings of schooners on the dungeon wall may date back more than 100 years. Every Monday to Saturday, park experts offer demonstrations in traditional island baking, gardening, weaving and crafting. Most demonstrations take place at

10 am and 2 pm. There is a $4 user fee for visitors 17 and over.

Estate Catherineburg Sugar Mill

In 1986, the National Park Service restored this windmill on Centerline Rd. The mill dates from the mid-18th century and is an excellent example of barrel-vaulting construction techniques. Just imagine the talent of the slave masons who built this tower and the lust for money that drove their masters. This is a quiet place with no restricted visiting hours, guards or tours.

Cinnamon Bay Archaeological Dig

Located on the beach at Cinnamon Bay Campground, this excavation is the site where Dr Ken Wild (☎ 340-693-5230) unearthed a Taíno presence on the island that dates back 500 years. The site consists of a 200-year-old rubble-construction building that serves as a laboratory and three square holes about 4 feet deep where Wild believes he has found a ceremonial site with a chieftain's seat. There are tours Tuesday, Thursday and Saturday at 1 pm, and you can also volunteer to work on the site, sifting the sand and possibly uncovering items like fishbones from a feast or a bowl with a dog head on it.

Beaches

Except in a few cases, you will need a car to reach these beaches, unless you have the good fortune of staying in the vicinity.

Honeymoon Beach If you follow the Lind Point trail from Salomon Beach past a point of rocks, you reach Honeymoon Beach, a long thin strand. For a shorter walk, park in the visitors' parking lot at the Caneel Bay resort and follow the shoreline west away from the resort buildings. There are few folks here and good shade. Snorkeling is fair off the rocks to the west.

Caneel Bay This is the main beach in front of the dining terrace at the Caneel Bay resort. The resort has seven beaches, but this is the one they permit visitors to use. There is a float here for swimmers, and fair snorkeling off the point to the east. You must sign in as a visitor at the guardhouse when you enter the resort property. Travelers can use the hotel's restaurants and bars. Jogging addicts sometimes come to the beach, then jog the resort grounds and trails before returning for a dip. Because the resort has so many beaches and the grounds are so expansive, all the beaches are tranquil. Beach chairs are for resort guests only.

Hawksnest Bay The bay here is dazzling to behold, a deep circular indentation between hills with a broken ring of sand on the fringe. Some scenes from the film *Christopher Columbus: The Discovery* were shot here. Because the main beach lies right along the North Shore Rd and is the closest public beach you can reach by car from Cruz Bay, this beach can get busy, particularly after school when St Johnians come to cool off. On winter mornings, Hawksnest is at its quietest and shadiest.

There are changing facilities, tables and BBQ pits. Snorkelers will find the reef just a few strokes off the central beach. If you prefer to be alone, swim around the rocks at the west end of the beach to a secluded strand tucked under a cliff. You can make a similar swim at the east end of the main beach to Oppenheimer's Beach.

Oppenheimer's Beach Also called Little Hawksnest and Gibney's, this strand lies on the eastern edge of Hawksnest Bay. To get here, take the dirt road to the left just after you pass the public beach at Hawksnest. This is not a National Park Service beach. The land and house on the property belonged to Dr Robert Oppenheimer, one of the inventors of the atomic bomb. His daughter committed suicide and left the land and beach house to the children of St John.

Longtime expats favor this beach because they can bring their dogs and horses (illegal on park land). Islanders also use this beach for communal beach parties to benefit social and environmental causes.

Jumbie Bay *Jumbie* is the common word for ghost in the Creole dialect of the Caribbean, and this beach east of Oppenheimer's has a plethora of ghost stories associated with it. Look for the parking lot on the North Shore Rd that holds only three cars. From here, take the wooden stairs down to the beach. Few people know about this place (or can find it), so some nudists find it a safe sanctuary. Snorkeling is best off the left end of the beach.

While you are here, consider stories of how rampaging slaves during the revolt of 1733 cut up the local plantation owners and stuffed them down a well here. The murders were in retaliation against a slave master who allegedly buried slaves in the sand up to their necks on the beach and used the exposed heads as bowling pins.

Trunk Bay This long, gently arching beach is the most popular strand on the island. The National Park Service has lifeguards, changing facilities, toilets, telephones, picnic facilities, showers, snorkel rental, a snack bar and taxi stand. No question, the beach is scenic, but it often gets packed. Everyone wants to try the underwater snorkeling trail that maintains a fair selection of fish. Entrance costs $4 for adults, free for children.

Cinnamon Bay The next bay east of Trunk Bay, this exposed sweeping cove is home to the Cinnamon Bay Campground (see Places to Stay). The beach has amenities including showers, toilets, a restaurant and grocery store. The least populated part of the beach lies to the east of the gift shop. You can rent sailboards and sea kayaks here. And there is a small island offshore that you can swim to for sunbathing. Be careful during winter months, when wind and swells can roll in from the northeast.

Maho Bay This should not be confused with the small beach servicing Stanley Selengut's eco-tent campground (see Places to Stay; that beach is Little Maho Bay around the point to the east. Maho Bay beach lies alongside the North Shore Rd east of Cinnamon Bay. Come here for protected waters when other north shore beaches are taking a beating from the northeasterly winds and swells in winter. The calm and shallow water makes this a popular place for families with young children. The snorkeling is over turtle-grass beds, where you might see hawksbills and green turtles feeding in the early morning.

Francis Bay A popular yacht anchorage because of the calm seas, this bay also boasts a long arch of broad sand around its fringe. There are bathrooms, picnic tables and BBQ facilities here, but few people. Francis Bay is a great beach for walking or embarking on a trail hike (see 'Hiking on St John'), but don't be surprised if you run into a clutch of wild donkeys, goats or even a horse, which hang around to scavenge in the garbage cans.

Leinster Bay This bay adjoins the grounds of the ruined Annaberg Plantation at the northeast end of the island, and the beach has been named Waterlemon Beach after an island in the bay. To get here, park in the lot at the plantation and follow a dirt road/trail around Leinster Bay. The sandy part of the beach is about half a mile along the shore to the east.

To reach the best snorkeling, continue past the beach on the trail until you are adjacent to the offshore islet, Waterlemon Cay. If you are a strong swimmer, head out to the island and explore the cay's reef fringe. You will probably not be alone here; Leinster Bay is a popular anchorage for yachts. Dive operators bring snorkeling tours here as well, so watch out for moving boats. Some folks claim this is the best snorkeling on St John, but the East End is arguably better.

Activities

Cinnamon Bay Water Sports Center (☎ 340-776-6330), at the campground, rents a good selection of **windsurfing** equipment for all ages and abilities for about $12 an hour. Lessons cost $40. The hotel water-sports operations at Caneel Bay and the Westin Resort also rent equipment.

Snuba of St John (☎ 340-776-6922), at Trunk Bay, runs hourly trips on the reef using dry snuba helmets. The tour runs $40.

The best value for renting **snorkeling** gear is at the Cinnamon Bay Water Sports Center (☎ 340-776-6330), at the campground. You pay about $4 a day plus a $25 deposit. You can also rent kayaks here for as little as $10 an hour; sailboats go for $20 and up.

The Caneel Bay resort (see Places to Stay) has the most **tennis** courts on the island, a tennis instructor and a pro shop. Nonguests pay $10 an hour. Lessons cost $65 an hour.

Places to Stay

Camping St John has been known for decades as a mecca for tropical campers. The national park land, as well as scores of undeveloped coves and beaches, creates extraordinary settings in which to get back to nature. Yet the camping opportunities available on St John are far from living the life of Robinson Crusoe. St John camping areas are not like the wilderness or free-form commune experiences backpackers may have seen on the islands of Thailand or the coast of Oaxaca. Almost all campers stay in well-developed areas with hundreds of other like-minded souls.

However, the island is big enough and wild enough that experienced tropical campers can get off the beaten path on day hikes or overnight. As on the other US Virgin Islands, the beaches on St John – with the exception of national park beaches – are public property and therefore campable, as long as you can get to them without trespassing. Have a look at the National Park Service's island map and the maps and lists of beaches in this chapter to find out the park boundaries and possible

sites for day hikes and overnights. Before you go hiking off, take some time to network with other tropical campers and long-term islanders. St John's divemasters are good sources of local knowledge, as are the long-term expats who show up for happy hour at Woody's Seafood Saloon in Cruz Bay and at Skinny Legs at Coral Bay.

The only place you can legally camp on national park land is at the Cinnamon Bay Campground. A ranger boat usually makes a pass along the beaches and coves of the park before sunset and early in the morning to make sure no one is violating the camping taboo. Punishment for camping violations is eviction and/or a fine.

When you camp, be exceptionally cautious in your use of open fires. Always keep them contained and below the tide line. The trade winds and arid climate of St John create conditions that are ripe for wild fires, especially on the East End. Insect repellents are a must: Do not risk an encounter with a mosquito carrying dengue or the maddening no-see-ums.

The *Cinnamon Bay Campground* (☎ 340-776-6330, 800-539-9998), about 6 miles east of Cruz Bay on the North Shore Rd (Route 20), has about 130 campsites in the national park. The setting is a mile-long crescent of sand at the base of forested hills. This operation is really a campers' village with a general store, snack bar and a restaurant. But the grounds are so expansive, and the vegetation so thick, you have more privacy than you might expect at a place that often has 400 to 500 guests.

There are three accommodation options at Cinnamon Bay. The cottages are 15x15-foot concrete shelters with two screened sides, electric lights, a propane stove, cooking and eating utensils, a water container, ice chest and ceiling fan. Outside is a picnic table and charcoal grill. The cottages have four twin beds and may be equipped with two extra cots or a crib. You can get a beachfront, water-view or forest location.

The tents are all 10x14 feet on a solid wood platform. Each tent comes with four cots, a propane lantern, propane stove, ice chest, water container, cooking and eating utensils. Of course, there's a charcoal grill and picnic table outdoors. You get a change of bed linens here twice a week, just as you do with a cottage rental. For those who want to rough it, there are bare sites that fit one large tent or two small ones. Each bare site has a picnic table and charcoal grill.

Everyone uses the public toilet facilities and cold-water showers. The high-season rate for the cottages (for two people) is about $105 to $135, depending on location. Tents run about $80, bare sites $25. You pay $15 for each additional person in the cottages and tents, $5 at the bare sites. Guests are limited to 14-day stays during high season, 21 days at other times.

Maho Bay Camps (☎ 340-776-6240, 800-392-9004), about 8 miles east of Cruz Bay on North Shore Rd (Route 20), is Stanley Selengut's award-winning ecosensitive tent resort. This resort has grown into a complex with 114 units. Each of the tents here is set on a platform on a steep forested hillside that overlooks Maho Bay, Francis Bay and the offshore islands. The tents are so far off the ground, and the surrounding vegetation is so thick, the effect is like living in a treehouse. When you want to access the beach, other tents, the toilets and showers or on-site outdoor restaurant or store, you follow a maze of boardwalks and stairs through the jungle. The hillside is steep and the complex vast, so be prepared for a lot of climbing.

The 16x16-foot tents actually look like canvas cottages with airy screened walls. Each tent has a private deck, table and chairs, two twin beds, a futon mattress, propane stove, cooler, water container, cooking and eating utensils, towels and bedding. Barbecue grills are built along the boardwalks for community use. The resort's 'green' philosophy includes water conservation: Community toilets are low-flush units, and showers have pull-chains for brief dousing. The beach offers only quiet water-sports rentals for snorkeling, sailing, windsurfing and kayaking. On-site environmentalists often organize recycling and conservation efforts. During the busy winter season, the tent cottages cost about $105 to $115 a night (for two people). Each extra person pays $15 a night. The minimum stay is seven nights during high season.

Harmony Studios, at Maho Bay Camps, are condo units. These 12 multistory units pepper the hillside above the tent camps. Here, you get a private bath, kitchen and deck in an ecosensitive building with solar-generated electricity, rainwater-collection and roof wind scoops for cooling. A lot of the construction materials come from recycled trash. Rates start at about $165 for a bedroom studio.

Hotels For a sense of space and old-school casual elegance, the *Caneel Bay* resort (☎ 340-776-6111, 800-928-8889) is still the reigning queen of USVI accommodations. Built around the ruins of an old sugar plantation, the resort covers 170 acres of national park land. There are no fewer than seven beaches here, along with landscaped rolling hills, miles of hiking and jogging trails, forests and rocky promontories. Cars are restricted to a satellite parking lot, and guests travel by foot or golf cart.

Only 166 guest quarters are spread around the property in units that are shaded and masked by the surrounding trees. Of course, the resort has all the luxuries you would expect, including a large pool, 11 lit tennis courts and gourmet restaurants like Equator (see Places to Eat). Rooms are elegant with plantation-style furnishings from Indonesia, but without TVs or cooking facilities. Rates start at $400, but tumble to $250 from May to November 15.

Places to Eat
Equator (☎ 340-776-6111), the gourmet restaurant set atop the ruins of the sugar mill at the Caneel Bay resort, has a menu that grows largely from the cuisine of cultures rooted in the tropic girdle of the earth. The Singaporean glass-noodle salad with seafood and crabmeat ($12) appeals to light diners. Indonesian *nasi goreng* (fried rice with chicken, prawns, veggies, satay and egg) is a popular entree for $32. Travelers should make reservations well in advance.

Le Chateau de Bordeaux (☎ 340-776-6611), on Centerline Rd near the center of the island on Bordeaux Mountain, has two dinner seatings (5:30 pm and 7:30 pm). There are sublime views of the BVI from the deck and the air-conditioned dining salon. Printed-fabric tablecloths and attentive service set the mood. Dinner items include a venison rack with a spicy bourbon glaze and a goat-cheese hollandaise for $35. Reservations are a must.

CORAL BAY & SOUTH ISLAND

Two hundred years ago, Coral Bay was the largest settlement on St John. Known originally as 'Crawl' Bay, presumably because there were pens or 'crawls' for sea turtles here, this settlement owes its early good fortune to the largest and best protected harbor in the Virgin Islands.

Today, Coral Bay's village center has dwindled to a school and a handful of shops, restaurants and pubs clustered around the base of a hill dominated by the Emmaus Moravian Church. Residents' homes lie scattered along the roads. Route 107 leads to Salt Pond Bay and the island's most remote beaches and coastal wilderness.

Emmaus Moravian Church

Built in 1783 as the second of two missions at Coral Bay, this large yellow church with its red roof (☎ 340-776-6291), at the intersection of Routes 10 and 107, is on the National Registry of Historic Places. It is an example of the importance of the Moravian Mission and Coral Bay in the history of the island. This land was once Caroline Estate, the plantation where the 1733 slave revolt broke out, resulting in the murder of the judge who owned the plantation and his 12-year-old daughter.

The Moravians arrived on the island in the 1750s. Once Coral Bay managed to prosper again after the slave revolt, the Moravian missionaries bent to the single-minded purpose of ministering to the slaves and teaching them to read. This building was a cornerstone of that dedication and continues to serve descendants of those slaves today. The church is not normally open to visitors, but you can come to Sunday morning services. Contemporary parishioners call their congregation Bethany Moravian Church.

Fort Berg

The ruins of this fort lie in the brush atop Fort Berg Hill on a peninsula that juts into Coral Bay. Danes built the fort in 1717 after Governor Erick Bridel seized the island from the British and fortified it with 9lb cannons mounted on the ramparts. Slaves reduced the fort to rubble during the revolt of 1733. The English built another battery here during their occupation in 1807–15, and a few iron cannons remain. The fort is on private land; you can ask at Skinny Legs restaurant about directions to the ruins and whether it is currently OK to intrude on private property.

Beaches

You have to hike into **Haulover Bay** beach via a trail off the East End Rd, 2 miles east of the settlement at Coral Bay. The beach is gravelly and exposed, and the swells can make for a rough entry and cloudy visibility. But if you come on a calm day, you will find spectacular snorkeling on the reef and coral heads – with no one else in sight and a superb view of the BVI to the east.

Several other rocky beaches in the vicinity offer comparable snorkeling and privacy. If you love to swim with the fishes, consider getting your flippers on at Hansen Bay, Long Bay or Privateer Bay.

The small **Salt Pond Bay** has calm waters, good snorkeling and protection from the trade winds. On a crowded weekend, you may see as many as 40 people here; on other days, it has just a few scattered couples or families. To reach this hideaway, drive or take the VITRAN bus (it turns around here) south from Coral Bay on Route 107. You will see a parking lot at the top of the hill and a broad trail leading down to the beach (a five-minute walk). Two hiking trails start at the beach (see 'Hiking on St John'). Valuables have been stolen from Jeeps and from off the beach here. One rumor claims that a mentally challenged

West Indian man hides in the brush and targets careless visitors for his thievery, but on three recent visits, I did not see him.

You reach the deserted **Great Lameshur Bay** and **Little Lameshur Bay** beaches by following the dirt Lameshur Rd (Jeeps only) along the south shore from Salt Pond Bay. The first cove you hit is Great Lameshur Bay, a stony beach that has excellent snorkeling among the rocks and on a reef. If you continue down the road less than a quarter-mile, you reach Little Lameshur Bay, with a wide, sandy apron, picnic facilities and toilets. Few people come here, and the snorkeling is good along the point to the left.

Horseback Riding
Caroline Stables (☎ 340-693-5778), in Coral Bay, offers beach rides, mountain trail rides, sunset rides and full moon rides on horses and burros. Rates run about $35 an hour.

Places to Stay
For the security of a designated campground without sharing the place with a cast of hundreds, head for **Camping at Hansen Bay** (☎ 340-693-5033) at the extreme northeast end of the island. The property is a short but wide strand of beach across the road from Vie's Snack Shack (see Places to Eat), a place of legendary West Indian cooking. The vivacious Vie runs this operation herself, and you can catch meals at the Snack Shack or fire up your own barbie on the beach. Vie has about six bare sites and a few wall tents. Some of the sites feature shade trees; others are out in the sun. There is an outhouse and solar shower on the premises. Rates are $35 a night for a two-person tent. Bare sites for two people run $20. The VITRAN bus from Cruz Bay stops about 2 miles short of Vie's. You will have a long, hot and hilly hike to the campground if you don't come by rental car or catch a ride with a friend. Make your reservations here early for high season.

Near the shores of Hurricane Hole, **Estate Zootenvaal** (☎ 340-776-6321) is at the remote northeastern end of St John. Robin Clair manages these four units overlooking a large crescent cove on Coral Bay.

Out of Africa

Mysterious petroglyphs discovered at Reef Bay (see 'Hiking on St John') on the south shore of the island have suggested to archaeologists that not all of St John's earliest inhabitants came from the well-known groups of Caribbean Indians.

One scholar, Dr Berry Fell, identified the carving of crescents and dots as belonging to the 'Tifanag branch of a medieval Libyan script used as early as the 1st century and as late as the 13th century.' In other words, the petroglyphs are evidence that African explorers may have been on these islands before the arrival of Columbus and may have marked Reef Bay as a ceremonial site. Such an interpretation supports similar speculation growing from the discovery of African pottery and skeletons at Hull Bay on St Thomas. However, the evidence is far from conclusive, and the debate as to whether African explorers passed through the Virgins before Columbus seems mired in white denial.

You can get one- or two-bedroom units perched on the hillside overlooking the cove. Each unit has a full kitchen, deck and a decor splashed with tropical fabrics. Fans cool the rooms. There is no air-con, telephone or TV. High-season rates start at $175 per day. The weekly rate starts at about $1250.

Concordia Eco-tents (☎ 340-693-5855, 800-392-9004), at Estate Concordia on a cliff above Drunk Bay, are probably the most imaginative and environmentally sensitive accommodations on the island. Maho Bay's resort developer, Stanley Selengut, now has more than six of these 'tent-cottages' on stilts, strung together by boardwalks on the steep hillside. In some ways, these units are an extension of the Maho Bay tent design, but there is more wood in these structures, covered with a synthetic fabric skin. The views are more dramatic here than at Maho Bay because the eco-tents are on tall stilts above the tropical dry forest at their feet. And unlike Maho Bay with its hundreds of vacationers, Concordia seems barely populated.

Each shelter is 16x16 feet and has a living area, camp kitchen, bedroom, 2nd-floor loft and private bathroom complete with a composting toilet and solar-heated shower. The tents' fans and lights run on a 12-volt solar-generated electrical system, and the shower water comes from a rain-collection cistern under the tent. The resort also has its own swimming pool, and it's a half-mile walk to the beach at Salt Pond Bay. Expect to pay about $120 a night for two people. Each additional guest pays $25 (units sleep five or six). Most guests come in a rental car, but you can get to and from Concordia on the VITRAN bus (between Cruz Bay and Coral Bay), which runs along this road and turns around a Salt Pond Bay.

Places to Eat
Vie's Snack Shack (☎ 340-963-5033), on the East End Rd, recalls the days 50 years ago when Coral Bay was an undiscovered backwater. Vie Mahabir opened this plywood-sided restaurant next to her house in 1979, just after the government paved the road. Her motive was to find a way to make a living while she stayed home to raise her 10 children. In the process, Vie has built herself a reputation as a treasured island storyteller and chef. She has even appeared in a Lands' End apparel catalog photographed on St John. But don't just come here to bask in Vie's celebrity glow; eat her conch fritters ($4), garlic chicken with johnnycake ($5) and homemade coconut tarts ($2). Many islanders confess to an addiction to her island-style beef pate. Vie's is generally open 10 am to 5 pm Tuesday to Saturday. Vie also has a small campground here (see Places to Stay).

The *Sputnik Restaurant (☎ 340-693-5340)*, next to Emmaus Moravian Church in Coral Bay, is the breakfast place of a traveler's dreams – cheery, welcoming and reasonably priced. Paul Van Loon started this gourmet breakfast cafe in 1998 and opens his door at 6 am every day but Sunday (7 am).

The Sputnik takes its name from the West Indian bar that occupies the same building. You can sit at cafe tables on the patio or interior booths. Both locations have a fresh feel, and the tones of Ella Fitzgerald seeping from the stereo set a lazy mood. Homemade muffins and bagels cost $1.50, herbal tea $1. Two eggs, home fries and toast costs $3.50. The clientele is a friendly mix of continentals and West Indians. If you get here in late morning, wander next-door to the bar and ask 'Jam' the bartender about the *vevés* (talismans) of obeah worship carved under the paint in the door frame.

Sweets', way down Route 107 and a hill away from the Concordia Eco-tents and Salt Pond Bay, is just a van parked more or less permanently near the bay shore in front of a clutch of West Indians' homes. You eat at a picnic table where you can watch anglers casting for bonefish in the shallows. The specialty here is the fried snapper for $2 and outrageously cold Coors beer ($2). Thick chicken soup runs $4. Bring bug spray in the evening.

Pickles Cyber Deli (☎ 340 693-5140), at the Route 20 and Route 107 intersection in Coral Bay, is a takeout spot for folks catching breakfast on the run. The deli is even more popular with the lunch crowd, who stop for sandwiches like the roast turkey and Swiss cheese with sun-dried tomato pesto on homemade wheat, pumpernickel or sourdough ($5 small, $7 large). This is also the place to get online. Computers rent for $3 for 15 minutes, $5 for a half-hour.

Skinny Legs (☎ 340-779-4982), past the fire station on the East End Rd in Coral Bay, is a cheeseburger-in-paradise pavilion on the edge of a small boatyard. A loyal following of cruising sailors, continentals and East End snowbirds frequent this place for the food, the bar scene and live music (see Entertainment). The grilled mahimahi sandwich (under $8) is the way to go. You won't find blenders or french fries here.

Miss Lucy's Bar & Restaurant (☎ 340-779-4404), on Route 107 on the way to Salt Pond Bay, offers a mix of West Indian and US standards. Come for the callaloo soup (crab base with okra, spinach and spices) for $5 and the bay view from the deck. Vegetarians flock to Lucy's for the 'local trimmings' platter ($6.50) of pigeon peas, rice, sweet potato, fungi, plantain and sautéed veggies. Entrees run more than $10.

Entertainment

Skinny Legs (see Places to Eat) is the laidback and funky creation of Doug Sica and Moe Chabuz. This place draws caravans of islanders and travelers to the East End for some hearty parties. The attraction is a steady diet of live entertainment from throughout the archipelago. Bluegrass, calypso, reggae, country and rock fuel the fire. The crowd is largely continental and ranges from six to 60 years old. Everybody dances.

St Croix

Cruzans (pronounced CREW-shuns), as the residents of St Croix call themselves, have a habit of referring to their island as the 'stepchild' of the US Virgin Islands. The origins of the image are rooted in St Croix's isolated location, 40 miles south of the other Virgins. Geographically, St Croix looks significantly different from the other isles.

Highlights

- Dining & shopping among the historic streets of Christiansted & Frederiksted
- Sailing out to Buck Island for a day of snorkeling, hiking & barbecuing
- Reliving the sugar cane days at the Estate Whim Plantation Museum
- Biking or horseback riding on the lush rain forest trails
- Hiking to the wild East End beaches from Point Udall, the easternmost point in the USA

With a land area of 84 sq miles, St Croix is larger than St Thomas, St John and Tortola combined. To a noticeable degree, St Croix lacks the filigree coastline and steep mountains associated with the other Virgins. St Croix has its harbors, beaches and hills, but these features seem subtle in comparison to what you find on the other islands. And St Croix has something the other Virgins lack: The southern third of the island is a fertile coastal plain that has earned the island the nickname 'Garden of the Antilles.'

For most of the island's colonial history, the plain was one of the best places in the Caribbean to grow sugar cane. Although the sugar industry has vanished, its golden age left the island with one of the largest collections of historic buildings in the West Indies. Today, travelers can explore the ruined and restored plantations that dot the island as well as the extensive historic districts of Christiansted and Frederiksted, which date back more than 250 years.

While St Croix's attraction seems at first glance to be largely historical, the island has other charms as well. This is why many snowbirds come to St Croix each winter to pass the 'season' in hillside villas and condo villages. There are just as many wild and beautiful beaches on St Croix as on the other Virgins, plus golf courses and dozens of world-class snorkel and dive sites. The island also features plenty of hiking, mountain-biking and horseback-riding trails.

Best of all, the Cruzans have a sophisticated culture. About 60,000 people live and work on this island. More than half are the descendants of former slaves; about 30% are second- or third-generation immigrants from Puerto Rico; quite a few are young, white Americans who come to run a lot of the island's restaurants, inns and sports operations. There are also recent immigrants here from the Leeward Islands and the Dominican Republic. Middle Easterners run many shops. Even a few of the Danish plantation families survive.

Economically, the island tunes itself to industry as well as tourism. The Hess Oil facility on the south side of the island, some small electronic factories and a senapol cattle ranch have replaced the sugar plantations and kept the standard of living high for Cruzans. Now, St Croix's southern coastal plain is dotted with housing developments and shopping malls. Surprisingly, except during rush hour along Centerline Rd, St Croix has the easygoing feel of a much-less-developed island.

History
Probably no place in the Caribbean can match St Croix for the sheer bluster behind the island's human occupation.

Early Peoples From tools found at Betty's Hope plantation, archaeologists trace the island's habitation back to about 2000 BC. These first inhabitants were Ciboney Indians. Artifacts discovered at Richmond Plantation show that the first wave of the Arawak Indians, the Igneri, arrived here from South America in about AD 100 and stayed until about 1200. Around 1300, a second wave of Arawak, the Taíno, displaced the Igneri and set up a community at Salt River Bay. The common name for the island at this time was 'Ay Ay.'

When Christopher Columbus arrived at Salt River Bay in November 1493 and named the island 'Santa Cruz,' the Indian community he encountered was a mix of Caribs and Taíno with the Caribs in control. These were the warriors who attacked the arriving Spaniards, killing one and wounding another.

The First Colonists Threatened by the fierce Caribs, the Spanish drove the Indians out of St Croix, and the island remained more or less ignored by humans until Sir Walter Raleigh touched here in 1587 on his way to North America with a party of settlers. In 1621, English colonists came to establish plantations for sweet potatoes, corn and tobacco, but the colony lasted just four months before the Spanish rounded up the English and carted them off to Puerto Rico.

By 1625, the English had re-established their colony on one section of the island while Dutch and French settlers made a separate colony to the west.

The combined population of the two colonies grew to about 600 by 1645, when war broke out between the groups following the murder of the Dutch governor in the English governor's house. After the Dutch governor received a mortal wound, the British invited his replacement to the English colony to make peace. Upon this visit, the Dutchman was arrested and publicly shot. The English colonists paraded the body through the streets in triumph and hung it in the village square. Terrorized, the Dutch left for St Eustatius and St Martin; the French fled to Guadaloupe.

In 1650, a Spanish force of 1200 soldiers arrived to ambush a large number of the English settlers by night. The remainder fled to other colonies in the Leeward Islands. In short order, the former Dutch colonists mounted a return only to be killed by a Spanish garrison left on the island. The French planters also tried to return in two ships. The Spanish ambushed the first ship, murdering most of the settlers. But when a second French ship appeared, the Spaniards retreated to Puerto Rico. Meanwhile, back in England, the remaining English settlers from St Croix warned Oliver Cromwell of the Spaniard's attempt to put a death grip on the West Indies, prompting Cromwell to launch his war on Spain and claim Jamaica as English.

On St Croix, the French were now clearly in control, and they moved quickly to establish a viable colony with about 300 settlers. Malaria wiped out two-thirds of the colony. To combat the pestilence, the French set fire to the entire island and retreated to their ships to watch her burn. For the next 45 years, French colonists came to suffer, die and burn the land of St Croix. Several times during this period, the islands changed hands between French entities including the Knights of Malta, the French West Indian Company and King Louis XIV. Finally, in 1695, the French colonists decided to abandon the island.

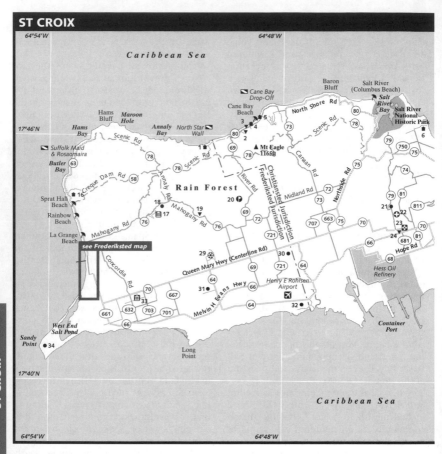

ST CROIX

Danish Colonization By 1725, rumors circulated throughout the West Indies that the British were planning to recolonize St Croix. Fearing a growing British presence in the region, Governor Moth of the Danish West India and Guinea Company in St Thomas urged his company to purchase the island. Nine years later, the French agreed to sell St Croix to help pay for their war against Poland.

In 1734, the Danes made big plans to colonize the third jewel of what would be their Virgin Islands colony for nearly two centuries. The Danish company quickly moved to create a number of financial incentives to attract settlers. Many who came to St Croix were British planters from St John, Tortola and Virgin Gorda, but the Danes solicited for settlers in Europe as well. In spite of two devastating hurricanes, St Croix become a lively place with about 300 plantations for sugar and cotton. By 1754, there were 7566 black slaves on the island, outnumbering the white planters by a ratio of about 10 to one.

In 1759, rumors of a planned slave rebellion shook St Croix. When the island's white government got wind of the alleged plot, the ringleaders were quickly rounded up,

[handwritten notes at top of page: "Left > Pass Gas station... 6pm Christmas Turner Maintenance - Homersa"]

ST CROIX

[Map of St Croix with coordinates 64°42'W and 64°36'W, showing Buck Island, Buck Island Channel, Green Cay, various bays, roads, and numbered locations]

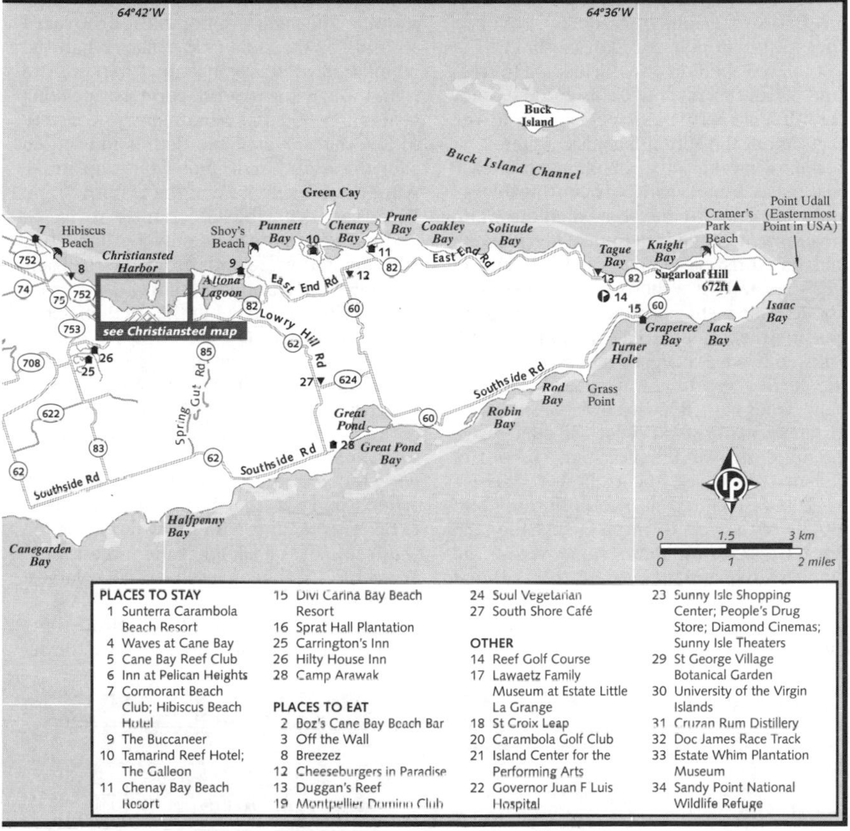

PLACES TO STAY
1 Sunterra Carambola Beach Resort
4 Waves at Cane Bay
5 Cane Bay Reef Club
6 Inn at Pelican Heights
7 Cormorant Beach Club; Hibiscus Beach Hotel
9 The Buccaneer
10 Tamarind Reef Hotel; The Galleon
11 Chenay Bay Beach Resort
15 Divi Carina Bay Beach Resort
16 Sprat Hall Plantation
25 Carrington's Inn
26 Hilty House Inn
28 Camp Arawak

PLACES TO EAT
2 Boz's Cane Bay Beach Bar
3 Off the Wall
8 Breezez
12 Cheeseburgers in Paradise
13 Duggan's Reef
19 Montpellier Domino Club
24 Soul Vegetarian
27 South Shore Café

OTHER
14 Reef Golf Course
17 Lawaetz Family Museum at Estate Little La Grange
18 St Croix Leap
20 Carambola Golf Club
21 Island Center for the Performing Arts
22 Governor Juan F Luis Hospital
23 Sunny Isle Shopping Center; People's Drug Store; Diamond Cinemas; Sunny Isle Theaters
29 St George Village Botanical Garden
30 University of the Virgin Islands
31 Cruzan Rum Distillery
32 Doc James Race Track
33 Estate Whim Plantation Museum
34 Sandy Point National Wildlife Refuge

tortured on the wheel, burned at the stake and hung. Terrorized into submission, the slaves bent to the Danish rule, and St Croix bloomed literally and economically for the next 60 years in spite of more devastating hurricanes.

During this epoch, the Danes moved their colonial capital from St Thomas to their new planned community of Christiansted. And by 1792, the island had 197 plantations and 22,000 slaves; 18,000 worked in the fields. The white population still numbered fewer that 3000. The same year, the Danish king declared further slave trade illegal, but 4000 more slaves arrived on the island by 1803. Describing this epoch in island history, the poet Philip Freneau wrote, 'If you have tears prepare to shed them now...no class of mankind in the known world undergo so complete servitude....' Meanwhile, sugar cane production soared to more than 40 million pounds of sugar per year. Windmills and oxen mills dotted the landscape.

Emancipation & Revolt Things began to turn sour for the Cruzan economy after two brief British occupations (in 1801 and also

1807–15). England's Parliament abolished slavery in 1834, and the freeing of slaves in the British Caribbean colonies provoked cries for freedom in the Danish islands. The 1848 slave rebellion ensued, leading to freedom for all slaves on St Croix and the other Danish Virgin Islands (see History in the Facts about the Virgin Islands chapter).

Following the slave rebellion, an uneasy peace was established between the blacks and whites on St Croix, but when the white government banned traditional black festivities on Christmas 1852, riots broke out in Christiansted. As if these waves of riots had not devastated the island enough, an earthquake struck in 1867, overwhelming Frederiksted to such a degree that a US warship was carried by a tidal wave over the tops of palm trees and deposited a considerable distance inland. And what the tidal wave did not destroy in Frederiksted, a labor riot did: In 1878, black anger about repressive wage laws resulted in a mob burning and looting of the port town, an event called the Fireburn. During these same years, the Danish government moved the colonial capital back to St Thomas, a clear sign that most observers had doubts about a positive future for St Croix.

US Purchase & Hurricanes Depopulation ensued. By the beginning of the 20th century, the island's population hovered around 15,000 souls (95% black), half the population of nearly a century earlier. And even though sugar production was peaking at about 19,000 tons per annum, prices were so low that poverty and depression settled over the island and fields went unplanted. After the US purchase of the Danish Virgin Islands in 1917, the US tried to revive St Croix's plantation economy by importing laborers and merchants from Puerto Rico. A Puerto Rican community took root around Frederiksted, but the tired one-crop economy withered.

The island's fortune changed during the 1960s, largely because of tax incentives to US corporations – part of a plan by the US government to industrialize the island. Some small manufacturing plants have located here, but it is the Hess Oil refinery, which arrived in 1962, that has truly changed St Croix. This facility, with its own port on the south side of the island, is the largest refinery in the Caribbean and one of the largest in the world.

Consistent with the island's history, life on modern St Croix has remained turbu-

Women cultivating sugar cane (1941)

Fireburn Queens

During and after slavery, plantation workers had a tradition of choosing a 'queen' for each plantation. This tradition came from West Africa and was simply an extension of the matriarchal society existing in the blacks' former homelands. In a sense, communities of plantation laborers on St Croix took the place of African tribes, and each plantation community chose a woman who was intelligent and fearless to be its queen.

When unrest erupted in October 1878 over a labor dispute, three plantation queens – Mary, Agnes and Mathilda – led their constituents off the plantations and brought the growing unrest of laborers gathered in Frederiksted to a climax. Looting had broken out in town when Queen Mary arrived and reportedly said, 'The town is not lighted up yet? You are too slow. We must have light.'

Eventually, most of Frederiksted blazed and fires rose on plantations across the West End, as each of the three queens led a legion to burn the crops and machinery that oppressed them. By the time the governor brought the riot under control, Frederiksted and 50 of the 87 West End plantations had been ravaged. Three whites and 100 blacks lost their lives.

Danish authorities charged the three 'Queens of the Fireburn' as ringleaders. The women would surely have been executed had it not been for popular support in Denmark for the queens' actions to right the wrongs of the plantation system. Ultimately, the women went to Denmark to serve prison sentences. But before they returned to St Croix, they were received by the king and queen of Denmark as working-class heroines. Back on the island, the queens ended their days as market vendors.

lent. A series of devastating hurricanes have raked the island in recent years. In 1989, Hurricane Hugo damaged or destroyed about 90% of island structures and left more than one-third of the population homeless. Since then, St Croix has weathered attacks from equally vicious category-four Hurricanes Marilyn (1995) and Lenny (1999). Stricter building codes after each hurricane have gone a long way to limit the destruction caused by the most recent storms, but everyone on the island can tell you horror stories about their personal ordeals surviving these monstrous hurricanes. In fact, regeneration in the face of adversity seems to be a defining quality of the Cruzans. They rise from the rubble.

Orientation

Shaped like a meat cleaver, St Croix stretches 28 miles from the end of the handle in the east to the tip of the blade in the west. At its widest, the island spans 7 miles from north to south. A chain of hills, several rising more than 900 feet, characterizes virtually the entire north coast of the island. Among these hills, Mt Eagle overlooking the northwest coast (1165ft) is the highest. The south side of the island, where both the airport and huge oil refinery lie, is a broad, low plain. You will find the main town, Christiansted, at midisland on the north shore, where the handle of the meat cleaver joins the blade. Frederiksted, the island's other historical town, sits at the West End.

Two major roads connect the two towns via the coastal plain. The older of these roads is Route 70, named Queen Mary Hwy but commonly referred to as Centerline Rd. Shopping malls and housing developments line this artery. There are plenty of stoplights and lots of traffic on this highway during morning and afternoon rush hours. If you are in a hurry, you can take the four-lane limited-access Route 66 between the two towns. The island airport lies just south of this road, as does the Hess Oil refinery. For scenic coastal drives, and to access the best island beaches and snorkeling and diving sites, head east or west from Christiansted along the north shore. Route 82,

East End Rd, runs all the way to Point Udall, the easternmost point in the US.

Cruzans still refer to neighborhoods on the island by the names of St Croix's ancestral plantations. These evocative names, such as 'Lower Love,' 'Catherine's Hope,' 'Sweet Bottom,' 'Betsy's Jewel' and 'Morning Star,' add a touch of romance and intrigue to Cruzan locales. You'll see the names and borders of these plantations printed on most maps of the island.

The St Croix Hotel & Tourism Association (☎ 340-773-7117) and the Virgin Islands Department of Tourism Visitors Bureau (see below) offer several free maps to visitors. You can pick up these maps at displays in most inns and restaurants on the island, as well as at the visitors center in the Old Danish Scale House on the Christiansted waterfront. The best of these maps is a four-color affair published by the Government of the Virgin Islands of the United States. There are also color road maps of the island and the towns in the front pages of the telephone book.

Information

Tourist Offices For travelers' information on the island, head to the visitors bureau (☎ 340-773-0495) in Christiansted, at 52 Company St near Market Square. It's open 8 am to 5 pm weekdays and on weekends when cruise ships arrive in Frederiksted. Visit its Web site at www.st-croix.com.

You can pick up more information and tickets to visit the National Park Service buildings (including the fort) at Kings Wharf in Christiansted, in the Old Danish Scale House (☎ 340-773-1460) adjacent to Fort Christiansvaern, open from 8:30 am to 4:30 pm daily.

Tourism information is harder to come by in Frederiksted. There is a tourist information booth in a kiosk near the cruise ship pier, but it's only open when a ship is in port. The airport has a tourist bureau booth (☎ 340-778-1061) as well, staffed during business hours daily.

Money St Croix is an easy place to take care of your money needs. Chase Manhat-

tan, Citibank, First Bank, Scotiabank and Banco Popular de Puerto Rico are all on the island. Most have a number of branch offices, both in the towns and along Centerline Rd. All of the banks have central locations in the vicinity of King and Company Sts in Christiansted. Although hours may vary slightly, most banks are open 9 am to 2:30 pm Monday to Thursday and from 9 am to 5 pm Friday.

Post & Communications You will find Christiansted's main post office (☎ 340-773-3586) at the corner of Church and Company Sts in the center of town. There is also a post office in the Gallows Bay Shopping Center and one in Frederiksted on Fisher St. All of these offices are open 8:30 am to 4:30 pm weekdays and 8:30 am to noon Saturday.

The Usual Suspects (see Places to Eat under Christiansted) has Internet access; online rates are $5 for a half-hour.

Bookstores & Libraries In Christiansted, you can check out Trader Bob's Bookshop (☎ 340-773-6001) in the Gallows Bay Shopping Center for a full-service bookstore. The Bookie (☎ 340-773-2592), 3 Strand St, has a good selection of papers and magazines and a few paperbacks. Kallaloo (☎ 340-773-3378), 15 Church St, near the post office, is the place to come for poetry readings and books by West Indian writers.

The Florence Williams Public Library (☎ 340-773-5715), King St at Kings Cross St, began as the home of a wealthy merchant-planter in 1838 but has been largely replaced by a newer structure.

Newspapers The *St Croix Avis* is the island's daily paper and the place to turn for local, national and international news. Travelers with a sense of humor will want to have a look at the *Island Melee,* which advertises 'none of the truth none of the time' and offers spoofs of island politics and current events as well as an entertainment section with risqué personal ads. *St Croix This Week* is an excellent free monthly tabloid that covers the island's tourist attractions from art to water sports.

Laundry There are plenty of laundries around the island, but travelers favor the Blue Angel, up the hill in Christiansted on Queen Cross St, between Hill and East Sts. Plan on $1.50 a wash.

Medical Services & Emergencies The Governor Juan F Luis Hospital (☎ 340-776-6311) is a sophisticated health care facility next to the Sunny Isle Shopping Center on Centerline Rd in midisland.

The People's Drug Store is a popular operation with stores at the Sunny Isle Shopping Center (☎ 340-778-5537) and at 1A Kings St (☎ 340-778-7355) in the center of Christiansted.

Call ☎ 911 for police, fire and ambulance.

Dangers & Annoyances As Caribbean islands go, St Croix is safer than most. However, plenty of Cruzans envy the real or imagined wealth of visitors to St Croix. The island still lives in the shadow of the day in the early 1970s when Black Power warriors massacred nine people on what is now the Carambola Golf Course.

Within the last decade, villains attacked a tourist couple on a remote beach: The attackers killed the woman's companion and raped her before she swam out to sea to be rescued by a fisherman.

Lonely beaches are no place to go without a group of friends. In particular, stay away from the Sandy Point Wildlife Refuge at the southwest corner of the island. Columbus Beach at Salt River Bay also has a dodgy reputation. In Christiansted, the area west of King Cross St is littered with strip clubs, rowdy bars, prostitution, drugs and vagrants. Avoid this area after dark. A similar red-light district exists in Frederiksted on King St for three blocks south of the intersection with Market St.

Organized Tours

St Croix vendors offer a number of island tours. St Croix Safari Tours (☎ 340-773-6700) has a 25-passenger open-air bus that departs Kings Wharf in Christiansted for a narrated tour of the island's major attractions. The trip lasts 5½ hours and costs about $35.

St Croix Heritage Tours (☎ 340-778-6997) offers walking tours of Christiansted and Frederiksted as well as customized tours to island attractions like Whim Plantation. Prices are based on the customized tour you request, but plan on $10 for one of the town walking tours.

St Croix Water Sports (☎ 340-773-7060), at Hotel on the Cay on Protestant Cay, offers reef tours aboard its semisubmersible *Oceanique* for $20.

Biplane Bob's three-passenger WACO (☎ 340-690-7433), at the airport, comes complete with a video system to record your flight. Bob is only on the island during the winter months. Rates are about $100 an hour for two passengers.

Also see Salt River National Historic Park, later in the chapter, for kayak tours of Salt River Bay.

Special Events

The visitors bureau (see Tourist Offices, earlier) in Christiansted is the place to go for information on St Croix's festivals and celebrations.

The St Croix Agricultural Festival, in mid-February, takes place at the fairgrounds on Centerline Rd. The three-day event features island crafters, food stalls with superb examples of West Indian and Puerto Rican cooking, flora exhibitions and livestock contests. Of course, there is plenty of entertainment from bands that come from around the Virgin Islands.

During the St Patrick's Day Parade, on March 17, Cruzans become adopted Irish for a day. Bands and floats process through Christiansted while islanders dress in green and find this day a perfect excuse to forget work and kick back at the beaches and pubs.

The St Croix Half-Ironman Triathlon (☎ 340-773-4470) takes place in early May and features qualifying spots for the Ironman World Championship in Kona, Hawaii. The event also provides qualifying spots for the Subaru Ironman Canada and the Isuzu Ironman USA Lake Placid triathlons.

Danish West Indies Emancipation Day is July 3, and Cruzans celebrate this event with

ST CROIX

a holiday from work, beach parties, family gatherings at places like Cramer's Park and plenty of fireworks over the fort and harbor in Christiansted.

The Crucian Christmas Fiesta runs from December 17 to January 7. This event puts a West Indies spin on the holiday shopping hype that seems to have spread the world over. Most of the decorations and events focus on Christiansted and a ballfield east of town. There is a Christmas village, a lot of musical performances and, of course, a Santa.

Getting There & Away

The Henry E Rohlsen Airport, off Route 66 on the southwest end of the island, can handle jumbo jets and has a new expanded terminal. But direct service to St Croix from the US has been an on-again, off-again proposition for years. Most travelers fly here via connecting flights through San Juan, Puerto Rico or St Thomas. St Croix gets its most frequent air service from American Airlines. Continental, Delta, TWA, United and US Airways also have connecting flights to St Croix.

For travel within the Caribbean, flyers look to American Eagle flights operating out of Puerto Rico. These flights tend to be expensive when not booked as a leg on a longer flight, but prices have come down in recent years. Fares can drop as low as $90 one way and $160 roundtrip. Air Sunshine flies to Tortola and San Juan. Cape Air is the new player here, with 14 flights a day between St Croix and San Juan, six flights a day between St Croix and St Thomas. Gulfstream International also flies the San Juan–St Croix run. Vieques Airlink flies to the island several times a week from San Juan or Fajardo in Puerto Rico. LIAT offers service to the other Lesser Antilles, as does Coastal Air Transport.

Seabourne Aviation's (☎ 340-773-6442) floatplanes commute between Charlotte Amalie and Christiansted (about $60 each way). The seaplane float is next to the Annapolis Sailing School on the waterfront in Christiansted. Bohlke International Airways (☎ 340-778-9177) has charter service

between St Croix and St Thomas and San Juan.

See the Getting There & Away chapter for more details.

Getting Around

To/From the Airport A taxi is the easiest way to make this trip. The fare for two passengers going between Christiansted and the airport is $10, $8 to Frederiksted. Additional passengers pay $4 to $5 more. Cabs are readily available at the airport.

You can also get bus service between the airport and the two major towns. Buses run about every 40 minutes and cost $1 for passengers under 55 years old; the senior fare is 55¢.

Bus VITRAN operates buses between Christiansted and Frederiksted. The bus route starts at Tide Village east of Christiansted and ends at Fort Frederik in Frederiksted. Look for the VITRAN bus stop signs at the end of the routes and at intermediate stops, mostly on Centerline Rd.

Buses travel this route seven days a week between the hours of 5:30 am and 9:30 pm, departing their stops at 40-minute intervals. The fare for people under 55 is $1; seniors pay 55¢; transfers cost 25¢. You must have exact change. If you're desperate for more bus information, try calling ☎ 340-773-1290 between 9 am and 4 pm weekdays. You may reach a person but will likely get an answering machine.

Car St Croix has several car rental agencies, but none of them seem to have many cars. Book ahead for a vehicle if you can. You can sometimes get cars for about $30 a day with unlimited mileage, but don't be surprised to hear vendors quote rates of $45 and up (shop around).

Some of the best rates on new vehicles are offered by Centerline Car Rentals (☎ 340-778-0450). Gold Mine Car Rental (☎ 340-773-0299), located in a Christiansted jewelry shop, offers a three-day special for $80.

Also try Avis (☎ 340-778-3995), Budget (☎ 340-778-9636), Olympic (☎ 340-773-8000) and Thrifty (☎ 340-773-7200).

Taxi Because taxis are not metered, you must set your fare before leaving. Ask your driver for a look at the rate sheet or get yourself a copy of the free *St Croix This Week,* which lists the rates between principal places on the island. Note that a surcharge of $1 to $1.50 applies to cabs called between midnight and 6 am. The minimum fare within town limits is $2. The taxi stand in Christiansted is at Kings St near Government House; in Frederiksted, it's at Market Square.

The following taxi services get good marks from islanders: St Croix Taxi Association (☎ 340-778-1088), Frederiksted Taxi Service (☎ 340-772-4775) and Cruzan Taxi Association (☎ 340-773-6388).

Bicycle If you stay off Centerline Rd (which is packed during rush hour) and refrain from travel during the heat of the day, you may find bicycling an invigorating way to get around St Croix. St Croix Bike and Tours (☎ 340-772-2343), in Frederiksted, offers rentals and guided bike excursions. You can rent a KHS mountain bike with full or front suspension. Rentals run $25 for the first day, $15 for a half-day, $10 for each additional day.

CHRISTIANSTED

Pressed between hills and a shallow, reef-protected harbor, Christiansted on St Croix's north coast is not only the island's major town but also a traveler's delight.

For decades, Christiansted's greatest appeal lay in its six-block historic district (set aside for preservation in 1952), which includes well over 100 residential, commercial and government buildings from the 18th and 19th centuries of Danish colonial rule. Here, the well-preserved fortress, flanked by gold, pink and brown West Indies neoclassic buildings, evokes the days when Christiansted was the capital of the Danish Virgin Islands and St Croix plantocracy society was awash in gold. In recent years, Christiansted has evolved from its status as an anachronism into a vibrant entertainment district with a broad range of accommodations, shopping opportunities, dining experiences and nightlife that draws a fresh mix of upscale Cruzans and visitors to downtown.

With its historical significance, cleanliness, walkability and array of dining and entertainment opportunities, Christiansted embodies almost everything many travelers hope for in a West Indies town. Here you can kick back at a waterfront brewpub or in a courtyard restaurant and make friends with the West Indians at the next table. Christiansted, whose population has declined from 5000 to 2500 since its sugar cane heyday, is an intimate community where a chef might wave you in off King St to sample her soup, and then remember your name days later when she sees you again at a jazz club.

History

Upon the Danish purchase of St Croix from the French in 1733–34, the Danish governor Frederick Moth designed Christiansted using Norway's picturesque town of Christiania (now Oslo) as a model. This new town would rise on the rubble of the ramshackle French outpost of Bassin and would take its name from the reigning Danish monarch, Christian VI.

Moth drew up a town with a fort on its waterfront to protect the nearby commercial buildings of the Danish West India and Guinea Company and a rectangular grid of streets where the town was subdivided into building sites. Surveyors laid out the first street, Strand Gade (Strand St) in 1735. The building code allowed for the construction of wood or masonry structures in a straight line along the street fronts. These structures could be two or three stories high built on masonry footings with shingled or tile roofs.

Thrilled with the development of the modern town and the burgeoning prosperity of this garden isle, the Danes moved the capital of the Danish West Indies here from St Thomas in 1755, where it remained until 1871. Christiansted grew rapidly during the last decades of the 18th century, and by 1800, the town's population reached 5284.

Many of the town's 18th-century buildings might have been lost to modernization

ST CROIX

ST CROIX

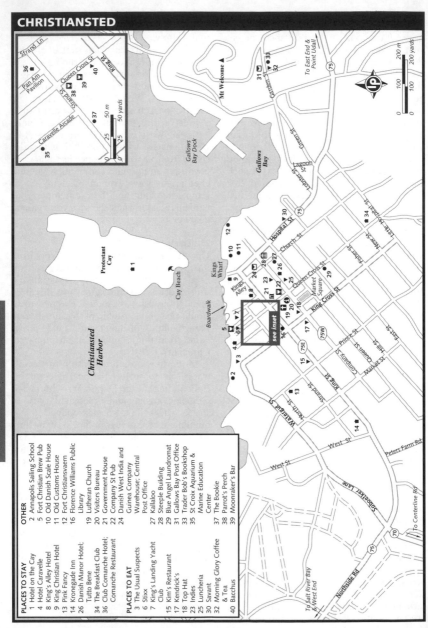

CHRISTIANSTED

Strand Ln

36 Pan Am Pavilion

Queen Cross St

King St

40

39

38

Strand St

37

Caravelle Arcade

35

0   25   50 m
0   25   50 yards

Mt Welcome

Garden St

31

32   33

To East End &
Point Udall

(75)

N

0   100   200 m
0   100   200 yards

Gallows
Bay Dock

Gallows
Bay

Lagoon St

Hospital St

30

(75)

12

10   9

11

Church St

28

27

26

25

24

23

22

21

Green St

Lagoon St

New St

Little Hospital St

Fisher St

34

Christiansted Harbor

Protestant
Cay

1

Cay Beach

Boardwalk

Kings
Wharf

Kings
Alley

5

6   7

4

3

2

see inset

19   20   18

16

17

15

13

14

Queen Cross St

King Cross St

Market Street
Square

29

(75W)

(75E)

(75W)

Prince St

Company St

Queen St

Market St

King St

Hill St

East St

North St

Strand St

Water Gut St

West St

West St

Peters Farm Rd

Sebastian Lane

To Salt River Bay
& West End

Northside Rd

(75)

To Centerline Rd

(70)

PLACES TO STAY
1   Hotel on the Cay
4   Hotel Caravelle
8   King's Alley Hotel
9   King Christian Hotel
13   Pink Fancy
14   Kronegade Inn
26   Danish Manor Hotel;
     Tutto Bene
34   The Breakfast Club
36   Club Comanche Hotel;
     Comanche Restaurant

PLACES TO EAT
3   The Usual Suspects
6   Stixx
7   King's Landing Yacht
     Club
15   Kim's Restaurant
17   Kendrick's
18   Top Hat
23   Indies
25   Luncheria
30   Savant
32   Morning Glory Coffee
     & Tea
40   Bacchus

OTHER
2   Annapolis Sailing School
5   Fort Christian Brew Pub
10   Old Danish Scale House
11   Old Customs House
12   Fort Christiansvaern
16   Florence Williams Public
     Library
19   Lutheran Church
20   Visitors Bureau
21   Government House
22   Company St Pub
24   Danish West India and
     Guinea Company
     Warehouse; Central
     Post Office
27   Kallaloo
28   Steeple Building
29   Blue Angel Laundromat
31   Gallows Bay Post Office
33   Trader Bob's Bookshop
35   St Croix Aquarium &
     Marine Education
     Center
37   The Bookie
38   Parrot's Perch
39   Moonraker's Bar

if the sugar industry had not gone into serious decline in the 1820s. As the island fell into economic hard times, Christiansted settled into dormancy, and little changed here for almost 200 years.

Since the 1960s, tourism has altered the function of a lot of Christiansted's buildings, as inns, restaurants, pubs and boutiques moved into town. But to a large degree, the old façades remain. Fort Christiansvaern, the old Danish commercial and government buildings and 27 acres at the heart of the town are under the direct administration of the National Park Service.

Orientation

Kings Wharf stands at the heart of Christiansted. Most of the historic buildings preserved by the National Park Service border this wharf. The historic district stretches southwest of here along a grid of narrow one-way streets.

The main arteries through town are King St (eastbound) and Company St (westbound). You will find most of the restaurants, pubs and shops along these streets, as well as on the cross streets and alleys. Gallows Bay is the new shopping district across the harbor to the east. The area west of King Cross St is a red-light district.

Kings Wharf

This is the commercial landing where, for more than 250 years, ships landed with slaves and set off with sugar or molasses. The heart of Christiansted's historic district, the wharf is now home to a harborside boardwalk, small hotels, restaurants, shops, pubs, water tour operators and the ferry to Protestant Cay. The wharf is the natural place for any walking tour of the town to begin.

Old Danish Scale House

The current Scale House, with its two-story, yellow-masonry construction and hipped roof dates from 1856. This is the site where the Danish weighed hogsheads of sugar for export; imports were also weighed here, to levy duty. You can see the scales as you enter the building. The 2nd floor was the weighmaster's office, while the rear of the

building once garrisoned Danish soldiers. Now, this building is an information center for the National Park Service (☎ 340-773-1460), where you can pick up brochures describing the national park buildings and historic Christiansted, as well as buy an entrance ticket ($2) for the national park properties. It's open 8:30 am to 4:30 pm daily.

Fort Christiansvaern

Built of masonry and yellow Danish brick that came to the islands as ballast in sailing ships, this fort took shape between 1738 and 1749 over the ruins of a French bastion. Fort Christiansvaern (Christian's Defenses) is a four-point citadel and the best preserved of the five Danish forts in the West Indies. Its ramparts surround a central courtyard.

Though Danish soldiers quartered here until 1878, and the walls have protected citizens from the onslaught of pirates, hurricanes and slave revolts, the fort's guns have never been fired in an armed conflict. After 1878, the fort served as a prison and courthouse for the island. Visitors touring the fort will find cannons in place on the ramparts, plus a magazine, soldiers quarters furnished in period decor, prison cells and a kitchen, as well as a small military museum. All the buildings are 8:30 am to 4:30 pm daily and require a $2 admission ticket for people over six years old. Park in the lot next to the fort ($2 for two hours).

Old Customs House

The yellow brick and masonry building with its sweeping 16-step entrance stairway stands between the fort and the Old Danish Scale House at Kings Wharf. The building served as the Danes' customs house for more than a century. Begun in 1750, the building evolved over decades; the 2nd floor was added around 1830. This floor was once the town's post office. The Park Service sometimes holds art exhibitions on the 1st floor, and the 2nd floor holds offices.

Danish West India and Guinea Company Warehouse

Just across the intersection of Hospital and King Sts from the Old Customs House stands a three-story neoclassical building with dormers set into the steep, hipped roof and a courtyard surrounded by a wall. Today, this building functions as the town's central post office, but it began life in 1749 as the headquarters and warehouse for the Danish West India and Guinea Company.

The courtyard here was the site of one of the West Indies' most active slave markets until the abolition of the slave trade in the early 19th century. The building has also served as military quarters and as the office for the Panama Telegraph Company early in the 20th century.

Steeple Building

The white building with the Georgian steeple, across Company St from the Danish West India and Guinea Company Warehouse, was St Croix's first house of worship, the Church of Lord God of the Sabaoth. Lutherans erected this edifice between 1750 and 1753, adding the steeple four decades later. In 1831, the government converted the building into a military bakery. It has been modified several times since then and put to use as a hospital and school.

Today, the Steeple Building houses the National Park Service Museum, with exhibits depicting life in old St Croix. There are Taíno relics, agricultural exhibits and a model of a working sugar plantation. Like other National Park Service buildings, this one is open 8:30 am to 4:30 pm daily. Your $2 admission ticket to the fort gains you entrance here as well.

Government House

This three-story, U-shaped building, mixing neoclassic and baroque elements, fills a full quarter of a block between King and Company Sts, just west of the other historic buildings at Kings Wharf. Begun as a private home in 1747, Government House evolved into one of the most elaborate governor's residences in all of the Lesser Antilles. Various Danish governors bought up surrounding townhouses and joined them together to form the current structure, which has galleries of colonnades surrounding a grassy courtyard and ornamental garden.

Visitors can enter via the sweeping staircase on King St and explore the huge 2nd-floor reception hall, which is still used for some formal government functions. The period furnishings are gifts from the Danish government. It's open 8:30 am to 4:30 pm daily; admission is $2.

Lutheran Church

Just beyond Government House as you move west on King St stands Christiansted's oldest church. Begun in about 1740 as the Dutch Reformed Church, this one-story, cruciform-plan house of worship became the property of the Lutherans in the early 1830s, when they moved here from the Steeple Building. The building is remarkable not only for its age, but also for the unusual three-tier Gothic tower added over the entranceway years after the original construction. This is still an active parish. Call ☎ 340-773-1320 for current service times and opening hours.

Market Square

Frederik Moth laid out Market Square in 1735 as the site for the town's produce market. The site still attracts some fruit and vegetable vendors (especially on Saturday morning) around the intersection of Company and Queen Cross Sts. Restored colonial townhouses and reproductions of period buildings form a shopping arcade called Market Square Mall, where minivans pick up and drop off passengers from cruise ships docked in Frederiksted.

St Croix Aquarium & Marine Education Center

This small aquarium (☎ 340-773-8995), in the Caravelle Arcade, looks a bit like a pet shop from the outside, but inside it's pure entertainment. Biologist Lonnie Kaczmarsky will take you on a half-hour tour of his tanks. The largest is 500 gallons and shows you an array of local sea creatures, ranging from a sea horse and a blue-headed wrasse to lobsters and a nurse shark.

As you travel among the tanks, you learn about species identification, feeding habits, mating behavior, reef conservation, diving and snorkeling tips and local sea lore. Lonnie's passion is infectious, and kids love the hands-on Discovery Room. The aquarium is open 11 am to 4 pm Tuesday to Saturday; admission is $4.50 for adults, $2 for children.

Protestant Cay

This small triangular cay, less than 200 yards from Kings Wharf (a five-minute ferry ride, $3 roundtrip), is the site of a small resort called Hotel on the Cay (see Places to Stay, later) whose beach bar/restaurant and wide sandy beach are open to the public.

There is a water-sports operation here, and you can rent a beach chair for $2. The beach offers protected swimming and snorkeling off the north side, as well as a vista that looks out over the sailboat anchorage, Fort Christiansvaern and Kings Wharf. Burgers at the beach bar run under $6. No West Indies port has such a perfect little oasis so close at hand.

Activities

There are three free, lighted public tennis courts at Canegata Park. More outdoor activities are listed in the Activities sections throughout this chapter.

Diving If you are a scuba enthusiast and you miss the north shore dives at Cane Bay Drop-Off, North Star Wall and Salt River Canyon, you may have blown your trip to the islands. Great wreck dives around St Croix are Truck Lagoon, the *Suffolk Maid* and *Rosaomaira*. Frederiksted Pier is an exceptional dive as well. One of the best things about diving St Croix is that while almost all the dive operators offer boat dives, many of the most exciting dives, such as Cane Bay, involve beach entries with short swims to the reef. On the deep side of the reef (just 100 to 200 yards offshore), there is a wall that drops off at a 60-degree slope to a depth of more than 12,000 feet. All the operators listed below charge $40 to $50 for one-tank dives, about $75 for two tanks and about the same for night dives.

Dive St Croix (☎ 340-773-3434, 800-523-3483), at the King Christian Hotel at Kings Wharf, is the underwater arm of popular Milemark Watersports.

St Croix Ultimate Bluewater Adventures (☎ 340-773-5994, 887-789-7282) is in the Caravelle Arcade next to the aquarium.

VI Divers (☎ 340-773-6045, 800-544-5911), at the Pan Am Pavilion, is the oldest dive operator on the island.

Fishing Sportfishing enthusiasts head for the waters north of the island for a long season of good fishing that runs from September to June. Kingfish, wahoo and bonito are usually the biggest catches, but sometimes the boats hook into marlin, yellowfin tuna and swordfish. Four-hour charters run about $400 on most of the boats, $700 for 8 hours.

Ruffian and *Shenanigans* (☎ 340-778-8974) both run out of the St Croix Marina in the Gallows Bay neighborhood east of Christiansted.

Captain Pete's *Louie G* (☎ 340-773-1123) also runs out of the St Croix Marina; the trip is free if you come home empty-handed.

Also at the St Croix Marina, the fishhawk Captain Bill Schmidt and his 38-foot Bertram special *Fantasy* (☎ 340-773-0917) await.

Sailing Most travelers combine their sailing adventures with trips to Buck Island aboard the big, 49-passenger catamarans operated by Milemark and Big Beard (see the 'Buck Island Tours' boxed text), but you can charter crewed boats for a tailor-made excursion on the water. You can also book a learn-to-sail package that includes a Christiansted hotel and daily instruction in your own 24-foot sloop.

Belinda Charters (☎ 340-773-1614) offers day trips for six on a 36-foot sloop with snorkeling gear and a catered lunch ($75 per person for 6 hours).

If sailing is not your cup of tea, consider booking a cruise aboard the 34-foot trawler yacht *Lisa* (☎ 340-713-9084).

Annapolis Sailing School (☎ 800-638-9192) has its base at the foot of King Cross St across from the Holger Danske Hotel. You can book a three-day, four-night learn-to-sail vacation with them (including your room) for about $950 single, $1300 double. The five-day program costs about $1350 single, $1850 double.

Windsurfing & Parasailing St Croix can be nirvana for board sailors. The problem is that there is no sailboard shop on the island. A few of the hotels offer older sailboards for novices. Those seeking instruction or board rental head for St Croix Water Sports (☎ 340-773-7060) on Protestant Cay.

Hotel on the Cay on Protestant Cay offers parasail rides for about $30.

Hiking If you pick up a copy of the *St Croix Avis,* you will often find articles about nature hikes on the island written by Professor Olasie Davis (☎ 340-692-8040), who teaches ecology at UVI in St Croix. This knowledgeable man is the dynamo behind the island's active St Croix Hiking Club (☎ 340-773-8409), which stages monthly hikes.

Travelers who want a tailor-made hike can contact island guides and herbalists Lamumba or Olu (☎ 340-772-0827, 340-778-6164), who will lead you on trails through the steeps of the rain forest for a fee of about $25.

Caribbean Adventure Tours (☎ 340-773-4599) offers a three-hour tidepooling hike on the northwest coast and a hike and picnic to Isaac Bay on the East End. Both trips cost $45.

The St Croix Environmental Association (☎ 340-773-1989) offers a hike to a different location daily. Hikes go from 9 to 11:30 am. You need a five-day advance reservation, and there's a four-person minimum.

Places to Stay

Before Hurricane Hugo hit St Croix in 1989, there were nearly 2500 guestrooms on the island. Today, only about 1000 of those rooms remain. Nevertheless, the accommodations industry is healthy again, and travelers can find a variety of places to stay while visiting St Croix. Prices listed are based on the winter high season unless otherwise noted.

The *Breakfast Club* (☎ 340-773-8642, 18 Queen Cross St) offers more than you might expect for the price. This villa with nine rooms sits on the hillside overlooking Christiansted just four blocks from the center of town and near the laundry. All rooms have a bath plus kitchen, and there is a shared hot tub on the deck with a great harbor view. In high season, singles start at about $65, doubles $75, including a gourmet breakfast.

Kronegade Inn (☎ 340-692-9590), on Route 75 near the western end of Christiansted, has 15 modern rooms with tile floors, kitchenettes and lots of space. Unfortunately, this inn is not in the best section of town. The security fence and indifferent staff do not add to the ambience. Room rates are about $85.

Pink Fancy (☎ 340-773-8460, 800-524-2045, 27 Prince St) is a B&B set in a 1780s Danish townhouse. There are 13 rooms here in four buildings, a pool and a bar where your hosts serve complimentary drinks each evening. All rooms include air-con and a kitchenette. Rates run from $70 to $130 for a couple, depending on the season, continental breakfast included.

The *Danish Manor Hotel* (☎ 340-773-1377, 800-524-2069, 2 Company St) is the best value of the downtown hotels. This pink hotel built around a courtyard in the heart of the restaurant district is also home to Tutto Bene (see Places to Eat), the island's premier Italian restaurant, and cooking smells waft through the hotel. There are 34 rooms, some with kitchenettes and sea views (distant). Rates start at $85 for a double.

Hotel Caravelle (☎ 340-773-0687, 800-524-0410, 44A Queen Cross St) has long been a leader in value among the downtown Christiansted hotels. Located on the waterfront, this property with 43 rooms was remodeled in 1995. The rooms have the usual amenities, including air-con and cable TV, and you can take advantage of the pool with sundeck overlooking the harbor. Rates run $110 to $150, but the hotel offers several package deals.

King Christian Hotel (☎ 340-773-6330, 59 Kings Wharf) is the three-story, sand-color building that looks like a Danish warehouse (which it was 200 years ago) right next to the National Park Service sites at the heart of Christiansted's waterfront. Many of the island's most popular dive operations and tour boats have offices on the 1st floor. The 39 rooms include refrigerators and safes as well as the usual amenities. There is a small pool, but most guests take the ferry to the beach at Protestant Cay. Rates start at $150 for a double, but a sea view will cost you $35 extra.

Club Comanche Hotel (☎ *340-773-0210, 800-524-2066, 1 Strand St*) is a downtown hotel set in a 250-year-old Danish mansion. There are 22 rooms here with air-con and TV. Some have cooking facilities. There is a saltwater pool on the premises with a small deck. The good news about this hotel is that it's in the heart of Christiansted's entertainment district; the bad news is the area can be noisy. Rates run $125 and up for a double.

King's Alley Hotel (☎ *340-773-0103, 57 King St*) has 35 rooms above a gallery of shops and restaurants right on the harbor. This is a new property that imitates a 19th-century Danish great house with colonial-style mahogany furniture and vaulted ceilings to match. French doors open onto a view of the King's Alley shops and cafes as well as the harbor and seaplane landing. There is also a freshwater pool. Rates run $110 to $170.

Hotel on the Cay (☎ *340-773-2035, 800-524-2035*), on Protestant Cay, is experiencing a comeback after more than a decade under the control of some shady characters. The location on this sandy islet in the center of Christiansted Harbor could not be better, and a three-minute ferry ride puts town at your fingertips. The 55 rooms come with private balconies, kitchenettes, TV and air-con. Rates are $150 and up, but you can stay here off-season for under $100. The broad, protected beach with all its water-sports vendors attracts a crowd for good reason.

St Croix saw the building of many resort condominiums and villa compounds during the last three decades of the 20th century. Some of these *rental accommodations* are time-share operations; some have individ-

ual owners. Most of these units are available as weekly rentals. High-season rates hover in the range of $110 to $160 per day, $650 to $900 per week. Rates can go as high as $3500 for a private mountainside palace. If you are interested in a condo or villa rental, consider the following developers and property management agencies.

American Rentals & Sales	☎ 340-773-8472
Antilles Resorts at Colony Cove	☎ 800-524-2025
CMPI Vacation Rentals	☎ 800-496-7379
Island Villas	☎ 800-626-4512
The Reef	☎ 800-595-2581
Sugar Beach	☎ 800-524-2049
Sunterra Resorts	☎ 888-503-8760

Places to Eat

St Croix, and Christiansted in particular, is known for imaginative, upscale dining. Note that many of the island's most popular restaurants are closed on Monday.

Morning Glory Coffee & Tea (☎ *340-773-6620*), across from the post office in Gallows Bay, is a bright deli that caters to snowbirds and businessfolk coming into town from the East End. Breakfast is the big attraction here. You can get a 12oz cup of fresh-roasted flavored coffee for under $2. The tropical French toast stuffed with banana, berries and granola costs $6.

Luncheria (☎ *340-773-4247, 6 Company St*) will prove a delight whether you eat here or take out. The setting is a shaded courtyard with picnic and cafe tables. House specialties like the chimichanga run about $8, but you can get tacos or enchiladas here for under $5.

Kim's Restaurant ☎ *340-773-3373, 45 King St*) is the place to come for dynamite West Indian cooking and friendly conversation with cook and manager 'Big Kim' about life for regular folks in the Virgin Islands. The ambience is fresh and dainty with peach-and-white tableclothes and a courtyard. Stewed or curried conch will cost you $12. Don't miss a bowl of her callaloo with lobster, conch, clams and fungi for $4.

King's Landing Yacht Club (☎ *340-773-0103*), on the boardwalk at the heart of the waterfront, has the ambience of a Mediterranean cafe. Prices here are cheap for St Croix, with sandwiches such as the veggie pita running about $6. Locals say it's best to come here for breakfast, when an egg sandwich costs $3.50 and local bush tea runs $1. Tourists love the crab races on Monday at 5:30 pm.

Stixx (☎ 340-773-5157), next to the old sugar mill at the waterfront end of the Pan Am Pavilion, is a two-level bar and restaurant that gets packed with tourists, especially for the Friday-night crab races (5:30 pm). The big draw here is the pizza by the slice ($1.50 and up) or the pie ($12 for a large cheese).

The Usual Suspects (☎ 340-773-6464), on the water at King Cross St, does a Caribbean interpretation of Humphrey Bogart's gin mill in *Casablanca*. Musician/raconteur/pilot/sailor/expat Jon Renck runs this show and can play a mean jazz guitar at just about any moment of the day. Lunch items like the veggie melt are popular for under $7.

Breezez (☎ 340-773-7077), at Club St Croix a mile west of Christiansted, is a popular lunching place for folks spending the day at the beach. This poolside operation serves up a Cajun chicken zydeco salad for under $8; burgers cost about $6. It serves a popular Sunday brunch with pasta jambalaya for under $9.

Comanche Restaurant (☎ 340-773-2665), on the 2nd floor of Hotel Comanche where the pedestrian bridge spans Strand St, has been a Christiansted institution for almost 40 years. The ambience is definitely Margaritaville, with peacock chairs and open-air seating that looks down on the town. Folks come for the local fish seared in tropical fruit glazes. Lunch costs under $8; dinner will run you $16 and up.

Bacchus (☎ 340-692-9922), on Queen Cross St between Strand and King Sts, has established itself as one of St Croix's gourmet restaurants. The setting is the 2nd floor of a historic townhouse, and the bait is the most complete wine list on the island. An endive salad runs $9. The eggplant Napoleon is considered a low-priced entree at $17.

Tutto Bene (☎ 340-773-5229, 2 Company St), at the Danish Manor Hotel, is quite possibly the most romantic of all St Croix's restaurants. Kelly Odem and her husband, Smokey, manage this intimate Italian bistro with exceptional personal attention to detail and their customers. Pizzas with three toppings cost about $8; pasta dishes like the cappelini with shrimp and papaya run $16 to $19.

Savant (☎ 340-713-8666), on Hospital St south of the fort parking lot, rocks Christiansted with its upscale fusion cookery in a colonial townhouse, which also has outdoor seating. The menu combines Caribbean, Mexican and Thai recipes and changes regularly. Dinner entrees run $17 and up.

Top Hat (☎ 340-773-2346), on Company St between Queen Cross and King Cross Sts, is chef Bent Rasmussen's top-drawer eatery on the 2nd floor of a restored townhouse. Over the last three decades, Bent has built his reputation on Scandinavian specialties and local lobster. Most entrees run $20 or more.

Indies (☎ 340-692-9440, 55-56 Company St) creates its own world of tropical elegance in an antique stable yard ringed with orchids, herbs and colonial architecture. The menu changes nightly, but you can expect to see offerings like yellowfin tuna with mango salsa and rum-fried plantains for $22. The biggest social scene here is sushi night on Friday evening (see Entertainment).

Chef David Kendrick's award-winning *Kendrick's* (☎ 340-773-9199), on King Cross St at Company St, has long set the standard for Cruzan gourmands. You can sit inside the colonial cottage or eat in the courtyard. The pasta dishes like fettuccine with medallions of lobster, jalapeños and fresh cilantro run more than $22. You can dine light on champagne gazpacho (under $5) or lobster nachos (under $13).

Entertainment

The best way to find out what's up is to check the entertainment section of *St Croix This Week* and the daily *St Croix Avis*. In general, there is a healthy collection of gin mills you can depend on for a good time week in, week out. St Croix has the largest 'out' gay population in the Virgin Islands and has begun to gain a reputation for its gay scene among travelers in the know.

Indies (see Places to Eat) attracts an over-25 crowd after work. They get pumped over sushi and French wines every Friday evening. This is the night when St Croix's young professionals, travelers and upscale Cruzan gays descend on the restaurant's bar for the California platters (about $10) and progressive jazz. There are a lot of welcoming and pretty people here in fine threads. Indies may well be the place to come if you are looking for a date for Saturday.

Steel pan aficionados head for *Hotel on the Cay* (see Places to Stay) on Tuesday night and Sunday afternoon. The same group goes to *Club Comanche* (see Places to Eat) on Friday evening.

The Usual Suspects (see Places to Eat) has a cybercafe; online rates are $5 for a half-hour. For nightly entertainment, you get Jon Renck on the guitar and vocals or a piano player. The crowd is 35 and up.

The *Fort Christian Brew Pub* (☎ 340-713-9820), on the boardwalk at King's Alley, pours drafts of the Virgin Island's only homebrew, Foxy's Lager. The beer takes its name from the legendary 'party mon' on Jost Van Dyke. There is a happy hour here between 4 and 7 pm that attracts young continentals working on the island and rafts of travelers drawn to the waterfront. This place can be a good spot to gain some local knowledge or get invited to a party. You pay $2.50 a pint for a brew at happy hour, $3 at other times.

The *Company St Pub* (☎ 340-773-6880, 54 Company St) is a friendly place to soak up brews with a local crowd. The clientele is largely under 30, racially mixed and from a wide band of social classes. The management runs a lot of beer promotions here, so you can quaff your suds cheaply if you opt for the special of the week.

The *Parrot's Perch* (☎ 340-773-7992, 43 BC Queen Cross St), is the 2nd-floor, open-air club that beckons to St Croix youth after about 10 pm. There is live music or a DJ here virtually every night. The tunes tend to

be rock, reggae or hip-hop. The crowd is under 25 and on the hunt for fast times and romance. Saturday is Latin night.

Moonraker's Bar (☎ 340-773-9581), on Queen Cross St between Strand and King Sts, is where you find hip islanders after their late dinners. This is a 2nd-floor jazz club where the scent of Cuban cigars and champagne linger in the air. The crowd is a mix of black and white, straight and gay. Almost everyone is dressed to the nines and is planning on staying out until sunrise. Makeup and cocktail dresses rule, ladies! Nobody wears shorts. There's a lot of flirting at the bar and plenty of easy chairs and dark tables if you want to retreat for more serious conversation.

Shopping

There are a few shops catering to the cruise ship arrivals in Frederiksted, and Centerline Rd has an almost endless collection of shopping plazas and mini malls serving the needs of island residents. But for travelers, shopping on St Croix is synonymous with Christiansted. The ambience could hardly be more fetching, with historic colonial buildings, shady arcades, galleried sidewalks, cooling trade winds, sea views, a wealth of imaginative restaurants and the lilt of calypso pouring from a host of boutiques and shops. There are more than 30 Cruzan shopkeepers specializing in gold, gems and handcrafted jewelry. A similar number sell decorations and objets d'art. Crafts, fashions, cosmetics and T-shirts are popular as well.

Many of the old townhouses and warehouses between Strand Gade and the waterfront open into courtyards or shopping pavilions. These include the complexes at Market Square, the Pan Am Pavilion, Caravelle Arcade, the Boardwalk and King's Alley. King's Alley, which opened in 1996, has 20 shops. The Gallows Bay residential and commercial development on the east side of the harbor attracts a lot of snowbirds to the hardware store, bookstore, boutiques and cafes.

For some uniquely Cruzan purchases, consider buying a bottle of Cruzan Estate

Diamond rum or a gold or silver bracelet with a 'Cruzan hook' from the Caribbean Bracelet Company (☎ 340-692-9000) in King's Alley. Check in the gourmet food stores for Jaquie's Jams, island-made fruit preserves.

Jane Akin (☎ 340-713-8419), Mark Austin (☎ 340-713-9842) and Maria Henle (☎ 340-773-7376) are among the island's score of respected artists with galleries.

FREDERIKSTED

Once Frederiksted was the island's major commercial port, but today most goods arrive on the island at the oil refinery's artificial harbor on the island's south side.

Except on Wednesday and Thursday, the most common days for cruise ship arrivals at the town pier, Frederiksted looks the part of a classic Caribbean outpost. It seems an almost motionless village of colonial buildings lying beside a painted turquoise sea. Although Cruzans rarely flock to this small town, and most cruise ship passengers stay here for only a few hours, Frederiksted is no ghost town. Slightly more than 1000 people live here today, about the same number as resided here two centuries ago, and they can show travelers a good time. Not only does Frederiksted pack a first-rate collection of Victorian colonial architecture into its historic district, it also has an unexpected collection of interesting shops and some of the most romantic restaurants on the island. There is also a bar scene, a vibrant gay community and uncrowded beaches.

History

From the beginning of the sugar cane industry on the island, merchant ships from England's North American colonies found this western end of St Croix a convenient point for transshipping cargoes of slaves, cane and finished goods without paying duty to the Danish government in Christiansted. To stop illegal traffic at this spot, nicknamed 'Freedom City,' the Danes decided to create an official port with a fort as a deterrent to the smuggling. As a consequence, surveyor Jens M Beck laid out the four-by-three-block grid in 1751. Construction of Fort Frederik, at the north end of the grid, began in 1752, and both town and fort owe their names to King Frederik V, Denmark's reigning monarch at the time.

The town prospered slowly, but by the last decades of the 18th century, both King and Queen Sts were thriving residential areas for dockworkers who staffed the warehouses on Strand St. During this era, the island began to cement its relationship with the US as Yankee ship captains were regular visitors to the port. Affection for the Americans grew so strong that the cannons of Fort Frederik fired a tribute to Yankee ships when the Yanks arrived at Frederiksted flying the new US flag after the outbreak of the American Revolution.

Dramatic events highlight Frederiksted's history during much of the 19th century. First came the recession in the sugar industry. Next came the slave revolt of 1848, when the black leader General Budhoe and a legion of slaves gathered outside the fort and threatened destruction of the island until Governor Peter von Scholten issued his Proclamation of Emancipation, which freed all the slaves in the Danish West Indies. Then came the hurricane of 1867 and its associated tidal wave that actually carried the US warship the USS *Monongahela* into the town.

Finally, on October 1 and 2, 1878, former slaves, angered by the planters' refusal to pay wages of more than 5¢ to 7¢ a day, went on an island-wide rampage called the Fireburn, which reduced Frederiksted to ashes. The burned neoclassic colonial buildings were rebuilt or replaced during the end of the 19th century, giving Frederiksted's historic buildings the Victorian look you see today, with structures trimmed with sawn balusters and decorative latticework.

Some Spanish-speaking immigrants from Puerto Rico began arriving and settling in Frederiksted during the 1920s, and the town is still a magnet for St Croix's Spanish-speaking residents. Immigrants from the Dominican Republic operate a collection of rough bars in the red-light district on the south end of King St.

Frederiksted Pier

There is nothing historic about this long concrete pier that heads out to sea from the north end of Strand St, where the Old Customs House and Fort Frederik provide a governmental welcome to the town. But when the pier is in full repair, two cruise ships can dock here at once to offload thousands of tourists. On days when the ships are in, the visitors bureau information booth (☎ 340-772-0357) opens to assist travelers from 8 am to 5 pm. The booth is closed most other days. During the quiet times, snorkelers and divers gravitate to the pier's pilings, which attract an extensive collection of marine life such as schools of sea horses.

Old Customs House

This building dates from the days when the Danes were serious about collecting taxes on imports and exports, and it continued to function as a customs house until recent years. It was badly damaged during Hurricane Hugo in 1989 but has been carefully restored since then. The 1st floor with its colonnades is an example of Danish civil architecture from the 18th century. The 2nd-floor gallery and hipped roof were Victorian additions. For years, the Virgin Islands government has talked about making the Old Customs House a visitors center, but the plan has made no headway, and the building serves as office space for other government agencies.

Fort Frederik

The traditional deep red color of this fort (☎ 340-772-2021) at the foot of the town pier is what most visitors remember about the little citadel; it is a truly threatening paint job obviously meant to dissuade smugglers of another era. This rubble and masonry fort came to life between 1752 and 1760 and owes its trapezoidal design to classic Danish military architecture of the period.

The seaward-facing west curtain is protected by projecting bastions and a heavy breastwork with gun platforms. The east wall contains a sally port and a single bastion to protect the fort from onland

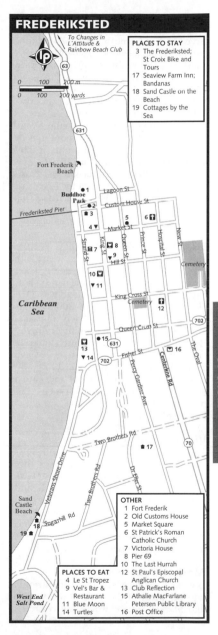

FREDERIKSTED

To Changes in
L'Attitude &
Rainbow Beach Club

Fort Frederik
Beach

Buddhoe
Park

Frederiksted Pier

*Caribbean
Sea*

*Sand
Castle
Beach*

Sugarhill Rd

*West End
Salt Pond*

Veterans Shore Drive

Two Brothers Rd

Strand St

Lagoon St

Custom House St

Market St

Queen St

Prince St

Hill St

Hospital St

New St

Cemetery

King Cross St
Cemetery

Queen Cross St

Fisher St

Percy Gardiner Ave

Centerline Rd

The Oval

Dr Fisher St

Two Brothers Rd

Two Brothers Rd

PLACES TO STAY
3 The Frederiksted;
 St Croix Bike and
 Tours
17 Seaview Farm Inn;
 Bandanas
18 Sand Castle on the
 Beach
19 Cottages by the
 Sea

PLACES TO EAT
4 Le St Tropez
9 Vel's Bar &
 Restaurant
11 Blue Moon
14 Turtles

OTHER
1 Fort Frederik
2 Old Customs House
5 Market Square
6 St Patrick's Roman
 Catholic Church
7 Victoria House
8 Pier 69
10 The Last Hurrah
12 St Paul's Episcopal
 Anglican Church
13 Club Reflection
15 Athalie MacFarlane
 Petersen Public Library
16 Post Office

ST CROIX

attacks. Following the US purchase of the US Virgin Islands in 1917, the fort has served as a jail, courthouse, police station, fire station and telephone exchange. In 1976, island conservationists restored the fort for the celebration of the US bicentennial. The Virgin Islands Division of Planning and Natural Resources manages the property.

If you go inside, you will see a few exhibits depicting life in the colonial Danish military and photos and memorabilia depicting some of St Croix's more destructive hurricanes. While the fort claims to be open 8:30 am to 4:30 pm weekdays, it was closed almost every time I stopped by. Locals say the fort tends to open when the cruise ships are in (usually Tuesday and Wednesday). Call to make sure it's open before visiting.

Buddhoe Park

This small, tree-shaded park lies outside the eastern ramparts of Fort Frederik. Today, it's a good place to escape the sun on a hot day, but on July 3, 1848, this land was a wild place when Moses 'General Budhoe' (also spelled 'Buddhoe') Gottlieb led 'all the Negroes in this part of the country in revolt.' Bells sounded from every church and plantation on the island, and 6000 to 8000 slaves, all armed with machetes and bludgeons, congregated here in front of the gate to Fort Frederik to demand and receive their freedom. (See the boxed text 'Caught in Freedom's Storm.')

Victoria House

This large residence at 7-8 Strand St sits back from the sidewalk and rises three stories as one of the most elaborately detailed buildings in the Virgin Islands. Largely destroyed in the 1878 fire, the house has been rebuilt with Victorian gingerbread, including a great deal of ornamental latticework. The house remains a private residence and is not open to the public.

Market Square

If you go east on Market St from Strand St into the heart of the small town, you will find Market Square, where the corners of the blocks have been cut away at the intersection of Market and Queen Sts to make room for vendors. This has been Frederiksted's marketplace for 250 years, but don't expect a lot of vendors now that most islanders shop at the supermarkets on Centerline Rd. On most days, you will find fresh produce in the market shed on the southeast corner, and this can be a good place to pick up a mango to quench your thirst.

St Patrick's Roman Catholic Church

This Catholic church at 5 Prince St (☎ 340-722-5052) lies on Market St, a block east of Market Square. It's interesting because of its unusual synthesis of architectural styles. Built in 1848, this church, with the three-story brick bell tower, is basically Gothic Revival, but the gabled ends of the nave and transept are reminiscent of the Spanish Mission style. A high masonry wall encloses the church and its cemetery. You can call for scheduled masses in English or Spanish.

St Paul's Episcopal Anglican Church

This church (☎ 340-772-0818) dating from 1812 is the oldest house of worship in the town. It lies slightly more than a block south of the Old Danish School House at 28 Prince St. Although much of the church roots in Danish colonial neoclassicism, the most outstanding part of the structure is its crenellated English Gothic bell tower.

Athalie MacFarlane Petersen Public Library

Also called the Bell House for its second owner, this building at the south end of Strand St (☎ 340-772-0315) dates from 1803. There is not only a small library in this building but also a cultural center that supports local arts and crafts events. This is a good stop if you want a look inside Frederiksted's Victorian buildings; the ornamental staircase where owner GA Bell added bells to represent his children is an interesting piece of Victoriana. It's open 9 am to 5 pm weekdays; admission is free.

Caught in Freedom's Storm

On July 2, 1848, large numbers of slaves on St Croix (led by Moses 'General Budhoe' Gottlieb, a free black and skilled sugar boiler on the La Grange plantation) rose up in arms, taking over buildings in Frederiksted and overrunning plantations. Whites on the island immediately fled to the island forts and ships in the harbor. Bells of alarm and the hoot of conch-shell horns rung out across the island, calling 8000 blacks to congregate outside the fort in Frederiksted. Here, the slaves tore down the whipping post and ransacked the judge's house. They threatened to burn Frederiksted and the rest of the island unless the government granted colony-wide freedom for all slaves.

In the capital of Christiansted, Danish Governor Peter von Scholten felt the urgency of the situation. He also felt personal pressure from his black mistress, Anna Elizabeth Heegaard. After consultation with his advisors, he headed by carriage to face the mob in Frederiksted. He arrived late in the afternoon, just as black women were gathering the dry tops of sugar cane and piling it against the fortress walls, preparing to set the bastion on fire. With barely a moment to reflect, von Scholten made his famous Proclamation of Emancipation that began 'All unfree in the Danish West India Islands are from today free....'

Both overjoyed and suspicious, gangs of blacks refused to disperse and roamed the island randomly burning and wrecking property. Defying the governor's orders, Danish soldiers killed protesting blacks. Weeks of rioting, looting and burning ensued. Throughout the days of chaos, Gottlieb traveled the island on horseback with a Danish major pleading for an end to the unrest. But not even the respected 'General' could end the violence.

Finally, thousands of troops came from St Thomas and Puerto Rico to squelch the rampage. For his part, Moses Gottlieb found himself thrown in jail, but he was later released and deported to Trinidad. For freeing the slaves, Governor Peter von Scholten was recalled to Denmark, where he was tried (but acquitted) for treason. Anna Elizabeth Heegaard never saw the governor again.

Beaches

Fort Frederik Beach is the public strand just north of the fort and the pier. When the prevailing trade winds are blowing, this beach remains as sheltered as a millpond; you can swim off the beach for some excellent snorkeling around the pier.

Sand Castle Beach is the nickname for the strand in front of the Sand Castle on the Beach (see Places to Stay), less than a mile south of Frederiksted along the waterfront road. This is a gay-friendly hotel, and the serene beach out front is a friendly place to meet other gay people.

Activities

Scubawest (☎ 340-722-3701, 800-352-0107), at 330 Strand St, is a **diving** operator offering wreck dives near shore and trips to explore the outer reaches of the town pier.

For **mountain biking**, Mike McQueston at St Croix Bike and Tours (☎ 340-772-2324), near the pier, will rent you a bike to cruise the back roads or beaches and will even deliver your bike to your hotel. You can also book a historic/nature tour of the coastal West End with Mike or get pumped up on his rain forest trail ride.

One of the least-used free **tennis** courts is right next to Fort Frederik.

Places to Stay

With its out-of-the-mainstream, laissez-faire ambience, Frederiksted is the center for gay life on St Croix. All of the hotels listed here are gay-friendly.

The Frederiksted (☎ 340-772-0500, 800-524-2025, 20 Strand St) calls itself 'a modern inn with old island charm.' There are 40 rooms here on four floors built around a courtyard and small pool. Many of the rooms have patios that overlook the anchorage and cruise ship dock just up the street. Rooms have tiled floors and standard hotel-style furnishings and a refrigerator. A bar and restaurant are on the premises. Rates in season start at $85 for a double.

The *Seaview Farm Inn* (☎ 340-772-5367, 800-792-5060), on Estate Two Brothers just south of Frederiksted, overlooks the Caribbean (at a distance) from the crest of a low hill. Although the eight suites are in a two-story building that looks more like a motel than a country inn, the rooms themselves are romantic, with four-poster beds, bright fabrics, private verandas and kitchens. Roland and Dulcy Kushmore are welcoming hosts who seem to know everyone on the island. The open-air restaurant (see Places to Eat) is one of the most popular stops for steak-lovers on the island. Rates start at $110 during winter and spring.

Cottages by the Sea (☎ 340-772-0495, 127A Estate Smithfield), right on a quiet beach about a mile south of Frederiksted, has 20 units. Dick Mercure and Vicki McFee operate this cottage compound. All rooms have kitchen, TV, air-con, bath and private patio. Rates for a cottage during the prime winter/spring season start at $120 for a couple.

Sand Castle on the Beach (☎ 340-772-1205, 800-524-2018, 127 Estate Smithfield) lies on the beach about a mile south of Frederiksted center. This multistory, four-building establishment with 23 rooms states that it has been 'proudly serving the gay and lesbian community for 20 years.' Rooms come with kitchenettes and air-con; most have sea views. In addition to swimming off the long beach, you can also sun or take a dip in the freshwater pool. There is also a video library and gas grills for cookouts. High-season rates run $115 to $250.

Places to Eat

Without a doubt, *Turtles* (☎ 340-772-3676, 625 Strand St) is the most charming deli/cafe on the island. Tom Kosh and Tom Pinchbeck run this shady little spot where you can grab a small table on the beach and eat major-league deli sandwiches like Cajun-style eye round beef on 10 different types of homemade bread for under $7. The beer and fruit juices here are icy-cold, and you can buy the cheeses and lunchmeats if you want to take a stock of treats back to your quarters.

Vel's Bar & Restaurant (☎ 340-772-2160, 29 King St) seems like the restaurant in Ernest Hemingway's short story 'A Clean, Well-Lighted Place.' It serves both West Indian and Latin cuisine. Stewed chicken costs under $7; fried plantains cost $1.

Changes in L'Attitude (☎ 340 772-3090) is on the beach about a mile north of Frederiksted. Travelers and islanders gather on weekends to make this their headquarters for a day at the beach. With Tex-Mex cuisine, this restaurant definitely appeals to a lot of Jimmy Buffett fans, who come for specials like the catfish (under $11) as well as free beach chairs, changing rooms and showers.

Bandanas (☎ 340-772-5367), at Seaview Farm Inn a mile south of town in estate Two Brothers, draws a big crowd for weekend dinners. A piano player performs in this open-air pavilion on weekend nights, and Roland Kushmore presides over the sizzling filet mignon that runs $20 and up, depending on the size of your steak. There is also a popular Sunday brunch here; consider ordering Dulcy's waffle hearts, plain or blueberry heart-shaped waffles with bacon or sausage ($8).

Blue Moon (☎ 340-772-2222, 17 Strand St) offers Caribbean, vegetarian and Cajun cuisine in the ambience of a restored colonial warehouse. Entree prices reach beyond $20 for the fish offerings, and you may want to make reservations if you come Friday night for live jazz or for the Sunday jazz brunch. Both events are very popular.

Le St Tropez (☎ 340-772-3000, 227 King St) is without a doubt worthy of its name. The owners, Daniele and Andre Ducrot, and their chef Willie are transplants from the Côte d'Azur, and they bring all the spirit and sophistication of the Mediterranean to this bistro. There are only 15 tables in this intimate terrace restaurant that drips with the sound of Louis Armstrong and the scents of coq au vin (chicken cooked in red wine; $19). Call early for reservations. Daniele does not hire musicians to entertain you, but she says 'If people want live music, I can sing.' *Mais oui!*

Entertainment
Friday is the big night at *Blue Moon* (see Places to Eat), when both locals and continentals jam this place for live jazz and the chance to find romance. The crowd is 25 to 45 years old.

On Sunday afternoon, *Rainbow Beach Club* (☎ 340-772-0002), less than a mile north of Frederiksted on Route 63, has live reggae and R&B in a beachside setting. The scene draws a lot of the island's hard bodies to party on, dude.

The local gay crowd mixes with the straight people at Blue Moon and at Unise Transburg's *Pier 69* (☎ 340-772-1441, 69 King St), which is popular with lesbian couples and singles.

The Last Hurrah, King St at Hill St, rocks out with gay men on Saturday night and when the cruise ship (and US Navy) crews hit town. The scene is a 19th-century townhouse with an interior courtyard, bar and lots of twinkling lights. The music tends toward heavy house. Sometimes they have drag shows.

Club Reflection (☎ 340-772-5559), Strand St at Queen Cross St, has bars, dance floors and quieter spots spread around the different rooms, each with its own atmosphere. A seaside patio offers a place to cool off after a workout on the dance floor. The music and the owner, Paul Brancoccio, are very New York. Some of the lesbians on staff are trying to organize a women's night here. The cover charge is usually $5.

WEST ISLAND
The area west of Christiansted has two very distinct sides to its topography and character. First, there are the wild mountains and beaches of the so-called rain forest area along the north shore. This is the site of some of the island's most dramatic scenery, spectacular diving and popular resorts. South of the mountains is the broad coastal plain that was once host to a majority of the sugar plantations. Today, the area is largely a modern commercial and residential zone where most of St Croix's population lives. But sprinkled among the few patches of undeveloped land bordering Centerline Rd are some remarkable heirlooms from the colonial era, including the Whim Plantation.

Estate Whim Plantation Museum
Just a few miles outside Frederiksted on Centerline Rd lies one of St Croix's most striking evocations of its colonial sugar cane history. Only a few of the original 150 acres of Whim Plantation survive as the museum (☎ 340-772-0598), but the grounds thoroughly evoke the days when 'King Cane' ruled the island. The fully restored and furnished neoclassic great house, 95 feet long and 35 feet wide, stands at the heart of the museum grounds. For the purposes of cooling, it has only three rooms, which are ventilated by huge windows. Walls built of coral, limestone and rubble bonded with a mortar of molasses insulate the house and have given it the strength to stand up against hurricanes since the 1790s.

As you tour the grounds, you'll see wind and animal mills as well as steam engines used for grinding cane. Buildings like the cookhouse (where they serve johnnycakes), bathhouse, watch house, caretaker's cottage and slave quarters are also on the grounds (some are restored to their vintage state); others function as exhibit galleries and the museum store.

The tombstone of Anna Heegaard, the black companion of Governor von Scholten, is also on the grounds. Whim is open 10 am to 4 pm Monday to Saturday; guided tours leave every half-hour. Admission is $6 for adults, $1 for children.

Cruzan Rum Distillery
If you are curious about how the Nelthropp family, one of the last of the Virgin Island distillers, make their popular product in handcrafted oak barrels, stop by the Cruzan Rum Distillery (☎ 340-692-2280).

ST CROIX

The factory lies about 2 miles east of Whim Plantation off of Centerline Rd on Route 64. The guided tour takes about 20 minutes, after which you get to sip some of the good stuff. You can get good buys on specialty rums like 'tropical banana' in the company store. It's open 9 am to 11:30 am and 1 to 4:15 pm weekdays. Admission is $4 for adults, $1 for minors.

St George Village Botanical Garden

If you continue east on Centerline Rd after leaving the Cruzan Rum factory, you soon see St George Village Botanical Garden (☎ 340-692-2874) on the north side of the highway. This 16-acre park built over the ruins of an Indian settlement and a colonial sugar plantation does for the flora and fauna what Whim Plantation does for the grandeur of plantation days. Your self-guided tour takes you on trails among the ruins of the rum factory, great house, shops, dam and aqueduct. There are 1000 species of tropical plants, including a profusion of orchids and hibiscus as well as the much-admired cactus garden. The garden is open 9 am to 5 pm daily except federal holidays. Admission is $5 for adults, $1 for children

Caledonia Rain Forest

Most of St Croix's rain falls over the mountains at the northwest corner of the island, producing a thick, damp forest of tall mahogany, silk cotton and white cedar. Although this area is commonly called 'rain forest,' only about 40 inches of rain fall here per year. That's actually less than half the amount a true rain forest receives, but no matter. This place looks the part, with clouds, dripping trees, earthy smells, slick roads and muddy trails.

The best hiking, mountain biking and off-road exploring is here along the unpaved tracks of the Creque Dam Rd (Route 58) and the Scenic Rd (Route 78). If you don't have the time, inclination or vehicle to do off-road exploring, you can still see the rain forest by following the Mahogany Rd (Route 76) as it dips through the steep hills and valleys.

St Croix Leap

Tucked into a steep hillside at the heart of the rain forest on the Mahogany Rd is the unusual outdoor woodworking and sculpture studio called St Croix Leap (☎ 340-772-0421). Here, master sculptor 'Cheech' leads a band of apprentice woodworkers in transforming chunks of fallen mahogany trees into all manner of art and housewares. The studio is open daily and is free. Bring your bug repellent.

Lawaetz Family Museum

Less than a quarter-mile beyond the entrance to St Croix Leap lies this plantation museum. Look for the light-blue sign for 'Little La Grange' (☎ 340-772-1539) and follow the dirt track up the hill between ruins of the old sugar mill and factory to the great house.

Set amid virtual jungle and steep hills, this plantation belies the myth that sugar cane could only be raised on St Croix's coastal plain. For the most part, the place and its furnishings retain the ambience of the plantation when it became the Lawaetz family homestead slightly more than 100 years ago. Now, family heir Irene Lawaetz acts as your hostess, giving you a guided tour of the house. New trails have been opened to make the grounds an exceptional place for hiking, losing yourself in bird songs and kicking back for a picnic lunch. It's a rustic place that stands in contrast to Whim Plantation's grandeur. La Grange is open 10 am to 4 pm Tuesday to Saturday. Admission is $6 for adults, $2 for children.

Doc James Race Track

The Doc James Race Track (☎ 340-778-1395) stands just south of the airport on Route 64. This is an old and small-scale thoroughbred-racing operation that is open sporadically. Call for a racing schedule and post time.

Sandy Point National Wildlife Refuge

In the 1980s, the US Fish & Wildlife Service (☎ 340-773-4554) purchased almost 400 acres that include the peninsula and beaches of Sandy Point at the extreme southwest end of St Croix. The area is a nature reserve with at least 3 miles of vacant beaches. These beaches are some of the most important nesting grounds for the mammoth leatherback sea turtle. Hawksbill and green turtles nest here as well. The Fish & Wildlife rangers constantly monitor the beaches during the nesting season from February to July, and the beach may well be closed when the 1000lb leatherbacks are coming ashore at night to lay their eggs.

To see the turtles, you may be able to join one of the night tours sponsored by the Fish & Wildlife Service or perhaps even volunteer for beach patrol. By day, birders enjoy the area, as it is a nesting ground for endangered brown pelicans, terns and oyster catchers. While Sandy Point is a wild and beautiful area, locals know it as a place that attracts a bad element. Car break-ins are commonplace, and not so long ago a murder and rape took place here (see Dangers & Annoyances, earlier).

Salt River National Historic Park

The Salt River Bay estuary, about 4 miles west of Christiansted on Route 80, is the only documented site where Christopher Columbus landed on US soil. More importantly, Salt River is the site where, on November 14, 1493, Native Americans first tried to repel European intruders (see History in the Facts about the Virgin Islands chapter). Not only is Salt River the site where the Caribs first drew Spanish blood, the shores are also the site of some of the earliest French, English and Danish colonial efforts.

In 1993, almost 700 acres of land surrounding the entire estuary gained the status of National Historic Park & Ecological Reserve. The park is most easily viewed from a parking lot at the western entrance to the bay – built on top of the ceremonial ball court and Carib village that the Spaniards invaded more than 500 years ago. With modern yachts moored in the bay and the parking lot beneath your feet, it is difficult to picture either the Caribs or Columbus here.

Prowling for Pirates

Although St Croix was never a favorite haunt of pirates, after the French abandoned the island, some buccaneers did find the island's Salt River Bay a good place to hide from prying eyes and storms. In 1717, a notorious Jamaican pirate named Martell was hiding at Salt River Bay when an English warship, the *Scarborough*, arrived on the prowl for pirates. For days, the ships traded shots while the English warship blockaded the entrance to the anchorage. Finally, one of the pirate ships tried to break out but wrecked on the reef. That night the remaining pirates disappeared into the island interior...after setting fire to their flagship and leaving 20 black slaves to burn to death aboard.

Probably the best way to see the bay is on a kayak tour sponsored by Caribbean Adventure Tours (see Activities, later). You can get a sense of the diversity of birds here, ranging from peregrine falcons to roseate terns, and then lose yourself in red mangrove canals or head to sea like a Carib fishing party. To find the various archaeological sites around the bay, join one of the hikes occasionally sponsored by the St Croix Environmental Association (☎ 340-773-1989), which cost $20 for adults, $12 for children.

Beaches

The **La Grange, Rainbow and Sprat Hall Beaches** are north of Fort Frederik Beach on Route 63. They're all actually the same beach, but you can get a beer at the south end, where there are several pubs and restaurants. Young Cruzans and continentals make this a party scene on weekends.

Plenty of travelers head for palm-fringed **Hibiscus Beach**, less than 2 miles west of Christiansted off Route 75. There are two hotels with a beachside restaurant and bars here, and good snorkeling on the reef joining the coast at the west end of the beach. When the wind swings northeast, there may be an undertow here.

Lying about 4 miles west of Christiansted off Route 80 on the west side of Salt River Bay, **Salt River (Columbus Beach)** is the place where Columbus (actually his men) landed in 1493. There are definitely safer and prettier beaches than this.

A long, thin strand along Route 80 about 9 miles west of Christiansted, **Cane Bay** marks the border between some of the best reef dives on the island and the steep hills of the rain forest. This beach is a favorite with adventure travelers and sports-minded locals. There are several small hotels, restaurants, bars, dive shops and even some shade trees. Every month the island's young and restless (both Cruzans and continentals) head here on the night of the full moon to party till they drop. It's a great time, if you have the stamina.

Activities

Diving & Kayaking Cane Bay Dive Shop (☎ 340-773-9913, 800-338-3843), on the North Shore Rd (Route 80), is the largest equipment, sales, rental and service operator on the island.

Caribbean Adventure Tours (☎ 340-773-4599) runs kayak tours of Salt River Bay for $45 (three hours); half-day kayak rentals are also available for $30 at the Salt River Marina on the west side of the bay. During the company's 'Moonlight' kayaking trip, you paddle through the river's luminescent water while the knowledgeable guides share St Croix's local legends, folktales and ghost stories.

See Christiansted for more on diving along the north shore.

Bird-Watching If you know where to look, you can see a lot of the more than 200 species of birds in the Virgin Islands. The West End Salt Pond at Sandy Point on the southwest tip of the island is a good spot for seabirds like egrets and the brown pelican. (You can also see these birds in abundance around Great Pond off the Southside Rd.) You may also see several species of grebes

and herons. The rain forest trails along Scenic Rd lead you into the territory of parakeets, canaries and hawks like the 'killy killy' sparrow hawk. Hummingbirds and bananaquits are common around the flowering ruins of many of the island's old estates, including the St George Village Botanical Garden.

Golf St Croix offers three of the four golf courses in all of the Virgin Islands. The Carambola Golf Club (☎ 340-778-5838) is the big enchilada. This Robert Trent Jones course has been ranked among the top 12 resort courses in the world. The 18-hole, 6834-yard, par-72 course spreads out through a valley on the edge of the rain forest on Route 69 about a mile south of the Carambola Resort. Rates vary with the season; during the fall, you pay as little as $50 for a round and $18 for a cart. Winter and spring rates rise above $60. The clubhouse was the site of the Fountain Valley Massacre of the early 1970s (see Dangers and Annoyances, earlier).

Horseback Riding Paul & Jill's Equestrian Stables (☎ 340-772-2880, 340-772-2627), 1½ miles north of Frederiksted on Route 63, offers trail rides that lead through hidden plantation ruins and the rain forest to hilltop vistas. Kerry's Northshore Horseback Rides (☎ 340-778-8510) at Cane Bay leads parties into the rugged hills along the northwest coast. Equus Rides (☎ 340-778-3502, 340-772-4771) operates in the same area. Rates at all of the stables are $20 and up.

Places to Stay

Rates in this section are based on high-season occupancy unless otherwise noted.

Cormorant Beach Club (☎ *340-778-8920, 800-548-4460, 4126 La Grand Princesse*) overlooks an attractive beach about 2 miles west of Christiansted. This is a gay-friendly resort hotel with pool, tennis, restaurant and beach bar. Many rooms have cooking facilities. Rates start at $135. Also see Entertainment, later.

Hibiscus Beach Hotel (☎ *340-442-0121, 800-442-0121, 4131 La Grande Princesse*) stands just up the mile-long beach from the Cormorant Beach Club. The 38 rooms spread through a collection of beachfront, colonial-style villas amid a coconut grove. Each room comes with a private patio or balcony. There is a popular beachfront bar and restaurant here, too, with a view across the water to Christiansted. Rates for a double start at $170.

The *Inn at Pelican Heights* (☎ *340-713-8022, 888-445-9458, 4201 Estate St John*) has six spacious rooms and suites overlooking the ocean about 3 miles west of Christiansted. Phyllis and Fred Laue offer all the amenities, including private kitchens, telephones and a pool. Phyllis also serves breakfast. Rates start at about $110 for a couple.

Carrington's Inn (☎ *877-658-0508*), on Herman Hill, overlooks Christiansted. Roger and Claudia Carrington provide personalized attention, including a cooked breakfast each morning, bathrobes, full concierge service and cookies at bedtime. The five poolside rooms offer guests a ceiling fan and air-con, direct-dial telephone, refrigerator, coffee-maker and access to a fax machine, copier and Internet service. Rates start at $150.

Hilty House Inn (☎ *340-773-2594*), on a hilltop about 2 miles south of Christiansted, rises from the ruins of an old plantation. The main house and great room are actually set in the estate's old rum factory. The ancient cookhouse serves as the site for two of the six guest apartments, and a huge pool overlooks a lush valley and the distant Caribbean. Jaquie and Hugh Hoare-Ward are two of the most gracious hosts on the island. Locals and travelers often arrive for Jacquie's gourmet dinner served once a week in the great room. Rates for a couple start at about $120.

Sprat Hall Plantation (☎ *340-772-0305, 800-843-3584*), on Route 63 north of Frederiksted, is a colonial great house on a sugar plantation. Joyce and Jim Hurd have operated this plantation inn for more than 50 years and are full of island lore. Set on a hillside of this rural plantation overlooking the sea, the great house dates from the 17th century, with antique furnishings to match. Most guests stay in a small clutch of cottages surrounding the great house, where you can get gourmet candlelit dinners. Rates for a double start at $120.

The *Waves at Cane Bay* (☎ *340-778-1805, 800-545-0603*), on the North Shore Rd at the east end of Cane Bay, is a small, kid-friendly hotel that molds to the laid-back personalities of owners Suzanne and Kevin Ryan. You can snorkel or scuba right off the rocks out front or lounge in the saltwater pool. The Ryans also offer free snorkel gear, baby-sitting and horseback riding. All rooms have kitchenettes, air-con and cable TV. Rates are $140 and up.

The *Cane Bay Reef Club* (☎ *340-778-2966, 800-253-8534*), on the North Shore Rd near the Waves, is a little like having your own villa on the beach. There are nine rooms here. All suites include kitchens and private patios virtually hanging over the sea. There is a pool for bathing and a seaside sundeck. The bar/restaurant at waterside is a popular place with continentals and travelers (see Places to Eat). Rates start at $150.

Sunterra Carambola Beach Resort (☎ *340-778-3800*), off the North Shore Rd west of Cane Bay, is the former Rockefeller resort, and it's posh. If you stay here, you stay in one of the red-roofed villas on the mountainside overlooking Davis Bay. There are 150 suite-sized rooms with all the trimmings. Three restaurants, a world-class golf course, an on-site dive operator and tennis courts cater to the guests. Rooms go for $200 or more.

Places to Eat

Across from Wendy's at the Sunny Isle traffic light on Centerline Rd, *Soul Vegetarian*

Party Piggies

The wildest place to eat on the West End is the *Montpellier Domino Club* (☎ 340-772-9914), off Route 76 in the rain forest. This is the home of the beer-drinking pigs Tony, Toni, JJ, Oreo and Shirley. The club is set in a series of open-air pavilions beneath the dripping vegetation, and the cuisine is modern West Indian with fried chicken, fish and pork offerings (around $10).

Weekend afternoons and evenings pack in the customers with live entertainment such as calypso bands. The tourists line up to pay $1 to watch the pigs gnaw open cans of nonalcoholic brewskis and swill the contents. It costs you $2 a can to feed the pet pigs and $3 to shoot a video. These porkers used to drink the real thing until offspring were born suffering the symptoms of alcohol withdrawal.

Some folks come to wonder at the monument of the late Buster, the party piggy who started the whole show with owners Rufus and Norma George more than two decades ago. And a few people actually come to play dominoes.

(☎ 340-778-4080) is the place Cruzans come when they want to eat vegan or vegetarian. This restaurant lacks the colonial ambience of a lot of the island's best eateries and is a bit of a drive from most places travelers stay, but you cannot beat the North African bulgar or the callaloo. Eat in or take out. You can get a multicourse veggie dinner for under $7.

Off the Wall (☎ 340-778-4771), on the North Shore Rd at the eastern end of Cane Bay, is an open-air pub and a favorite place for both local and transient divers and beach bums to chill. Nachos, quesadillas and pizza are popular fare, with a lot of items on the menu for under $8. This place hops with live jazz on Saturday night.

Boz's Cane Bay Beach Bar (☎ 340-778-5669), on the hillside above Cane Bay

beach, offers a similar scene. Conch fritters and homemade onion rings are popular light fare (under $5). You get jazz on Tuesday and reggae to accompany the jumping Sunday brunch. Dinner entrees can exceed $10.

Entertainment

Performing Arts On Route 79 just north of the Sunny Isle Shopping Center, the *Island Center for the Performing Arts* (☎ 340-778-5272), is St Croix's venue for theater, cabaret and performances by local and internationally recognized classical ensembles and pop music stars. Visitors have included the Boston Pops, José Greco, the Debussy Quartet and the Temptations.

The *Caribbean Community Theater* (☎ 340-778-3596), at the Island Center, is a very active local theater troupe, performing more than four shows annually in the Sidney Lee Theater.

Caribbean Dance Company (☎ 340-778-8824) usually performs its big February show at the Island Center. The company takes pride in its capacity to preserve and perform African-Caribbean traditions of storytelling, music and dance.

The *Landmarks Society* (☎ 340-772-0598), at Estate Whim Plantation on Centerline Rd, sees itself as the keeper of St Croix's historical and cultural heirlooms and traditions. The organization regularly sponsors fund-raising events to support island preservation efforts. Many of these events, such as candlelight concerts, occur on the grounds of Whim Plantation. The society also sponsors house tours at regular intervals during the year.

Bars & Clubs Every month, *Boz's Cane Bay Beach Bar* (see Places to Eat) is the locus for St Croix's infamous Cane Bay Full Moon Party. Hundreds of people come here to shake their booty to the rhythms of 'de steel drums, mon.' While there is definitely a predominance of under-30 types in shorts and T-shirts at this bash, it appeals to all ages, races and genders. Some throw a tailgate party to rival a Penn State football championship. Boz's also has a steel band during its Sunday brunch.

The **Cormorant Beach Club** (see Places to Stay) is a major gay party on Friday nights with dancing to house, techno and classic R&B.

Cinema At the Sunny Isle Shopping Center on Centerline Rd, *Diamond Cinemas* (☎ 340-778-5200) has two screens. *Sunny Isle Theaters* (☎ 340-778-5620), in the same shopping complex, has six screens. Both theaters show first-run Hollywood films.

Shopping

Estate Whim Plantation Museum (see earlier) and Estate Mt Washington (☎ 340-772-1026), 2 miles north of Frederiksted off Route 63, sell mahogany reproductions of colonial Cruzan furniture like planters' chairs. St Croix Leap (also listed earlier) has handmade items like clocks, mirrors and natural-form tables.

EAST ISLAND

The scalloped coastline, steep hills and dry climate of the East End deterred the area's development until St Croix's roads improved during the second half of the 20th century. Then, the developers began marketing East End property as sites for vacation condo villages, resorts and seasonal homes. Today, the East End is largely an upscale territory that appeals to snowbirds, who come each winter to relax among their kind.

The yacht club and the Virgin Islands' only casino are out this way, as are a number of lively restaurants and bars. But you do not have to be a member of the upper class to enjoy the East End. Most of the best free campsites are here, as are the sea gardens of Buck Island Reef National Monument.

Buck Island Reef National Monument

With about 30,000 visitors a year, Buck Island is probably the most-visited single attraction on St Croix. This small island (176 acres, a mile long by a half-mile wide) lies

1½ miles off the northeast coast of St Croix and sits at the center of an 880-acre marine sanctuary. US President John F Kennedy guaranteed the protection of this sanctuary by naming it the first US underwater national monument in 1961. Since then, the National Park Service has worked to control uses and preserve the natural habitat of both the island and its surrounding reefs. Here is a prime example of a complete, wild Caribbean ecosystem.

A number of brochures and guidebooks tout the sea gardens and the snorkeling trail off the east end of Buck Island as the best reef dive in the Caribbean. Such descriptions are stretching the case, but the reef here, with its elkhorn coral grottos, healthy collection of tropical fish (from blue tang to barracuda) and marked trail is a first-rate snorkeling site that is accessible and safe for novice divers. Do not come here expecting *Blue Lagoon* serenity. During the late fall and winter, the trade winds often blow hard at Buck Island, creating a significant chop on the reef and cloudy visibility. Scuba divers find wreck and coral dives in 30 to 40 feet of water off the north coast.

Diving is not the only attraction here. Buck Island itself is a potent lure. West Beach and Dietrichs Point have protected beaches, sheltered swimming, toilets and picnic sites with tables and cooking grills you can fuel with driftwood. The hiking trail that circles around the west end of the island is a moderate walk through tropical dry forest, bromeliads, guinea grass and giant tamarind trees. The walk takes about 45 minutes and leads to an observation point on the island's 340-foot ridge.

Another reason to visit Buck Island is simply the trip itself. Most visitors travel here aboard tour boats from Christiansted, 5 miles to the west. These tour boats (see the 'Buck Island Tours' boxed text) may be large powerboats, dive boats, sleek catamarans or smaller sailboats. Pick the one that fits with your sense of a day or half-day adventure with sea and sun. Make sure you reserve your trip ahead of time because these trips are usually fully booked.

ST CROIX

Buck Island Tours

Several tour operators carry passengers to Buck Island. Most boats leave from Kings Wharf. Expect to pay about $30 to $50 per person, including snorkeling gear. The following are some of the most popular tour operators.

Milemark Watersports (☎ 340-773-2628) offers half- and full-day trips aboard a large dive boat or catamaran, leaving from Kings Wharf.

Big Beard Adventures (☎ 340-773-4482) offers a similar service to Milemark's, leaving from the Pan Am Pavilion.

Teroro II (☎ 340-773-3161) has multihull sailboats, leaving from Green Cay Marina, east of Christiansted.

Diva (☎ 340-778-4675) is a 35-foot sailboat that carries six passengers, based at Christiansted.

Point Udall

The territorial government paved the road (about 1½ miles) from Cramer's Park (see Beaches) to Point Udall in 1999 and built a monument at the end of the road to celebrate the millennium. Publicists claim that Point Udall is the easternmost geographic point in the US territory, and on December 31, 1999, St Croix staged a huge millennium party here with bands, dignitaries and plenty of rum as the first spot in the US to welcome 2000.

The millennium passed, and Point Udall is once again a serene place. As you face into a 25-knot trade wind, the vista from the promontory more than 225 feet above the surf-strewn reefs and beaches is enough to make some travelers hear symphonies in their heads. Others simply like the challenge of hiking the steep trails down the hillside to the isolated beaches on the south side of the point, where you can pitch a tent or sunbathe, swim and snorkel with no one looking over your shoulder.

Great Pond Bay

This area on the southeastern side of the island bracketed by Routes 62, 624 and 60 is just about the last undeveloped coastal lowland area on the island. The large salt pond here, called Great Pond, hosts dozens of varieties of migratory and wading waterfowl such as egrets. The Boy Scout Camp Arawak (see Places to Stay) is over on the western end of this wilderness, and you can find hiking trails from the camp leading to both the Great Pond and the bay.

Beaches

Cramer's Park This is an attractive public beach on Route 82. There are grills, picnic tables and a few shelters here. The park can get crowded with Cruzans on holidays and weekends. Most of the time, though, Cramer's Park is quiet. The facilities have recently been rebuilt, and you can now count on working toilets and a telephone. Do not count on fresh running water; bring your own. You can pitch a tent here free of charge and without a permit.

Buccaneer Beach A crescent beach sheltered from the trade winds and popular with tourists, Buccaneer Beach is in front of the Buccaneer Hotel, about 2 miles east of Christiansted off the East End Rd (Route 82). If you are not a guest of the hotel, you must pay $4 to enter at the hotel gatehouse. You can take advantage of the changing facilities and beach restaurant, but the beach chairs and towels are reserved for hotel guests.

Shoy's Beach This long crescent of sand just east of Buccaneer Beach is just as protected as the hotel beach but less touristy and free. Lots of upscale Cruzans come here on weekends. Head off the point at the west end of the beach for good snorkeling. To get to Shoy's, go to the gatehouse at the Buccaneer, but instead of following the road into the hotel, take the road that veers off to the right; check in with the guard to the gated community and follow the road to the beach. There are no facilities here.

Chenay Bay This beach lies a mile east of Shoy's as you head toward Point Udall on Route 82. The Chenay Bay Beach Resort is here with its bar/restaurant and watersports concession renting kayaks. Swimming at Chenay Bay is protected, and the water is shallow, which makes this area popular with families and children.

Reef Beach Travelers will find Reef Beach at Tague Bay in front of Duggan's Reef restaurant, about 7 miles east of Christiansted on Route 82. The water is a little rough at Reef Beach, as the trade winds sometimes blow onto the beach. A lot of the sunbathers here are snowbirds and short-time guests staying in the condo developments in the surrounding area. For strong swimmers, there is good snorkeling on the offshore reef.

Isaac Bay & Jack Bay These two secluded beaches are near the southeast tip of the island. They are popular with Cruzans and the young continentals working on the island. Nudism and topless bathing are common at Isaac Bay. The most popular route to get to these beaches is to take the steep trail south from Point Udall. You can also follow the unnamed road east from Route 60 through the ruins of the vacation homes destroyed by Hurricane Hugo. A path leads along the shore from the end of the road. Swimmers should be careful of the riptides.

Grapetree Bay This broad, long beach lines the shore in front of the Divi resort. You can park at the resort and head down to the 1000-foot strand. There is good snorkeling off the east end.

Activities
If you are serious about **windsurfing**, bring your own board to the island (there are no windsurfing shops) and head for Chenay Bay or Shoy's Beach.

A **golf** course slightly less challenging than Carambola (see West Island, earlier) is the oceanside, rolling 18-hole course at the Buccaneer Hotel. The greens fee is $30 for nonguests; carts rent for $18 during the fall. During the high season, expect to pay more.

Golfers on a budget will love the Reef Golf Course (☎ 340-773-8844) on Route 82 at Tague Bay. This 9-hole course stretches 3000 yards. Greens fees are $18 for 18 holes, $30 with a cart. You can rent clubs for only $8. There is also a driving range here ($2.50 for a bucket of balls).

The Reef Golf Course also has **tennis** courts that rent for $4 an hour. You pay $5 per hour per person at the two courts of the Tamarind Reef Hotel and the Chenay Bay Beach Resort. The Buccaneer Hotel has the most courts on the island (eight) and a pro on staff. Nonguests pay $8 per hour.

You can play formal wicket **croquet** like plantation gentry at the Tamarind Reef Hotel. The fee is $8 for 1¼ hours.

Places to Stay
Although condo and villa construction have encroached on the East End wilderness in recent decades, this area offers the island's best off-the-beaten-track camping and a few spacious resorts.

Camping As is the case throughout the USVI, territorial law states that the beaches of the islands are public space, so you can camp on any of them. On holidays such as Easter, Labor Day, Emancipation Day/Fourth of July, a lot of Cruzans camp. On St Croix, most campers head to the East End due to the generally dry conditions there.

Coakley Bay, off Route 82, can become a tent city on holiday weekends. But there are no facilities here.

Isaac Bay and *Jack Bay* (see Beaches) appeal to backpackers who favor hiking to the remote beach on the trail starting at Point Udall.

Cramer's Park (see Beaches) is a popular camping spot on the far east side of the island.

Camp Arawak (☎ *340-773-7377*), on Route 62 at Great Pond Bay, is a Boy Scout camp just 3 miles south of Christiansted. The camp is on one of the largest undeveloped tracts of coastal wilderness on the south coast, which includes Great Pond, the adjacent bay and the ruins of Fareham Plantation. There are no facilities here open to the public, but you can camp for free when it's not being used by the Scouts or the National Guard.

Hotels Overlooking Green Cay from the north shore about 4 miles east of Christiansted, the *Tamarind Reef Hotel* (☎ *340-773-4455, 800-619-0014*) is one of the island's newest hotels, and it offers a lot for a 46-room property. All rooms come with a kitchenette and private patio or balcony with a sea view. There are two beaches, protected by offshore reefs, and a large pool. The popular Galleon restaurant (see Places to Eat) is here along with tennis courts and a croquet course. Rates start at about $160 for a double during high season.

Chenay Bay Beach Resort (☎ *340-773-2918, 800-548-4457*), on the North Shore Rd, rises above the swells at Chenay Bay. This complex of 50 efficiency cottages may well be the favorite destination of vacationing families on St Croix. Sports equipment for snorkeling and kayaking are free, as is tennis. Kids under 10 stay (and sometimes eat) free. In season, rates start at about $185.

The Buccaneer (☎ *340-773-2100*), on the East End Rd, 2 miles east of Christiansted, set the standard for VI beach resorts back in the 1950s and still supplies plenty of luxury. There are 134 rooms in a complex of buildings and cottages surrounding the main three-story hotel that overlooks a cove and beach. The Buccaneer is geared for the active resort guest, with golf, tennis, water sports and a health spa. There are four restaurants, too. Celebrities including Michael Jackson have long favored this resort. Expect to pay $210 and up during high season, but call for special packages.

Opened for the millennium, the *Divi Carina Bay Beach Resort* (☎ *340-773-9700, 800-554-2008*), on Route 60 at Grapetree Bay on the southeast coast, is St Croix's new premier resort.

There are 120 oceanfront rooms here and 20 one-bedroom villas. Data ports, VCRs and voice mail are offered, along with all the other top-end trimmings. Guests can choose from two restaurants, two pools, a 1000-foot beach, tennis courts or the island's only casino for entertainment. Rates run about $210 and up.

Places to Eat

Cheeseburgers in Paradise (☎ *340-773-1119*), near Green Cay Marina on the East End Rd, is an ever-popular stop for snowbirds and travelers. The setting here is a roadside field with a small bar and kitchen building surrounded by a collection of open-air tables, some shaded with large umbrellas. The cuisine is light and informal Tex-Mex. The ambience says 'picnic.' Nachos and the 'world famous cheeseburger' run about $7.

The *South Shore Café* (☎ *340-773-9311*), at Great Pond, is a gourmet bistro with an open-air setting. Most of Diane Scheuber's cuisine is Italian, but you can get prime rib and veggie specials for lunch and dinner. Diane makes her own bread and ice cream. Most dinners will run you $15 or more.

Duggan's Reef (☎ *340-773-9800*), on the East End Rd overlooking the beach and Buck Island, has been Frank Duggan's celebrity restaurant since 1983. Stop by for lunch or dinner and you might see Senator Ted Kennedy, actor Bill Murray or baseballer Roger Clemens at a neighboring table. Dinner prices are moderate, with several pasta dishes under $17. New York Knicks star Walt Frazier likes the 'island style' fish ($21).

The Galleon (☎ *340-773-9949*), less than 2 miles east of Christiansted at the Green Cay Marina, is the choice of East Enders who are in the mood for fine French and Northern Italian dinners. *Escalopes de veau aux crevettes* (veal with shrimp) is a popular entree. Diners say you should not miss out on the *gravlax* (cured salmon with dill and pepper). Expect to pay more than $60 for two without cocktails or wine.

Entertainment

Cheeseburgers in Paradise (see Places to Eat) has live entertainment starting at about 6:30 pm Thursday to Sunday.

The Virgin Islands' first casino opened in 2000 at the **Divi Carina Bay Resort** (see Places to Stay). Slots and the usual games are here in a plush but virtually windowless 10,000-sq-foot setting. The casino is open noon to 4 am weekdays, to 6 am weekends. Players will feel out of place if they do not dress the part of a high roller.

Tortola

Viewed from St Thomas, Tortola oozes a sense of enchantment with its high mountains glowing purple in the mist. Yet most travelers coming to the BVI view Tortola more as a jumping-off place than a destination.

Tortola is a big diamond in the rough, offering a lot to travelers willing to take the time to penetrate its crusty façade. Although Tortola is virtually the same size as its close neighbor to the west, St John, it is not nearly as pristine. The island is both the

governmental and commercial center of the BVI as well as the air and ferry hub for the eastern end of the Virgin Islands. More than 14,000 of the BVI's 19,000 citizens live and work here, and the south shore of the island is a thickly settled mix of commercial development, industrial sites, marinas, hotels and West Indian homes. Tortola's urban center, Road Town, lacks the polish and colonial architecture that characterize Christiansted and Charlotte Amalie. And unlike its sister islands of St Thomas, St Croix and St John, Tortola has little in the way of ruins or architecture to evoke its colonial past.

But as singer Jimmy Buffett insinuates in his anthem to Cane Garden Bay, anyone who misses the beaches and nightlife on the north shore of Tortola has missed a land of peace and plenty. This is the territory of welcoming islanders, moderately priced guesthouses, mountainside villas, beachfront restaurants, compact West Indian settlements and some world-renown bars including Quito's Gazebo and Bomba's Surfside Shack.

Meanwhile, the other 40 islands of the BVI beckon for exploration. Each offers its own version of an undeveloped tropical oasis, and they're accessible through the extensive ferry system or by yacht from one of more than 15 charterboat operations based on Tortola.

History

New archaeological excavations in the area of Josiahs Bay seem to document Native American habitation of Tortola back more than 2000 years. Discoveries of pottery on the island suggest that Tortola hosted Ciboney, Igneri and Taíno communities during the same period those Indians settled on St Croix, St Thomas and St John. Although no definitive record exists, many historians speculate that Tortola was the island that Columbus called Santa Ursula when he sailed past in 1493. The island got its present name around 1515, when outriders from Puerto Rico passed this way in search of gold. They called the island Tortola, which means 'turtle dove' or 'land of the turtle dove' in Spanish. Today, most of the doves that gave their name to the island are gone from Tortola, but you can still hear them on the neighboring Guana Islands (off East End), where their distinctive cooing fills the air.

Privateers, Explorers & Pirates No one of record settled on Tortola during the 16th century, but explorers passed by the island because Tortola marks the north edge of one of the broadest passages between the Caribbean and the Atlantic. Sir Jack Hawkins used this broad passage in 1542 and again in 1563 when he brought the first cargo of slaves from Africa to Hispaniola. He had Sir Francis Drake with him on a third trip in 1568, and Drake returned in 1585. On this trip, Drake navigated the pass south of Tortola with 25 ships and more than 2000 men on their way to a successful attack on Santo Domingo (the Sir Francis Drake Channel was named in the process).

In 1595, Drake returned with an aging John Hawkins to use the waters off Tortola as a staging area for an unsuccessful attack on the Spanish at Puerto Rico. The attack was not only a military failure but also wounded Hawkins, who died aboard Drake's *Defiance* and was buried at sea off Tortola. A year later, the Earl of Cumberland passed this way and summed up his impression of the Virgins as 'a knot of little islands, wholly uninhabited, sandy, barren, craggy.' The islands appeared just as desolate when Captain John Smith passed by 10 years later on his way to Virginia.

Such desolation and so many harbors adjacent to one of the most favored trade routes in the West Indies made Tortola the perfect hideout for pirates

during the 17th century. They hid along the island's coast and ravaged passing ships with small, fast attack sloops they called 'filibusters.' This was the era of Blackbeard (Edward Teach) and dozens of other renegade captains. According to legend, the first half of the 17th century saw buccaneers – probably from a number of European nations – build a rough and ready settlement at Sopers Hole on West End.

British Colonization & Plantations The island was formally claimed by Holland in 1648, when the Dutch West India Company established a settlement and built a fort on the site that is now the Fort Burt Hotel. In 1666, a band of British drove the Dutch out and claimed the island for England. A French force quickly displaced this group, but the English returned in 1672. During the last decades of the 17th century, some English families came to Tortola from Anguilla to raise cattle and grow cotton, sugar, ginger and indigo. The first census conducted in 1717 identified 159 whites and 175 blacks on Tortola.

Although the 18th century was a time of almost ceaseless wars between the powers of Western Europe, Tortola flourished as colonists began to flood the island. Just three years after the first census, the BVI

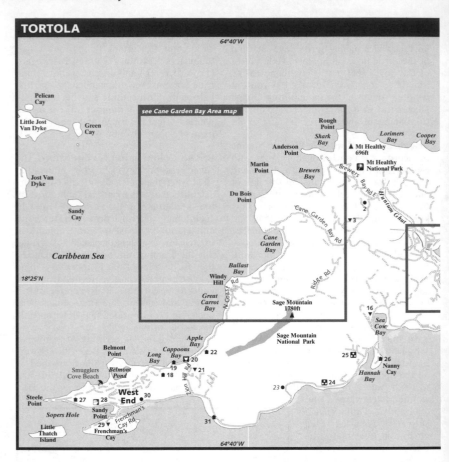

TORTOLA

Pelican Cay

Little Jost Van Dyke

Green Cay

Jost Van Dyke

Sandy Cay

64°40'W

see Cane Garden Bay Area map

Rough Point

Shark Bay

Anderson Point

Martin Point

Brewers Bay

Du Bois Point

▲ Mt Healthy 696ft

Mt Healthy National Park

Lorimers Bay

Cooper Bay

Brewers Bay Rd E

Plantation Ghut

▼ 2

Cane Garden Bay Rd

▼ 3

Caribbean Sea

Cane Garden Bay

18°25'N

Ballast Bay

Windy Hill

Great Carrot Bay

N Coast Rd

Ridge Rd

Sage Mountain 1780ft ▲

16 ▼

Sea Cow Bay

Sage Mountain National Park

Belmont Point

Apple Bay

Cappoons Bay

Long Bay

Smugglers Cove Beach

Belmont Pond

Zion Hill Rd

■ 22

25 ☒

▣ 20

19 ●

▼ 21

■ 18

★ 26

Nanny Cay

Hannah Bay

Steele Point

Sopers Hole

Little Thatch Island

West End

■ 27

☐ 28

Sandy Point

29 ▼ Frenchman's Cay

● 30

Frenchman's Cay Rd

☒ 24

23 ●

★ 31

64°40'W

population soared to 1122 whites and 1509 blacks. Among these new settlers were an enterprising group of English religious dissidents known as Quakers, famed for their work ethic, business acumen and devotion to pacifism. These Quakers under the leadership of Joshua Fielding and William Piggott established plantations throughout the BVI in 1727.

Anglican and Methodist settlers arrived as well, and by 1740, Tortola was almost totally divided into plantations producing sugar, molasses, rum, cotton, lime juice, ginger, indigo, coffee, pimentos and mahogany. Thirty-five years later, the slave population grew to more than 6000.

Prosperity for the planters did not translate into ideal social conditions on the island. King George's heavy taxes and an unequal distribution of wealth caused a 'peasants' uprising' in 1753. When George Suckling arrived in 1778 to take the post of Chief Justice of the Virgin Islands, he found 'the indolent and base preying upon the vitals of the industrious and virtuous,' and 'the island presented a shocking scene of anarchy.' However, some plantation owners possessed a nobility of spirit. The Quaker planter

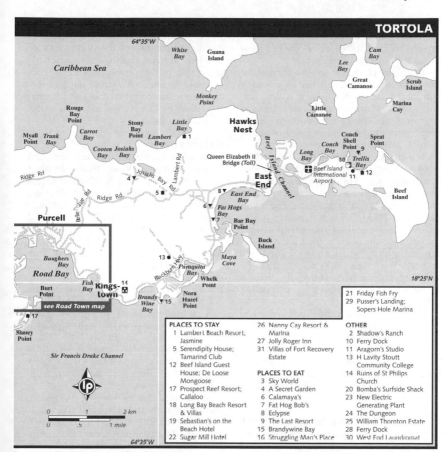

TORTOLA

64°35'W

Caribbean Sea

White Bay
Guana Island
Cam Bay
Lee Bay
Great Camanoe
Scrub Island

Monkey Point

Rouge Bay Point
Stony Bay Point
Little Bay
Hawks Nest
Little Camanoe
Marina Cay

Myall Point
Trunk Bay
Carrot Bay
Lambert Bay
Conch Bay
Conch Shell Point
Sprat Point

Cooten Bay
Josiahs Bay
Long Bay
Trellis Bay

Ridge Rd
Queen Elizabeth II Bridge (Toll)
East End
Beef Island International Airport

Ridge Rd
East End Bay
Fat Hogs Bay
Bar Bay Point
Beef Island

Purcell

Baughers Bay
Maya Cove
Buck Island

Road Bay
Fish Bay
Kings-town
Paraquita Bay
Whelk Point
18°25'N

Burt Point
Brandy Wine Bay
Nora Hazel Point

see Road Town map

Slaney Point

Sir Francis Drake Channel

0   1   2 km
0   .5   1 mile

64°35'W

PLACES TO STAY	26	Nanny Cay Resort & Marina	OTHER		21	Friday Fish Fry

PLACES TO STAY
1 Lambert Beach Resort; Jasmine
5 Serendipity House; Tamarind Club
12 Beef Island Guest House; De Loose Mongoose
17 Prospect Reef Resort; Callaloo
18 Long Bay Beach Resort & Villas
19 Sebastian's on the Beach Hotel
22 Sugar Mill Hotel

26 Nanny Cay Resort & Marina
27 Jolly Roger Inn
31 Villas of Fort Recovery Estate

PLACES TO EAT
3 Sky World
4 A Secret Garden
6 Calamaya's
7 Fat Hog Bob's
8 Eclypse
9 The Last Resort
15 Brandywine Bay
16 Struggling Man's Place

21 Friday Fish Fry
29 Pusser's Landing; Sopers Hole Marina

OTHER
2 Shadow's Ranch
10 Ferry Dock
11 Aragorn's Studio
13 H Lavity Stoutt Community College
14 Ruins of St Philips Church
20 Bomba's Surfside Shack
23 New Electric Generating Plant
24 The Dungeon
25 William Thornton Estate
28 Ferry Dock
30 West End Laundromat

Samuel Nottingham, for example, freed all of his slaves and in 1778 and gave them the land that was Long Look Plantation.

19th-Century Troubles The island attained its economic peak about 1805, when Tortola exported 2500 barrels of sugar and the island's population swelled to 1300 whites and about 9000 blacks. But the disruption of trade caused by the Napoleonic Wars, the end of the slave trade in 1807 and then the development of the sugar beet in Europe spelled economic disaster for Tortola. By 1815, less than one-fifth of the island remained under cultivation. Indolence, gambling and begging were commonplace among the population, and the island seethed with tension.

At one point, a planter named William Hodges shot his slave Prosper for letting a mango fall from a tree. Although a court found Hodges guilty of murder, and officials hung Hodges behind the Road Town jail, the case galvanized hatred and suspicion between the races on Tortola. This animosity reached its peak in 1831, when rumor spread of a slave plot to revolt, murder all the white males on the island, seize ships in

TORTOLA

the harbor and sail off to Haiti with the white females as concubines. With this 'discovery,' more than 500 whites packed their belongings and fled Tortola.

Three years later, the English Parliament emancipated all slaves in British colonies. Afterward, the black population fled Tortola as well. Many sailed aboard schooners known as 'blackbird hunters,' which carried freed blacks to Trinidad where a booming economy demanded laborers.

The blacks who remained found their lives just as miserable as they had been under slavery, and in 1853, a new cattle tax and the beating of a black man by a white man brought revolt to the island. The revolt started in Road Town, but before it was over, it had engulfed the entire island, leaving the cane fields burned, the mills destroyed and the great houses looted and torched. While the blacks retreated to the bush to hide from British forces that arrived to punish the rioters, nearly all of Tortola's whites left the island.

For the next five decades, Tortolians eked out a living through fishing, subsistence farming, cattle raising and rum making. By 1893, there were only two whites on the island, the doctor and the deputy governor. Blacks had now claimed positions as merchants, mariners, elected officials and government workers.

A Sailor's Paradise In the early 20th century, the establishment of an experimental agricultural station for growing and ginning cotton brought a new sense of optimism to the island. In the wake of the station's success, a sugar factory moved to the island. But Tortola and the other British Virgin Islands remained depopulated, forgotten islands well into the 1960s, when modern sailors discovered the fair winds, pristine anchorages and welcoming people in the BVI. A number of bareboat yacht-charter companies led by the Moorings began locating their operations on Tortola.

Soon sailors came by the tens of thousands from the US and Europe to charter cruising sailboats. And in the wake of the sailors came restaurants, bars, resorts and real estate developers. The 1980s and '90s saw rampant development on Tortola, including the creation of the Wickhams Cays commercial zones and the construction of a cruise ship pier. Probably 90% of the commercial buildings and homes on the island date from the boom of the last 25 years. And those buildings come in a hodgepodge of shapes and sizes.

Orientation

At 21 sq miles in area, Tortola is the third-largest island in the Virgin Islands archipelago after St Croix and St Thomas. Tortola lies less than 2 miles east of St John, across a windswept and current-ripped channel called the Narrows. This long, thin, high island stretches 14 miles from west to east (if you include the appended Beef Island) but is rarely more than 2 miles wide from north to south. The altitude of Tortola's mountain spine creates steep slopes that come almost to the water's edge on both the north and south shores of the island.

Sage Mountain near the western end of the mountain range is the highest point in all of the Virgin Islands at 1780 feet. A fringe of scalloped bays ring the island. The deepest of these bays on the south shore is the harbor for the BVI's largest town and capital, Road Town.

The ruggedness of Tortola's topography makes for slow travel around the island. Plan on spending at least 45 minutes to travel the 14 miles from Sopers Hole at the West End to the airport on Beef Island on the East End. In traffic, you can easily spend 25 minutes traveling between the airport and Road Town. Crossing over the island from the south shore to the north shore involves a slow trek on switchback roads. The trip from Road Town to Cane Garden Bay, less than 3 miles as the crow flies, will take you about 20 minutes. The main roads on the island, Blackburn Hwy and Waterfront Dr, run along the south shore of the island. Ridge Rd is a scenic drive along Tortola's mountain spine. From here, secondary roads leading to beaches like Brewers Bay and Josiahs Bay branch off to the north.

Most travelers will find the fold-out color maps sponsored by AT&T perfectly adequate for navigating Tortola and Road Town. These maps come in every packet of tourist information from the BVI Tourist Board, and you will find the map among the brochures displayed at most hotels and restaurants. For a more detailed, topographical road map with the island and Road Town drawn to scale, contact International Travel Maps (☎ 604-687-3320) in Vancouver, BC, Canada.

Information

Tourist Offices The BVI Tourist Board (☎ 284-494-3864, 800-835-8530) is in the Akara Building in Road Town on Wickhams Cay 1 (look for the banner on the building), facing the Village Cay Hotel and the cruise ship dock. There is also a small office (☎ 284-494-7260) at the ferry terminal in Road Town. The offices are open 9 am to 5 pm weekdays.

Money Barclays, Scotia and Chase Manhattan Banks are all on Wickhams Cay 1 in Road Town. Banco Popular is on Main St near the customs office. All these banks have ATMs, and most are open 8 am to 4:30 pm Monday to Thursday and 8 am to 5:30 pm Friday. You will also find a Barclays ATM on the wharf at Sopers Hole, West End.

Post & Communications The main post office (☎ 284-494-4996) stands at the south end of Main St in Road Town. It is open 8 am to 4 pm weekdays, 9 am to 1:30 pm Saturday. There are small regional offices at Cane Garden Bay, Carrot Bay, East End and West End.

The Carib Wave Internet Café (☎ 284-494-7579), on the 2nd floor next to the Shirt Shack on Main St, offers complete Internet and email access. This place is as much a computer service and repair center as it is a cafe. The rates ($8 for 15 minutes, $12 for 30 minutes) are pretty steep, but you get a free cup of coffee or tea while you surf.

Travel Agencies Tortola has a number of travel agencies in Road Town. International travelers use Travel Consultants Ltd (☎ 284-494-2777) in the Simmonds Building at 30 Decastro St on Wickhams Cay 1.

Bookstores & Libraries The Book Store (☎ 284-494-3921), on Wickhams Cay 1, has books for all ages. Books Etcetera (☎ 284-494-6611), in the Ellen L Skelton Building at Road Reef in Road Town, is a newcomer to the book scene.

You will find the main public library (☎ 284-494-3701) on the 2nd floor above the Rite Way Food Market on Fleming St between Main St and Waterfront Dr.

Newspapers The *Island Sun* has been around for more than 40 years. It comes out twice a week and costs 35¢. Another major news source is the *BVI Beacon,* which costs 50¢ and comes out every Thursday. The free *Limin' Times* is a weekly entertainment tabloid that gives you the best sense of where to find the action throughout the BVI.

Laundry Your best bet in Road Town is Sylvia's (☎ 284-494-2230) on Fleming St. This place is centrally located and is a dry cleaner and laundry. Expect to pay $1.50 to wash, $2 to dry. You can also try the West End Laundromat (☎ 284-495-4463), on Waterfront Dr just east of Sopers Hole. If you are in need of a wash in Cane Garden Bay, there's a laundry in the back of Rhymer's Hotel.

Medical Services & Emergencies Peebles Hospital (☎ 284-494-3467), at the south end of Main St, has 40 beds and complete emergency services.

Specializing in cosmetic and reconstructive surgery, the Bougainvillea Clinic (☎ 284- 494-2181) operates a pair of villas on Russell Hill in Road Town.

In an emergency, call ☎ 999 for the police, fire department, ambulance or VISAR (Virgin Islands Search & Rescue).

Cay Pharmacy (☎ 284-494-8128), on Wickhams Cay 1 in Road Town, is well stocked and easy to find.

Dangers & Annoyances Tortola has little street crime. Nevertheless, the usual rules of

TORTOLA

cautious conduct for travelers apply here. There are parts of Road Town, the south shore and the East End that are extensive West Indian neighborhoods where the bars, clubs and restaurants cater strictly to local clientele. Frequently, groups of men gather in the streets outside these places and convenience stores to drink and flirt with passing women. Such places and gatherings are best left to the people who are familiar with each other and the neighborhood.

Road Town can be a desolate place even on a Saturday night. Main St is particularly quiet after dark and unsupervised by police.

Long Bush Rd in the northwest corner of town has a number of rowdy West Indian bars and clubs. Don't make yourself a target for a desperate person by walking in this area after dark. Most of the bars and restaurants that appeal to travelers are on Wickhams Cay 1 and along the waterfront in Road Town. Stick to this area and you will be safe unless you are strolling around alone.

As with the USVI, cars take the left-hand lane in the BVI. Drivers should be careful of cattle wandering the roads. These animals are a particular hazard at the East End and

Magic Mushrooms

Psychoactive mushrooms (psilocybin) grow wild on Tortola. If you travel in frisky circles, someone will tempt you with 'shrooms' or shroom tea (Bomba's Surfside Shack serves it at the monthly full-moon party). Shrooms are legal to possess and consume in the BVI but illegal to sell.

There are dozens of species of psilocybin or 'magic mushrooms.' The effects of their ingestion resemble a short LSD trip, producing significant physical, visual and perceptual changes. The primary distinguishable feature of most psilocybin mushrooms is that they bruise blue when handled.

Psilocybin mushrooms have been used for thousands of years by Native Americans. The first European record of their use showed up in the 16th-century writings of a Spanish priest who wrote about the Aztec's use of both mushrooms and peyote. By the mid 1960s, mushrooms were being studied and used recreationally. In 1968, possession of psilocybin mushrooms was made illegal in the US.

Depending on how much and how recently you have eaten, mushrooms generally take 30 to 60 minutes (up to two hours) to cause a reaction. The primary effects of shrooms last four to six hours when taken orally. For many people, there is an additional period of time when it is difficult to fall asleep and reality is skewed.

In the onset, mushrooms are likely to cause a feeling of anticipation or anxiety. There may be an energy burst and the sense that things are different than usual. As the effects intensify, a wide variety of perceptual changes may occur: pupil dilation, visuals, mental stimulation, new perspectives, quickly changing emotions (lots of laughter), possible paranoia and confusion. Closed-eye visuals are extremely common; open-eye visuals are common for some people and are more likely at higher doses.

Many people experience nausea and/or vomiting during mushroom trips, especially with higher doses. Other possible negative effects include anxiety and frightening thoughts and visions. Mushrooms, like LSD, can precipitate strong, temporary changes in an individual's experience of life and reality. Recent experiences, especially strong ones, can have a substantial effect. Physically or psychologically unsettling events in the days before a mushroom trip can blossom into more serious distress. You should be prepared for the possibility of difficult or frightening mental states. Depending on the strength and size of the dose, Tortola's shrooms can give you anything from a mild high to a wall-melting, commode-hugging bad trip. Note that mixing shrooms with alcohol is asking for trouble.

all along Ridge Rd. If you drive at night on Tortola roads, sooner or later you will have a brake-screeching close encounter with a cow. Be vigilant and drive very slowly.

Here is a second reason to drive with exceptional care: The government has booby-trapped most roads with speed bumps.

Organized Tours

The taxi drivers have a corner on this market. The best place to get a cab for a tour is the BVI Taxi Stand (☎ 284-494-7519), at the Road Town Jetty on Waterfront Dr. You pay about $25 an hour.

You can also try Travel Plan Tours (☎ 284-494-2872), on Wickhams Cay 1, for a three-hour tour of the island ($25), snorkel trips and out-island excursions.

Special Events

Tortola plays host to an almost endless list of yacht races, including the Annual Spring Regatta (☎ 284-494-3286), but land-based celebrations are hard to come by.

The grand exception to this statement is the BVI Summer Festival (☎ 284-494-7963), which occurs over three weeks at the end of July and the beginning of August. During this time, Tortola rocks from the West End to the East End, celebrating its African-Caribbean heritage. Festival events feature everything from a beauty pageant and car show to 'rise & shine tramps' (noisy parades led by reggae bands in the back of a truck that start at 3 am) to horse racing.

The festival dates back 166 years to August 4, 1834, when British officials read the proclamation for the abolition of slavery in the British Virgin Islands under the Sandbox tree in Road Town. Since then, islanders have commemorated Emancipation Day each year on the first Monday of August. The celebration of August Festival (which includes the public holidays Festival Monday, Tuesday and Wednesday) is an important historical and cultural event in the BVI.

Getting There & Away

Air In the midst of a 1000-foot runway extension and terminal expansion, Tortola's Beef Island International Airport (☎ 284-494-3701) is the BVI's major point of entry. However, because the airport will not have the ability to accommodate large jets, there are no direct flights from Europe or North America. Travelers coming from overseas arrive at San Juan, Puerto Rico, or St Thomas and take smaller aircraft to Tortola.

For years, American Eagle has had the most flights in and out of Beef Island (about 14 flights a day to and from San Juan) with its propjets. Tickets cost $55 one way, $110 roundtrip if you fly weekdays, otherwise they are $132/$155. In 2000, Cape Air became real competition, offering a dozen flights a day. One-way tickets cost $94; roundtrip tickets cost $109 to $175. One of the attractive features of Cape Air is you can always get on one of its scheduled flights: If one plane is full, the airline simply adds a second aircraft to the run. Cape Air also flies about six times a day between St Thomas and Tortola. Air Sunshine and Continental also fly the San Juan-St Thomas-Tortola route.

For travel to other islands in the Lesser Antilles, you can fly LIAT. There are flights from Tortola to Antigua, St Kitts, St Martin, St Thomas and San Juan.

See the Getting There & Away chapter for more information.

Ferry There is regular ferry service between Tortola, St Thomas and St John. The fare to St Thomas is about $23/44 one way/roundtrip. The BVI have an extensive network of ferries between Tortola and Virgin Gorda ($19 roundtrip), Jost Van Dyke ($15 roundtrip) and Peter Island ($15 roundtrip). Also see 'Interisland Ferries' in the Getting Around chapter.

Getting Around

To/From the Airport There is a taxi stand at the airport, and the government sets the rates. Expect to pay $15 (for one to three passengers) to reach Road Town and most of the resorts on the eastern half of the island. You pay about $20 for a cab to Cane Garden Bay or the West End. When you're ready to return to the airport, you can call

TORTOLA

the BVI Taxi Association (☎ 284-494-2322) or Turtle Dove Taxi (☎ 284-494-6274).

In general, hotels do not send courtesy vans to and from the airport, but some charterboat companies like the Moorings offer free pickup and drop-off.

Local ordinances prohibit you from renting cars at the airport, but your company may let you drop your car off there.

Car Tortola has a complete array of car rental companies, but do not be surprised if they tell you they're closed on the weekend. This situation is not necessarily as big a problem as it might seem, as many of the island's hotels have rental cars on the property or can make arrangements to have one waiting for you. If you are leaving during the weekend, you can drop the car at an airport lot without a checkout.

Expect to pay around $38 to $45 a day for a Suzuki Samurai. Large vehicles run $55 or more with unlimited mileage, but car rates drop off during the summer and fall. Jeep-style vehicles are your best bet on this island, as many island roads are steep and/ or rough. Law requires that the rental agencies charge you $10 for a temporary (three months) BVI driver's license. Sometimes the car rental folks charge you for this document; sometimes they don't.

Some popular agencies on the island are Avis (☎ 284-494-3322), Dollar (☎ 284-494-6093), Hertz (☎ 284-495-4405), Jerry's Car Rental (☎ 284-495-4111) and National (☎ 284-494-3197).

Taxi Taxis on Tortola are usually Asian-built vans. Rates are set by the government (see To/From the Airport), but you will find that different drivers quote you different prices for the same trip, so it is reasonable to negotiate. Expect to pay about $10 from Road Town to Cane Garden Bay or either end of the island. Road Town to Josiahs Bay will cost you $15, as will a trip to places along the northwest end of the island like the Bomba Shack.

Scato's Bus Service (☎ 284-494-2365) roams the island with its pickup trucks equipped with bench seats in the bed and an awning overhead. There is no set schedule. Passengers wishing for a ride just stand by the side of the road and hail the driver as he or she approaches. Expect to pay between $1 to $4, depending on the length of the ride.

ROAD TOWN

Road Town looks, smells and sounds like the boomtown it is. The BVI capital takes its name from the island's principal harbor, Road Bay, which has served as a 'roadstead' (staging area) for fleets of ships for centuries. By day, the town's roads are a clot of traffic that stirs up dust and shakes your spine with the winding of transmission gears. Even the harbor seems on the verge of chaos with the comings and goings of scores of charter yachts, ferries and occasional cruise ships.

Some of the island's most economical lodgings stand on the hills overlooking Road Town and on the back streets. Most of the town's pubs and restaurants of interest to travelers are strung out along Waterfront Dr. Despite the name, little of this road actually skirts the sea in Road Town, and the town (perhaps because of hurricanes) largely turns its back to the harbor.

Any traveler seeking shade and quiet should retreat to Main St, Road Town's primary shopping venue. This narrow street that winds along the western edge of town is a collection of wooden and stone buildings – including churches, a prison and a museum – dating back about 200 years. Historic preservation is afoot in this neighborhood, and there are some attractive shops and cheap eateries. But the renaissance of Main St is a work in progress, and travelers should not come here expecting anything like the polish you find in Charlotte Amalie or Christiansted.

Orientation

For such a small community, Road Town can be daunting for the traveler to navigate upon first arrival. The difficulty comes partly from mule-paths-turned-paved-streets that twist, turn and change names capriciously. The two different segments of Main St, for example, are separated by Pickering Rd.

ROAD TOWN

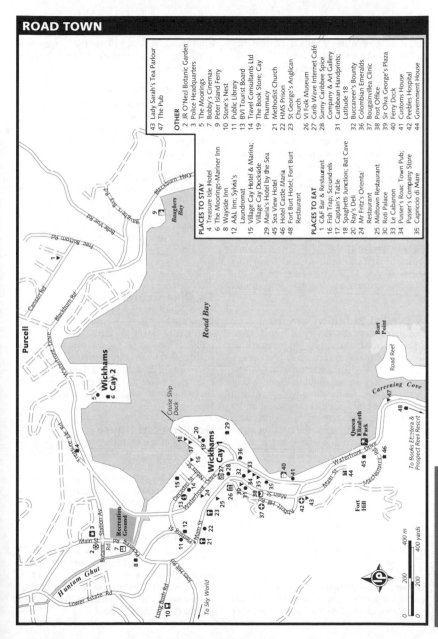

43 Lady Sarah's Tea Parlour
47 The Pub

OTHER
2   JR O'Neal Botanic Garden
3   Police Headquarters
5   The Moorings
7   Bobby's Cinemax
9   Peter Island Ferry
10 Stone's Nest
11 Public Library
13 BVI Tourist Board
14 Travel Consultants Ltd
19 The Book Store; Cay
    Pharmacy
21 Methodist Church
22 HMS Prison
23 St George's Anglican
    Church
26 VI Folk Museum
27 Carib Wave Internet Café
28 Sunny Caribbee Spice
    Company & Art Gallery
31 Caribbean Handprints;
    Latitude 18
32 Buccaneer's Bounty
36 Colombian Emeralds
37 Bougainvillea Clinic
38 Post Office
39 Sir Olva George's Plaza
40 Ferry Dock
41 Customs House
42 Peebles Hospital
44 Government House

PLACES TO STAY
4   Treasure Isle Hotel
6   The Moorings–Mariner Inn
8   Wayside Inn
12 A&L Inn; Sylvia's
    Laundromat
15 Village Cay Hotel & Marina;
    Village Cay Dockside
29 Maria's Hotel by the Sea
45 Sea View Hotel
46 Hotel Castle Maria
48 Fort Burt Hotel; Fort Burt
    Restaurant

PLACES TO EAT
1   C&F Bar & Restaurant
16 Fish Trap; Scoundrels
17 Captain's Table
18 Spaghetti Junction; Bat Cave
20 Ray's Deli
24 Mr Fritz's Oriental
    Restaurant
25 Midtown Restaurant
30 Roti Palace
33 Le Cabanon
34 Pusser's Roac Town Pub;
    Pusser's Company Store
35 Capriccio di Mare

TORTOLA

Furthermore, Main St, despite its name, has become a seldom-traveled byway. Most traffic follows Waterfront Dr around the harbor and skirts the old town.

The flatness of the terrain on which most of the town is situated, as well as the density of the buildings, make it difficult to get your bearings from geographic landmarks like the waterfront. Basically, if you can see the water, you are on the outskirts of town. Finding specific buildings is also a bit of a challenge because few places have precise street addresses. Both Tortolians and this guide describe locations as being on a certain street near some prominent landmark like the post office or traffic roundabout.

The traffic roundabout at the heart of town is the best landmark. It's the easiest place to see and hear (screeching brakes, revving engines). Most of Road Town's principal arteries lead to and from this heart. If you know the location of the roundabout and consult a map, you should be fine.

JR O'Neal Botanic Gardens
This garden (☎ 284-494-4997), on Botanic Rd at Main St, about two blocks north of the town's main roundabout, is a 4-acre refuge from Road Town's traffic, noise and heat. Benches are set amid indigenous and exotic tropical plants along with an orchid house, a lily pond, a small rain forest and a cactus grove. The herb garden is rife with traditional bush medicine plants. The garden is open from about 8 am to dusk daily. A $2 donation is requested.

HMS Prison
Located at the heart of Main St, these stark, white rubble walls date back to the 18th century and mark the oldest building in Road Town. The fortress is still a working jail, and you can hear muffled voices, singing and radio music from the cells as you walk by at night.

St George's Anglican Church
Just to the south of the prison, this neat Anglican chapel (☎ 284-494-3894) is another survivor of the 18th century but was rebuilt in the early 19th century following a hurricane. Inside is a copy of the 1834 Emancipation Proclamation that freed Britain's slaves in the West Indies.

Methodist Church
Flanking the north side of the prison, this working Methodist house of worship (☎ 284-495-9619) dates from 1924. It's a fine example of classic West Indian timber-framed construction.

VI Folk Museum
This small museum north of the post office on Main St is in a traditional West Indian house and contains pre-Columbian, plantation-period and marine artifacts as well as a gift shop. The museum claims to be free and open 8:30 am to 4:30 pm weekdays, but it was closed every time I stopped by. If you get inside, let us know what you've discovered.

Sir Olva George's Plaza
Once Road Town's primary street market, this shady square, stretching between the waterfront ferry terminal and the post office, is now a courtyard with ficus trees surrounded by the customs house and other government buildings. It's a good place to relax and watch the local citizens go about their business while you're waiting for a ferry.

Government House
Standing at the extreme south end of Main St like one of those imperial symbols you may have seen in Penang and Rangoon, this whitewashed manor is a classic example of British colonial architecture. It is the home of England's appointed governor and is not open to the public.

Queen Elizabeth Park
This small community park bordering the western side of the harbor south of Government House is a good place to cool off in the trade winds while eating takeout food from one of the local eateries like the Roti Palace (see Places to Eat).

Fort Burt

Only the foundations and the magazine remain of this small fort that once guarded the mouth of Road Harbour. It was constructed by the Dutch and later rebuilt by the English, who claimed the islands in 1672. The Fort Burt Hotel (see Places to Stay) and its restaurant now crown the site.

Activities

In the minds of **sailing** enthusiasts, the British Virgin Islands are the charterboat capital of the world, with about 15 bareboat charter companies offering hundreds of cruising sailboats for rent. In addition, dozens of crewed charter yachts sail the waters of the BVI. For a complete list of chartering options, see the chapter Yacht Charter Basics. The following are well-known daysail operators. Generally, rates start at about $50 per person for a half-day, $85 for a full day.

Dual Bliss (☎ 284-496-7149), at Village Cay Marina, offers daysails aboard its new catamaran, including hot lunches and drinks. *Patouche II* (☎ 248-494-6300), at the Pub in Road Town, is a 48-foot catamaran. Lunch and drinks are free to passengers on daysails. *Tamarin II* (☎ 284-495-9837), at Village Cay Marina, is a 55-foot fast cat. *White Squall II* (☎ 284-494-2564), at Village Cay Marina, takes you sailing on an 80-foot traditional schooner.

Powerboat Rentals (☎ 284-495-9993), at Village Cay Marina, rents 18- to 28-foot outboards with bimini tops and VHF radios. Rates start at about $120 a day. Sea kayaks rent for about $30 a day.

For **kayaking**, Last Stop Sports (☎ 284-494-1843), at the Moorings and Nanny Cay, offers great rates with kayaks starting at $18 a day.

With more than 20 premier **diving** sites, the BVI bring big business to dive operators, and several of them are based on Tortola. In general, expect to pay about $55 for a one-tank dive, $85 for two tanks. Underwater Safaris (☎ 284-494-3235), at the Moorings dock and at Cooper Island, is a PADI five-star facility.

Bicycling on Tortola can be particularly hair-raising along the heavily trafficked roads of the south shore, but the back roads along the north shore can be delightful as long as you enjoy hill climbs. Last Stop Sports (see above) is the best place to rent well-maintained trail bikes. Rates start at $20 a day.

The larger resorts like the Treasure Isle Hotel, Lambert Beach Resort, Long Bay Beach Resort, Nanny Cay Resort & Marina and the Prospect Beach Resort have **tennis** courts for their guests.

Places to Stay

One of Tortola's big attractions for independent travelers on moderate budgets is the number and variety of guesthouses and villa rental opportunities available across the island. Backpackers and resort seekers will not be disappointed either.

The *Wayside Inn* (☎ 284-494-3606), on Pickering Rd across from the Recreation Ground, is the island's most economical offering. This is a small, no-frills inn inside a building that has been hard used by hurricanes and guests. The rooms are sparsely furnished, and you will get only cold water from the taps and showers. Most rooms share baths. Rooms start at $30.

A&L Inn (☎ 284-494-6343), on Fleming St between Main St and the roundabout, has 14 modern rooms on the 2nd floor over the inn's small bar. Each modern, spacious room has air-con, TV and fridge. Rates run $75 to $90, and the location is within walking distance of the 'action' in Road Town.

The *Hotel Castle Maria* (☎ 284-494-2553), on the hillside of MacNamara Rd on the west end of town, can't be beat for value and cleanliness. This 30-room property has the look of an art deco mansion. All rooms have bath, air-con, TV, fridge, telephone and balcony. Some rooms have kitchenettes. The secluded pool, restaurant and bar are gay-friendly. A single room in season starts at about $80. You will pay about $150 for a quadruple with a harbor view in the winter.

The *Sea View Hotel* (☎ 284-494-2483), on Waterfront Dr and MacNamara Rd at the

TORTOLA

west end of town, is an excellent stop for the budget traveler. Ishma Christopher, a charming West Indian matriarch, will welcome you to this clean oasis featuring about 20 small rooms as well as efficiency apartments. All rooms have private bath, air-con and TV. Some rooms have a porch with a garden or sea view. There is a small pool, a deck, bar and breakfast service. You must sample or buy some of Ishma's homemade hot-pepper sauce, which she bottles in recycled rum containers. Rooms run about $70 to $170, but the rates come down if you book for more than a few days.

Maria's Hotel by the Sea (☎ 284-494-2595) is on the harbor (no beach) at Wickhams Cay 1. If you like watching the coming and going of charter yachts from a seaside pool and sundeck, this expansive three-story operation with 38 units may be for you. Rooms have 1st-class amenities, including air-con, balconies and kitchenettes. High-season rates run from about $105 to $250.

Village Cay Hotel & Marina (☎ 284-494-2771), on Wickhams Cay 1, has 21 rooms and adjacent condo facilities overlooking the yacht slips in Road Bay. The rooms have all the 1st-class amenities of a resort at a fraction of the price, and there is a large freshwater pool and deck on the premises. With rates running about $125 to $190, this small hotel is a popular place for yacht charterers to 'chill' before or after going to sea.

The *Fort Burt Hotel (☎ 284-494-2587)* rises on the ruins of a 300-year-old fort guarding a steep hillside above Waterfront Dr. Pusser's, the restaurant and clothing company, gave this old place a face-lift in 2000 (including data ports), and it's now a 1st-class business hotel. The 12 rooms have all the amenities; most have sea views and some even have private pools. There is a gourmet restaurant on site (see Places to Eat). Rates run about $125 to $370.

The Moorings–Mariner Inn (☎ 284-494-2332), at Wickhams Cay 2, stands adjacent to the docks supporting the Moorings' mammoth fleet of charter sailboats. Most guests here are folks leaving on or returning from yacht charters. The 40 rooms in this two-story building have balconies, air-con

and all the 1st-class amenities. A swimming pool is on the property. Rates run $175 and up in high season.

Treasure Isle Hotel (☎ 284-494-2501, 800-437-7880) is just across Waterfront Dr from the Moorings. A popular stop for yacht charterers, this place is a hillside oasis of shade trees and flowers laid out around a sundeck and pool. Each of the 40 rooms has a harbor view, air-con, bath and fridge. Rates for a double during the winter run $185 and up.

The British Virgin Islands Tourist Board (☎ 294-494-3134, 800-835-8530) puts out an excellent illustrated booklet called *Intimate Inns, Hotels & Villas* with descriptions of more than 40 **rental properties** in the BVI. The greatest concentration of rentals on Tortola is at Long Bay on the northwest end of the island. A&J Rental Apartments (☎ 284-494-1422) offers apartments overlooking Road Town for $600 a week in the winter.

Places to Eat

Tortolians like to eat out, and the island has plenty of restaurants to meet the needs of every wallet. The variety of island cuisine is another matter. Two-thirds of the restaurants on the island subscribe to a similar menu and offer grilled chicken, conch, fish and lobster. Recently, a fresh crop of restaurants and internationally schooled chefs have begun to bring more imagination and sophistication to island menus.

Capriccio di Mare (☎ 284-494-5369), a cafe set on the porch of a classic West Indian house across from the ferry dock, is a magnet for both locals and travelers. Breakfast includes fresh pastries and cappuccino for under $3. For lunch, you can order pasta ($6) or pizza (about $9 a pie).

The *Midtown Restaurant (☎ 284-494-2764),* on Main St, attracts a local following for breakfast, lunch and dinner. This place is a storefront operation right out of the 1950s, with a dining counter and menu board hung over the grill. Johnnycakes cost about $3. Eggs, bacon, toast and coffee runs less than $4. Lunch and dinner feature curried conch and beef, baked chicken, whelk and salt fish (all about $7).

Ray's Deli (☎ *284-494-6165*), on Wickhams Cay 1 across from Spaghetti Junction, is a clean, air-conditioned shop. The prices are terrific, and there are a couple of tables in the shade outside. Cold drinks run under $2, and you can get a mini veggie pizza for $3.

Roti Palace (☎ *284-494-4196*), on Abbott Hill Rd, has some of the best roti on the island. Its on a side street that leads up the hill off Main St near the Sunny Caribbee Spice Company. The establishment is a bit cramped and smells like Bombay's restaurant district. A mammoth chicken roti runs $7, conch $12, lobster $18. Try the veggie roti for about $8.

Mr Fritz's Oriental Restaurant (☎ *284-494-5592*), in the Denmark Building on Waterfront Dr, is just about your only stop in the BVI for Asian food…but you won't see an Asian face anywhere near the kitchen. The cuisine at this patio restaurant is classic Cantonese fare with a West Indian spin. The prices are not cheap, with fried rice running $9 to $12. Friday afternoon happy hour features platters of jerked pork ribs (Jamaican not Chinese) for $4, $6 and $12.

Lady Sarah's Tea Parlour (☎ *284-494-4244*), a quiet tearoom in the Harbour House on Waterfront Dr at the west end of town, offers a touch of refined elegance at reasonable prices. This place is in a neat, air-conditioned building surrounded by a collection of boutiques. Portia Harrigan's cuisine is basically light fare such as salads, wraps and sandwiches (under $8) as well as teas and desserts.

Pusser's Road Town Pub (☎ *284-494-3897*), a landmark on Waterfront Dr, is an English-style pub popular with travelers and locals. Pizza, burgers and salads are the big things here, in an air-conditioned, lively atmosphere. Small pizzas start at about $7. I recommend the smoked turkey and Gouda sandwich ($8).

The Pub (☎ *284-494-2608*), on the waterfront near Fort Burt, has been a Road Town institution for years. You can dine on the deck at the harbor's edge on steaks, ribs, lobster and fresh fish. Lots of folks show up on Tuesday for all-you-can-eat pasta (about $10).

Spaghetti Junction (☎ *284-494-4880*) has moved from its former location on Waterfront Dr to an attractive frame building hovering at water's edge on the north side of Wickhams Cay 1. John Schultheiss and April Ridi have breathed new life into this old standby. The cuisine is a mix of Italian and Caribbean. People love the mahimahi fish sticks (under $7) and the fettuccine Alfredo ($14). The Bat Cave bar (see Entertainment) has a lively scene.

Village Cay Dockside (☎ *284-494-2771*), a harborside terrace restaurant at Village Cay Marina, serves steaks, ribs, lobster and local fish to the tourist trade. Most entrees run $18 and up. The lunch menu features burgers and salads for around $8.

The **Fish Trap** (☎ *284-494-3626*) is an open-air seafood restaurant at the Columbus Centre on Wickhams Cay 1. This is not only a popular lunch and dinner spot, it is also a late-night party venue, abutting Scoundrels nightclub (see Entertainment). Todd Hill runs this eatery, which is popular with travelers and local expats. The changing menu includes lobster, burritos and Teriyaki chicken. Consider the sweet potato chowder ($6) and grilled tuna with mango chutney ($20).

Le Cabanon (☎ *284-494-8660*), on Waterfront Dr next to Pusser's, is a tropical French bistro created by a young Parisian, Christophe Boisgirard. The scene is very chic, with an open-air terrace carved from a classic West Indian house. The cuisine is imaginative, with French West Indies offerings, including sea scorpion in Creole sauce ($19). The chef, Sabastian, flies in all of his provisions from the French Island of St Martin.

The **Captain's Table** (☎ *284-494-3885*), dockside at Inner Harbour Marina, offers continental cuisine such as escargot, fresh fish and live lobster. This restaurant definitely aims for the tourist trade and has prices to match. Most entrees cost more than $20.

Fort Burt Restaurant (☎ *284-494-2587*), at the Fort Burt Hotel (see Places to Stay), is a gem. Since Pusser's took over, the hillside terrace restaurant has garnered the reputation as the most romantic dining experience on Tortola. Dinners include seafood in puff pastry, filet Admiral Nelson and fresh lobster. Most entrees here are priced under $25.

C&F Bar & Restaurant (☎ *284-494-4941*), in Purcell Estate just east of Road Town, is worth the trouble it takes to find it (a cab is your best bet the first trip). Tortolians claim this is West Indian cuisine at its best, and they show up in droves to consume BBQ and curry dishes from chef Clarence Emmanuel. Grilled dolphin with peas and rice runs about $18, but the seafood platter with conch, scallops and shrimp in lime butter or curried butter costs $12.

Entertainment

Tortola has a lively nightlife, especially if you like drinking and dancing. Check out the free weekly tabloid *Limin' Times* to find out the local scoop when you're on Tortola.

Bars & Clubs For years, ***The Pub*** (see Places to Eat) was the most happening gin mill in Road Town, but times have changed, and the younger crowd has headed elsewhere. Nevertheless, this is still a good place to meet charterboat crews and network with the regulars, who are mostly middle-age expats. On Friday night, Ruben Chinnery performs his steel pan calypso music from 6 to 9 pm.

Pusser's Road Town Pub (see Places to Eat) attracts an early-evening crowd of sailors and expats. Drink specials are a big draw, for example, 5¢ glasses of John Courage Ale on Thursday nights.

Le Cabanon (see Places to Eat) is possibly the hippest place on the island to drink and cruise. It's a place to sip wine or martinis, not slug down beer in your shorts and T-shirt. The scene is very chic with low lights, the scent of French cooking and Brazilian or French jazz filtering through the open-air terrace. The music gets friskier as the night unfolds. The crowd is mostly under-25 expats, including many Europeans. Folks dress in funky tight cocktail dresses and loose continental clothing.

The ***Bat Cave*** at Spaghetti Junction (see Places to Eat) is a backroom bar off the restaurant. There is a pool table here and a small deck at harborside to catch the trade winds. You'll find lively conversation and a pulsing sound system that pumps out classic rock. The crowd is a mix of travelers and expats between 25 and 40.

Scoundrels, next to the Fish Trap (see Places to Eat), is a smoky dance cave and currently the favored cruising and dance scene for expats and travelers. On weekdays, $2 beers between 10 and 11 pm draw the crowd. On Friday night, the DJ plays a mix of '80s and '90s dance music, and the crowd ranges from 16 to 50 years old. The pool table appeals to the youth, while more mature folk hang around the open-air bar and tables at the Fish Trap. This is a good place to network for jobs or look for apartments if you've just hit town. It's also quite a pickup scene.

Stone's Nest (☎ *284-494-5182*), across from the power plant on Long Bush Rd, is the most popular West Indian club on the island. This places draws live acts every weekend from St Thomas and 'down island.' Some nights you get wild reggae; other nights it's disco. There is always a crowd, but surprisingly the dress for this venue is casual (shirts and slacks). You will see some heavy drinkers here, and things can get pretty rowdy after midnight. It helps to bring West Indian friends along. Don't walk the streets in this neighborhood alone after dark.

Gay & Lesbian Venues While a fair number of islanders and travelers on Tortola are gay, West Indian taboos on the lifestyle are crumbling slowly. You are not likely to meet many 'out' gays or lesbians on the island, nor are you likely to see public displays of affection among gay couples. Some upscale gay travelers head for the sanctuary of the Cooper Island Beach Club (see the Out Islands chapter). Gay men, many of whom

Old Customs House (c 1750) in Christiansted, St Croix

St Croix houses

Divi Carina Bay Beach Resort, St Croix

Cormorant Beach, St Croix

Reggae, calypso, Quelbe and fungi bands perform throughout the islands.

Vibrant colors of West End, Tortola

Bayside dining at West End, Tortola

Snack shack, Tortola

are resort workers, find kindred spirits in the low-key ambience of the Hotel Castle Maria bar (see Places to Stay).

Cinema On Pickering Rd across from the Recreation Ground, ***Bobby's Cinemax*** *(☎ 284-494-2098)* is the only theater on the island, featuring an almost endless list of action films.

Shopping
If you love the antique alleys full of pretty things in Charlotte Amalie or the hip boutiques of Christiansted, you may be disappointed by the variety of shops and the ambience of many of the shopping districts on Tortola. However, Tortola is capable of providing you with a shopping fix. Storekeepers stay open 9 am to 5 pm weekdays and 9 am to 1 pm Saturday. BVI shops are not duty-free.

Main St and the Wickhams Cay 1 area have the most shops of interest to travelers. As you walk north on Main St from the post office and Sir Olva George's Plaza, have a peek in Buccaneer's Bounty (☎ 284-494-7510), a gift shop dedicated to pirate memorabilia. Caribbean Handprints (☎ 284-494-3717) is across the street, specializing in locally designed silk-screened fabric by the yard. A bit farther north, where Main St makes a sharp left turn, Latitude 18 (☎ 284-494-7807) sells upscale resort wear, watches and sunglasses.

Slide across the street to one of Tortola's most famous shops: Sunny Caribbee Spice Company & Art Gallery (☎ 284-494-2178) has a complete array of island-made spices like 'mango fire.' They also sell West Indian art and body-care products like coconut shampoo. The building, a born-again West Indian cottage, is a visual delight.

A footpath runs south from Main St near Sunny Caribbee to Tortola's other famous shopping venue. Pusser's Company Store (☎ 284-494-2467) faces the harbor on Waterfront Dr and sells a complete line of tropical/nautical clothing and accessories. You can buy the company's Pusser's Rum (the blend served on Her Majesty's Royal Navy

ships for 300 years), a rigging knife, a tote bag or an antique doll.

A few steps to the east lies Colombian Emeralds (☎ 284-494-7477), at Romasco Place on Wickhams Cay 1. There is a reason this operation has stores throughout the Caribbean: good gems at excellent prices.

CANE GARDEN BAY AREA
On the north shore, just a 15-minute drive over the mountains from Road Town, Cane Garden Bay is a turquoise cove ringed by a semicircle of steep hills. A West Indian settlement is here, complete with church, laundry and police station. The settlement is the oldest and most-developed holiday destination on the island. Many of the island's most popular guesthouses are here, along with legendary restaurants and bars.

Sage Mountain National Park
At 1780 feet, Sage Mountain is the Virgin Islands' highest peak. This 92-acre park is laid out with gravel paths and has the attractive Mountain View restaurant at the trailhead.

The park is not a rain forest in the true sense because it receives less than 100 inches of rain a year. However, the lush area possesses many of the characteristics of one and offers cooling breezes and spectacular vistas of both the US and British Virgin Islands. Travelers should keep an eye open for the 20-foot-tall fern trees that have not changed since the days of dinosaurs. Hummingbirds, kestrels and martins are a few of the birds you may see. The park is open from dawn to dusk, and admission is free.

North Shore Shell Museum
You can't miss this funky restaurant and museum (☎ 284-495-4714) at Carrot Bay. The place has so many shells it looks like it was built from a mound of beached conch (also see Places to Eat). Admission is free.

Callwood Rum Distillery
Just off the North Coast Rd at the west end of Cane Garden Bay stands a stone plantation building dating back more than 300 years. The distillery still produces rum under

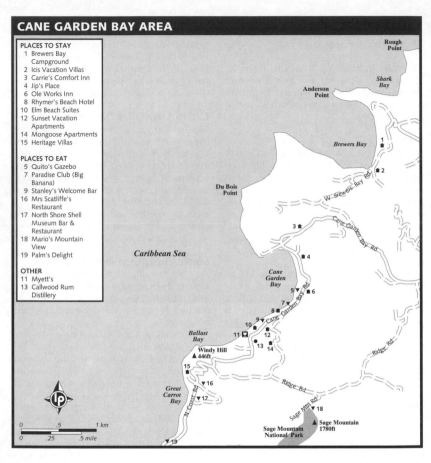

CANE GARDEN BAY AREA

PLACES TO STAY
1 Brewers Bay
   Campground
2 Icis Vacation Villas
3 Carrie's Comfort Inn
4 Jip's Place
6 Ole Works Inn
8 Rhymer's Beach Hotel
10 Elm Beach Suites
12 Sunset Vacation
   Apartments
14 Mongoose Apartments
15 Heritage Villas

PLACES TO EAT
5 Quito's Gazebo
7 Paradise Club (Big
   Banana)
9 Stanley's Welcome Bar
16 Mrs Scatliffe's
   Restaurant
17 North Shore Shell
   Museum Bar &
   Restaurant
18 Mario's Mountain
   View
19 Palm's Delight

OTHER
11 Myett's
13 Callwood Rum
   Distillery

the label Arundel, in much the same fashion it did centuries ago, using copper vats and wooden aging casks. There is a small store where you can buy rum or join a tour ($1). The distillery is open to visitors 8:30 am to 6 pm Monday to Saturday.

Beaches

Tortola's most famous and popular beach is **Cane Garden Bay**. The gently sloping crescent of sand stretches for almost a mile with a backdrop of steep green hills. The waters inside the barrier reef make for a popular yacht anchorage. There are water-sports

vendors and a host of beachfront restaurants, bars and guesthouses. On most nights and weekends, Cane Garden Bay is a party scene with a congenial mix of West Indians, sailors and travelers grooving to all manner of live music. Recently, cruise ships arriving in Road Town in the middle of the week have begun bussing their passengers over to Cane Garden for the day. Even the local restaurant and bar owners are not thrilled by the crowds.

Travelers like **Brewers Bay**, a palm-fringed bay on the north shore east of Cane Garden Bay. There are two beach bars, a campground, guesthouse and good snorkeling on the coral heads that pepper the bay. The beach is always tranquil because getting here involves an expensive cab ride as well as a brake-smoking ride down steep switchbacks.

Activities

Brewers Bay has excellent snorkeling. Cane Garden Bay Pleasure Boats (☎ 284-495-9660) rents 18- to 28-foot outboards with bimini tops and VHF radios. Rates start at about $120 a day. Sea kayaks rent for about $30 a day.

Places to Stay

Tortola's only commercial camping area is **Brewers Bay Campground** (☎ 284-494-3463), on the north shore, barely 2 miles from Road Town. Nevertheless, campers' biggest complaint about Brewers Bay is it's difficult to reach. Those 2 miles on the map turn into about 7 miles when you scale and descend a mountain. Public transportation to the bay is virtually nonexistent, and a taxi here will cost you more than $10 from almost any place on the island except neighboring Cane Garden Bay ($5).

Owner Noel Callwood has about 20 prepared sites under the sea grape trees and tall palms right on the beach. Each site comes with a wall tent mounted on a wooden platform, two cots, a gas stove, ice chest, lantern, linens, cooking utensils, drinking water and sun/rain fly over the tent. The showers, toilets and washing facilities are in one central building. Sites generally rent for $35 but cost less for long-term stays between April 1 and December 20. A few bare sites rent for $15 a night.

The Bamboo Bar is the camp's beachside watering hole, where campers come together over cold water, soda and beer. Campers are a mix of youthful backpackers, 'crunchy' couples and a few families. The extensive reef system offshore in the bay makes for excellent snorkeling, and exploring the reef is the major daily activity for campers.

Next to the settlement church, **Jip's Place** (☎ 284-495-4543) has a single one-bedroom apartment with living area, kitchenette, bath, fan and patio with sea view. This place is simple and clean, offering you the lowest price in Cane Garden Bay at about $65 for two.

Sunset Vacation Apartments (☎ 284-495-4751), near the Callwood Rum Distillery at the west end of Cane Garden Bay, has 10 spacious one and two-bedroom apartments in a two-story ranch-style building. There is no sea view here, as the road is set back 100 yards from the beach, but each apartment has a private balcony to catch the breeze. All apartments include maid service, private bath and fans. The convenience store/small bar on the property has the cheapest beer ($2.50) in Cane Garden Bay. The one-bedroom units for two people run about $90 per night, $600 per week.

Rhymer's Beach Hotel (☎ 284-495-4820), on the beach in the center of the settlement at Cane Garden Bay, is probably the oldest of the area's inns. The big pink concrete building with its restaurant, bar, beauty salon and laundry show signs of hard use over a lot of seasons. Rooms are mostly studios with kitchenettes, bath, air-con and private patio with sea view. Expect to pay about $90 for two people.

The **Elm Beach Suites** (☎ 284-494-2888), just a few yards west along the beach from Rhymers, offers one of the warmest welcomes on the island. Elvet Meyers and Lianna Jarecki have five one-bedroom suites in this two-story, beige-and-violet guesthouse. You get bright fabrics, nice wicker furniture and cable TV in the suites and air-con in the bedrooms. The patios have expansive sea views. The associated beach bar (see Entertainment) should not be missed. Winter rates start at about $100.

Carrie's Comfort Inn (☎ 284-495-9220), perched on the hill above the east end of the bay, is another good value. There are 16 one-bedroom apartments in this two-story motel-style building. The units are spacious and airy, freshly decorated with colorful fabrics and spotlessly maintained. Individual balconies give you a bird's-eye view on the bay and beach that lie one-eighth of a mile down the steep hill. In season, you will pay $100 to $150.

Ole Works Inn (☎ 284-495-4838), across the street from Quito's Gazebo bar/restaurant, cannot be beat for ambience. Reggae master Quito Rymer has created this inn of 18 small rooms within the walls of a 320-year-old rum factory. All rooms have air-con, fridge and private bath; most have private balconies. Rooms that look to the hillside or coconut grove start at about $110 for a double. A sea view will cost you $150 and up during the winter. Noise from Quito's bar across the street can be a problem if you are a light sleeper.

Elroy and Sandra Henley designed and built the three-story *Mongoose Apartments (☎ 284-495-4421)* on the hillside farm that Elroy's mother once worked. Each of the six units has a living room, full kitchen, bath and bedroom as well as a private balcony. Large ceiling fans cool the rooms, and the beach is just a two-minute walk through a coconut palm grove. Winter rates are about $125.

Heritage Villas (☎ 284-494-5824), high on Windy Hill between Cane Garden Bay and Great Carrot Bay, has a pool, sundeck and nine apartments that seem to hang out in thin air from the surrounding hill. If you like the feel of a self-contained (but shared) oasis with a restaurant and bar, here's an intriguing possibility. The villas are spacious with all the amenities and great views of the sunset over Jost Van Dyke and St Thomas. You will need a car to get around from here. Rates run about $145 to $200.

Icis Vacation Villas (☎ 284-494-6979), at Brewers Bay, are some of Tortola's newest accommodations, but the grounds surrounding the villas give you the feel of being on an old plantation. The one- and three-bedroom villas and studios lie inland about a one-minute walk from the beach. All units have a private patio, air-con, full kitchenette and cable TV. There is an open-air restaurant and bar on the property. Rates run $130 to $275.

For *rental accommodations*, Ronneville Cottages (☎ 284-494-3337) at Brewers Bay has units starting at less than $700 a week. Stanley's Welcome Villas (☎ 284-495-2990) offers mountainside villas east of Cane Garden Bay for about $900 a week.

Places to Eat

Rhymer's (see Places to Stay) is a hotel beach bar that caters to the crews off yachts who are sick of cooking aboard. The dinner menu includes fish, ribs and conch (around $16), but the big attraction these days is breakfast. You can get a scrambled egg croissant for $3.50, French toast for $4.50. A side order of eggs or bacon costs less than $2.

The *Elm Beach Bar*, at the Elm Beach Suites (see Places to Stay), is the smallest and perhaps the most welcoming of all the beachfront eateries on Cane Garden Bay. Try the fruit platters (under $9) or get the BBQ ribs with Jamaican festival sauce and coconut curried rice (about $10).

Stanley's Welcome Bar (☎ 284-495-9424), on the beach, has been popular with yacht crews and surfers for years. This is a cheeseburger-in-paradise ($7) kind of place that also serves pasta, salads, fresh fish, steak and lobster. Grilled king fish runs $15.

Mario's Mountain View (☎ 284-495-9536), high on the mountain at the entrance to the trails at Sage Mountain National Park, serves entrees like chicken roti ($9) and curried conch ($12). The view here of Tortola and the surrounding islands is memorable. So is the wit and welcome of chef Audrey Frank.

Mrs Scatliffe's Restaurant (☎ 284-495-4556), in a two-story house about a hundred yards up a bushy street off the North Coast Rd, is a Carrot Bay institution. Mrs S cooks up West Indian favorites like chicken in coconut (about $16) and stages lively fungi band performances on many evenings.

Paradise Club (☎ 284-495-4606), also known as the Big Banana, is one of the larger, busier and louder restaurant/bars at Cane Garden Bay. You can get dishes like coconut shrimp, BBQ chicken and ribs for under $17. A lot of folks show up for happy hour on Friday, when fried chicken wings are 25¢ each.

Quito's Gazebo (☎ 284-495-4837), on the beach, is a legendary pub (see Entertainment). The owner sings calypso and reggae ballads almost every night. Rotis (under $6) make for popular light luncheons. Conch, grilled snapper and steak run about $20.

The *North Shore Shell Museum Bar & Restaurant* (☎ 284-495-4714), at Carrot Bay, is a zany mix of fascinating (but tiny) museum and eatery. The chef specializes in cracked conch and grilled lobster. Most dishes (except lobster) run about $16. The waitstaff often lead the patrons in making fungi music by blowing and banging on conch shells. Dinner reservations are a good idea.

The *Palm's Delight* (☎ 284-495-4863), on the water's edge at Carrot Bay, has great cheap eats and local ambience. This is a family-style West Indian restaurant. The menu includes pates, rotis, fish Creole and 'honey stung' chicken, all for under $10. Friday night is a lively scene, with families eating on the patio and a bar crowd watching cricket or baseball on the TV.

Entertainment

The *Elm Beach Bar* (see Places to Eat) is worth checking out if you are looking for an intimate and welcoming beachside bar to kick back with a few friends and friendly Tortolians. The hosts blend their own spiced rum called Seven Dwarfs. One of the BVI's most beloved calypsonians, Reggie George, plays his steel drums and sings on Friday and Saturday evenings. On Memorial Day, the bar rocks when it becomes the official Tortola headquarters for crews racing in Foxy's Woodenboat Regatta.

Quito's Gazebo (see Places to Eat) takes its name from its preeminent act, Quito Rymer & the Edge. These guys have been on tour with the likes of Ziggy Marley. You can dance up a storm to Quito's reggae rhythms, and hundreds pack the restaurant on weekends to do just that. The crowd ranges from 16 to 60 and is a rich blend of travelers, expats, yacht crews and West Indians.

Myett's is the competition down the beach. It draws a lot of people off the charterboats and features local bands Friday through Monday nights. Very different kinds of bands play here: You get reggae bands covering a lot of UB40 songs like 'Red, Red Wine,' blues and even country &. western. I once heard a weird steel pan

version of 'No Woman No Cry' here. (You can skip their food.)

You can get more sophisticated reggae at the *Paradise Club* (the Big Banana; see Places to Eat). Popular Tortolian bands like O-2 and X-Treme crank out contemporary reggae and funk to a mix of tourists and West Indians.

The North Shore Shell Museum at Carrot Bay and Mrs Scatliffe's nearby are the places to go for *fungi music.* The proprietors put on a show for the dinner guests.

WEST ISLAND

The western end of Tortola draws a large number of travelers, as it is the site of many resort hotels and villa rentals, a couple of spectacular beaches, vistas of the offshore islands, distinctive restaurants and legendary bars.

Fort Recovery

This fortification near the West End is the BVI's oldest intact structure. It has a turreted gun emplacement with 3-foot-thick walls that date from Dutch construction in 1660. The Villas of Fort Recovery Estate (see Places to Stay) now surround the fort.

William Thornton Estate

The ruined walls and foundations of this plantation great house lie unpreserved and unguarded in Pleasant Valley. The estate was once home to the designer of the US Capitol Building in Washington, DC. (See the boxed text.)

Mount Healthy National Park

This small preserve of less than an acre stands above Brewers Bay and features Tortola's only intact remains of a stone windmill, once part of an 18th-century sugar plantation. Admission is free.

The Dungeon

Built in 1794 by the Royal Engineers, this is a ruined fort located halfway between Road Town and West End. It was dubbed the Dungeon because its underground cell holds remnants of what might be prisoners' graffiti.

William Thornton

When British Prime Minister Winston Churchill was asked where the British Virgin Islands were, he reportedly replied that he had no idea, but he should think they were as far from the Isle of Man as possible. But those like Churchill who imagined the British Virgin Islands as the ultimate backwater from which nothing of consequence would proceed, might consider this: One of the BVI's prominent Quakers during the 18th century was Dr William Thornton. His professional career bloomed as a Philadelphia doctor. Later, he moved on to design the US Capitol building and become the first US Secretary of Patents.

Sopers Hole

A major anchorage on the West End, this is the site of a 16th-century pirate's den. The main ferry terminal for vessels going to and from the USVI is here. Recent years have brought the development of the Caribbean-style Sopers Hole Marina and shopping wharf, which includes a restaurant and a bank.

Beaches

Lying to the west of Little Carrot Bay, the beach at **Apple Bay** has long been 'the surfing beach.' On many maps, Apple Bay includes Cappoons Bay, home of the infamous surfer bar, Bomba's Surfside Shack (see Entertainment, later).

Long Bay is an attractive mile-long stretch of white-sand beach that spreads west of Apple Bay. A top-end resort and clutch of rental villas line its eastern portion. The western end offers slightly less development and good swimming. Beach joggers come here for workouts during the early morning and evening.

An undeveloped beach at the northwestern tip of Tortola, **Smuggler's Cove** used to be a secluded patch of island where you could risk topless or nude sunbathing without prying eyes or offending the modesty of islanders. Now the dirt track to the beach gets clotted with rental Jeeps and folks trying to escape the predictable scenes at their beach resorts.

During the late 1990s, Hollywood staged a remake of *The Old Man and the Sea* here. An old Cadillac that was a film prop is still on the beach. You'll find good snorkeling here. Take care of your valuables, as the vegetation hides parked cars and thieves from the view of folks on the beach.

Activities

This side of the island is popular for **sailing**. King Charters (☎ 284-494-5820), at Nanny Cay, offers daysails on its 46-foot motor yacht. *Karula* (☎ 284-495-4381), at West End, offers daysails on a 50-foot catamaran.

For **diving**, Blue Water Divers (☎ 284-494-2847), at Nanny Cay, has a 47-foot catamaran and a 42-foot striker to get you there. Baskin in the Sun (☎ 284-494-2858), at the Prospect Reef Resort and on Peter Island, will take you out aboard 30-, 42- and 55-foot boats.

Pelican Charters (☎ 284-496-7386), at the Prospect Reef Resort, takes you out **fishing** for blue and white marlin on a 46-foot Chris Craft. Rates are $600 for a half-day, $950 for the day. Persistence Charters (☎ 284-495-4122), at West End, fishes from a 31-foot tiara. Charters cost $400 for a half-day, $700 for a full day.

Boardsailing BVI (☎ 284-494-0422), at Nanny Cay and Trellis Bay, is the biggest **windsurfing** operator on the islands, with loads of gear for beginners to advanced sailors. Last Stop Sports (☎ 284-494-1843), at Nanny Cay, has boards for $18 a day. Hi Ho (☎ 284-494-0337), at the Prospect Reef Resort, has similar rates and offers board sales and instruction. It also sponsors a large competition in June.

The Prospect Reef Resort (☎ 284-494-3311) lets nonguests play on their two **tennis** courts for $10 per hour.

Shadow, a friendly West Indian man you might well meet at the Elm Beach Bar at

Cane Garden Bay, offers **horseback riding** through Sage Mountain National Park or down to the beach from Shadow's Ranch (☎ 284-494-2262) in Todman's Estate. Rates run $25 an hour.

Places to Stay

The ***Jolly Roger Inn*** *(☎ 294-495-4995)*, on the north side of Sopers Hole next to the ferry dock, is the place to drop your bags if you arrived via the ferry. This popular restaurant and bar has five clean rooms that were redecorated in 2000. Most rooms share baths. There is no beach or pool, but the place has a great waterfront location and it is an easy walk to the beach. Rates start at about $60 for a single room with shared bath.

Sebastian's on the Beach Hotel *(☎ 284-495-4212)*, at Little Apple Bay, is well known for its friendly staff and reasonable prices. All 26 rooms have a sea view, balcony, private bath, fridge and fan. There's a restaurant here as well (see Places to Eat). Winter rates run $130 and up.

Nanny Cay Resort & Marina *(☎ 284-494-2521, 800-742-4276)*, on Nanny Cay, 2 miles west of Road Town, describes itself as 'an island unto itself,' and the description fits. This 42 room resort has two pools, two restaurants, a tennis court, marina, windsurfing school, dive shop, mountain bike center, boutiques and a mini market – a self-contained pleasure dome on a 25 acre islet. Rooms have kitchenettes, private balconies and wooden cathedral ceilings. Winter rates start at $170 for a standard studio.

Prospect Reef Resort *(☎ 284-494-3311, 800-356-8937)*, just beyond Fort Burt on the western border of Road Town, is Tortola's largest resort. There are 137 rooms, studios and villas here with all the amenities you expect from a large (44 acres), self-contained seaside resort…except a beach and universal air-conditioning. The resort compensates for its lack of beach by running a regularly scheduled glass-bottom ferry to Peter Island 3 miles across Sir Francis Drake Channel, but you have some great swimming options closer to home in the Olympic lap pool and the specially constructed tide

pools. Tennis, diving instruction, fishing and yacht charters are at your doorstep here. Rates for doubles run from about $160 to $450 during the winter season.

The ***Sugar Mill Hotel*** *(☎ 284-495-4355)*, on Apple Bay, is in a league of its own for ambience, intimacy and customer service. This boutique resort rises from the ruins of the Applby Plantation that gave Apple Bay its name. The centerpiece of the property is the gourmet restaurant (see Places to Eat). Twenty-one 1st-class studios and suites hide on the steep hillside among mahogany trees, bougainvillea and palms. There is a pool up on the hill and a small beach. Winter rates start at about $190 and go to $650.

The ***Villas of Fort Recovery Estate*** *(☎ 284-495-4354, 800-367-8475)*, on the southwest coast, have the privacy and isolation that some travelers crave. Here, one- and four-bedroom villas spread out on a private beach in the shadow of the old fort's martello tower. There is also a pool in a garden setting of hibiscus, oleander and palms. Everything is top drawer, and the views of St John and Norman Island to the south and west are expansive. High-season rates run about $275 and up.

Long Bay Beach Resort & Villas *(☎ 284-495-4252, 800-729-9599)* spreads out along the bay of the same name at the northwest end of the island. This is a large resort with more than 70 rooms plus additional private homes and rental villas secreted among the vegetation of a north-facing hill. With several pools, tennis courts, jogging trails, restaurants and bars, this place can keep you entertained for a week. Expect to pay about $280 to $400 for a double in high season, depending on location, style and amenities.

As for ***rental accommodations,*** Bananas on the Beach (☎ 284-495-4318), at Little Apple Bay, has vacation apartments for about $850 per week during the winter but $500 during the summer and fall. Casa Caribe (☎ 284-495-4318), on Little Apple Bay, has four deluxe waterfront villas with full kitchens and telephones. Rates run $1175 a week and up. At Long Bay, Purple Pineapple Rental Management (☎ 284-495-4848) has one- and five-bedroom villas and condos available from $700 to $5000 a week. Grape Tree Vacation Rentals (☎ 284-495-4229), at Long Bay, has villas for $850 to $2000.

Places to Eat

Jolly Roger (see Places to Stay), near the West End ferry landing, has a hearty pub scene in the evening and serves food long after most of the competition's kitchens have closed. Pizza is the popular beer chaser here. A 12-inch pie runs $12. A veggie roti and salad costs under $9. Lots of folks staying in the surrounding villas order takeout.

Struggling Man's Place (☎ 284-494-4163), about 1½ miles west of Road Town on Sea Cow Bay, has West Indian cooking and a sea view. Not much more than a converted fisherman's shack, this small restaurant has a funky ambience, with friendly service and a nice mix of West Indians and travelers. Try the pumpkin soup ($4) or curried mutton (about $12). Don't miss the free guavaberry brandy at the bar.

Sky World (☎ 284-494-3567), perched on a mountaintop about a mile north of Road Town (via Joes Hill Rd), has a 360-degree view of the BVI. *Gourmet* magazine once featured the island dishes of this restaurant. Consider the pureed mango soup ($8) and the prawns in garlic/ginger ($10). Entrees like ribeye steak run about $20. The view of almost the entire BVI is worth the trip.

Callaloo (☎ 284-494-3311), overlooking the lagoon at Prospect Reef Resort, specializes in Caribbean gourmet cuisine. Dinner entrees include local shark and grilled lamb chops. Most meals run $20 and up.

The *Friday Fish Fry*, in the clearing opposite the Apple Bay Restaurant on Zion Hill Rd, is a great community gathering that draws a lot of folks from the surrounding West Indian settlement, expats and travelers staying on the north shore. For $8, you'll get grilled snapper or flying fish with sweet potato, peas and rice. Bring your own beverage.

Pusser's Landing (☎ 284-495-4554), on the waterfront at Frenchman's Cay, offers outdoor harborside seating and Margaritaville ambience. There are nightly all-you-can-eat specials: Tuesday is shrimp ($19), Friday is roast pig ($16), Saturday is BBQ ($16). The best deal is the daily happy hour from 5 to 7 pm, when chicken wings go for 25¢ each.

Sebastian's on the Beach (see Places to Stay) has been a favorite of travelers for years and offers beachfront dining for all three meals. The prices are moderate: You can get chicken wings for $5, a veggie casserole for $15 and ginger chicken for $16.

Sugar Mill Hotel (see Places to Stay) is a diner's delight. Owners Jeff and Jinx Morgan, contributing writers for *Bon Appetite* magazine, oversee the menu, cooking and presentation of meals in the restored boiling house of the plantation's rum distillery. Here you dine by candlelight on haute cuisine like wild mushrooms in puffed pastry or leg of lamb with roasted peppers, spinach and feta filling. Entrees start at $21. Reservations are a must.

Entertainment

The most famous bar on Tortola would have to be *Bomba's Surfside Shack* – see the boxed text.

Pusser's Landing (see Places to Eat) offers live entertainment almost every night of the week. There is usually a lively after-work crowd here most days for the happy hour specials like cheap chicken wings and $1 discounts on all drinks. On Saturday night, all Caribbean beers cost $2. Depending on the night, you get live steel pan, calypso, reggae or fungi music. The crowd is a mix of local expats, travelers and sailors off charterboats.

The *Jolly Roger* (see Places to Eat) has bands Friday and Saturday nights. The music is either West Indian or country & western and draws 30-somethings from the surrounding West End villas. There is still much talk on the island about an event that occurred here in 1999: Lois McMillen, a frequent island visitor to her parents' villa, came to dance one night and was found dead on a beach the next day. Four visiting American men were arrested for the crime and were still in prison awaiting their trial at press time.

Booze, Bras & the Bomba Shack

The best-known pub on Tortola is Bomba's Surfside Shack (☎ 284-495-4148) at Cappoons Bay – a rival of Foxy's on Jost Van Dyke and Duffy's Love Shack in Red Hook for the distinction of being the most-fabled watering hole in the islands. But this place is a different beast.

Visually, the Bomba Shack looks a lot like a pig pen. It started as a surfer's bar in the 1970s and is nothing more than a nailed-together collection of beach flotsam and jetsam covered with graffiti scrawled by decades of party animals or painted by the West Indian owner Bomba Callwood himself. One of Bomba's typical signs challenges 'sexy' females to get naked for Bomba and win a free T-shirt. He claims this is not exploitation, 'just a lot of fun.' And apparently plenty of free spirits take Bomba up on his offer, as the décor of the bar consists of ceilings strung with hundreds of bras and panties.

The big attraction here is the full-moon party Bomba throws once a month. The party features an outdoor barbecue, live reggae, plenty of dancing in the dirt and hordes of youthful drunks. To top it off, Bomba serves free psychoactive mushroom tea (see the 'Magic Mushrooms' boxed text, earlier). Five hundred people can show up for one of these bacchanals. While plenty of people (especially males) come away saying they have never been to a better party, a lot of women look back on their experience at the Bomba Shack with horror and regret at the poor choices they made under the influence of mushrooms and rum punch.

Many female expats and seasoned travelers in the islands refuse to patronize the bar. They claim the scene degrades women and takes advantage of unsophisticated teenage girls on vacation, who seem drawn to the place like moths to a flame…while the sharks circle in the shadows.

Shopping

If you like the ambience of a seaside West Indian settlement (the way many people imagine it in their dreams), the shopping complex at Sopers Hole Marina is the place to come. The keystone here is another Pusser's store and restaurant, but you can shop in several boutiques like the Sea Urchin (☎ 284-494-6234), selling beach wear. The Caribbean Corner Spice House (☎ 284-495-9567) has products to compete with Sunny Caribbee of Road Town. Zenaida's (☎ 284-495-4867) sells sarongs and straw bags as well as funky jewelry.

On your way to the West End and the Sopers Hole Marina, stop at Nanny Cay for Arawak Designs Boutique & Gift Shop (☎ 284-494-5240), featuring island-made batik fashions.

EAST ISLAND

Tortola's eastern end is a mix of steep mountains, remote bays, the airport and thickly settled West Indian communities. A few resorts, charter-yacht marinas, quiet beaches and an exceptional collection of restaurants call to travelers.

Ruins of St Philips Church

The walls of this church on the north side of Blackburn Hwy in Kingstown, east of Road Town, are all that remain of a community of freed slaves established in 1833 as the 'Kingstown Experiment.' Most of the worshippers here were survivors from the wreck of a slave ship (in about 1815) who were given this reservation and place of worship after working for some years as plantation laborers.

Beef Island

This large isle off the eastern end of Tortola can be reached via the bridge from East End. The island is best known for being the site of the BVI's main airport, which is in the throes of a major expansion. The southern half of the island is a large mountain. For years, developers have been hoping to

TORTOLA

build a resort on this prime real estate, but environmentalists' challenges have derailed their plans. You will finds some hiking trails crisscrossing the large, bush-covered hill.

Beaches

An undeveloped gem on the north shore near East End, **Josiahs Bay** is a dramatic strand at the foot of a valley that has excellent surf with a point break in winter. A small beach bar is here, surrounded by acres of empty space. Several charming and inexpensive guesthouses lie inland on the valley slopes. While there is precious little shade at the beach except under a few sea grape trees, the privacy and wildness of Josiahs appeal to travelers who want to veer off the beaten path and a have a rental Jeep to get there.

East of Josiahs Bay, **Lambert Bay** used to be called Elizabeth Beach before the

Lambert Beach Resort developed it in the late 1990s. If you make the trek down the steep hill to the resort and park in its lot, you will find a wide, palm-fringed beach. In winter, when there is an Atlantic Ocean swell coming out of the north, the undertow here and at Josiahs Bay can be dangerous.

Located on the northwest end of Beef Island, **Long Bay** is an undeveloped beach that Tortolians have long kept for themselves. Probably the least visited strand on the island, the secluded beach with sheltered waters borders a nesting area for terns and a salt pond that attracts egrets. Unfortunately, the nearby airport runway is a frequent source of whining propjet noise. Except on Sunday, when West Indian families have family picnics at the beach, you are likely to have Long Bay to yourself.

Trellis Bay, a broad semicircular beach east of the airport on Beef Island, is a crowded yachting anchorage with a small island (and restaurant) in the center of the bay. Trellis Bay is also the landing for Virgin Gorda's North Sound Express ferry and home to a water-sports operator, sculptor's studio, restaurants, a general store and funky guesthouse.

Activities

You can go **sailing** on the *Golden Spirit* (☎ 284-495-1479), at Fat Hogs Bay, which offers day and dinner sails on its luxury catamaran.

Jolly Mon Boat Rentals (☎ 284-495-9916), at Maya Cove, rents 26-foot speedboats for $275 a half-day, $350 full day.

High Sea Adventures (☎ 284-495-1300), at Fat Hogs Bay, has a 25-foot powerboat for **snorkeling** trips ($55 half-day, $80 full day).

UBS Dive Center & Lounge (☎ 284-494-0024), at the Harbour View Marina on the East End, specializes in personalized **diving** excursions.

Places to Stay

The *Serendipity House* (☎ 284-495-1488), on Josiahs Hill about half a mile from the beach, is one of the best values on Tortola. Canadians Carol and Bill Campbell have welcomed travelers here since 1990 with the

---

Sailing, Carib Style

You can take daysails on *Gli Gli*, an authentic replica of a traditional Carib Indian dugout canoe. A daysail (9 am to 3 pm) costs $65 per person (five-person minimum) and includes a lunch featuring traditional Carib dishes. For information and reservations, call Aragorn Dick-Read (☎ 284-495-1849) at his sculpture studio on Trellis Bay.

Carib Indians Jacon Fredericks and John Francis, who participated in the canoe's construction, are often on hand to guide the tours. Tours also include viewing of a video showing the construction and parts of the *Gli Gli*'s 1997 expedition. The *Gli Gli* was built to make its maiden voyage in 1997 as part of the Gli Gli Project – a celebration of Carib culture. The canoe's initial three-month expedition lasted from May to August 1997 and included a voyage from Dominica to Guyana. Along the way, the voyagers sought out the remaining Caribs on the various islands and in the Orinoco River Delta to introduce the expedition to them and learn from their collective cultural knowledge.

invitation to 'spend a vacation, not a fortune.' There are one-, two- and three-bedroom options in the hillside compound. You get a full kitchen, bath, TV and VCR, an outdoor gas grill and a pool here. The poolside studio (about $425 a week) has the charm of a doll's house. One-bedroom apartments rent for around $100 a night or $600 a week. Children are welcome.

Tamarind Club (☎ 284-495-2795) lies just 100 yards down the hill from Serendipity House. In 2000, Dawn Rosenberg took over these red-roofed West Indian–style villas around a central garden and pool, and brought fresh energy and creativity to the property. The pool with swim-up bar is large, and the open-air restaurant serves a mean and economical Sunday brunch (under $9). Nine rooms surround the garden/pool. Each room has a private bath and veranda; some have air-con and TV. Rates run $100 to $165.

The *Beef Island Guest House* (☎ 284-495-2303) is on Trellis Bay next to De Loose Mongoose restaurant (see Places to Eat). It's about a five-minute walk to the airport and therefore an excellent choice for travelers planning a late arrival or early departure. Set on a thin beach among a grove of low coconut palms, the one-story guesthouse looks more like a contemporary West Indian home than an inn, but the guest rooms have unexpected distinctive character, with beam ceilings and carpeted floors. All rooms come with private bath and fans. Winter rates for a double run about $120 per day, $700 per week.

Family-friendly *Lambert Beach Resort* (☎ 284-495-2877), on a long, white strand of beach near the northeast corner of the island, is one of Tortola's newest resorts (1998). Most of the 38 units are large, one-bedroom suites in a four-unit villa. The pool, with its swim-up bar, waterfalls and huge children's pool must be the largest resort pool on the island. The tennis courts are free, as are bodyboard and kayak rentals. The new Jasmine beachfront restaurant (see Places to Eat) gets high marks for its value and creativity. You can get a gardenview room here for about $140 in season.

For *rental accommodations*, Josiahs Bay Cottages (☎ 284-494-6186), next door to the Josiahs Bay Plantation, has a clutch of octagonal villas and suites for rent starting at about $900 per week. Over the Hill Cottages (☎ 284-495-2322, 800-952-9338), on Little Bay, lists rentals for $700 to $1600 a week.

Places to Eat
De Loose Mongoose (☎ 284-495-2302), at the Beef Island Guest House (see Places to Stay), makes a great breakfast stop if you are waiting for a flight or the North Sound ferry. Try the banana pancakes for about $7. You pay the same price for a great quesadilla at lunch.

A Secret Garden (☎ 284-495-1834), at Josiahs Bay Plantation, is one of the most delightful places to eat on Tortola. Outdoor tables are set amid the distilling buildings of the old plantation (now an art gallery and boutique). Owner Kim Peters Millman opened her cafe in 1999 and offers an exceptionally imaginative menu that ranges from the Asian tuna burger ($11) to Bajan flying fish pie ($12) – herb-encrusted flying fish pan-fried and topped with tomatoes, onions and gravy, crowned with a sweet potato topping and baked to bubbling.

Fat Hog Bob's (☎ 284-495-1010), at Maya Cove, is basically an upscale rib shack with a 100-foot porch at seaside. The baby-back ribs, marinated in Guinness Stout, start at $15, but you can eat salt fish cakes for $6.

Jasmine (☎ 284-495-2877 ext 207), at the Lambert Beach Resort (see Places to Stay), on a secluded beachside terrace, is several cuts above most hotel restaurants and an excellent value. The cuisine here is imaginative and international. Try the Guyanese garlic pork ($15).

Eclypse (☎ 284-495-1646), at Penn's Landing Marina on Fat Hogs Bay, has a hip, eclectic menu featuring fusion cuisine. The setting is a tranquil seaside patio with candlelight and jazz. I recommend the Santa Fe crabcakes appetizer for about $10. You can get some veggie entrees for under $17.

Calamaya's (☎ 284-495-2126), at Hodge's Creek Marina, a few miles east of Road

Town on Blackburn Hwy, serves an eclectic menu of Mediterranean and Caribbean cuisine. This cafe sits on a deck overlooking a shimmering cove with a view of Peter Island. Chef David Pugliese has made this restaurant the third jewel in his collection of gourmet eateries on the island (he and his wife, Cele, also run Cafesito and Brandywine Bay). For a light meal, try the Caribbean Caesar salad with lobster (under $14).

The Last Resort *(☎ 284-495-2520),* on an islet in Trellis Bay, is reached by boat from the Trellis Bay ferry dock. The restaurant features a changing dinner buffet of fish such as baked mahimahi and red meat options. The big attraction is the cabaret act with owner Tony Snell following dinner. The dinner and cabaret are popular with cruising sailors, but landlubbers can call for ferry service from the resort's hotline telephone at the Trellis Bay ferry dock. Expect to pay around $23 for the buffet.

Brandywine Bay *(☎ 284-495-2301)* lies a mile east of Road Town and overlooks Sir Francis Drake Channel. This is chef David Pugliese's signature restaurant. Here you can eat haute Mediterranean dishes served on a breeze-cooled terrace. Entrees run $15 to $45 and include offerings like *bistecca alla fiorentina.*

Shopping

Don't miss Aragorn's Studio (☎ 284-495-1849) on the beach at Trellis Bay, where sculptor Aragorn Dick-Read works his magic on metal, wood and silkscreen. He is one of the builders of the traditional Carib sailing canoe *Gli Gli,* which followed the old Carib routes in South America a few years back. (See the boxed text.)

Virgin Gorda

Until the 1960s, when Laurence Rockefeller began construction of his resort at Little Dix Bay, Virgin Gorda ('Fat Virgin' in Spanish) was a place lost in daydreams of its colonial glory. Today, this 10-mile-long, 1-mile-wide island is the second-most-developed island in the BVI, with about 2500 residents. For many citizens and travelers alike, Virgin Gorda is a land of milk and honey.

Virgin Gorda's wide variety of landscapes presents a visual feast and an array of adventures. At the north end of the island, you can explore the almost totally enclosed bay of North Sound and its ring of protecting cays by kayak, sailboard, sailboat or Boston Whaler. On another junket, you can hike to the summit of Gorda Peak National Park for its cool breezes, bromeliads and vistas of the entire archipelago. Beach walkers spend days on the sweeping, sand-rimmed bays of the island's western side. And for a rock scramble, you can explore the mammoth granite boulders – including the famous Baths – and the Copper Mine National Park at the south end of Virgin Gorda. There are also tons of places to snorkel.

Most accommodations for travelers on Virgin Gorda are in a score of sophisticated resorts. There is no visible poverty on the island, virtually no crime and no rampant commercialism. The businesses and homes in the settlements of Spanish Town, the Valley and Gun Creek have spacious grounds, a profusion of flowers and well-tended structures. Sure, you will probably come across a roaming brood of chickens sooner or later, but they will be snowy white and an islander will have named them all. There are no camping facilities and very few rooms on the island for travelers with a tight budget.

Highlights

- Visiting the Baths at sunrise or sunset
- Exploring North Sound by water
- Hiking to Virgin Gorda Peak for a picnic
- Dining to jazz riffs at Chez Bamboo
- Trekking to remote Devil's Bay or Spring Bay

History

Virgin Gorda hosted Igneri, Taíno and Carib Indians just as the other Virgin Islands did to the west. After leaving St Croix in 1493, Christopher Columbus sailed north and anchored to the southeast of Virgin Gorda. He named the island the Fat Virgin because when viewed from this anchorage, to him its silhouette resembled a full-bodied woman sleeping on her back. In the years following, Spanish adventurers moved east through the Virgin Islands looking for Indians to enslave and precious metals. Some stumbled upon the copper deposits on Virgin Gorda and began a mining operation, but this mine never resulted in a viable colony, and Virgin Gorda remained simply a stopping place for buccaneers and foreign fleets. One of these fleets belonged to

VIRGIN GORDA

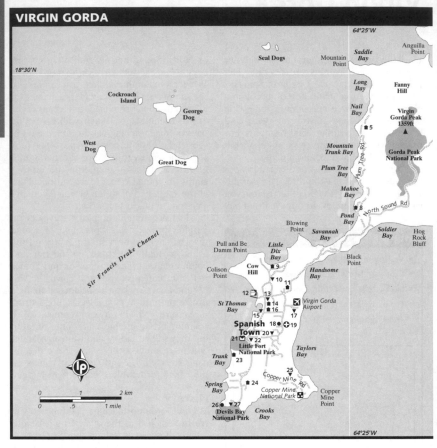

England's Earl of Cumberland, who assembled his ships and soldiers at Virgin Gorda before his successful but brief (five months) conquest of Puerto Rico in 1596.

By 1680, British planters had moved their cattle-raising operations from Anguilla to Virgin Gorda. And during the 1690s, the BVI had enough colonists to warrant their own deputy governor and a representative council. In 1717, Virgin Gorda was the most populated of the BVI, with 317 whites and 308 blacks. As the BVI continued to prosper, England eventually granted the islands increased status as a colony. When

the crown appointed Abednego Pickering the first Lieutenant Governor of the Leeward Islands, he chose Virgin Gorda as his capital. But Pickering converted to the Quaker faith, and shortly after his conversion, he shifted his capital to Tortola, where a colony of Quakers had developed. Nevertheless, Virgin Gorda continued to thrive. Large plantations on the island produced sugar cane, ginger, indigo and cattle. And by 1812, the island's population reached an all-time peak of 8000 citizens.

The copper mine that lay dormant during the glory days of 'King Cane' reopened in

VIRGIN GORDA

Mosquito Island
Blunder Bay
Malone Bay 4
Prickly Pear Island 1
Vixen Point
North Sound
Beach
Camelia Point
Robin Bay
Gun Point
Gun Creek
Great Hill
Joe Bay
South Sound
Mattie Point
Little Bay
South Sound Bluff
Eustatia
Eustatia Sound
■2
■ 3
Biras Hill ▲ 432ft
Biras Creek
6 ▼
▲ 7
Berchers Bay
Deep Bay
Oil Nut Bay
Pajaros Point
Berchers Bluff
Caribbean Sea

64°20'W
18°30'N

PLACES TO STAY		
2	Saba Rock Resort; Pirate's Pub	
3	Bitter End Yacht Club & Resort; Clubhouse Steak & Seafood Grille	
4	Leverick Bay Resort; Light House; Pusser's Company Store; Kounda's Digital Jammin'	
5	Nail Bay Resort; Dog & Dolphin Bar & Grill	
7	Biras Creek Resort	
8	Mango Bay Resort; Katiche Point; Giorgio's Table	
9	Little Dix Bay	
11	Old Yard Inn	
14	Bayview Vacation Apartments; Chez Bamboo	
16	Wheel House; Travel Plan	
23	Fischer's Cove Beach Hotel	
24	Guavaberry Spring Bay	

PLACES TO EAT		
1	Sand Box	
6	Fat Virgins Café	
10	Thelma's Hideout	
13	New Dixie's Bar & Restaurant	
15	Spanish Town Café; Bath & Turtle; Yacht Harbour; BVI Tourist Board; Island Drugs Center; Stevens Laundromat	
17	Flying Iguana	
20	Crab Hole Bar & Restaurant	
22	Rock Café	
25	Mine Shaft Café	
27	Mad Dog; Top of the Baths	

OTHER		
12	Ferry Dock	
18	Virgin Gorda Community Library	
19	Nurse Iris O'Neal Clinic	
21	Post Office	
26	The Baths	

1840. Forty professional miners from Cornwall, England, and 150 islanders worked the copper pit, erecting the stone-shaft building and smelting house whose ruins are now a national park. In 1867, the mine finally closed for good.

Over the centuries, as many as 10,000 tons of ore had been extracted. Meanwhile, the struggling plantation economy had all but collapsed, and both whites and blacks abandoned the Fat Virgin in droves. By the beginning of the 20th century, Virgin Gorda's population had declined to about 600 souls.

In the late 1950s and early 1960s, Laurence Rockefeller's resort at Little Dix Bay brought jobs, roads and utilities to the island. Yachts and other exclusive resorts followed. Soon, the giant granite rock formations of Virgin Gorda's Baths were the BVI's biggest tourist attraction, drawing day-trippers from as far afield as St Thomas. Jet setters such as Virgin Atlantic Airways heir Richard Branson arrived to carve out private retreats. In 1999, *Sports Illustrated* magazine used Virgin Gorda and its satellite cays as its primary setting for the famous swimsuit issue.

To Columbus, the island resembled a large woman on her back.

Orientation

Virgin Gorda lies 8 miles east of Tortola. Its serpent shape running northeast to southwest makes it a particularly easy place to navigate. Prominent Virgin Gorda Peak (1359ft) dominates the northern half of the island. The southern half of the island is a rolling plain called 'the Valley.' The island's main settlement, Spanish Town, lies on the western shore of the Valley; the airport is a mile to the east. The granite formations of the Baths and the ruins of the historic copper mine lie near the southern tip of the island. The main highway, called North Sound Rd for much of its length, runs along the spine of the island.

Most travelers will find the map in this book or the fold-out, color maps sponsored by AT&T perfectly adequate for navigating Virgin Gorda.

Information

The BVI Tourist Board (☎ 284-495-5181) is in the Yacht Harbour mall in Spanish Town. The offices are open 9 am to 5 pm weekdays.

Barclays Bank is in the Yacht Harbour mall as well, open 8:45 am to 3 pm Monday to Wednesday, 9:30 am to 3 pm Thursday and 8:45 am to 5 pm Friday.

The post office (☎ 284-495-5234) lies just off Lee Rd south of the Yacht Harbour and the boatyard in Spanish Town. It is open 8 am to 4 pm weekdays and 9 am to 1:30 Saturday.

If you want to get online or check your email, head for Kounda's Digital Jammin' (☎ 284-495-7013), on the 1st floor of the Leverick Bay Resort. Rates are 45¢ a minute, $1.25 to log on.

The island's primary travel agent is Travel Plan (☎ 284-495-5586), in the courtyard at the Wheel House guesthouse across from Yacht Harbour.

There are no bookstores on this island, but most of the resorts and villas keep collections of used paperbacks. You will find the Virgin Gorda Community Library (☎ 284-495-5516) opposite the clinic, on the ridge near the airport in the Valley.

A lot of people on the island and visiting yachts use Stevens Laundromat (☎ 284-495-5525) at Yacht Harbour. Washes cost $3, $2.50 to dry.

For medical help, the Nurse Iris O'Neal Clinic (☎ 284-495-5337) is on the ridge road in the Valley near the airport. The nurse lives here and answers the phone 24 hours a day. She is available for a consultation from 9 am to 4:30 pm. A doctor usually visits the clinic each weekday from 9 am to noon.

For drugs and medical needs, head to the Island Drugs Center (☎ 284-495-5449) at Yacht Harbour. The store is open 9 am to 6 pm Monday to Saturday.

Call ☎ 999 for police on Virgin Gorda; ☎ 911 gets you the fire department.

Organized Tours

Potter Gafford Taxi Service (☎ 284-495-5329) will give you (up to three people) an island tour for about two hours ($60).

Andy Flax at the Virgin Gorda Tour Association (☎ 284-495-5252) charges $20 per person.

Special Events

Held on the four days preceding the Christian Lent, the Virgin Gorda Easter Festival

(☎ 284-495-5181) is a true carnival event. Spanish Town around Yacht Harbour fills with mocko jumbies, scratch bands, calypsonians, a food fair, vendors' booths, parades and floats.

Getting There & Away

Air Air Sunshine has at least three flights a day between Virgin Gorda and San Juan, Puerto Rico, St Thomas and St Croix. Continental Connection also flies the San Juan to Virgin Gorda route, as does Vieques Airlink. Air St Thomas services Virgin Gorda from Charlotte Amalie.

Expect to pay about $102 one way or $190 roundtrip between Virgin Gorda and San Juan, $170 roundtrip to St Thomas or St Croix.

See the Getting There & Away chapter for more information.

Ferry There is regularly scheduled ferry service between the resorts on Virgin Gorda's North Sound and Trellis Bay on Tortola ($20 one way, $40 roundtrip). There is also service between Spanish Town and Road Town, Tortola (see 'Interisland Ferries' in the Getting Around chapter). The fare runs $10 one way, $19 roundtrip.

Getting Around

To/From the Airport The Virgin Gorda Airport (☎ 284-495-5621) is on the east side of the Valley. You can count on taxis waiting at the airport when flights are arriving. Expect to pay about $7 for a ride into Spanish Town; $15 or more will get you to the resorts along the island's northwest beaches. You will pay about $20 if you need to reach one of the water taxis at the Bitter End (see Ferry, below).

Car Virgin Gorda has several car rental companies, but you probably haven't heard of them. Nevertheless, they are very accommodating and will generally deliver your car to you wherever you want it; drop-off arrangements are equally flexible. Expect to pay around $45 a day for a Suzuki Sidekick, but car rates drop off during the sum-

mer and fall seasons. Repeat visitors recommend the following agencies: Speedy's Car Rental (☎ 284-495-5240), L&S Jeep (☎ 284-495-5297) and Mahogany Car Rentals (☎ 284-495-5469).

Taxi Cab rates on Virgin Gorda are some of the highest in the Caribbean. Rates from the northwest beach resorts or Gun Creek to Spanish Town can be as high as $15 for a 3-mile trip. Potter Gafford Taxi Service (☎ 284-495-5329) and Mahogany Run Taxi Service (☎ 284-495-5469) are the major services on the island.

Ferry The Bitter End Yacht Club runs a water taxi to Gun Creek. From here, you can walk the trails (half a mile) to the Biras Creek Resort or the Fat Virgins Café. The water taxi departs Gun Creek every hour on the half-hour from 7:30 am to 10:30 pm. Return boats leave on the hour. Passage is free if you are a guest at the Bitter End or plan to eat and shop there.

SPANISH TOWN & THE VALLEY

More of a settlement than a town, the commercial center of Virgin Gorda probably gets its name from a corruption of the English word 'penniston,' not as a reference to the 16th-century Spanish presence on the island. Penniston is a blue woolen fabric long used for making slave clothing on the island, and islanders referred to their settlement as Penniston well into the 1850s.

The yacht harbor dredged here in the 1960s (as an adjunct facility to the Little Dix Bay resort) is the heart of Spanish Town. Many of the island's businesses, government buildings and restaurants stretch along Lee Rd as it skirts the yacht harbor from the ferry dock (north) to the post office (south). Today, a patchwork of homes and businesses spreads out from this center, so it's impossible to identify where Spanish Town stops and the surrounding area of the Valley begins. Spanish Town is a sleepy place. Nevertheless, the settlement offers low-key but interesting shopping, dining and nightlife with a fresher mix of West

Indians, expats and travelers than you get at the island's resorts.

The Baths

This collection of giant boulders jumbled at seaside near the southwest corner of the island marks a national park and the BVI's most popular tourist attraction. The rocks form a series of grottoes that flood with seawater.

While the Baths are a site to stir the imagination, the place is generally overrun with tourists. By 10 am each morning, a fleet of visiting yachts has moored off the coast and tourists have been shuttled in from resorts and cruise ships as far away as St Thomas. Come at sunrise or sunset if you want to wonder at the Baths in private. It can be a sublime experience, but make sure to lather up with insect repellent.

Yacht Harbour

The dredged harbor here at Spanish Town came as a result of Laurence Rockefeller's construction of Little Dix Bay. Today, the development is known as Yacht Harbour and contains many of the island's most popular and essential shops as well as places to eat, a bank and a tourist office. While the style of this mall seems more like what you would find in Southern California than in the West Indies, Yacht Harbour is well kept without being sterile or banal.

Copper Mine National Park

Located near Virgin Gorda's southwest tip, these impressive ruins (which include a chimney, boiler house, cistern and mine shaft house) are now a national park and protected area. These ruins mark a mine worked by Cornish miners between 1838 and 1867. Signs now forbid visitors from scrambling around the ruins and mine shaft because of the possibility of injury, but you don't need to climb on the ruins to enjoy them. Many travelers find the ruins are better viewed at a distance as a backdrop to the sea roiling on the rocks a hundred feet below. The rugged hillside and coastline on this part of the island make an excellent place for a picnic.

Little Fort National Park

There is little left of this garrison south of the Yacht Harbour, save some crumbling walls. It was the site of a Spanish stronghold, but the attraction today is a 36-acre wildlife sanctuary. Wild orchids and tall silk cotton trees rule.

Wild orchid

Beaches

Virgin Gorda has at least 14 of them, and beachcombing is a primary attraction for island visitors.

The most famous natural setting in the BVI, **the Baths** are more of an attraction than a beach...although plenty of people come here to swim, stroll and dabble their toes in the water (see earlier).

Neighboring the Baths to the north, **Spring Bay** is a narrow beach broken into segments by the presence of large boulders just like at the Baths. You will find white sand, clear water and good snorkeling off the boulder enclosure called the 'Crawl.' This place is a national park, too. Spring Bay is far less crowded than the Baths, except when the Little Dix Bay resort brings in a gang of revelers for a BBQ and beach party (usually on Thursday).

If you really want to get away from people and find your own rugged interface between boulders, sand and water, head south of the Baths on one of the two trails that leads to **Devil's Bay**, a 20-acre national park at the very southern tip of Virgin Gorda. The easy trail departs from the traffic roundabout at the Baths. The rugged trek follows the beach south from the Baths. This trail involves scaling boulders, wading and climbing ladders. The beach here is a secluded crescent, but if you want even more privacy, continue on a shoreside trail to the smaller beach among the boulders.

For an unpopulated, longer strand, head north from Spring Bay to **Trunk Bay**. This is a place for sun, sand and swimming, but not snorkeling.

Little Dix Bay is a perfect crescent of sand on the fringe of what is usually a perfectly calm bay. To get here, enter through the gates of the resort and tell them you are going to the beach.

North of the Valley, **Savannah Bay** features more than a mile of white sand, largely protected by a barrier reef from the worst of the northerly swells that come during the winter. Except for the beaches of Anegada, no other beach provides such opportunities for long, solitary walks. Sunsets here can be fabulous.

Taylors Bay, a beach off Copper Mine Rd on the southeast side of the island, sees few visitors. Facing east, Taylors Bay can have some rough surf. It is probably the best place to come for sunbathing in the buff because the chance of offending anyone is quite slim.

Activities

The 44-foot schooner *Spirit of Anegada* (☎ 284-496-6825), at Yacht Harbour, carries six passengers on full- and half-day **sailing** adventures. Rates are $55 for a half-day, $85 for a full day.

Double 'D' (☎ 284-495-6150), at Yacht Harbour, offers half-day sails for $50, full days for $70, on a 50-foot sloop.

Euphoric Cruises (☎ 284-495-5542), at Yacht Harbour, rents 21- and 24-foot Robalo speedboats for around $250 a day.

The resorts at Biras Creek, Little Dix Bay and Nail Bay have **tennis** courts for their guests. The Little Dix Bay resort (☎ 284-495-5555) has the most courts (seven). They are free to guests and cost $20 an hour for nonguests. You cannot make reservations; just show up and hope for an empty court.

The lack of traffic and relatively gentle terrain (except for Virgin Gorda Peak) make this island an inviting place for **bicycling**. You can rent trail bikes from Lucy and Orville Thompson at K&T Bike Rental (☎ 284-495-5398) in the Valley. Rates are $5 an hour, $20 a day, with better prices for multiple days.

Alex Parillon (☎ 284-495-5100) offers **horseback riding** on the mountain and in the Valley. Expect to pay $25 an hour.

Places to Stay

The accommodations on Virgin Gorda are almost entirely aimed at the top-end traveler. Furthermore, there are no camping facilities, and police will run you off if they catch you trying to camp out on a deserted beach. Rates here are based on the high, winter season.

The *Wheel House* (☎ 284-495-5230), across the street from Yacht Harbour, has the least expensive rooms on the island. This guesthouse has 12 units above a restaurant in a concrete-block building with a spacious 2nd-floor veranda. Rooms are clean and brightly decorated with tropical fabrics, and the grounds are meticulously maintained. Each room has a bath, TV, air-con and phone. Prices run about $85.

The *Bayview Vacation Apartments* (☎ 284-495-5329), behind Chez Bamboo restaurant, can be a good deal if you are traveling with three or four people. Each apartment has two bedrooms, a full kitchen, dining facilities and an airy living room. Sliding doors open to sea and garden views, and there is a roof deck for sunbathing. Rates run $95 to $135 a day.

Fischer's Cove Beach Hotel (☎ 284-495-5252), near the southwest end of the island, is a small collection of triangular-shaped beachfront cottages and a main hotel building with studio apartments. All rooms have a private bath, TV, phone, refrigerator and porch. Some have air-con and kitchens. Rates start at about $150 per night, but you can save more than 25% if you rent for a week or more.

The *Old Yard Inn* (☎ 284-495-5986, 800-653-9273), on North Sound Rd at the north end of the Valley, has a reputation for hospitality and personal service. Although the inn is not on the beach, its large pool, garden setting and health club give the place the feel of an oasis, and you can get a free shuttle to nearby Savannah Bay if you want waves and snorkeling. Each of the 14 rooms has cedar paneling, rattan furnishings, a huge shower and private balcony/patio. Some rooms have air-con and refrigerators. Rates run $145 to $245.

Guavaberry Spring Bay (☎ 284-495-5227), about a mile south of Spanish Town near the Baths, is a serene resort set among giant boulders and lush vegetation. Octagonal pods are perched among the trees of a low hill with a view of Sir Francis Drake Channel. Each of these 'homes' has two bedrooms, a private bath, living room, kitchen and broad sundeck. Rates run about $160 to $210.

Little Dix Bay (☎ 284-495-5555, 800-928-3000), north of the Valley on the west coast, looks every bit as polished and serene as it did 40 years ago. There are 98 rooms here in villas poised in a coconut grove along a half-mile crescent of sugar-sand beach. The lush grounds are redolent with well-tended flowers, and the thatched conical roofs of the public buildings give the resort the feel of a South Seas resort without being corny. Rooms are spacious and furnished with elegant fabrics and wicker furniture fit for the Sultan of Brunei. You get all the physical amenities here except TV. The resort has tennis courts and a water-sports/diving operation. Rates run about $550 to more than $1500.

For *rental accommodations*, Priority Property Management (☎ 284-495-5201), in the Valley, offers one- to three-bedroom luxury condos and villas on the beach for $2100 to $4100 a week. Also try Virgin Gorda Villa Rentals Ltd (☎ 284-495-7421, 800-848-7081), in the Valley. Its one- and five-bedroom villas rent for $1300 to $8400 a week. If you're looking for a tropical estate of your own to accommodate a clan of seven, consider Toad Hall (☎ 284-495-5397) at the Baths, for about $4500.

Places to Eat

The *Wheel House* (see Places to Stay) is a breakfast stop for locals. You can get West Indian lunches and dinners here, too. Try the chicken served curried or with native sauce (under $10).

The *New Dixie's Bar & Restaurant* (☎ 284-495-5640), across from the ferry dock, is a great cheap-eats diner. Come for breakfast and get two eggs, toast and coffee for $3. At lunch, you can score a fish burger for $3.50. Beer and ice cream cost $2. Cricket plays on the TV all day.

Spanish Town Café (☎ 284-495-5555 ext 201), at Yacht Harbour, is a deli that makes a popular breakfast stop for cruising sailors and locals. Croissants or bagels with cappuccino cost under $4. Fruit salad runs just $2. Gourmet sandwiches such as shaved, smoked turkey start at about $5.

The *Mad Dog* (☎ 284-495-5830) is an airy pavilion set among the rocks where the road ends at the Baths. There is often a gathering of local expats and tourists here. Ham-and-cheese sandwiches and shrimp salad cost $5.

The *Crab Hole Bar & Restaurant* (☎ 284-495-5307), in the south valley, is a small place specializing in West Indian dishes. Locals swear by the curried-chicken rotis and callaloo, which run around $6.

Thelma's Hideout (☎ 284-495-5646) is on the side road leading to Little Dix Bay resort. Seating is in an open-air courtyard, and there is a stage where a band plays West Indian rhythms some nights during high season. Thelma will serve you bacon, eggs, orange juice and coffee for breakfast, but most travelers come here for the conch stew ($12 for lunch, $18 for dinner). Make dinner reservations here by 3 pm.

The *Bath & Turtle* (☎ 284-495-5239), at Yacht Harbour, is a patio tavern surrounded by the mall. Some diners come for Caribbean dishes (over $12), seafood and pasta, but pizza goes for less than $13 and burgers cost about $10. I like the fiesta quesadilla (black and refried beans) for $7.50.

The *Mine Shaft Café* (☎ 284-495-5260), on Copper Mine Rd at the southeast end of the island, is a hilltop pavilion with views of both the Atlantic Ocean and Drake Channel. A lot of patrons come for the jerked chicken wrap ($10) and the flying fish in fresh salsa ($16). There is also a lively bar scene here (see Entertainment).

The *Flying Iguana* (☎ *284-495-5277)* overlooks the Atlantic near the airport at midisland and offers largely West Indian cuisine in a dining room adjoining a small art gallery. Monday is BBQ night (everything is under $16).

The *Rock Café (☎ 284-495-5482)* is an upscale restaurant and club among the boulders at the traffic circle south of Spanish Town. There is a cave feeling about the interior of this place, but it also has a popular terrace bar (see Entertainment) on top of the boulders. The restaurant is popular with West Indians, expats and travelers staging a big night out. The cuisine is mostly Italian with entrees like penne Caprese and homemade gnocchi. Expect to pay around $20 for a dinner.

Top of the Baths (☎ 284-495-5497), on the hillside above the Baths, offers indoor and outdoor dining to a clientele who often come from visiting yachts. If you come for lunch, a veggie burger will cost you $6, fish & chips $11. Babyback ribs are about $19 on the dinner menu, but most dishes run over $22.

Chez Bamboo (☎ 284-495-5752), on Lee Rd just north of Yacht Harbour, is a gourmand's delight. This bistro (in a converted West Indian home and yard) is open for dinner only and serves French Creole Caribbean cuisine. Specialties include bouillabaisse and jambalaya penne pasta with desserts like chocolate bourbon mint cake. A lot of entrees run over $25, and desserts cost $7 and up, but you can eat off the appetizer menu that includes a conch tortilla for about $10. You may want to make reservations, as this restaurant is popular with locals, expats and yacht crews.

Entertainment

Most of the resort hotels have live West Indian music playing during and after the dinner hour. You will find more frisky folk haunting the gin mills in the Valley. All of the following are also places to eat (see above).

The *Bath & Turtle*, also called 'The Pub,' is in yacht Harbour mall. This courtyard restaurant pushes back the tables and becomes the hottest nighttime venue for expats working on the island and travelers. The crowd ranges from the college set to older yacht captains ready to kick up their heels. Local bands play Wednesday and Sunday nights and cover classic reggae and dance tunes.

The *Mine Shaft Café* always has a fired-up crowd for happy hour, but once a month the place really rocks. Owner Elton Sprauve throws a full-moon party here that seems to draw all the young and young-at-heart. The bait is live music under the stars, warm breezes, cheap rum punch and beer and grilled meats.

Chez Bamboo has developed into a hip after-dinner destination. This bistro usually features jazz and blues on Friday night. Calypsonians play here some other nights each week. Bands like Natural Magic set up under the tree in the courtyard, and the dance gang hits the floor in the restaurant after the tables are pushed back. The crowd is largely couples and groups of friends, mostly expats and travelers.

The *Rock Café* (see Places to Eat) is without a doubt the most lively night scene on the island for West Indians. The management brings in bands and DJs Wednesday to Sunday nights, including popular BVI acts like Heavy B. The crowd on the Le Tequila terrace bar is largely under 30, an even mix of West Indians, expats and tourists. The music is a mix of West Indian, house and hip-hop.

Shopping

With the exception of gift shops and boutiques in most of the resorts and the Pusser's Company Store (☎ 284-495-7369) at Leverick Bay selling tropical apparel, just about the only place to shop is in the Yacht Harbour mall in Spanish Town. You'll find exotic perfumes at Flamboyance (☎ 284-495-5946), handcrafted jewelry at Margo's Jewelry Boutique (☎ 284-495-5237), crystal and coins at the Artistic Gallery and locally produced Coppermine-brand fabric and clothing at the Virgin Gorda Craft Shop (☎ 284-495-5137).

NORTH & EAST ISLAND

The northeast end of Virgin Gorda features the spectacular scenery of North Sound and steep mountain slopes rising up to Virgin Gorda Peak. The region is also home to most of the island's luxury resorts.

Gorda Peak National Park

This mountain park contains a wide variety of trees and plants typical of a semi-rain forest. At 1359 feet, Gorda Peak is the island's highest point. The park protects all of the island above 1000 feet and creates a nature preserve of 265 acres. Both of the trails leading to the summit branch off the North Sound Rd and are well marked.

If you are coming from the Valley, the first trailhead you see marks the start of the longer trail (about 1½ miles). This trail makes a moderate climb to the summit, where you will find a few picnic tables, an observation tower and portable toilet. The second trailhead is farther north along the North Sound Rd. From here, you have a relatively easy half-mile climb to the summit.

Beaches

The strand of gently curving beach and vivid blue water at the Mango Bay Resort is called **Mahoe Bay**.

Mountain Trunk Bay, Nail Bay and **Long Bay** lie north of Mahoe Bay and run nearly undisturbed for about a mile all the way to rugged Mountain Point. Resort and villa development along these strands has taken some of the former privacy away. Waters are generally calm.

You will find **Berchers Bay**, a reef-protected beach, on the ocean side of the Biras Creek Resort. It is your best beach option if you are staying at or visiting Biras Creek or the Bitter End Yacht Club.

You need a boat to access Prickly Pear Island in North Sound. On the south side of the island, you find **Vixen Point**, with a long, broad stretch of white sand, sheltered swimming and a beach bar. There is also a secluded beach on the north side of Prickly Pear.

Activities

For **sailing** and **boating**, Bitter End Yacht Club (☎ 284-494-2745, 800-872-2392), on North Sound, rents Freedom 30 sloops for $2,625 a week and up. You can take off on a cruise or daysail around North Sound and stay at the dock at night. The Nick Trotter Sailing School (☎ 284-494-2745) is also at the Bitter End. It offers lessons and rentals of mistral sailboards and a variety of small sloops.

Nick Trotter also has 12-foot Boston Whalers for rent. These boats have 8-horsepower engines and rent for about $20 an hour. They are excellent craft for exploring North Sound. The school has sea kayaks at the same rate. The Leverick Bay Resort (☎ 284-495-7421) rents dinghies with outboards and kayaks for similar rates.

Dive BVI (☎ 284-495-5513), at Yacht Harbour and Leverick Bay, has four fast boats that take you **diving** at any of the sites in the BVI. Kilbride's Sunchaser Scuba (☎ 284-495-9638), at the Bitter End Yacht Club, is the creation of BVI diving pioneer Burt Kilbride. The staff offers trips to the wreck-strewn Horseshoe Reef of Anegada as well as popular night dives.

Many of the resorts offer sailboard rentals, but the Nick Trotter school has by far the most equipment and great **windsurfing** conditions nearby.

Places to Stay

The *Mango Bay Resort* (☎ *284-495-5673*), at Mahoe Bay, is a compound of five Italian-style luxury villas. The respected Giorgio's Table restaurant is on the property, and there's great snorkeling along the reef just off the beach. A studio with small porch and kitchenette runs about $120, but you'll pay about $250 or more for a one-bedroom villa.

Nail Bay Resort (☎ *284-494-8000, 800-871-3551*) is on the grounds of a 147-acre sugar plantation in the shadow of Virgin

Gorda Peak. Probably no other BVI resort offers such a range, from standard hotel rooms and suites to apartments and seaside villas with as many as five bedrooms. Most of these units are privately owned and managed by the resort. All rooms come with aircon, TV and VCR, phone, private bath and balcony. There are three secluded beaches here, which are great for strolling, but the centerpiece of the resort is the Dog & Dolphin Bar & Grill with its waterfall and swim-up bar overlooking Drake Channel. Rates run $120 to $600. You will want a rental Jeep if you stay here, as Nail Bay is at the end of a long, rough road.

Leverick Bay Resort (☎ 284-495-7421, 800-848-7081), on North Sound near the settlement of Gun Creek, is a resort that mixes hotel, condo, villa and marina accommodations. The best deal here is to take one of the 14 rooms in the hotel. Each has aircon, private balcony, bath, TV, phone, fridge, coffee-maker and toaster. There is a beach, pool, tennis court, dive shop, spa, restaurant, market and boutiques on the property. Expect to pay $150 for one of the hotel rooms.

Saba Rock Resort (☎ 284-495-7373) is on the tiny island of the same name just off the Bitter End Yacht Club in North Sound. For years, this used to be the Pirate's Pub, a raucous little bar tucked in the former house of Burt Kilbride, a dive master and pioneer expat on the North Sound. But in 1999, developers knocked down the pub and basically submerged Saba Rock beneath a boutique resort with eight hotel rooms, a restaurant, two bars and a gift shop. While the gritty, funky charm of the pub is becoming a fading memory, the new resort replaces it with some of the friendliest and most efficient staff on Virgin Gorda. Rooms are typical of luxury hotels and include private balconies. A free water shuttle ferries guests here from the Bitter End. You will pay $250 for the sense of exclusivity that comes with staying on the Rock.

The *Bitter End Yacht Club & Resort (☎ 284-494-2745, 800-872-2392),* at the east end of North Sound, is in a class of its own. This all-inclusive resort started as a beach bar and collection of five cottages in the 1960s. Now, it has 95 hillside villas, multiple restaurant/bars and docks that have everything from outboards to cruising yachts that you can live aboard. Almost every week has some kind of theme, usually related to sailboat instruction and racing for beginners and professionals. This is a great place for an active couple or families who like to spend their days with a mix of hiking, windsurfing, diving, fishing and sailing. Some of the villas have air-con; others are open to the trade winds and hardly need fans to keep you cool. All accommodations have 1st-class amenities but no TVs. Rates start at about $585 and go to $770. These rates are for two people and include three meals a day and unlimited use of the resort's fleet of boats.

Biras Creek Resort (☎ 284-494-3555, 800-223-1108), on the eastern shore of North Sound, is an oasis for up to 70 guests that can only be reached by boat. The 140-acre property fills a narrow isthmus between North Sound and the open Atlantic. Staying in one of the suites on the beach is like living a Robinson Crusoe existence but with air-con, maid service and a gourmet restaurant at your back. There are excellent trails among the sea grape tree forest for hiking and biking. Good snorkeling lies right offshore. You pay about $650 to $1300 for the exclusivity of this place, and you can tie up your yacht at the resort's dock.

Katiche Point (☎ 284-495-5672), at the Mango Bay Resort, is a collection of five suites set on the crest of a seaside bluff and built around a dramatic great house. The compound will cost you about $11,000 per week.

Places to Eat

The *Fat Virgins Café (☎ 284-495-7052),* on the south side of Biras Creek, is the budget diner's delight of North Sound. Travelers must come by boat to this little bistro (and little boutique) that rises from the wharf of the boatyard on the west side of Biras Creek. You can get a jumbo hot dog here for under $4; burgers cost under $6. Consider the roti stuffed with curried chicken and the daily West Indian specials. Beers cost $2.50. There is often acoustic music from an islander named Jackson, who the staff say is 'like de weather – you never know when he gone show up.'

The *Light House* (☎ 284-495-7369) overlooks the marina at Leverick Bay. Lots of folks show up for lunch to sample the gazpacho and conch chowder (under $4). You can get large pizzas for $10 and up.

The *Sand Box* (☎ 284-495-9122), a laid-back beach bar on Prickly Pear Island, is a great lunch stop for boaters. You can play some beach volleyball, take a dip and eat in your bathing suit. Conch fritters run under $8 and come with fries. The chicken and fish sandwiches cost about the same. Dinners like the sautéed mahimahi start at around $18.

The Bitter End Yacht Club (see Places to Stay) has three restaurants that overlook North Sound. The *Clubhouse Steak & Seafood Grille* is the most popular. You can get an a la carte menu here, but most people order the buffet ($38); it's monumental in both variety and substance. Roasted meats and fowl are a specialty. Make reservations early.

By the sea at the Mango Bay Resort, *Giorgio's Table* (☎ 284-495-5684) serves fine Italian dishes, including Mediterranean appetizers, fish, veal and beef filet in a pavilion built on the rocks at the tip of a peninsula. For lunch, an exotic salad like insalata Caprese or a margherita pizza run around $12. Dinner entrees like lobster Catalana cost $25 or more.

Biras Creek (see Places to Stay) overlooks North Sound from an elegant, tiki-style pavilion. The cuisine is an international buffet with entrees like honey-coated brochette of *gambas* (shrimp) or scallops and Bajan-style flying fish. You need reservations, and the buffet runs $55. There is a dress code here.

Entertainment

The *Pirate's Pub*, at Saba Rock Resort in North Sound (see Places to Stay), is not the funky old bar that lured travelers for more than two decades to this islet off the Bitter End Yacht Club. Long the haunt of characters in cut-offs, T-shirts and sweat-stained ball caps, the pub has been reincarnated as a spit-and-polish operation at the new resort. Most of the regulars have vanished to barfly Valhalla, but the pub is still worth a visit at happy hour to meet Jemme Hankey behind the bar and get beer and well drinks for $2.50. The clientele is largely crews and guests off visiting charter yachts.

Jost Van Dyke

For the last 400 years, the island of Jost (pronounced Yoast) Van Dyke has been an oasis for seafarers and adventurers. This small island less than 5 miles north of Tortola has developed a reputation that far exceeds its mere 4 sq miles of land. Measuring about 4 miles from west to east, and 1 mile from north to south, Jost and its

Highlights

- Kicking back with Foxy Callwood at his Tamarind Bar
- Camping in the shade of palm trees at White Bay
- Kayaking or sailing for a picnic on Sandy or Green Cay
- Tying on the feed bag for the pig roast at Sidney's Peace and Love
- Eating fresh coconut bread with your morning coffee at Christine's Bakery

primary satellite cays of Little Jost Van Dyke, Green Cay and Sandy Cay constitute a retreat of mountains, beaches and coves to delight travelers seeking a simpler world. The ebb and flow of the tide measure time. Chords from a guitar and homespun calypso rhythms drift out to sea on the breeze.

Jost first started to develop its reputation during the early 17th century, when the Dutch pirate (whom the island is named after) used it as his base of operations. In the 18th century, Jost and Little Jost became the homesteads of Quakers escaping the religious tyranny of England, and Quaker surnames like Lettsome and Callwood still survive among the islanders who descend from freed Quaker slaves.

Fewer than 200 people live in the shadows of 1000-foot peaks like Majohnny Hill and throw their cast nets for fish off Pull and Be Damm Point. Electricity only arrived in 1991. But since the 1960s, modern sailors have been discovering the island's charms, when they stopped here to clear customs. And since the late 1960s, calypsonian and philosopher Foxy Callwood (see the boxed text 'One Foxy Fella') has been the Lorelei wooing mariners to stay. His annual Foxy's Woodenboat Regatta at the end of May and his New Year's Eve party draw a cast of thousands.

In response, islanders have developed a low-key resort trade with a score of bars, restaurants and shops catering to visitors, who generally arrive by yacht. A few guesthouses, villas and a primo campground cater to the handful of landlubbers who make their way here by ferry from St John or Tortola. So far, the green hills of this island remain undisturbed by the development that has beset many of the other Virgins. But if you talk to Foxy, he'll tell you 'da times dey are a changin.' Just a few years ago, Jost only had two telephones; now its businesses have Web sites, and tourists can rent Jeeps to buzz about the island.

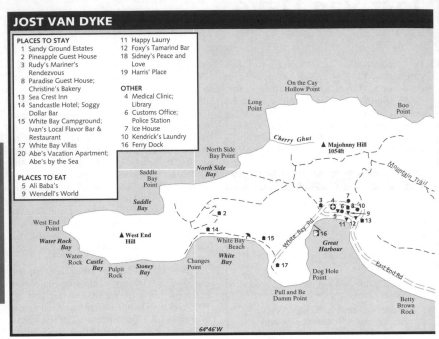

JOST VAN DYKE

PLACES TO STAY
1 Sandy Ground Estates
2 Pineapple Guest House
3 Rudy's Mariner's
    Rendezvous
8 Paradise Guest House;
    Christine's Bakery
13 Sea Crest Inn
14 Sandcastle Hotel; Soggy
    Dollar Bar
15 White Bay Campground;
    Ivan's Local Flavor Bar &
    Restaurant
17 White Bay Villas
20 Abe's Vacation Apartment;
    Abe's by the Sea

PLACES TO EAT
5 Ali Baba's
9 Wendell's World

11 Happy Laurry
12 Foxy's Tamarind Bar
18 Sidney's Peace and
    Love
19 Harris' Place

OTHER
4 Medical Clinic;
    Library
6 Customs Office;
    Police Station
7 Ice House
10 Kendrick's Laundry
16 Ferry Dock

On the Cay Hollow Point
Long Point
Boo Point
Cherry Ghut
▲ Majohnny Hill 1054ft
Mountain Trail
North Side Bay Point
North Side Bay
Saddle Bay Point
Saddle Bay
West End Point
Water Rock Bay
▲ West End Hill
Water Rock
Castle Bay
Pulpit Rock
Stoney Bay
Changes Point
White Bay Beach
White Bay
■ 2
■ 14
▲ ■ 15
White Bay Rd
3 4 7
6 8 10
5 9
11 12 13
□ 16
Great Harbour
East End Rd
■ 17
Dog Hole Point
Pull and Be Damm Point
Betty Brown Rock

64°46'W

Orientation

Ferries to Jost Van Dyke land at the stone pier in Great Harbour, which lies midway along the south shore of the island. Great Harbour is the island's main settlement; you'll find the customs office, police station, school, church and most of the shops and restaurant/bars here.

The island's main road runs along the south shore. If you follow it over the hill to the west for about a mile, you reach White Bay, the campground and the Sandcastle Hotel. If you go east for about 2 miles, you reach a small settlement and restaurant/bars at Little Harbour. If you follow the road farther northeast, you reach Diamond Cay National Park and a number of secluded snorkeling sites.

You really don't need a map to navigate Jost Van Dyke, but the fold-out color map you get in every packet of tourist information from the BVI Tourist Board should be sufficient.

Information

Travelers will find brochures and postings of the island events at the customs office (☎ 284-494-3450), next to the police station on the waterfront at Great Harbour. Customs is open 8:30 am to 3:30 pm weekdays and 9 am to 12:30 pm Saturday. Sometimes the agent is in her office Saturday and Sunday afternoons.

There are no banks on Jost. If you need cash, you must take a ferry to Sopers Hole at Tortola's West End, where there is a Barclays Bank ATM. You can drop off outgoing mail at the customs office if you already have stamps on your letters.

You will find some used paperbacks for sale at the Ice House on Back St. The small Jost Van Dyke Public Library is on Back St.

Kendrick's Laundry is on Back St behind Foxy's. You pay about 75¢ a pound for drop-off service. Expect to pay $3 to wash and dry.

For medical services, there is a clinic next to the school and library on Back St. The

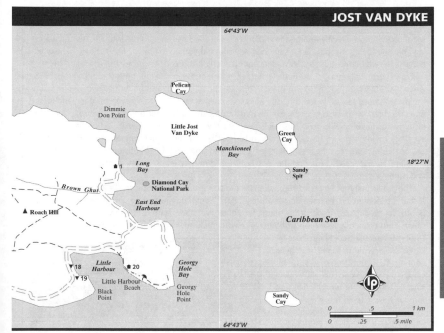

JOST VAN DYKE

doctor comes once a week, usually on Thursday. The nurse stays on the island and lives above the clinic. For police, fire and medical emergencies, call ☎ 999. The police station is beside the customs office on the waterfront.

Jost has quite a collection of hiking trails that lead over the mountains to the rugged north shore and isolated east and west ends. It is easy to get lost on these trails, and in 1999, a tourist died from a heart attack while lost in the bush. Get local knowledge from island hikers and/or hire a local to take you on a guided hike.

Special Events
Foxy's Woodenboat Regatta (☎ 284-495-9258) takes place at the end of May every year on the US Memorial Day weekend. The regatta draws classic wooden yachts from all over the Caribbean for four days of light racing and heavy partying. Currently, Foxy is building a classic island sloop

to race in the regatta and to teach island kids seafaring skills.

New Year's Eve parties on Jost are wildly popular with the yachting crowd. Hundreds of boats show up in the harbors. Party Central is Foxy's Tamarind Bar at Great Harbour, where there is constant live reggae and calypso. The other island beach bars are full of action as well.

Getting There & Away
The easiest way to get to Jost is by ferry from West End on Tortola. It costs about $8 one way, $15 roundtrip. You can also take a ferry from Red Hook, St Thomas, which stops to pick up and drop off at Cruz Bay, St John. Tickets are about $20 one way, $40 roundtrip (see 'Interisland Ferries' in the Getting Around chapter).

Getting Around
Catch Greg Brat's water taxi (☎ 284-495-9401) or travel by land with Ceto's Taxi

One Foxy Fella

Mention you have recently returned from the BVI in a casual conversation at some first-world watering hole and there's a good chance someone will ask, 'Did you go to Foxy's? How's Foxy?' The question will have the tone of a traveler ruminating on a long lost friend. And Foxy has legions of them.

Foxy (born 'Philiciano') Callwood started life as one of seven children on Jost Van Dyke in 1938. Since then, this barefoot man with the dreadlocks, chocolate skin and guitar has become probably the most famous person in the BVI. The keys to Foxy's celebrity are his irreverent, deep and infectious laughter, the persistent twinkle in his eye and the ability to offer up a melody or piece of philosophy to make each person he meets feel worthy. Best of all, the man exudes a disarming euphoria owing more to his guitar than to the bottle of beer he has forgotten on your table. 'I always happy,' you can hear him telling himself and anyone who will listen, as the troubadour wanders around Foxy's Tamarind Bar in a T-shirt and ragged jeans. 'I am so happy my cup is full and running over.'

The public first met Foxy in 1968, when his mother set up a booth on the beach for a festival at Jost and proclaimed it 'Mama's Booth & Foxy's Bar.' 'Somebody told us to put a little kitchen on da booth, so we did,' says Foxy. 'Den Mama left, and I was stuck with it.' Soon word spread among sailors about this jolly fellow on Jost Van Dyke who could make up a calypso melody in the time it took you to crack a cold beer from his cooler. Sailors and travelers have been coming to listen to Foxy sing his calypso and bask in his glow ever since. Many of the world's rich and famous have passed this way, but remembering actress Liv Ullman's visit really spreads a smile on Foxy's face: 'Dat girl she top 'em all,' he chuckles. 'And I ain't sayin' no more.'

Randy Peffer and Foxy

The first Foxy's Woodenboat Regatta took place in 1974, and as Foxy's reputation spread, he has prospered. He has a boutique selling Foxy memorabilia, a huge two-story restaurant addition tucked behind his open-air bar, and his own private-label rum. Then there is Foxy's Lager, brewed and bottled in St Croix. He authorized the use of his name on the product under an agreement stating, according to him, 'Dat if I think it tastes like s, h, i…, dey takin' my name off of dere.' Every day, Foxy executes the taste test, and so far he claims the lager is ambrosia.

'I ain't no friggin' businessman,' claims Foxy. 'I'm an entertainer, a people person.' And lots of islanders agree. Over the years, they have seen Foxy pass the hat and make large donations for funds to build a high school on the island and for building an island sloop to teach local kids about their heritage. He will tell anyone who will listen, 'Don't put all these hillsides in condos; educate our young people to grow mangos up dere or build and sail boats. Don't teach dem to become welfare paupers; we never been paupers here.' Then he adds a calypso rhyme that sums up his attitude: 'Good, better, best; never let it rest until the good is better, and the better is best!'

And how did Foxy get his crafty nickname? He isn't saying. But one island woman has this to say: 'What would you call a fella dat done gone out with two sisters at da same time, and dem not even carin'?'

Service (☎ 284-499-6585). If you are feeling rich, rent a vehicle from Paradise Jeep Rental (☎ 284-495-9477) in Great Harbour for about $45 a day.

GREAT HARBOUR

The main settlement of Jost Van Dyke stretches about 400 yards along the beach and extends about 100 yards back to the foot of the mountains. Kick off your shoes and stroll through a place that seems to be waking up after 100 years of sleep. Then hit the restaurants and bars.

Great Harbour Beach

The broad beach borders the main road and the island's primary settlement. While perfectly adequate for sunbathing and close to many of the island's manmade attractions, this beach isn't good for swimming (shallow water, turtle grass and isolated patches of dead coral).

Activities

Island innkeepers can make arrangements with water-sports vendors on Tortola to meet your diving, sailing and boating needs.

Ceto of Ceto's Taxi Service (☎ 284-499-6585) is also a skilled bonefishing guide. Expect to pay about $250 for a half-day.

Places to Stay

The offerings on Jost Van Dyke are likely to explode, as a number of islanders are in the midst of planning or building guesthouses. Check a current copy of the BVI Welcome guide online (www.bviwelcome.com) for an up-to-date list of places to stay before planning your trip to Jost. Below is my list of the tried and true.

Travelers frequently have difficulty making reservations for a stay on the island because they rely on the mail to receive brochures, exchange money and transfer confirmations. Forget the mail. Written messages going to/from Jost can take months. Phone calls, email (although addresses are in constant flux) and credit card transfers are the only way to nail down your accommodations. Some backpackers just show up and hope they will find a campsite or room.

This is a reasonable practice May through December, but you could easily be disappointed during the winter.

Rudy's Mariner's Rendezvous (☎ 284-495-9382) is a bar, restaurant and convenience store rolled into one at the west end of the beach. Rudy George now has five units, some overlooking the harbor. Each room has a kitchen and private bath. Expect to pay about $80 to $125 a night.

The *Paradise Guest House (☎ 284-495-9281)*, on the 2nd floor above Christine's Bakery, has several basic rooms with a shared porch, air-con and private bath. Rates run about $85 in winter.

Sea Crest Inn (☎ 284-495-9024) is on the waterfront just east of Foxy's. The gracious Ivy Chinnery Moses has four large studio apartments, each with a kitchenette, air-con, TV, queen-size bed, private bath and balcony. Rates run $130 and up in winter.

Places to Eat & Drink

Since most of Jost's businesses cater to the crews off visiting yachts, almost all of the restaurants and bars stand by on VHF radio channel 16 to take lunch and dinner reservations and announce nightly events.

Christine's Bakery (☎ 284-495-9281), just inland from the customs office in Great Harbour, is the kind of out-island bakery you dream about. Christine does not start baking when the roosters wake up, but she's got the settlement filled with the scents of banana bread, coconut and coffee by 8 am, which is just about as early as anyone starts to move around here. Coffee runs $1; an egg sandwich costs $2.50. Muffins and coconut bread cost $1.50. You can fill yourself for the day on the pancakes, eggs, bacon and coffee breakfast ($7). Come early if you want a loaf of fresh bread; Christine is usually sold out by 9:30 am.

Wendell's World is another low-cost eatery. You'll recognize this place as the yellow-and-orange shack on the beach at Great Harbour. Ice cream – a rare luxury in the out islands – runs about $2.50 a scoop.

Happy Laurry (☎ 284-495-9259) is a green shack on the beach. Shirley serves sandwiches, burgers and honey-dipped chicken. One of the best deals is her peas, rice and beans for under $6. The beer here is the cheapest on the island ($2.50).

Rudy's Mariner's Rendezvous (see Places to Stay) specializes in lobster and local fish. You can sit on the patio and enjoy stewed conch for about $16.

Ali Baba's (☎ 284-495-9280), near Rudy's, has a lazy, down-island atmosphere on its open-air patio. The Monday night pig roast costs $20.

Foxy's Tamarind Bar (☎ 284-495-9258), at the east end of the beach, is the place of legends. The yachting crowd has been pausing here for almost four decades and raising hell on the beach. Local bands play several nights a week in season and draw a mix of islanders and party animals off the boats. The light fare is a mix of rotis ($12) and burgers (about $8). I like the veggie roll-up for $6 and the veggie lasagna for $14. Expect to pay over $25 for most dinner entrees, and make reservations by 5 pm. If you want to hear Foxy sing his highly improvisational calypso, he does a set or two Monday to Saturday at 10 am and 6 pm.

Shopping
The Ice House across Back St from Christine's Bakery has two charming proprietors, Daisy and Joyce Chinnery. Ask Joyce for her fresh mangos and mango chutney ($3.50). Foxy now has a shop attached to his restaurant that sells all manner of Foxy souvenirs, including T-shirts, hats and shorts. There is even some very pricey jewelry, some crafted from allegedly authentic Spanish doubloons.

AROUND GREAT HARBOUR
Beyond Great Harbour, Jost remains largely steep mountains and bold, undeveloped coast except for the campground, bars and inn at White Bay and the harborside restaurants at Little Harbour.

White Bay
This is by far Jost's most attractive strand of beach. The long, white beach near the southwest end of the island lies pressed to the sea by steep hills. A barrier reef shelters the water from swells and waves, which makes for good swimming and a protected anchorage. White Bay has a popular camping area, a couple of entertaining beach bars, a small hotel and restaurant. All of the above are attractive to sailors and the backpacking set.

Little Harbour
The east side of Little Harbour has a thin, steep strand of white sand that is agreeable for sunbathing and swimming in water totally protected from wind and waves.

The three nearby beach bars and restaurants make this a popular stop for yachts that descend on the harbor, especially on weekends.

Diamond Cay National Park
Travelers who follow the road all the way to the east end of Jost will see a tiny offshore island at the southern end of Long Bay. This is the 1¼-acre Diamond Cay National Park. Pelicans, boobies and terns nest here. There is good snorkeling on the coral heads in shallow Long Bay as well as along the south side of Little Jost Van Dyke. Be *very*

John Lettsome

Dr John Coakley Lettsome was a Quaker born on Jost Van Dyke in the 18th century. After freeing his slaves, Lettsome went on to found the London Medical Society in England and the Royal Humane Society for the protection of animals. He also was a strong voice in scientific circles for vaccination as a means to prevent the spread of disease. Lettsome is best remembered today for the comic-irony of his doggerel:

> I, John Lettsome
> blisters, bleeds and sweats 'em.
> If, after that, they please to die,
> I, John Lettsome.

careful of the boats and dinghies moving through the anchorages here.

Sandy Cay & Green Cay

If you have a boat or kayak, you might want to check out the small Sandy Cay off the southeast coast of Jost. It is the quintessential desert island, with a broad apron of sand on the west side and good snorkeling on the fringe reef both north and south of the island. There are also some short hiking trails. The island is a favorite picnic stop for yachts, so you probably won't have the place to yourself.

Even smaller is Green Cay, an islet off the east end of Little Jost, featuring adjacent Sandy Spit with its lone coconut palm rising above the beach. This is a terrific place to stop for lunch or a swim if you are kayaking in the vicinity of Little Jost Van Dyke.

Places to Stay

On the east end of the bay of the same name, *White Bay Campground* (☎ 284-495-9312) is the creation of Ivan Chinnery. He has a mix of bare sites and platform tents in the shade of palms and sea grape trees on the fringe of the beach. This campground is one of the most popular stops for young backpackers in the Virgin Islands. It also has a small beach pub (see Places to Eat & Drink). Expect to pay at least $25 for a bare site, $40 for 8x10-foot tents (two persons), but these rates may dip as low as $15 out of season. There are also a couple of basic cabins that run $50 to $60 a night. Showers and toilets are on the property.

Abe's Vacation Apartment (☎ 284-495-9329), on the west side of Little Harbour, has three bedrooms, a full kitchen, dining room, fans and TV/VCR on the 1st floor. This apartment is behind Abe's restaurant (see Places to Eat & Drink). You can rent single rooms in this apartment for $85; the whole place will run you $150 a night in season.

Pineapple Guest House (☎ 284-495-9401), on the hill rising above the west end of White Bay, belongs to Greg Bratt (who runs the water taxi). This place is still

coming together; expect to pay around $85 for a new room with a private bath, fan and sea view.

The *Sandcastle Hotel* (☎ 284-495-9888), at the west end of White Bay, is a gem. Owners Debby Pearse and Bruce Donath moved to Jost Van Dyke from Concord, Massachusetts, and offer their guests a choice of four beachside and garden cottages or two new garden rooms, all set within 70 feet of the shore. There are no phones or televisions in any of the guestrooms. A restaurant and the infamous Soggy Dollar Bar are on the premises. Winter rates run $170 to $220 per night.

For *rental accommodations*, Sandy Ground Estates (☎ 294-494-3391), on the hillside at the east end of the island, has eight luxury villas with a private beach overlooking Little Jost Van Dyke. There is a small shop on the premises, and good snorkeling and hiking right out your front door. High-season rates run $1650 a week for two people. White Bay Villas (☎ 410-626-7722), on the hill at the east end of White Bay, has three large villas with all the amenities. Expect to pay $1650 to $3600 a week

Places to Eat & Drink

Ivan's Local Flavor Bar & Restaurant at White Bay Campground (see above) is an excellent place for young travelers to network. The Thursday night cookouts (about $14) draw a crowd, but you can get sandwiches here for under $5. Beers cost $3 at the honor-system bar.

Abe's by the Sea (☎ 284-495-9329), on the east side of Little Harbour, offers a full breakfast with ham, two eggs, homemade bread, juice and coffee for $6. The pig roast on Wednesday night during the winter is the big event ($20) and often features live fungi music.

Harris' Place (☎ 284-495-9302), in Little Harbour, also offers a full breakfast ($8.50). Amiable Cynthia Jones now runs this harborside pavilion. The best bargains are at lunch, when a burger runs under $4. There is a Monday night lobster feast for $40. Most dinner entrees run around $20.

Sidney's Peace and Love (☎ *284-495-9271*), on the water at Little Harbour, cooks up a burger and fries for $8. Lobster for lunch runs $25, about $10 less than you pay at dinner. Pumpkin soup is the best value on the menu for $5. The Monday night pig roast ($15) is very popular. Sunday, Tuesday and Thursday nights feature a ribs/chicken/pig BBQ for about $20. There is live reggae and music here for dancing every night except Wednesday and Friday. Saturday night rocks with crews off the charter yachts in attendance. T-shirts left behind by visiting revelers decorate the rafters. Beers and drinks cost $2 at happy hour. A popular T-shirt for sale here proclaims 'Time flies when you ain't doin' shit.'

The ***Soggy Dollar Bar*** (☎ *284-495-9888*), at the Sandcastle Hotel, takes its name from the sailors who swim ashore from their yachts to spend wet bills for a 'cold pop.' The restaurant offers a fixed-price gourmet candlelit dinner for about $32 per person. Ruben Chinnery sings calypso on most Sunday afternoons, when lots of yachts stop by for lunch.

Yachts swarm in the Great Harbour at Jost Van Dyke.

Though often full of tourists, the Baths at Virgin Gorda are great for snorkeling.

Marina Cay is a private 6-acre islet, housing Pusser's Marina Cay Resort.

Roseate flamingos have been reintroduced to Guana Island.

Endangered red-legged tortoises, Tortola

Colorful fairy basslet

Graysby, the great camouflager

Fileclam off Peter Island

Pillar coral and blue chromis, off Northwest Tobago Point

Anegada

Sometimes referred to as the 'Mysterious Virgin' or 'Ghost Cay' because of its remote location and killer reef, Anegada takes its name from the Spanish word for 'drowned' or 'flooded.' But whatever you call the easternmost Virgin Island, it's the place to come to for shipwrecks, sharks, lonesome beaches and creatures that go bump in the night.

Lying about 20 miles to the northeast of Tortola and 12 miles from Virgin Gorda, Anegada does not look like the tall, steep

---

Highlights

- Snorkeling at Loblolly Bay
- Camping at Mac's Place
- Spotting endangered iguanas on the north shore
- Kayaking the south shore amid wading birds, fish & sea turtles
- Joining the evening BBQ party at the Anegada Reef Hotel

and verdant islands travelers associate with the Virgins. The Mysterious Virgin is a coral atoll stretching about 12 miles from west to east and at most 3 miles from north to south. The island is so low (at its highest, 28 feet above sea level) that mariners often cannot see it to get their bearings until they are trapped in a maze of coral reef that extends miles off the shore. Since the early days of colonization, Anegada's Horseshoe Reef has snared more than 300 ships. Some of these wrecks are legendary, such as that of the HMS *Astrea,* a 32-gun British frigate, and the *Paramatta,* an English steamship.

Taíno and Caribs used the island for conch fishing and feasting. No doubt the Indians stopped here on their interisland travels to replenish water supplies – Anegada has a series of deep natural wells, or 'shelf holes,' that bubble up freshwater and seem to rise and fall with the tides of the neighboring salt water. Some early settlers tried to establish cotton plantations on the island, but the crops failed in its arid, windswept weather and its soil, which is a mix of clay, limestone, sand and plant fiber.

In the 17th century, the island became the legendary haunt of pirates, including Billy Bones and Normand. The reclusive settlers who followed in their wake subsisted on fishing, vegetable plots and salvaging the wrecks on the reef. A writer for the Royal Geographic Society described the scene this way after visiting the island in the early 1830s:

> The great object, however, always was and still is the wreck of vessels, and the indolence of the inhabitants is only thoroughly roused by the cry of *vessel on the reef.* Scarcely is the news announced than boats of every description, shallops and sailing vessels, are pushing off with all haste toward the scene of the action.

Today, about 170 people live on Anegada. Some are the descendants of the pirates and wreckers; a few are descendants of Portuguese immigrants who came here three

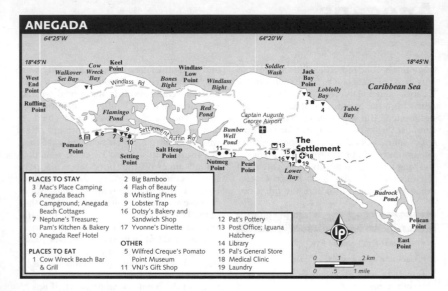

ANEGADA

PLACES TO STAY
3 Mac's Place Camping
6 Anegada Beach
   Campground; Anegada
   Beach Cottages
7 Neptune's Treasure;
   Pam's Kitchen & Bakery
10 Anegada Reef Hotel

PLACES TO EAT
1 Cow Wreck Beach Bar
   & Grill

2 Big Bamboo
4 Flash of Beauty
8 Whistling Pines
9 Lobster Trap
16 Dotsy's Bakery and
   Sandwich Shop
17 Yvonne's Dinette

OTHER
5 Wilfred Creque's Pomato
   Point Museum
11 VNJ's Gift Shop

12 Pat's Pottery
13 Post Office; Iguana
   Hatchery
14 Library
15 Pal's General Store
18 Medical Clinic
19 Laundry

generations ago. Many of the adults survive on lobster and conch fishing. While Anegadians are clannish, they are just as welcoming as folks from other corners of the BVI.

During the 1960s, a real-estate developer named Kenneth Bates seemed to have worked a sweetheart deal with the BVI government for building a marina and hotel complex at the west end of the island. He succeeded in constructing an airport, part of a hotel and maintenance buildings before the islanders drove him off. What Bates could not accomplish in the way of stirring up tourism for the island, local Lowell Wheatley did, building the low-key Anegada Reef Hotel at Setting Point in the 1970s.

Visitors began returning with stories of a wild island. They spoke of salt ponds rife with wading birds, wild orchids, century plants, blooming cacti and epiphytes. They talked about reclusive rock iguanas that could weigh up to 70 pounds and a population of more than 2000 wild goats and hundreds of stray cows roaming the island. Divers claimed they never saw so many sharks and large fish in one place. The BVI government responded by declaring much

of the island a wilderness sanctuary, fostering a project for the reintroduction of flamingos to the salt ponds and building a nursery to protect some young rock iguanas from predators.

Growing outside interest has led islanders to develop a small clutch of restaurants, beach bars and guesthouses. Still, going to Anegada is an adventure, not a vacation. The island is just the kind of place that appeals to backpackers, hikers and fishers. Anegadians have built several primitive and inexpensive campgrounds on wilderness beaches.

Orientation

Shaped like a long sliver of mango stretched west to east, Anegada constitutes about 15 sq miles of extremely flat land covered with scrub brush. The island's horizon holds very few visual landmarks except for a few clumps of casurina and coconut trees. Anegada's main road starts at the airport in the center of the island and swings by the Settlement, where most islanders live. The road heads west to most of the popular restaurant/bars, the yacht anchorage at Setting Point and a number of nice beaches, the best of which run along the north coast from Cow Wreck Bay to Loblolly Bay. Trails and Jeep tracks lead to the East End and interior of the island. If you plan to explore these areas, it's a good idea to let someone know where you are headed. Make sure to take plenty of water and possibly a handheld VHF radio for emergencies.

The best maps of Anegada are the map in this book and the map in the flyer distributed by the Fly BVI air-taxi service (☎ 284-495-1747). The flyer is available at the Beef Island International Airport, tourist offices and some hotels and guesthouses on Tortola and Anegada.

Information

The best source of local knowledge on the island is probably Romalia Smith, who staffs the desk at the airport when a flight is due in or out. She also drives a van for her husband's business, Toni's Taxi (☎ 284-495-8027). Sue and Lowell Wheatley, the proprietors of the Anegada Reef Hotel, are also good sources of information.

Keep in mind that there are no banks on Anegada, and some businesses do not accept credit cards. Plan accordingly.

The post office is part of the police office (☎ 284-495-8057) in the government administration building at the west end of the Settlement. The building is open 8 am to 4 pm weekdays and 9 am to 1:30 pm Saturday.

In recent years, many businesses and some residences have gotten telephones and email on Anegada. However, many islanders still use VHF marine radios in their houses and cars as their primary means of communication.

You can choose from a small assortment of newspapers, magazines and paperback books at Pal's General Store in the Settlement. The library is next to the power station just west of the Settlement.

Anegada has no local paper. Citizens generally post notices and advertisements on utility poles along the road.

Romalia Smith runs the laundry (☎ 284-495-8049, or 'Osprey' on VHF channel 16). If you do it yourself, you pay $2 to wash and $2 to dry. A drop-off load costs $15.

The island clinic (☎ 284-495-8049) is on the east side of the crossroads in the Settlement. The resident nurse is always on call. She opens the clinic weekdays 9 am to noon and 1 to 4 pm. The doctor comes once a week on Monday or Wednesday morning.

In an emergency, call ☎ 999, or even better, hail the Anegada police or clinic on VHF channel 16.

Anegada has some fierce mosquitoes. 'Gallon Nippers' can appear in swarms thick enough to kill wild goats. Be prepared with strong repellent. Stinging red ants and aggressive wild cattle can also be a problem, especially for trekkers and campers.

Special Events

The Tortola to Anegada Sailboat Regatta (☎ 284-495-8002), also known as the 'Booze Cruise,' takes place in August each year. The race currently draws 80 vessels or more for a beat to windward followed by an enormous beach party at the Anegada Reef Hotel.

Getting There & Away

The Captain Auguste George Airport lies a mile northwest of the Settlement in the center of the island. Fly BVI (☎ 284-435-9284) and Clair Acro (☎ 284-495-2271) both have scheduled flights between Tortola and Anegada on Monday, Wednesday, Friday and Sunday. Roundtrip fares are about $60, $40 for children. You can also get charter flights to and from Anegada with these air-taxi services.

The Bitter End Yacht Club (☎ 284-494-2746) usually runs a weekly day trip to Anegada from Virgin Gorda (about $60). You can book a one-day excursion from Tortola to Anegada with Speedy's (☎ 284-495-5240) for about $110. There is no regularly scheduled ferry service to Anegada.

Getting Around

If you're renting a car, expect to pay about $70 for a pickup-jitney that carries 12 people at the Anegada Reef Hotel (see Places to Stay). You will pay around $40 for a Suzuki Samurai at DW Jeep Rentals (☎ 284-495-9677) in the Settlement.

Tony's Taxi (☎ 284-495-8037, or 'Silver Bird' on VHF channel 16) waits for your inbound flight, and Tony will give you a three-hour tour of the whole island for about $45. He will run you across the island to the beach or Mac's Place Camping for about $4. In addition, shuttle jitneys run to the beaches from the Anegada Reef Hotel for $6 roundtrip.

Renting (or bringing) a bicycle is definitely the way to get around Anegada if you plan to stay for some time and you feel like you have the stamina to ride on rough, dusty roads in the hot sun. The place for trail-bike rentals is the Anegada Reef Hotel (see Places to Stay).

THE SETTLEMENT
This collection of houses and small businesses stands on the hardscrabble soil of a nearly treeless section of the island. The community centers on a crossroads and a neighboring boat jetty near the southeast corner of the island. This is a West Indian village with all the hallmarks of out-island existence. The Settlement is a picture of dead cars (you can get them on the island, but you can't get them off), hurricane-damaged structures, laundry drying in the breeze and folks singing to themselves as they feed the goats and chickens.

Iguana Hatchery
The BVI National Parks Trust is trying to protect some of the endangered juvenile rock iguanas from predators. You'll see the six cages of young lizards just to the left of the Government Complex west of the Settlement. Rondel Smith, the caretaker, has spent years helping scientists radio-tag and track the rock iguanas in the wild. He is a great source of information about the species, its favorite haunts and its chances for survival on the island.

Places to Eat
Anegada pitches most of its restaurants to tourists off visiting yachts, leaving a lack of 'down-home' eateries where travelers can find islanders enjoying local cooking at moderate prices. There are, however, a few places to help you manage your food budget and escape the tide of tourists.

Dotsy's Bakery and Sandwich Shop (☎ 284-495-9667), in the Settlement, features fresh-baked breads and desserts. Breakfasts, local fish and chips, chicken, burgers and pizza attract a local following. Lunch prices are in the $6 range.

Yvonne's Dinette (☎ 284-495-8027), in the Settlement on the road to the jetty, is a neat West Indian house with five pink tables. For totally 'old school' local recipes, do not miss the trigger fish, doctor fish or grunt served with ground provisions (vegetables, plantains and sweet potato).

Shopping
Pat's Pottery (☎ 284-495-8031), at Nutmeg Point, has one-of-a-kind hand-painted platters, pitchers, mugs and bowls for sale. She also carries island-made dolls and Christmas ornaments.

VNJ's Gift Shop (☎ 284-495-9734) is another small crafter's outpost west of the Settlement. Vera specializes in hand-painted ceramics.

You can purchase homemade chutneys, jellies, preserves and papaya hot sauce at Pam's Kitchen & Bakery (see Places to Eat & Drink, later).

AROUND THE SETTLEMENT
Many of Anegada's attractions appealing to travelers – beaches, nature preserves, waterfront restaurants and accommodations – lie beyond the Settlement on the island's fringe.

Flamingo Pond
The large salt pond at the west end of the island hosts a flock of flamingos. These birds were once plentiful on Anegada and other cays in the BVI, but the flamingos were exterminated by hunters seeking their tender meat and feathers. In 1987, biologists reintroduced flamingos to the BVI. The scientists flew in birds from the Bermuda Aquarium and Natural History Museum and Zoo and set them in an appropriate habitat on Guana Island. The colony did not succeed, but in 1992 the biologists flew in 20 more birds from Bermuda. Some went to

Facing Extinction

The Anegada rock iguana, *Cyclura pinguis*, is a highly endangered species. A relatively large and stout member of its genus (males have been recorded at up to 6 feet in length and may grow to weigh 70lb), these iguanas are recognizable by dusty brown backs, which can be vertically barred with black chevrons. Females lay 12 to 16 eggs between May and June, and hatchlings can mature to reproductive size in three to four years. Once encompassing the Virgin Islands and Puerto Rico, the rock iguana's range has been cut down to Anegada, owing to development in these regions over the last century. Recent events have further threatened the rock iguana's existence.

In an 1885 ordinance pertaining to Anegada, the British Crown agreed to grant land to islanders with the proviso that landowners have their property boundaries surveyed. Not one Anegadian did so. However, they maintained their claim to the land, erecting stone walls that fenced off crops and livestock and delineated ownership boundaries. In 1961, under new legislation, the Crown assumed administration of most of the island and, along with the government of the BVI, leased all but 607 hectares to a Canadian development firm in 1968.

Before Anegadians' resentment and slim prospects for profit drove the Development Corporation of Anegada Ltd to abandon the island shortly after its arrival, the corporation's bulldozers had knocked massive holes in Anegada's network of stone walls. Goats, sheep, cattle, burros and swine began to range the cay freely. Anegada could no longer serve as a safe refuge for iguanas, as the feral livestock stripped the landscape of all palatable vegetation.

During the 1980s and early 1990s, the biologists Dr Skip Lazell and Dr Numi Mitchell worked with the BVI government to restore iguanas both on Anegada and to parts of their former range in the BVI. Eight iguanas from Anegada were relocated to Guana Island, and their descendants are thriving and reproducing; some of the offspring have been relocated to Necker Island as well. In 1993, the government of the BVI approved the establishment of an Anegada National Park in principle. But when the proposal for an Anegada National Park was released to the public, Anegadians grew enraged at the plan, which would claim disputed land for the government. Local anger still smolders, and consensus on ownership and property boundaries remains elusive. As a result, the National Park proposal has been tabled.

Some biologists feel that without the protection of a national park, the rock iguanas on Anegada may be extirpated within the next decade.

Guana, but most went to Anegada. In 1995, the Anegada colony had its first hatchlings, and by 2001 the flock had grown to more than 50. Now, biologists are hoping the flock will attract migrating birds to increase the gene pool.

You can see the birds wading on the far north side of what is now called Flamingo Pond, near the west end of the island. Please keep your distance: Flamingos require hundreds of feet of buffer between them and apparent threats such as humans. The BVI

National Parks Trust has now designated Flamingo Pond and its surrounding wetlands as a bird sanctuary, and you can see egrets, terns and ospreys nesting and feeding in the area.

Wilfred Creque's Pomato Point Museum

One islander, Wilfred Creque (pronounced CREEK-ee; ☎ 284-495-9466), has been collecting archaeological relics from Anegada and its reefs since the 1960s. This tiny museum is actually a separate room at the Pomato Point Restaurant, but the contents are intriguing. You can see doubloons and foreign money salvaged from wreck sites as well as cannons, gin bottles, musket balls, ship timbers, crockery from steamship lines and Taíno artifacts. The museum is usually open in the evening, when dinner guests can view the collection.

Beaches

At least two-thirds of Anegada's shoreline is beach. Nevertheless, some sections stand out. Open-air taxis run to the most popular beaches from the Anegada Reef Hotel and airport (see Getting Around, earlier).

Loblolly Bay lies on the northeast shore about 2 miles from the Settlement. The beach has two bars, the popular Mac's Place Camping, sun shelters and good snorkeling on the offshore reef.

Cow Wreck Bay stretches along the northwest end of the island and features good snorkeling and a popular bar named after the bay and beach.

Activities

For **diving**, stop at the Big Bamboo restaurant (see Places to Eat & Drink, later) and talk to owner Aubrey Levons about his north-shore dive service. He offers a 'shark tour' for about $50.

There is good **bonefishing** year-round on the flats around Setting Point and Salt Heap Point on the south shore. Captains Garfield and Kevin Faulkner are respected local guides. Rates start at about $200.

Lowell Wheatley at the Anegada Reef Hotel runs deep-sea charters on *Basic Lady*,

a 46-foot Hatteras sportfisherman. You can also fish with Captain Tim Jones and his first mate, Sue, on the *Whopper*. Rates run about $450 for a half-day.

You can fish for tarpon from the dock of the Anegada Reef Hotel, where you should inquire about exact rates and make arrangements for fishing guides. The hotel also sponsors a sportfishing tournament at the end of May, on the US Memorial Day weekend. The main targets are blue marlin, white marlin and wahoo.

For those interested in **kayaking**, sea kayaks (single and double) are for hire at the Anegada Reef Hotel. The rates are $35 per day for a single, $45 per day for a double. You get better rates for longer periods.

Bicycling is one way to get around the island. You can rent trail bikes at the Anegada Reef Hotel for about $18 a day.

Places to Stay

Anegada Beach Campground (☎ 284-495-9466), at Pomato Point near Pam's Kitchen & Bakery, has about 10 sites. Expect to pay at least $7 for a bare site, $26 to $36 for an 8x10-foot tent.

Mac's Place Camping (☎ 284-495-8020), at Loblolly Bay, is without question the premier camping experience on Anegada. The setting is in a shady grove of sea grape trees just above the beach line, where the landscape opens to the cooling trade winds. Expect to pay $15 for prepared bare sites, $35 or more for an 8x10-foot tent. Showers, toilets and grills are available. You also get a lookout tower, kitchen pavilion and an honor bar, where beers cost $3, sodas $1.50. The location is just a few steps from two beach restaurants.

Neptune's Treasure (☎ 284-495-9439), on the beach near Setting Point, is a restaurant, guesthouse and marina rolled into one. There are about six simple guestrooms with private baths. In season, a double will run you about $100 a night ($110 with air-con).

Anegada Beach Cottages (☎ 916-683-3352), at Pomato Point, are concrete beach bungalows on stilts. They each have one bedroom and all the amenities. You can expect to pay $140 and up during the winter. The Pomato Point Restaurant and Wilfred Creque's Pomato Point Museum are on the property.

Anegada Reef Hotel (☎ *284-495-8002*), at Setting Point, is the largest and best-known hostelry on the island. This seaside place has the feel of a classic out-island fishing camp you might find in a Hemingway novel. Islander Lowell Wheatley and his English wife, Sue (and their pet billy goat Charlie), welcome guests to 16 air-conditioned rooms or two-bedroom villas, many with a sea view. The hotel overlooks the island's yacht anchorage, and the fishing dock, restaurant and beach bar (see below) constitute the social epicenter of the island. Winter rates run about $180 to $270.

Places to Eat & Drink

Next to Neptune's Treasure at Pomato Point, ***Pam's Kitchen & Bakery*** (☎ *284-495-9237*) is a terrific breakfast stop. Try the cinnamon rolls ($2), and pick up a loaf of French bread for lunch ($3). Pam's home-made hot sauce ($5) gives quite a jolt to local conch and fish.

Whistling Pines, on the beach west of Setting Point, has a seaside deck with comfortable deck chairs and a killer sound system that features R&B as well as West Indian music. Come for the BBQ conch (about $16), or drink and dance with the boat crews who meander ashore to revel in the starshine.

Next door, the ***Lobster Trap*** (☎ *284-495-9466)* features a garden setting on the main anchorage's waterfront. The restaurant has a dinghy dock for boaters, and the specialty here is BBQ lobster (about $40). Reserve by 4 pm.

Anegada Reef Hotel (see Places to Stay) serves breakfast, lunch (burgers and sandwiches under $5) and dinner. Try the tuna melt ($4.50). Most entrees such as ribs and local fish run about $20 and up; grilled lobster costs $40. A lot of folks cruising in

yachts show up in the anchorage off the dock and make a beach party at the open-air bar while the fish and lobster sizzle on the grill.

Big Bamboo (☎ *284-495-2019*), at the west end of Loblolly Bay on the north shore, is Aubrey Levons' popular beach restaurant/bar. Tony's Taxi and the shuttle jitneys from the Anegada Reef Hotel seem to make an almost constant cycle between the airport, the yacht anchorage and the Big Bamboo. The restaurant specializes in island recipes for lobster, conch, fish and chicken. Most dinner entrees run $20 or more, but you can get sandwiches for under $6. Call ahead for dinner reservations or if you want lobster. Allegedly, quite a few celebrities have passed through here, including Princess Di, Brooke Shields and Andre Agassi. Some of them have left their autographs.

Flash of Beauty (☎ *284-495-8014),* on the east end of the beach at Loblolly Bay, is the Big Bamboo's competition. This is slightly more of a drinks-and-sandwich place than the Big Bamboo, but the menu and prices are similar. The restaurant closes at 6 pm; call ahead for reservations if you want to make certain the staff and provisions are on hand. The snorkeling right in front of the restaurant is excellent.

Cow Wreck Beach Bar & Grill (☎ *284-495-9461),* at Lower Cow Wreck Beach, is a beachside pavilion featuring lobster, conch and shellfish cooked over local wood on the outdoor grill. Rates are equivalent to the other beach bars. Call for reservations.

Neptune's Treasure (see Places to Stay) stands at the center of a compound built by the Soares family, originally Portuguese fisherfolk from the Azores. The menu here is more or less the same as at most of the island's waterfront restaurants, but this place offers an enclosed air-conditioned dining room. Expect to pay $20 for grilled swordfish, $18 for chicken.

Out Islands

With a territory including more than 40 islands, most of which are sparsely inhabited or totally uninhabited, the BVI lures travelers looking for their own private retreat. A few of the BVI 'out islands' (a Creole expression for remote or undeveloped cays), such as Necker Island and Little Thatch, are sanctuaries for the world's rich and famous. But the British Virgin Islands have an island

Highlights

- Snorkeling or diving at the *Rhone* shipwreck, the Indians & the Dogs

- Hiking the trails & beaches of wild Peter Island

- Dining on the terrace at the Cooper Island Club

- Drinking Painkillers & listening to live calypso on Marina Cay

- Partying with dead pirates on Norman Island

to suit every taste. Some you can access by ferry. Most will require you to charter a boat for a day or longer.

There are some islands that turn their back on travelers, but the islands listed in this chapter all welcome visitors.

LITTLE THATCH ISLAND

This private 54-acre island just off Tortola's West End accommodates up to 10 people. *Little Thatch* (☎ 284-495-9227) boasts a hilltop great room and an enormous 21x65-foot freshwater pool. The master bedroom cottage and four additional guest bedroom cottages circle the hilltop. A dock at the other end of the beach offers adventures and water sports; a 24-foot powerboat with your own captain is available for nearby island-hopping, picnics, snorkeling trips, water-skiing and light-tackle fishing. The beach staff maintains sailing dinghies, ocean kayaks, sailboards, body boards, snorkel gear and pool floats. If you'd rather stay on land, there are books, a music collection, board games, bikes, badminton, volleyball and table tennis. The island has email and fax facilities, personal laundry service and a daytime helicopter landing pad. Little Thatch's staff provides for every need, including gourmet dining. The rate per night runs $9200 and up. The management does not welcome casual visitors on boats.

A private launch service runs between Sopers Hole (Tortola) and Little Thatch for island guests. You can also come here by chartered helicopter from San Juan (Puerto Rico), St Thomas or Tortola.

GUANA ISLAND

Lying a mile off Tortola's northeast tip, this undeveloped island of steep green peaks is the seventh-largest island in the BVI. Guana takes its name from a rock formation called the 'Iguana Head' that juts out from a cliff at the northwest corner of the island. Quaker families settled here in the 18th century and cultivated sugar cane on

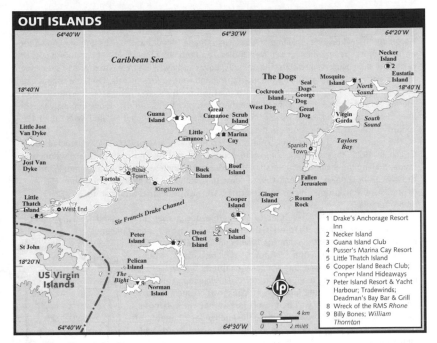

OUT ISLANDS

1 Drake's Anchorage Resort
   Inn
2 Necker Island
3 Guana Island Club
4 Pusser's Marina Cay Resort
5 Little Thatch Island
6 Cooper Island Beach Club;
   Cooper Island Hideaways
7 Peter Island Resort & Yacht
   Harbour; Tradewinds;
   Deadman's Bay Bar & Grill
8 Wreck of the RMS *Rhone*
9 Billy Bones; *William
   Thornton*

Guana's 850 acres. But the island's settlers found themselves at odds with the Quaker community at Fat Hogs Bay on Tortola and perhaps for good reason. The Guana brethren were fond of firing a cannon at other Quakers rowing past the island. Eventually, many of Guana's settlers were 'disowned' by the other Quakers or married out of the faith. The island was abandoned, and the land reverted to local ownership.

In the mid-1930s, Beth and Louis Bigelow bought the island, built a clubhouse called Dominica in a saddle on an island ridge and began inviting intellectuals and world travelers to 'rusticate' on their island. During this time, there was no electricity or hot water, and Guana's population never exceeded about 20 people, including the guests and caretakers. When the Bigelow's generation died out, Dr Henry Jarecki and his wife, Gloria, bought the island in 1975. Both ardent conservationists, the Jareckis saw the opportunity to establish Guana as a private nature preserve just when the Virgin Islands were being 'discovered' and their ecosystem laid waste by developers (see the boxed text 'Almost Eden'). During the last three decades, the Jareckis have added a number of stone cottages along the island ridge for guests who want an extraordinary tropical retreat, with seven pristine beaches, hiking trails, ruins of the sugar plantations and a menagerie of wildlife. Visiting mariners can anchor off the beach at White Bay and enjoy the excellent snorkeling in the bay and along the cliffs that stretch to Monkey Point. Note that Guana does not welcome uninvited visitors.

The **_Guana Island Club_** (☎ 284-494-2354, 800-544-8262) may be the oldest private-island resort in the entire Caribbean. The club accommodates up to 30 guests a day. The individual stone cottages are models of simple elegance. Cottages have no air-con, telephones or TV, but they have windswept private porches and spacious bathrooms.

OUT ISLANDS

Almost Eden

According to field biologist Dr James 'Skip' Lazell, Guana Island 'has the richest fauna known for an island of its size anywhere in the West Indies – and probably the world.' About 100 species of birds (including black-necked stilts, frigate birds, doves and owls) are here. There are 14 species of reptiles and amphibians, including the piping frog and four species of bats. One, the fishing bat, has a wingspan of 2 feet. Flora and insects that live on the island number in the hundreds of species. A large ground spider, generally but inaccurately called 'tarantula,' is one impressive specimen. Flowering trees like the frangipani, royal poinciana and tamarind abound. More than 125 species of fish have been counted in the island's coastal waters.

The exuberance of nature on Guana is no accident. When Henry and Gloria Jarecki bought Guana in 1975, they started a long-term program to restore and protect Guana's flora and fauna, making the island a private nature preserve and wildlife sanctuary. Every summer and fall, the Jareckis host dozens of scientists who come to Guana to document the condition of the island and propose ways to strengthen Guana's terrestrial and marine environments.

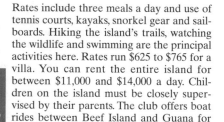

In general, the Jareckis have tried to extirpate exotic species on the island and reintroduce indigenous species that have been lost to indiscriminant hunting. Since the 1980s, scientists have reintroduced the once-native roseate flamingo (there is now a nesting colony), the Anegada rock iguana (see the Anegada chapter), the white-crowned pigeon and the red-legged tortoise. The flamingo colony has been touted in scientific journals as a conservation success story. The iguanas are doing so well that resort guests may see a 4-footer, nicknamed 'Hambone,' show up outside the kitchen for a handout of fruit before he sunbathes on a neighboring rock. Some lizards have all the luck.

Rates include three meals a day and use of tennis courts, kayaks, snorkel gear and sailboards. Hiking the island's trails, watching the wildlife and swimming are the principal activities here. Rates run $625 to $765 for a villa. You can rent the entire island for between $11,000 and $14,000 a day. Children on the island must be closely supervised by their parents. The club offers boat rides between Beef Island and Guana for island guests.

MARINA CAY

Lying just east of Tortola and Beef Island, Marina Cay is the perfect islet resort and has been declared the site of the fantasy Republic of Cuervo (as in the tequila). In 1953, this 6-acre knob poised above an apron of reef was the setting for Rob White's classic tropical memoir *Our Virgin Isle*. The book later became a film titled *Two on an Isle*, with Sidney Poitier and John Cassavetes. The anchorage here on the north side of the cay offers exceptional shelter. It is almost always packed with about 50 yachts, whose crews come ashore for drinks, entertainment and dinner. There is a small beach off the west end and good snorkeling on the shallow reef.

Pusser's Marina Cay Resort (☎ 284-494-2174) has no phones or TVs but rekindles a more genteel era with croquet and badminton. There is a dive shop, water-sports rentals and a sportswear store here. The hotel has four rooms and two villas that surround the great house, which has an intimate and cool library for relaxing. Rates run $175 to $450.

The open-air restaurant on a deck at the beach is very popular with yacht crews as well as travelers coming over for dinner from Tortola. Grilled yellowfin tuna, mahi-mahi and jumbo shrimp all run about $20. You can have them cooked in a choice of sauces from Trinidad, Martinique, Cuba and the Bahamas. Make reservations and come at 5 pm for the half-price Painkillers on the patio bar, which always features live calypso music in the evening.

A free ferry runs from Trellis Bay on Beef Island (see 'Interisland Ferries' in the Getting Around chapter).

THE DOGS

This clutch of six islands lies halfway between Tortola and Virgin Gorda. The Dogs take their name from a now-extinct monk seal known as *lobo marina* (sea wolf). These animals had colonies on the islands before hunters harvested them into oblivion. Today, the islands are protected by the BVI National Parks Trust, and they are sanctuaries for both birds and marine animals. The bridled tern, sooty tern, roseate tern and red-billed tropic bird nest here. Snorkeling around each of the islands is superior. Sometimes the schools of glassy sleepers can be so thick you are enveloped in a cloud of fish. Scuba divers will want to check out Joe's Cave, Flintstones and Wall-to-Wall just off the coast of West Dog.

A dive boat, charterboat or private yacht are the only ways to reach the Dogs. Pick up one of the moorings placed here by the BVI National Parks Trust. Come early in the day.

MOSQUITO ISLAND

This 125-acre island looks like a green gumdrop and guards the entrance to Virgin Gorda's North Sound. Mosquito takes its name from the Miskito Indian tribe who left relics here. This is a private island that remains largely an undeveloped, untended nature sanctuary with several good hiking trails. The south side of the island has a dock and a small, exclusive resort and restaurant.

Transient visitors are only welcome ashore if they have dinner reservations.

Drake's Anchorage Resort Inn (☎ 284-495-7045, 617-969-9913) has been a haven for wealthy yacht crews and rusticators since the early 1970s. Little has changed since I first bumbled in here decades ago. It's a low-key place where guests stay in frame cottages with no TV, radio or phones. But in 2001, the resort added air-con to the suites. The rooms are spacious and feature airy verandas and natural stone showers. The dining room is a small, simple waterside shelter. The cuisine has its roots in West Indian classics like grilled lobster. Expect to pay more than $25 for dinner, and remember that reservations are required (call on VHF channel 16).

Room rates (including meals) run $550 a night. You can rent the whole island for $8000 a day. If you're not traveling by yacht, take a cab to Virgin Gorda's Gun Creek settlement and have the taxi driver call the island on his VHF radio. A boat will meet you for the five-minute trip across North Sound.

NECKER ISLAND

This private island belongs to Richard Branson, famous balloonist and scion of Virgin Atlantic Airways, Virgin Records and Virgin Cola. *Necker Island* (☎ 800-557-4255 in the US, ☎ 44-171-313-6109 in the UK) lies about a mile north of Virgin Gorda and is one of the world's most luxurious retreats. There are 74 acres of private nature trails linking a selection of sandy beaches.

Atop the island's low hill, a magnificent great house, crafted with Balinese architecture, has 10 double bedrooms that open onto private balconies. An unobtrusive staff prepares meals, serves drinks and offers water-skiing and sailing. Spacious studios, each with one double bedroom and full facilities, stand about 500 yards from the great house. Necker Island can accommodate up to 26 guests for $14,000 to $24,000 a day. Hollywood celebrities such as Eddie Murphy come here. Don't even think of visiting unless you have a verifiable invitation.

Guests come by private helicopter (included in the rental) from St Thomas or Tortola.

FALLEN JERUSALEM

A 30-acre island lying half a mile southwest of Virgin Gorda, Fallen Jerusalem is a gem of a national park, overlooked by almost everybody. The island takes its name from its appearance: It is strewn with large boulders like those found at the Baths on Virgin Gorda, but here, the boulders appear to be the tumbled ruins of some ancient city with what look like clearly defined roads and foundations. Pelicans, noddies, boobies, gulls and terns nest here, but they will not disturb you on one of the small beaches. The entire fringe of the island makes for rewarding snorkeling (in calm weather). If you want to escape the almost relentless tourist traffic at the nearby Baths on Virgin Gorda, Fallen Jerusalem is a place to get away from it all.

You must come here on a dive boat, charterboat or private yacht. Pick up one of the moorings on the north side of the island. An ocean swell often stirs up the seas here, so come early when the winds are lighter and the swells are at their lowest.

COOPER ISLAND

Lying about 4 miles south of Tortola, Cooper Island is a moderately hilly cay, shaped something like an hourglass and stretching 1½ miles from north to south, a half-mile at its widest from east to west. The island is virtually undeveloped except for the Cooper Island Beach Club on Manchineel Bay. This bay has a long, narrow beach that is totally sheltered from the easterly trade winds; the shelter and the club's restaurant make this a popular anchorage for cruising yachts. You will find superb snorkeling off Cistern Point, and Underwater Safaris (☎ 284-494-3235, 800-537-7032) has a full-service dive shop here that also rents kayaks, sailboards and sunfish sailboats.

Once a private house, the **Cooper Island Beach Club** (☎ 284-494-3721, 800-524-4624) evolved into a restaurant in the 1970s. Since 1980, Toby Holmes and Steve Pardoe have run the restaurant here and have been building guestrooms. Now, there are 12 rooms, each with a kitchen, balcony and open-air shower. You will find bright fabrics throughout and a sea view outside each room. A double runs about $175 in winter.

The Beach Club is gay-friendly and is a popular destination for gay couples – with plenty of straight guests staying on the island and visiting off the yachts as well. The club offers a friendly bar and casual seaside dining among the palm trees. West Indian and international cuisine is served, with lunch entrees running about $9 for a salad platter. Dinner will cost you about $20 for grilled fish.

Ginny Evans runs **Cooper Island Hideaways** (☎ 513-232-4126), small villas with one or two bedrooms. Rates run about $1200 a week during the winter. The club runs a shuttle boat for guests between Road Town (Tortola) and the island. Other travelers must visit on a private yacht or charterboat.

SALT ISLAND

This T-shaped island, measuring a mile in both directions, lies just a dinghy ride west of Cooper Island. It is a forlorn place. About six West Indians live in the cottages on a narrow strand between the beach and the salt pond on the north shore. The salt-making (which gave the island its name) still goes on here, but watching seawater evaporating from a pond to leave a crust of salt is pretty subtle entertainment.

The big attraction here is the wreck of the RMS *Rhone*. The *Rhone* was the Royal Mail Steamer that crashed against the rocks off Salt Island's southwest coast during a hurricane in 1867. Now a national park, the steamer's remains are extensive and have become an exotic habitat for marine life (see the boxed text 'Wreck of the *Rhone*'). One of the most famous dive sites in all of the Caribbean, the wreck was a principal set in the film *The Deep*. A stone wall to the west of the settlement on Salt Island surrounds the graves of nine of the 124 souls who perished on the *Rhone*.

A lot of people come to the wreck aboard charterboats that either anchor off the beach at Salt Island Bay or pick up one

Wreck of the *Rhone*

On the morning of October 29, 1867, Captain Robert F Wooley of the RMS *Rhone* thought the hurricane season was over as his ship lay alongside another Royal Mail Steamer at Great Harbour on Peter Island. Wooley had planned to load cargo and coal for Britain in the shelter of the harbor at Charlotte Amalie, St Thomas. But an outbreak of cholera on St Thomas forced the *Rhone* and the other steamer, the *Conway,* to avoid the quarantine and get their fuel and cargo at a coaling station on Peter Island.

It was a sun-washed morning without the usual trade winds, and you could hear the calls of terns as they searched for fish in the shallows. The *Rhone* was virtually new. Built two years earlier, it was one of the new class of steamships England had designed and built to run the Federal blockade of the South during the American Civil War. Launched just months too late to run the blockade, the *Rhone* went into the fast packet trade between England and the West Indies. She was a greyhound, a steam-driven, steel ship 310 feet in length and 40 feet abeam. With her propeller churning, she could make 12 knots of speed, and when she spread the canvas on her schooner rig, she could motor-sail even faster. Soon she would be off to England again with 147 passengers.

Around 11 am, the barometer suddenly dropped about 2 inches, the sky grew leaden, and a fierce wind came out of the north. Both ships stoked their boilers and began steaming into the wind to prevent themselves from dragging anchors and blowing ashore on Peter Island. When the wind abated at about noon, the captain of the *Conway* cast off and headed north with hopes of finding shelter in the harbor at Road Town. But as she steamed across the Sir Francis Drake Channel, the *Conway* met harsh winds that carried away her masts and smokestack before driving her ashore on Tortola.

There are conflicting stories about what happened next aboard the *Rhone*. One chronicler claims the *Rhone* was trying to get her anchor up and head for deeper water when the cable parted, leaving the anchor and chain on the bottom of Great Harbour and the ship adrift. Another version of the story maintains that Captain Wooley cast off his anchor cable when he discovered his ship was dragging toward the shore. Whatever the case, the *Rhone* labored into deeper water. She cleared Deadman's Bay, then Blonde Rock, and turned southeast, hoping to put to sea and weather the storm or find a lee on the south side of Cooper Island or Virgin Gorda. According to legend, the crew lashed hysterical passengers in their berths.

But the storm was not the norther that Wooley imagined; it was a hurricane with winds that backed swiftly to the west and southwest just as the *Rhone* struggled to pass Salt Island. The ship was too close to the island, and the waves and southwest wind drove her ashore near the southern tip of Lee Bay. Seawater burst in and hit the hot boiler. Instantly, the boiler exploded, and the ship broke in half and sank. Only 23 of the 147 people survived by washing ashore on Salt Island.

The stern with its propeller now lies in 20 to 40 feet of water. The forward half of the ship lies nearby and intact under about 80 feet of water. Three years after the wreck, hard-hat divers salvaged copper, cotton, liquor, and $20,000 worth of money and gold as well as the skull of a large man from the wreck. Scuba divers were picking the wreck clean until the BVI National Parks Trust moved in to preserve the wreck in the 1970s.

of the moorings placed by the BVI National Parks Trust at Lee Bay near the wreck. Almost every dive shop in the Virgin Islands offers trips to the wreck of the *Rhone*. They generally cost $55 and up.

DEAD CHEST ISLAND

Just half a mile north of Peter Island, this island looks like a giant vermilion mushroom covering 30 acres of land. Reputedly the place where the pirate Blackbeard left

15 men with a saber and a bottle of rum to fight out their differences, this uninhabited island and its legend are the prototype for TV's survival shows and the setting that spawned the doggerel ending in 'yo ho ho and a bottle of rum.'

Today, the island is a national park and bird sanctuary for noddies, boobies, gulls and terns. There is good diving at Dead Chest West and Painted Walls, where sponges and cup corals light up the sides of canyons with brilliant yellow, crimson, red, blue, white and orange.

As with a lot of the national park islands, you must come here on a dive boat, charter-boat or private yacht and pick up one of the moorings. An ocean swell generally makes mooring here a rough ride.

PETER ISLAND

This lofty L-shaped island about 4 miles south of Road Town is the fifth largest of the BVI with 1800 acres. In the late 17th century, a group of slave traders from Brandenburg, Germany, first settled Peter Island after plans to build a plantation on St Thomas failed. Although the sugar cane plantation boom of the 18th century passed over Peter Island because of its unsuitable soil, several Tortolian planters with slaves successfully introduced cotton here. Soon after the first harvest, the plantations expanded and required more slaves. But the decline of the plantation system, compounded with the abolition of the slave trade, brought about the complete decline of Peter Island, which soon returned to its natural state.

In 1855, manufacturers set up a coaling station for the steam packets at Peter Island's Great Harbour. Settlers introduced a few small tobacco plantations in the early 1920s, which survived until retired British diplomat John Brudenell-Bruce established a large home on the island a decade later. In the late '60s, Norwegian millionaire Peter Smedvig fell in love with Peter Island and purchased most of the land. He shipped a set of luxury A-frame chalets to the island from Norway, and assembled them on Sprat Bay along with a clubhouse and marina that became the Peter Island Resort & Marina.

Now almost entirely owned by JVA Enterprise, Peter Island remains just about as wild as it was 500 years ago, except along the shores of Deadman's Bay and Sprat Bay where the resort sits. There are five pristine beaches, excellent diving and snorkeling sites and roads/paths for hiking and trail biking. Even if you are not a guest at the resort, you can visit for the day by taking a ferry from Tortola.

Places to Stay & Eat

Named one of the 'best places to stay in the world' by *Conde Nast Traveler*, **Peter Island Resort & Yacht Harbour** (☎ 284-495-2000) recently completed a multimillion-dollar renovation. The place has about 60 rooms in a variety of luxury configurations, ranging from villas and two-story clusters to the original A-frames. The resort offers all the amenities, including water sports, tennis, a fitness center and spa. The island's beach at Deadman's Bay is an idyllic palm-lined crescent. Winter rates start at $720 for a double and can go twice that high.

The **Tradewinds** restaurant features gourmet West Indian and continental cuisine (there's a dress code for dinner), with entrees like the grilled fish running $22 and up.

You can get a casual lunch and dinner at **Deadman's Bay Bar & Grill**, where a salad platter for lunch runs about $10. Both restaurants are popular with visiting yacht crews, so be sure to call on VHF channel 16 to make reservations.

Getting There & Away

Unless you come here aboard a private yacht or charter, the only way to reach Peter Island is via the Peter Island Boat (☎ 284-495-2000). This boat picks up guests on demand (who arrive in the BVI by plane) at the ferry dock at Trellis Bay (next to the airport on Beef Island). Expect to pay $25 roundtrip.

You can also catch the ferries that run back and forth between Road Town and Peter Island just about every hour from Baughers Bay (see 'Interisland Ferries' in the Getting Around chapter). Roundtrip tickets cost about $15.

PELICAN ISLAND

This small island about half a mile north of Norman Island is a favorite diving and snorkeling stop. Three pinnacles of rock called the Indians are the main attraction. Snorkeling is best in the shallows on the eastern side of the Indians if the seas are calm. The diving on the western side features 50-foot drops with elkhorn, stag and brain coral.

You must come here on a dive boat, charterboat or private yacht. Pick up one of the moorings placed here by the BVI National Parks Trust. Come early, when the winds are lighter and the mooring area is not crowded with other boats.

NORMAN ISLAND

The hype surrounding this island is almost too much for any place to bear. Since 1843, with the appearance of a slim travel volume entitled *Letters from the Virgin Islands,* writer upon writer has been alleging that Norman Island is the site of buried treasure. Some writers cite a letter of 1550, stating that 'Mr Fleming' recovered the treasure from a Spanish galleon, the *Nuestra Señora* (wrecked off the coast of North Carolina), and buried it at Norman Island – loot 'comprising $450,000 dollars, plate, cochineal, indigo, tobacco.' Other writers point to a story that the French pirate Normand left Anegada and settled here (giving the island his name) 'with his portion of the general booty' from ransacked ships. Apparently, Spanish rivals killed Normand but never found the treasure he and his mates left on the island.

Some chroniclers go so far as to say that Norman Island is the prototype for Robert Louis Stevenson's book *Treasure Island.*

The place sure fits the bill. At 2 miles long and a half-mile wide, Norman is the largest uninhabited island in the BVI. It lies about 6 miles southwest of Tortola. And if it is an evocation of piracy you are looking for, check out the water-filled Treasure Caves off Treasure Point (there are a few moorings for yachts), where Mr Fleming and the fictional Long John Silver allegedly hid treasure. You can find a more contemporary image of piracy in the anchorage at the Bight. Here, a black schooner lies at anchor flying a Jolly Roger flag. The schooner is the *William Thornton,* a floating restaurant and bar.

The snorkeling is good along both shores of the Bight. There tends to be a mob scene of sailboats, dinghies and swimmers clustered around the Treasure Caves (which are not the most impressive caves or snorkeling sites, unless you like bats).

Except for the beaches at the Bight and at Benures Bay on the east side, the island is so overgrown it is virtually impenetrable. Depending on the season and traffic, you may find a trail open between the beach at the Bight and Spyglass Hill. The hike takes about half an hour each way. But beware, though the island is uninhabited by humans, it has its share of wild goats and cattle. Some of these critters can be pretty threatening if you meet them on a narrow trail.

Places to Eat & Drink

On the beach at the Bight, *Billy Bones* (☎ 284-494-4770) is an open-air pavilion appealing to crews off the yachts that anchor or moor here. The restaurant is open for lunch and dinner and serves grilled meals with an emphasis on seafood and ribs. I like the curried veggie roti for under $14. Happy hour runs from 5 to 6 pm, and sometimes the staff passes out flyers offering free shots of rum for everyone in your crew. Make dinner reservations on VHF channel 16.

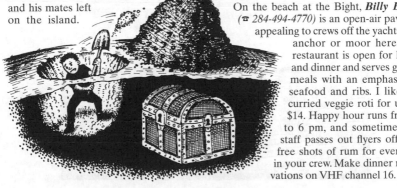

If you don't want to go ashore, try the **William Thornton**, also called the *Willie T* (*☎ 284-494-0183),* the Baltic trader-style schooner converted into a bar/restaurant and moored in the Bight. Shrimp Creole, ribs and steak are popular fare. Most of the entrees run in the $14 to $18 range.

Both Billy Bones and the *Willie T* often bring in live West Indian music on Friday and Saturday nights in high season, but mostly they just crank Bob Marley and Jimmy Buffett over high-voltage sound systems. Weekends at the Bight are always a huge party scene at both bars. In the afternoon, you can play volleyball, go on treasure hunts or participate in crab races at Billy Bones. The action can get really frisky when bare-chested maidens in speedboats blow in from St Thomas.

Getting There & Away

Almost everyone comes here by private boat or charter yacht. But you can also come out for dinner aboard the *Willie T* from the Fort Burt Marina at Road Town, Tortola. The launch departs Road Town at about 5 pm and returns when the gang is sated. (The trip is free because you are buying dinner and drinks.)

Classic Charters (☎ 284-494-5943) runs weekend overnight trips (you sleep on the boat) from Tortola to the Bight, bringing you to the *Willie T* for dinner and drinks. Expect to pay $120 (excluding dinner or drinks).

Glossary

accra – a fried mixture of okra, black-eyed peas, pepper and salt

back time – a Creole expression meaning 'good old days'

bareboat – a sail-it-yourself charter yacht usually rented by the week or longer

breadfruit – an introduced tree common throughout the Caribbean whose round, green fruit is prepared like potatoes

bush tea – tea made from the islands' leaves, roots and herbs. Each tea, with names like 'sorrel,' 'tamarind,' 'worry vine,' 'worm grass' and 'Spanish needle,' cures a specific illness, such as gas, menstrual pain, colds or insomnia.

BVI – British Virgin Islands

calabeza – pumpkin soup

callaloo – also spelled kallaloo; a soup made with dasheen leaves that resembles a creamy spinach soup

calypso – a popular Caribbean music essential to carnival

carambola – star fruit; a green-to-yellow fruit with a star-shaped cross section

carnival – the major Caribbean festival. Originally a pre-Lenten festivity blending African and Christian traditions, it is now observed at various times throughout the year.

cassava – yucca or manioc; a root used since precolonial times as a staple of island diets, whether steamed, baked or grated into a flour for bread

cassareep – a molasseslike sauce used in local recipes, made of cassava, water, sugar and spices

cay – an Arawak word meaning 'small island'

christophene – a common pear-shaped vegetable, like a cross between a potato and a cucumber, that is eaten raw in salads or cooked like a squash

continental – an individual from the US mainland

Creole – a person of mixed black and European ancestry; also the local pidgin language, which is a combination of English (or, elsewhere, French) and African languages; also the local cuisine, characterized by spicy, full-flavored sauces and a heavy use of green peppers and onions

dasheen – a type of taro. The leaves are known as *callaloo* and cooked much like spinach or turnip leaves, while the starchy tuberous root is boiled and eaten like a potato.

Daube meat – a pot roast seasoned with vinegar, native seasonings, onion, garlic, tomato, thyme, parsley and celery

dolphin – both a marine mammal found in Caribbean waters and a common type of white-meat fish (also called mahimahi). The two are not related, and 'dolphin' on any menu always refers to the fish.

down island – a Creole expression referring to the islands of the Lesser Antilles south of the Virgins

duppy – a ghost or spirit; also called a *jumbie*

flying fish – a gray-meat fish named for its ability to skim above the water

frangipani – a small tree with fragrant pink or white flowers called *plumeria*

fungi – a semihard cornmeal pudding similar to Italian polenta, added to soups and used as a side dish; also a Creole name for the music made by local scratch bands

gade – Danish for 'street'

ground provisions – roots used for cooking

gneps – a fruit the size of a large marble that yields a sweet, orange flesh

Ital – a natural style of vegetarian cooking practiced by Rastafarians

johnnycake – a cornflour griddle cake (sometimes baked)

jumbie – a ghost or spirit; also called a *duppy*

jump-up – a nighttime street party that usually involves dancing and plenty of rum drinking

limin' – from the Creole verb 'to lime,' meaning to hang out, relax, chill

mahimahi – see 'dolphin'

manchineel – a tree common to Caribbean beaches whose fruit and sap can cause a severe skin rash

mash up – a wreck, a car accident or a street riot

mauby – a bittersweet drink made from the bark of the 'mauby' or 'carob' tree, sweetened with sugar and spices

Maria Boombe – a dessert made of fried dough covered with powdered sugar

mocko jumbies – costumed stilt walkers representing spirits of the dead, seen in carnivals

native seasoning – homemade mixtures of salt, ground hot pepper, cloves, garlic, mace, nutmeg, celery and parsley

obeah – a system of ancestral worship related to voodoo and rooted in West African religions

out islands – islands or cays that lie across the water from the main islands of an island group

Painkiller – probably the most popular alcoholic drink in the Virgins, made with two parts rum, one part orange juice, four parts pineapple juice, one part coconut cream and a sprinkle of nutmeg and cinnamon

pate – a fried pastry of cassava or plantain dough stuffed with spiced goat, pork, chicken, conch, lobster or fish

paw paw – common Caribbean name for papaya

pepperpot – a spicy stew made with various meats, accompanied by peppers and cassareep

pigeon peas – brown, pealike seeds of a tropical shrub that are cooked like peas and served mixed with rice

plantain – a starchy fruit of the banana family that is usually fried or grilled like a vegetable

planters punch – a punch made of rum and fruit juice

rendezvous diving – service common to Virgin Island dive operators, where the dive boat picks you up from your chartered yacht and brings you back at the end of the day

rise & shine tramps – noisy parades led by reggae bands in the back of a truck starting at 3 am during BVI's Summer Fest

roti – West Indian fast food of curry filling (often potatoes and chicken) rolled inside flat bread

scratch band – a West Indian band that uses homemade percussion instruments such as washboards, ribbed gourds and conch shells to accompany a singer and melody played on a recorder or flute

snowbirds – North Americans, usually retired, who come to the VI for its warm winters

sorrel juice – a lightly tart, bright-red tea drink rich in vitamin C, made from the flowers of the sorrel plant

soursop – an irregularly shaped fruit with a cottony pulp that is fragrant yet bland or acidic in taste, hinting at guava and pineapple; used for puddings, ice cream, canned drinks and syrups

souse – a dish made of a pickled pig's head and belly, spices and a few vegetables

steel pan – also called 'steel drum,' it refers both to a percussion instrument made from oil drums and to the music it produces

strade – Danish for 'step street'

tamarind – the legumelike pod of a large tropical tree, or the juice made from the seeds

tannia – an edible tuber used in soups, also called 'blue taro'

USVI – United States Virgin Islands

welcoming arms staircase – a staircase that flares at the base

LONELY PLANET

You already know that Lonely Planet produces more than this one guidebook, but you might not be aware of the other products we have on this region. Here is a selection of titles which you may want to check out as well:

Bahamas, Turks & Caicos
ISBN 1864501995
US$19.99 • UK£12.99

Eastern Caribbean
ISBN 186450305X
US$19.99 • UK£12.99

Jamaica
ISBN 0864427808
US$17.95• UK£11.99

Diving & Snorkeling British Virgin Islands
ISBN 1864501359
US$16.99 • UK£10.99

Puerto Rico
ISBN 086442552X
US$15.95 • UK£9.99

World Food Caribbean
ISBN 1864503483
US$13.99 • UK£8.99

Available wherever books are sold.

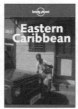

LONELY PLANET

Guides by Region

L onely Planet is known worldwide for publishing practical, reliable and no-nonsense travel information in our guides and on our Web site. The Lonely Planet list covers just about every accessible part of the world. Currently there are 16 series: Travel guides, Shoestring guides, Condensed guides, Watching Wildlife guides, Pisces Diving & Snorkeling guides, City Maps, Road Atlases, Out to Eat, World Food, Journeys travel literature and Pictorials.

AFRICA Africa on a shoestring • Cairo • Cairo City Map • Cape Town • Cape Town City Map • East Africa • Egypt • Egyptian Arabic phrasebook • Ethiopia, Eritrea & Djibouti • Ethiopian Amharic phrasebook • The Gambia & Senegal • Healthy Travel Africa • Kenya • Malawi • Morocco • Moroccan Arabic phrasebook • Mozambique • Read This First: Africa • South Africa, Lesotho & Swaziland • Southern Africa • Southern Africa Road Atlas • Swahili phrasebook • Tanzania, Zanzibar & Pemba • Trekking in East Africa • Tunisia • Watching Wildlife East Africa • Watching Wildlife Southern Africa • West Africa • World Food Morocco • Zimbabwe, Botswana & Namibia
Travel Literature: Mali Blues: Traveling to an African Beat • The Rainbird: A Central African Journey • Songs to an African Sunset: A Zimbabwean Story

AUSTRALIA & THE PACIFIC Auckland • Australia • Australian phrasebook • Australia Road Atlas • Cycling Australia • Cycling New Zealand • Fiji • Fijian phrasebook • Healthy Travel Australia, NZ and the Pacific • Islands of Australia's Great Barrier Reef • Melbourne • Melbourne City Map • Micronesia • New Caledonia • New South Wales • New Zealand • Northern Territory • Outback Australia • Out to Eat – Melbourne • Out to Eat – Sydney • Papua New Guinea • Pidgin phrasebook • Queensland • Rarotonga & the Cook Islands • Samoa • Solomon Islands • South Australia • South Pacific • South Pacific phrasebook • Sydney • Sydney City Map • Sydney Condensed • Tahiti & French Polynesia • Tasmania • Tonga • Tramping in New Zealand • Vanuatu • Victoria • Walking in Australia • Watching Wildlife Australia • Western Australia
Travel Literature: Islands in the Clouds: Travel in the Highlands of New Guinea • Kiwi Tracks: A New Zealand Journey • Sean & David's Long Drive

CENTRAL AMERICA & THE CARIBBEAN Bahamas, Turks & Caicos • Baja California • Belize, Guatemala & Yucatán • Bermuda • Central America on a shoestring • Costa Rica • Costa Rica Spanish phrasebook • Cuba • Dominican Republic & Haiti • Eastern Caribbean • Guatemala • Havana • Healthy Travel Central & South America • Jamaica • Mexico • Mexico City • Panama • Puerto Rico • Read This First: Central & South America • World Food Mexico • Yucatán
Travel Literature: Green Dreams: Travels in Central America

EUROPE Amsterdam • Amsterdam City Map • Amsterdam Condensed • Andalucía • Austria • Baltic States phrasebook • Barcelona • Barcelona City Map • Belgium & Luxembourg • Berlin • Berlin City Map • Britain • British phrasebook • Brussels, Bruges & Antwerp • Brussels City Map • Budapest • Budapest City Map • Canary Islands • Central Europe • Central Europe phrasebook • Copenhagen • Corfu & the Ionians • Corsica • Crete • Crete Condensed • Croatia • Cycling Britain • Cycling France • Cyprus • Czech & Slovak Republics • Denmark • Dublin • Dublin City Map • Eastern Europe • Eastern Europe phrasebook • Edinburgh • England • Estonia, Latvia & Lithuania • Europe on a shoestring • Europe phrasebook • Finland • Florence • France • Frankfurt Condensed • French phrasebook • Georgia, Armenia & Azerbaijan • Germany • German phrasebook • Greece • Greek Islands • Greek phrasebook • Hungary • Iceland, Greenland & the Faroe Islands • Ireland • Italian phrasebook • Italy • Krakow • Lisbon • The Loire • London • London City Map • London Condensed • Madrid • Malta • Mediterranean Europe • Mediterranean Europe phrasebook • Moscow • Munich • Netherlands • Normandy • Norway • Out to Eat – London • Out to Eat – Paris • Paris • Paris City Map • Paris Condensed • Poland • Polish phrasebook • Portugal • Portuguese phrasebook • Prague • Prague City Map • Provence & the Côte d'Azur • Read This First: Europe • Rhodes & the Dodecanese • Romania & Moldova • Rome • Rome City Map • Russia, Ukraine & Belarus • Russian phrasebook • Scandinavian & Baltic Europe • Scandinavian phrasebook • Scotland • Sicily • Slovenia • South-West France • Spain • Spanish phrasebook • St Petersburg • St Petersburg City Map • Sweden • Switzerland • Tuscany • Ukrainian phrasebook • Venice • Vienna • Walking in Britain • Walking in France • Walking in Ireland • Walking in Italy • Walking in Spain • Walking in Switzerland • Western Europe • World Food France • World Food Ireland • World Food Italy • World Food Spain
Travel Literature: After Yugoslavia • Love and War in the Apennines • The Olive Grove: Travels in Greece • On the Shores of the Mediterranean • Round Ireland in Low Gear • A Small Place in Italy

LONELY PLANET

Mail Order

Lonely Planet products are distributed worldwide. They are also available by mail order from Lonely Planet, so if you have difficulty finding a title please write to us. North and South American residents should write to 150 Linden St, Oakland, CA 94607, USA; European and African residents should write to 10a Spring Place, London NW5 38H, UK; and residents of other countries to Locked Bag 1, Footscray, Victoria 3011, Australia.

INDIAN SUBCONTINENT & THE INDIAN OCEAN Bangladesh • Bengali phrasebook • Bhutan • Delhi • Goa • Healthy Travel Asia & India • Hindi & Urdu phrasebook • India • Indian Himalaya • Karakoram Highway • Kerala • Madagascar • Maldives • Mauritius, Réunion & Seychelles • Mumbai (Bombay) • Nepal • Nepali phrasebook • Pakistan • Rajasthan • Read This First: Asia & India • South India • Sri Lanka • Sri Lanka phrasebook • Tibet • Tibetan phrasebook • Trekking in the Indian Himalaya • Trekking in the Karakoram & Hindukush • Trekking in the Nepal Himalaya
Travel Literature: The Age of Kali: Indian Travels and Encounters • Hello Goodnight: A Life of Goa • In Rajasthan • Maverick in Madagascar • A Season in Heaven: True Tales from the Road to Kathmandu • Shopping for Buddhas • A Short Walk in the Hindu Kush • Slowly Down the Ganges

MIDDLE EAST & CENTRAL ASIA Bahrain, Kuwait & Qatar • Central Asia • Central Asia phrasebook • Dubai • Farsi (Persian) phrasebook • Hebrew phrasebook • Iran • Israel & the Palestinian Territories • Istanbul • Istanbul City Map • Istanbul to Cairo • Istanbul to Kathmandu • Jerusalem • Jerusalem City Map • Jordan • Lebanon • Middle East • Oman & the United Arab Emirates • Syria • Turkey • Turkish phrasebook • World Food Turkey • Yemen
Travel Literature: Black on Black: Iran Revisited • The Gates of Damascus • Kingdom of the Film Stars: Journey into Jordan

NORTH AMERICA Alaska • Boston • Boston City Map • Boston Condensed • British Columbia • California & Nevada • California Condensed • Canada • Chicago • Chicago City Map • Florida • Great Lakes • Hawaii • Hiking in Alaska • Hiking in the USA • Las Vegas • Los Angeles • Los Angeles City Map • Louisiana & the Deep South • Miami • Miami City Map • Montréal • New England • New Orleans • New York City • New York City City Map • New York City Condensed • New York, New Jersey & Pennsylvania • Oahu • Out to Eat – San Francisco • Pacific Northwest • Rocky Mountains • San Francisco • San Francisco City Map • Seattle • Southwest • Texas • Toronto • USA • USA phrasebook • Vancouver • Virginia & the Capital Region • Washington, DC • Washington, DC City Map • World Food New Orleans
Travel Literature: Caught Inside: A Surfer's Year on the California Coast • Drive Thru America

NORTH-EAST ASIA Beijing • Beijing City Map • Cantonese phrasebook • China • Hiking in Japan • Hong Kong • Hong Kong City Map • Hong Kong Condensed • Hong Kong, Macau & Guangzhou • Japan • Japanese phrasebook • Korea • Korean phrasebook • Kyoto • Mandarin phrasebook • Mongolia • Mongolian phrasebook • Seoul • Shanghai • South-West China • Taiwan • Tokyo • World Food Hong Kong
Travel Literature: In Xanadu: A Quest • Lost Japan

SOUTH AMERICA Argentina, Uruguay & Paraguay • Bolivia • Brazil • Brazilian phrasebook • Buenos Aires • Chile & Easter Island • Colombia • Ecuador & the Galápagos Islands • Healthy Travel Central & South America • Latin American Spanish phrasebook • Peru • Quechua phrasebook • Read This First: Central & South America • Rio de Janeiro • Rio de Janeiro City Map • Santiago de Chile • South America on a shoestring • Trekking in the Patagonian Andes • Venezuela
Travel Literature: Full Circle: A South American Journey

SOUTH-EAST ASIA Bali & Lombok • Bangkok • Bangkok City Map • Burmese phrasebook • Cambodia • Hanoi • Healthy Travel Asia & India • Hill Tribes phrasebook • Ho Chi Minh City • Indonesia • Indonesian phrasebook • Indonesia's Eastern Islands • Java • Lao phrasebook • Laos • Malay phrasebook • Malaysia, Singapore & Brunei • Myanmar (Burma) • Philippines • Pilipino (Tagalog) phrasebook • Read This First: Asia & India • Singapore • Singapore City Map • South-East Asia on a shoestring • South-East Asia phrasebook • Thailand • Thailand's Islands & Beaches • Thailand, Vietnam, Laos & Cambodia Road Atlas • Thai phrasebook • Vietnam • Vietnamese phrasebook • World Food Thailand • World Food Vietnam

ALSO AVAILABLE: Antarctica • The Arctic • The Blue Man: Tales of Travel, Love and Coffee • Brief Encounters: Stories of Love, Sex & Travel • Chasing Rickshaws • The Last Grain Race • Lonely Planet...On the Edge: Adventurous Escapades from Around the World • Lonely Planet Unpacked • Not the Only Planet: Science Fiction Travel Stories • Sacred India • Travel Photography: A Guide to Taking Better Pictures • Travel with Children

LONELY PLANET

ON THE ROAD

Travel Guides explore cities, regions and countries, and supply information on transport, restaurants and accommodation, covering all budgets. They come with reliable, easy-to-use maps, practical advice, cultural and historical facts and a rundown on attractions both on and off the beaten track. There are over 200 titles in this classic series, covering nearly every country in the world.

 Lonely Planet Upgrades extend the shelf life of existing travel guides by detailing any changes that may affect travel in a region since a book has been published. Upgrades can be downloaded for free from **www.lonelyplanet.com/upgrades**

For travelers with more time than money, **Shoestring** guides offer dependable, first-hand information with hundreds of detailed maps, plus insider tips for stretching money as far as possible. Covering entire continents in most cases, the six-volume shoestring guides are known around the world as 'backpackers bibles.'

For the discerning short-term visitor, **Condensed** guides highlight the best a destination has to offer in a full-color, pocket-sized format designed for quick access. They include everything from top sights and walking tours to opinionated reviews of where to eat, stay, shop and have fun.

CitySync lets travelers use their Palm™ or Visor™ hand-held computers to guide them through a city with handy tips on transport, history, cultural life, major sights, and shopping and entertainment options. It can also quickly search and sort hundreds of reviews of hotels, restaurants and attractions, and pinpoint their location on scrollable street maps. CitySync can be downloaded from **www.citysync.com**

MAPS & ATLASES

Lonely Planet's **City Maps** feature downtown and metropolitan maps, as well as transit routes and walking tours. The maps come complete with an index of streets, a listing of sights and a plastic coat for extra durability.

Road Atlases are an essential navigation tool for serious travelers. Cross-referenced with the guidebooks, they also feature distance and climate charts and a complete site index.

LONELY PLANET

ESSENTIALS

Read This First books help new travelers to hit the road with confidence. These invaluable predeparture guides give step-by-step advice on preparing for a trip, budgeting, arranging a visa, planning an itinerary and staying safe while still getting off the beaten track.

Healthy Travel pocket guides offer a regional rundown on disease hot spots and practical advice on predeparture health measures, staying well on the road and what to do in emergencies. The guides come with a user-friendly design and helpful diagrams and tables.

Lonely Planet's **Phrasebooks** cover the essential words and phrases travelers need when they're strangers in a strange land. They come in a pocket-sized format with color tabs for quick reference, extensive vocabulary lists, easy-to-follow pronunciation keys and two-way dictionaries.

Miffed by blurry photos of the Taj Mahal? Tired of the classic 'top of the head cut off' shot? **Travel Photography: A Guide to Taking Better Pictures** will help you turn ordinary holiday snaps into striking images and give you the know-how to capture every scene, from frenetic festivals to peaceful beach sunrises.

Lonely Planet's **Travel Journal** is a lightweight but sturdy travel diary for jotting down all those on-the-road observations and significant travel moments. It comes with a handy time-zone wheel, a world map and useful travel information.

Lonely Planet's eKno is an all-in-one communication service developed especially for travelers. It offers low-cost international calls and free email and voicemail so that you can keep in touch while on the road. Check it out on **www.ekno.lonelyplanet.com**

FOOD & RESTAURANT GUIDES

Lonely Planet's **Out to Eat** guides recommend the brightest and best places to eat and drink in top international cities. These gourmet companions are arranged by neighborhood, packed with dependable maps, garnished with scene-setting photos and served with quirky features.

For people who live to eat, drink and travel, **World Food** guides explore the culinary culture of each country. Entertaining and adventurous, each guide is packed with detail on staples and specialties, regional cuisine and local markets, as well as sumptuous recipes, comprehensive culinary dictionaries and lavish photos good enough to eat.

LONELY PLANET

OUTDOOR GUIDES

For those who believe the best way to see the world is on foot, Lonely Planet's **Walking Guides** detail everything from family strolls to difficult treks, with 'when to go and how to do it' advice supplemented by reliable maps and essential travel information.

Cycling Guides map a destination's best bike tours, long and short, in day-by-day detail. They contain all the information a cyclist needs, including advice on bike maintenance, places to eat and stay, innovative maps with detailed cues to the rides, and elevation charts.

The **Watching Wildlife** series is perfect for travelers who want authoritative information but don't want to tote a heavy field guide. Packed with advice on where, when and how to view a region's wildlife, each title features photos of over 300 species and contains engaging comments on the local flora and fauna.

With underwater color photos throughout, **Pisces Books** explore the world's best diving and snorkeling areas. Each book contains listings of diving services and dive resorts, detailed information on depth, visibility and difficulty of dives, and a roundup of the marine life you're likely to see through your mask.

OFF THE ROAD

Journeys, the travel literature series written by renowned travel authors, capture the spirit of a place or illuminate a culture with a journalist's attention to detail and a novelist's flair for words. These are tales to soak up while you're actually on the road or dip into as an at-home armchair indulgence.

The new range of lavishly illustrated **Pictorial** books is just the ticket for both travelers and dreamers. Off-beat tales and vivid photographs bring the adventure of travel to your doorstep long before the journey begins and long after it is over.

Lonely Planet **Videos** encourage the same independent, tough-minded approach as the guidebooks. Currently airing throughout the world, this award-winning series features innovative footage and an original soundtrack.

Yes, we know, work is tough, so do a little deskside dreaming with the spiral-bound Lonely Planet **Diary** or a Lonely Planet **Wall Calendar**, filled with great photos from around the world.

TRAVELERS NETWORK

Lonely Planet Online. Lonely Planet's award-winning Web site has insider information on hundreds of destinations, from Amsterdam to Zimbabwe, complete with interactive maps and relevant links. The site also offers the latest travel news, recent reports from travelers on the road, guidebook upgrades, a travel links site, an online book-buying option and a lively traveler's bulletin board. It can be viewed at **www.lonelyplanet.com** or AOL keyword: lp.

Planet Talk is a quarterly print newsletter, full of gossip, advice, anecdotes and author articles. It provides an antidote to the being-at-home blues and lets you plan and dream for the next trip. Contact the nearest Lonely Planet office for your free copy.

Comet, the free Lonely Planet newsletter, comes via email once a month. It's loaded with travel news, advice, dispatches from authors, travel competitions and letters from readers. To sub-scribe, click on the Comet subscription link on the front page of the Web site.

Index

Text

99 Steps 98
11,000 Virgins 13–4

A

accommodations 55–6. See
  also individual locations
  camping 55, 138–9
  costs 37, 55
  guesthouses & inns 55
  hotels 55–6
  rentals 56
activities 40, 52–4. See also
  individual activities
AIDS 45
air travel
  airlines 65
  airports 42, 65
  baggage 68
  glossary 67
  interisland 75
  international 65–72
  tickets 66, 68
alcoholic drinks 51, 58–9
amphibians 22, 40
Anegada 225–31, **226**
  accommodations 230–1
  activities 230
  attractions 228–30
  history 226–7
  restaurants 228, 231
  shopping 228
  transportation 227–8
Anegada Reef Hotel 231
Annaberg Sugar Mill Ruins
  135–6
Apple Bay 198
Arawak 13, 145
archaeological sites 118, 136,
  141, 145, 169
architecture 27
art galleries 99, 107, 162
Athalie MacFarlane Petersen
  Public Library 164
ATMs 36

B

bananaquit 22, 127
bars. See pubs & bars
The Baths 210
beaches
  Anegada 230
  Jost Van Dyke 221, 222
  St Croix 165, 169–70, 174
  St John 128–9, 136–7,
    140–1
  St Thomas 108–9, 112–3,
    118
  Tortola 194–5, 198, 202
  Virgin Gorda 210–1, 214
Beef Island 201–2
belongers 25
Berchers Bay 214
bicycling 54, 77
  Anegada 230
  St Croix 165
  St John 129
  St Thomas 109–10
  Tortola 189
  Virgin Gorda 211
birds
  bananaquit 22, 127
  flamingo 22, 228–30, 234
  species of 22
  watching 54, 130, 170, 234
  white-crowned pigeon 22,
    234
bites 45–6
Blackbeard 14, 98, 179, 237–8
Blackbeard's Castle 92, 97–8,
  101, 103–4, 105, 106
Bluebeard's Beach 112–3
Bluebeard's Castle 92, 102
boats. See cruise ships;
  ferries; motorboats; yachts
  & sailboats
Bolongo Bay 109
Bomba's Surfside Shack 201
books 39–41.
  See also literature

C

Brewers Bay (St Thomas) 109
Brewers Bay (Tortola) 194–5
Bridel, Erick 121, 140
Buccaneer Beach 174
Buck Island Reef National
  Monument 173, 174
Buddhoe Park 164
buses 75–6
business hours 51

Caledonia Rain Forest 168
callaloo 57
Callwood, Foxy 217, 219,
  220, 222
Callwood Rum Distillery
  193–4
calypso 26
Camille Pissarro Gallery 99
camping. See accommoda-
  tions
Cane Garden Bay 193–7, **194**
Caneel Bay 136
canoe, Carib 202
Caribs 11, 13, 14, 15, 83,
  145, 169, 202, 205, 225
carnival 26, 90, 125–6,
  208–9
cars 76–7
  driver's license 35
  driving conditions 76
  gasoline 76
  insurance 77
  regulations 76
  renting 76–7
casinos. See gambling
Charlotte Amalie 92–107,
  94–5, 97
  accommodations 100–2
  attractions 95–100
  climate 20
  entertainment 105–6
  history 92–4
  restaurants 102–5
  shopping 106–7

Chenay Bay 175
children, traveling with 48, 68–9
Christiansted 153–62, **154**
  accommodations 158–9
  activities 157–8
  attractions 155–7
  entertainment 160–1
  history 153, 155
  restaurants 159–60
  shopping 161–2
Ciboneys 13, 83, 145, 178
cinemas 60. See also films
Cinnamon Bay 137
Cinnamon Bay Archaeological Dig 136
climate 19–20
clothing 29, 33, 46
Coki Bay 112
Columbus, Christopher 11, 13–4, 15, 83, 118, 121, 145, 169, 170, 179, 205
Columbus Beach 170
conduct 28–9
consulates 35
Cooper Island 236
Copper Mine National Park 210
coral 23, 33, 40, 49, 53, 60
Coral Bay 140–3
Coral World Marine Park & Underwater Observatory 112
Cormorant Beach 171
costs 37
Cow Wreck Bay 230
Cramer's Park 174
credit cards 36
Creole 29–30
Creque, Wilfred 230
crime 37, 46–7, 49
croquet 175
Crown House 97
cruise ships 72
Cruz Bay 120–1, 127–35, **128**

Cruz Bay Beach 128–9
Cruzan Rum Distillery 167–8
cultural events 51–2
currency 36
customs 35–6
cuts 45–6
cycling. See bicycling

D

dance 27, 60
Danish West India and Guinea Company 15, 83, 86, 93, 99, 121, 146, 153, 155–6
de Castro, Morris 17–8
Dead Chest Island 237–8
debit cards 36
deforestation 20
dengue 45
Devil's Bay 210–1
Diamond Cay National Park 222–3
diarrhea 44
Dick-Read, Aragorn 27–8, 204
disabled travelers 47–8, 68
discounts 37
diseases. See health
Divi Carina Bay Beach Resort 176, 177
diving & snorkeling 52–3
  Anegada 230
  guide 39
  Out Islands 235, 236–7, 239
  responsible 53
  safety 49–50
  St Croix 157, 165, 170
  St John 129, 137, 138
  St Thomas 109, 113–4
  Tortola 189, 195, 198, 202
  Virgin Gorda 214
Doc James Race Track 168
documents 34–5
The Dogs 235
Drake, Sir Francis 14, 107, 179
Drake's Seat 107
drinks 51, 58–9
driving. See cars
drugs 49. See also mushrooms, psychoactive

Duffy's Love Shack 115–6, 117, 134, 135

E

economy 24
education 25
Elaine Ione Sprauve Library & Museum 128
electricity 42
email 39
Emancipation Garden 95–6
embassies 35
emergencies 50
Emmaus Moravian Church 140
employment 54–5
endangered species 22, 33, 60, 229, 234
entertainment 59–60. See also individual locations
environmental issues 20–1
Estate Catherineburg Sugar Mill 136
Estate Concordia 141–2
Estate St Peter Greathouse & Botanical Garden 107
Estate Whim Plantation Museum 167
etiquette 28–9
exchange rates 36

F

Fallen Jerusalem 236
fauna. See wildlife
faxes 38
feral animals 21–2, 126
ferries 77–80
films 41. See also cinemas
fish 22
fishing 53–4, 114, 129, 157, 198, 221, 230
Flamingo Pond 228–30
flamingos 22, 228–30, 234
flora. See plants
food. See restaurants & food
Fort Berg 140
Fort Burt 189
Fort Christian 96
Fort Christiansvaern 155

Bold indicates maps.

Fort Frederik 163–4
Fort Frederik Beach 165
Fort Recovery 197
Foxy's Tamarind Bar 219, 220, 222
Foxy's Woodenboat Regatta 217, 219, 220
Francis Bay 137
Frank Bay 128–9
Frederik Church Parsonage 96
Frederik Lutheran Church 96
Frederiksted 162–7, **163**
Frenchtown 99
fungal infections 44
fungi (music) 26, 197

G

gambling 60, 177
gardens 107, 168, 188
gasoline 76
gays & lesbians
    resources & organizations 47
    travelers 47
    venues 106, 192–3
geography 18–9
geology 18–9
golf 54, 119, 170, 175
Gorda Peak National Park 214
Gottlieb, Moses 'General Budhoe' 162, 164, 165
government & politics 23–4, 40
Grand Hotel Complex 96
Grapetree Bay 175
Great Cruz Bay 129
Great Harbour 221–2
Great Harbour Beach 221
Great Lameshur Bay 141
Great Pond Bay 174
Green Cay 223
Guana Island 232–4
guesthouses. See accommodations

H

Haagensen House 98
Hans-Lollik Island 119
Hassel Island 107–8
Haulover Bay 140
Hawkins, Jack 14, 179

Hawksnest Bay 136
health 42–6
    cuts, bites & stings 45–6
    diseases 44–5
    guide 40
    insurance 34–5, 43
    travel & climate-related problems 43–4
heat, effects of 44
hepatitis 44–5
Hess Oil 18, 148
Hibiscus Beach 169–70
hiking 54
    Peter Island 238
    St Croix 158, 168
    St John 130–1
    Virgin Gorda 210–1, 214
history 13–8, 40. See also individual locations
hitchhiking 77
HIV 45
holidays 51
Honeymoon Bay 109
Honeymoon Beach 136
horse racing 168
horseback riding 54, 119, 141, 170, 199, 211
Hotel 1829 99, 101
hotels. See accommodations
Hull Bay 118–9
hurricanes 18, 19, 87, 149

I

Igneri 13, 145, 178, 205
iguanas 22, 226, 228, 229, 234
The Indians 239
indigenous peoples
    Caribs 11, 13, 14, 15, 83, 145, 169, 202, 205, 225
    Ciboneys 13, 83, 145, 178
    Igneri 13, 145, 178, 205
    Taíno 13, 14, 19, 83, 118, 121, 136, 145, 178, 205, 225
inns. See accommodations
insects 22, 40, 50
insurance
    car 77
    travel 34–5, 43
Internet

access 39
resources 39
Isaac Bay 175
itineraries, suggested 31–2
Iverson, George 83–4

J

Jack Bay 175
Jarecki, Henry & Gloria 233, 234
jellyfish 45, 49–50
jet lag 43–4
Josiahs Bay 202
Jost Van Dyke 217–24, **218–9**
    accommodations 221, 223
    activities 221
    attractions 221, 222–3
    history 217
    restaurants 221–2, 223–4
    shopping 221–2
    transportation 219, 221
Jumbie Bay 137
jumbies 29, 137

K

kayaking 129, 170, 189, 195, 223, 230
King, Cyril 17

L

La Grange Beach 169
Lambert Bay 202
language 29–30
laundry 42
Lawaetz Family Museum 168
legal matters 50–1
Leinster Bay 137
lesbians. See gays & lesbians
Lettsome, John 222
L'Hotel Boynes 98
Lind Point trail 130
Lindbergh, Charles 109
Lindbergh Bay 109
Lindquist Beach 113
literature 27. See also books
Little Dix Bay 205, 211, 212
Little Fort National Park 210
Little Harbour 222
Little Lameshur Bay 141
Little Magens Bay 118
Little Thatch Island 232

Loblolly Bay 230
Long Bay (Beef Island) 202
Long Bay (Tortola) 198
Long Bay (Virgin Gorda) 214

M

Mac's Place 230
magazines 41
Magens Bay 118
Maho Bay 137
Mahoe Bay 214
mail 37–8
mammals 21–2. See also
    individual species
manchineel tree 21
mangroves 20, 21
maps 33
Marina Cay 234–5
marine life 22
McMillen, Lois 200
measurements 42
mining 205, 206–7, 210
money 36–7
Montpellier Domino Club 172
Morningstar Bay 108
Mosquito Island 235
mosquitoes 22, 45, 50
Moth, Frederick 86, 146, 153
motion sickness 43
motorboats 129, 189, 195,
    202, 214
motorcycles 76–7
Mount Healthy National Park
    197
mountain biking 54, 165,
    168
Mountain Top 107
Mountain Trunk Bay 214
movies. See cinemas; films
mushrooms, psychoactive 21,
    184
music 25–7, 41, 60

N

Nail Bay 214
national parks 22–3, 48. See
    also individual parks
Necker Island 235–6

newspapers 41
nightclubs 60
Norman Island 239–40
North Shore Shell Museum
    193
North Sound 205
no-see-ums 50

O

obeah 29
offshore businesses 24
Old Danish Scale House 155
O'Neal (JR) Botanic Gardens
    188
Oppenheimer's Beach 136–7
orchid, wild 21, 210
Out Islands 232–40, **233**

P

packing 33
Paiewonsky, Ralph 18
painting 27
Paradise Point Tramway
    99–100
parasailing 158
passports 34
Pelican Island 239
Peter Island 238
petroglyphs 131, 141
phones 38
photography 41–2
pigeon, white-crowned 22,
    234
pigs 172
Pineapple Beach 112
pirates 14, 169, 179, 198,
    225, 239
Pissarro, Camille 27, 96, 99
planning 32–3
plantations 15–6, 135–6,
    144, 167, 168, 179–81
plants 21, 40. See also
    individual species
Point Udall 174
politics. See government &
    politics
Pomato Point Museum 230
population 20, 24–5
Portuguese man-of-war 50
postal services 37–8
Protestant Cay 157

pubs & bars 59–60
Pusser's Marina Cay Resort
    234–5

Q

Queen Elizabeth Park 188
queens, plantation 149
Quelbe 26

R

radio 41
Rainbow Beach 169
Raleigh, Sir Walter 21, 145
Red Hook 112–7
Reef Beach 175
regattas 185, 217, 219, 220,
    227
reggae 26
religion 29
reptiles 22, 40
restaurants & food 56–8. See
    also individual locations
    costs 37
    guides 40, 41
    safety 43
    vegetarian 58
Rhone, RMS 236–7
Road Town 186–93, **187**
rock iguana 22, 226, 228,
    229, 234
Rockefeller, Laurence 124,
    205, 207, 210
rum 17, 59, 60, 167–8,
    193–4

S

safety
    crime 37, 46–7, 49
    recreational hazards 49–50
Sage Mountain 19, 23, 193
sailing. See yachts & sailboats
Salomon Bay Beach 129
Salt Island 236–7
Salt Pond Bay 140–1
Salt River Beach 170
Salt River National Historic
    Park 169
Sand Castle Beach 165
Sandy Cay 223
Sandy Point National Wildlife
    Refuge 168–9

Bold indicates maps.

Sapphire Beach 113
Savannah Bay 211
Schmidt, Erik 83
scuba diving. *See* diving & snorkeling
sculpture 27–8, 168
Secret Harbour 112
senior travelers 48
The Settlement 228
Seven Arches Museum 96–7
sharks 49
shipwrecks 225, 236–7
shopping 60. *See also individual locations*
Shoy's Beach 174–5
Sidney's Peace and Love 224
slavery 15–6, 25, 86, 93, 121–2, 140, 146–8, 149, 162, 165, 181–2
Smuggler's Cove 198
snakes 22, 40
snorkeling. *See* diving & snorkeling
soca 26
soil erosion 20
Sopers Hole 198
Southey, Thomas 11
Spanish Town 209–13
special events 52
sports 60
Sprat Hall Beach 169
Spring Bay 210
St Croix 144–77, **146–7**
  accommodations 158–9, 165–6, 170–1, 175–6
  activities 157–8, 165, 170, 175
  attractions 155–7, 163–5, 167–70, 173–5
  entertainment 160–1, 167, 172–3, 177
  history 145–9, 153, 155, 162
  restaurants 159–60, 166–7, 171–2, 176–7
  shopping 161–2, 173
  transportation 152–3
St Croix Aquarium & Marine Education Center 156–7
St Croix Leap 168

St George Village Botanical Garden 168
St George's Anglican Church 188
St John 120–43, **122–3**
  accommodations 130–3, 138–9, 141–2
  activities 129, 130, 138, 141
  attractions 127–9, 135–7, 140–1
  entertainment 134–5, 143
  history 121–3
  restaurants 133–4, 139–40, 142–3
  shopping 135
  transportation 126–7
St Patrick's Roman Catholic Church 164
St Paul's Episcopal Anglican Church 164
St Philips Church 201
St Thomas 82–119, **84–5**
  accommodations 100–2, 110–1, 114–5
  activities 109–10, 113–4, 119
  attractions 95–100, 107–9, 112–3, 118–9
  entertainment 105–6, 111–2, 117
  history 83–7, 92–4
  restaurants 102–5, 111, 115–7, 119
  shopping 106–7, 112, 117
  transportation 90–2
St Thomas Reformed Church 98
steel pan 26–7
Steeple Building 156
stings 45–6
Stumpy Bay 119
sugar 15, 16, 135–6, 167
sunburn 44
surfing 54, 198
swimming 49–50, 52. *See also* beaches
Synagogue of Beracha V'Shalom V'Gimilath Chasidim 99

T

Taíno 13, 14, 19, 83, 118, 121, 136, 145, 178, 205, 225
taxes 37
taxis 81
Taylors Bay 211
Teach, Edward. *See* Blackbeard
telegraph 38
telephones 38
tennis 54
  St Croix 157, 165, 175
  St John 129, 138
  St Thomas 109–10, 114
  Tortola 189, 198
  Virgin Gorda 211
theater 60
theft. *See* crime
Thorton, William 197, 198
ticks 45–6
Tillett Gardens 107
time zone 42
tipping 37
tortoise, red-legged 22, 234
Tortola 178–204, **180–1**
  accommodations 189–90, 195–6, 199–200, 202–3
  activities 189, 195, 198–9, 202
  attractions 188–9, 193–5, 197–8, 201–2
  entertainment 192–3, 197, 200
  history 178–82
  restaurants 190–2, 196–7, 200, 203–4
  shopping 193, 201, 204
  transportation 185–6
tourism 17–8, 24, 33
tourist offices 33–4
tourist season 32
tours, organized 73–4, 81
transportation
  air travel 65–72, 75
  bicycling 54, 77
  buses 75–6
  cars & motorcycles 76–7
  cruise ships 72
  ferries 77–80

hitchhiking 77
taxis 81
yachts 61–4, 72–3
travel insurance 34–5
traveler's checks 36
trekking. See hiking
Trellis Bay 202
Trunk Bay 137, 211
turtles 22, 40, 60, 169
TV 41

U

University of the Virgin
Islands 25, 27, 48–9

V

Vessup Beach 113
VI Folk Museum 188
video 41–2
Virgin Gorda 205–16, **206–7**
accommodations 211–2,
214–5
activities 211, 214

attractions 209–11, 214
entertainment 213, 216
history 205–7
restaurants 212–3, 215–6
shopping 213
transportation 209
Virgin Islands National Park
127–8
visas 34
Vixen Point 214
von Scholten, Peter 86, 95,
97, 162, 165

W

water 21, 43
Water Island 108
Web sites 39
Westin Resort (St John) 132
White Bay 222
wildlife 21–2. See also feral
animals; individual species
conservation efforts 169,
234

dangerous 49–50, 126
guides 40
windsurfing 54
St Croix 158, 175
St John 138
St Thomas 113
Tortola 198
Virgin Gorda 214
women travelers 46–7
Wooley, Robert F 237
work 54–5

Y

Yacht Harbour 210
yachts & sailboats
chartering 61–4
crewing 72–3
guides & maps 40, 73
St Croix 157–8
St John 129
St Thomas 113
Tortola 189, 198, 202
Virgin Gorda 211, 214

Boxed Text

Air Travel Glossary 67
Almost Eden 234
Becoming an Island Park 124
Booze, Bras & the Bomba Shack 201
Buck Island Tours 174
Caught in Freedom's Storm 165
Considerations for Responsible Diving 53
Coral Ecology 23
Dastardly Dengue 45
Facing Extinction 229
Fireburn Queens 149
First Blood at St Croix 15
A High Wind Gonna Blow 19
Hiking on St John 130–1
The Hull Bay Find 118
Interisland Ferries 78–80

Island Proverbs & Witticisms 30
John Lettsome 222
Lone Eagle in Paradise 109
Magic Mushrooms 184
One Foxy Fella 220
Out of Africa 141
Party Piggies 172
Poison Apples 21
Prowling for Pirates 169
Rum by Gum 59
Sailing, Carib Style 202
The Secret of Callaloo 57
Wild Kingdom 126
William Thornton 198
Women: First from Chains 25
Wreck of the Rhone 237

MAP LEGEND

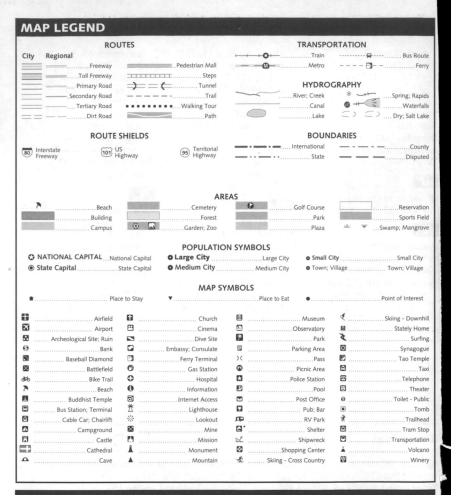

ROUTES

City | **Regional**

====== Freeway
====== Toll Freeway
—— Primary Road
—— Secondary Road
—— Tertiary Road
== == Dirt Road

Pedestrian Mall
Steps
Tunnel
Trail
•••••••• Walking Tour
Path

TRANSPORTATION

Train
Metro

Bus Route
Ferry

HYDROGRAPHY

River; Creek
Canal
Lake

Spring; Rapids
Waterfalls
Dry; Salt Lake

ROUTE SHIELDS

(80) Interstate Freeway
(101) US Highway
(95) Territorial Highway

BOUNDARIES

International
State

County
Disputed

AREAS

Beach
Building
Campus

Cemetery
Forest
Garden; Zoo

Golf Course
Park
Plaza

Reservation
Sports Field
Swamp; Mangrove

POPULATION SYMBOLS

◉ **NATIONAL CAPITAL** National Capital
◉ **State Capital** State Capital
◉ **Large City** Large City
◉ **Medium City** Medium City
● **Small City** Small City
○ **Town; Village** Town; Village

MAP SYMBOLS

🏠 Place to Stay
▼ Place to Eat
● Point of Interest

Airfield	Church	Museum	Skiing - Downhill
Airport	Cinema	Observatory	Stately Home
Archeological Site; Ruin	Dive Site	Park	Surfing
Bank	Embassy; Consulate	Parking Area	Synagogue
Baseball Diamond	Ferry Terminal	Pass	Tao Temple
Battlefield	Gas Station	Picnic Area	Taxi
Bike Trail	Hospital	Police Station	Telephone
Beach	Information	Pool	Theater
Buddhist Temple	Internet Access	Post Office	Toilet - Public
Bus Station; Terminal	Lighthouse	Pub; Bar	Tomb
Cable Car; Chairlift	Lookout	RV Park	Trailhead
Campground	Mine	Shelter	Tram Stop
Castle	Mission	Shipwreck	Transportation
Cathedral	Monument	Shopping Center	Volcano
Cave	Mountain	Skiing - Cross Country	Winery

LONELY PLANET OFFICES

Australia
Locked Bag 1, Footscray, Victoria 3011
☎ 03 8379 8000 fax 03 8379 8111
email talk2us@lonelyplanet.com.au

USA
150 Linden Street, Oakland, California 94607
☎ 510 893 8555, TOLL FREE 800 275 8555
fax 510 893 8572
email info@lonelyplanet.com

UK
10a Spring Place, London NW5 3BH
☎ 020 7428 4800 fax 020 7428 4828
email go@lonelyplanet.co.uk

France
1 rue du Dahomey, 75011 Paris
☎ 01 55 25 33 00 fax 01 55 25 33 01
email bip@lonelyplanet.fr
www.lonelyplanet.fr

World Wide Web: www.lonelyplanet.com *or* AOL keyword: lp
Lonely Planet Images: lpi@lonelyplanet.com.au